PENGUIN BOOKS

GOLDEN AFTERNOON

M. M. Kaye was born in India and spent most of her childhood and much of her early married life in that country. Her ties with India are strong: her grandfather, father, brother and husband all served the Raj, and her grandfather's first cousin, Sir John Kaye, wrote the standard accounts of the Indian Mutiny and the first Afghan War. When India achieved independence her husband joined the British Army, and for the next nineteen years she followed the drum to all sorts of exciting places she would not otherwise have seen, including Kenya, Zanzibar, Egypt, Cyprus and Berlin.

M. M. Kaye is known world-wide for her bestselling historical novels *The Far Pavilions*, *Shadow of the Moon* (both of which are published by Penguin) and *Trade Wind*, and for her detective stories, *Death in Kenya* and *Death in Cyprus*, and *Death in Zanzibar* and *Death in the Andamans* (which are published by Penguin as *House of Shade*). Penguin also publishes *The Sun in the Morning*, the first volume of her autobiography. M. M. Kaye has also written a children's story, *The Ordinary Princess* (1991).

M. M. KAYE

Golden Afternoon

being the second part of
SHARE OF SUMMER,
her autobiography

PENGUIN BOOKS

PENGUIN BOOKS

Published by the Penguin Group
Penguin Books Ltd, 27 Wrights Lane, London w8 5 tz, England
Penguin Putnam Inc., 375 Hudson Street, New York, New York 10014, USA
Penguin Books Australia Ltd, Ringwood, Victoria, Australia
Penguin Books Canada Ltd, 10 Alcorn Avenue, Toronto, Ontario, Canada m4v 3b2
Penguin Books (NZ) Ltd, Private Bag 102902, NSMC, Auckland, New Zealand

Penguin Books Ltd, Registered Offices: Harmondsworth, Middlesex, England

First published by Viking 1997
Published in Penguin Books 1998
3 5 7 9 10 8 6 4

Set in Monotype Garamond
Printed in England by Clays Ltd, St Ives plc

To
the friends of my youth,
most of whom are now dead,
but who live on in my memory.
And to
those happy highways where we went
and cannot come again.
With all my Love.

Contents

꠸꠸꠸꠸

List of Illustrations

Foreword

❧✦❧

Is it so small a thing
To have enjoyed the sun
To have lived light in the Spring
To have loved, to have thought, to have done.

Matthew Arnold

Well, no. Or not as far as I am concerned anyway, for I've had a wonderful life, and if I had to answer the question put to the music in popular song: 'If we could have it all again, would we — could we?' I could honestly say, 'Yes.' Even though it would mean reliving some truly agonizing black patches. For among the many unhappy lessons that life teaches us is that hearts don't break; even though they may crack so badly that however well the years mend them, the cracks are always there.

I used to think that I should never get over the loss of my father, 'Tacklow'. And I didn't, until a few years ago when something very odd, but reassuring, happened to me, and made me realize that I might not have to wait too long before I saw him again.

I was undergoing a five-week stretch in hospital, getting hell from angina, and there came a night when I thought I was dying (so, incidentally, did the nurses, one of whom telephoned my darling daughters at a hideous hour of the night to tell them to get there quickly if they wanted to see Mum alive). I've no idea how this transition was made, but quite suddenly I found myself standing in the dusk on one side of a wide, stony valley on the far side of which lay a long line of barren hills, rather like the Khyber hills on India's North West Frontier. It was getting very dark, but though the valley and the hills were in shadow, the sky still held the dregs of a yellow and gold sunset, and the whole scene was a study in sepia, as though it had been drawn on a sheet of brown packing-paper with a Conté pencil.

I looked down at my dress and saw that I wasn't wearing my long-sleeved granny-style nightgown any more. I was wearing a full-skirted cotton dress of the 1930s and 40s. And I knew in the same moment that I was young again. And not only young, but feeling incredibly happy and exhilarated as well. *Wonderfully* well! I could have danced my way across that desolate waste of broken ground and skipped over the boulders. It would soon be too dark to see, but there was still enough light to show me that there was a pass in those hills, and I knew without any doubt whatever that if I could reach it, I would be home and safe.

I had taken the first step when it occurred to me that perhaps I ought to check on the 'me' who was lying on her back in the blackness, behind me, being badgered by nurses. A nurse was holding each of her hands and one of them kept shouting, 'Can you *hear me*?' and telling her to press her hand, or make a movement — any movement — to show that she could hear her.

Well, of *course* I could hear her! But all I wanted was for everyone to leave me alone to get on with getting up to that pass. However, I thought that I'd get back into 'me' for a moment, just to see how things were with her, so I did — but 'me' was feeling truly awful, so I hastily abandoned her and started off, young and gay and supremely confident, to cross that shadowy valley and scramble up to the pass. But I hadn't gone far when, without warning, I was jerked out of it like a trout on a line and found myself in a brightly lit hospital room, full of people, and feeling far from well. It was a distinct shock . . . because I'd so nearly made it.

I learned later that my heart had stopped twice (hence that brief return into 'me' and back again, perhaps). Also that, as the heart unit that night had been pretty busy, and its electrical gadgets were in use, the doctors had restarted mine with the aid of one of those rubber plungers that you use to unblock kitchen sinks. Very *infra dig*!

I'm sure that the medical profession will be able to explain away that 'out-of-body' experience, but I don't have to believe them. I was there and they weren't, and the best thing about it was that wonderful feeling of happiness and well-being which by itself was enormously reassuring. I know now that when my number comes up I shall only have to cross the valley and find my nearest and dearest waiting to give me a hand if there are any tricky bits to be negotiated in the pass. And in the nature of things it can't be too long now before I meet them again.

I have told this story here partly because it explains why there was such a long gap between the first volume of my autobiography and this one. My apologies to the many readers who have been writing in during the past nine years, demanding to know when Vol. II will be coming up, and would I please get a move on with it? I'm truly sorry for the delay. I really did try, but it was ill-health and not idleness that caused the hold-up: cross my heart.

The other part was because not long after I'd had the curious experience, I described it to a dear friend, one Stanley Hall — who had more friends to the square inch than you would have thought possible. Stanley made me promise that I would write it down somewhere in my autobiography — 'And don't go leaving it too late,' he said. Well, this seems as good a place as any, though, alas, it's too late for Stan to read it here, for he crossed his own valley not long afterwards. I rather think his would have been a Mediterranean one within sight of the sea and with a heavenly palazzo somewhere in the offing. I wouldn't have chosen the one I landed up in, but I'm not complaining, since I reckon one gets what one deserves. And now, while I'm about it, I would like to give my special thanks to three people without whose help this book would never have got off the ground. My sister Bets for all the help and support she has given me; Carole Pengelly Parrish for her unfailing encouragement — not to say nagging — and for introducing me to Margaret Samuel, who has actually been able to translate endless pages of scruffy pencilled longhand and not only made sense of it but managed to turn it into type. My warmest thanks to you all. Especially Bets.

Northbrook, 1991–7   M. M. Kaye

❊ I ❊

'Exemption from oblivion'

Chapter 1

❧❧❧

How does one describe Memory? The *Shorter Oxford Dictionary*, which weighs around six and a half pounds and ought to know, goes into it at some length. According to its compilers, Memory is 'the faculty by which things are remembered'; 'recollection'; 'the fact or condition of being remembered'; 'exemption from oblivion' (I rather fancy that one); and, among other things, 'a memorial writing'; 'a record'; 'a history'; 'a tomb, shrine, chapel, or the like'. And by way of illustration, this information is followed up by a flurry of quotations; notably one from Chaucer (he of *The Canterbury Tales, circa* AD 1340–1400), which states briefly that he was 'yet in memorie and alyve'.

Well, so for the present, am I. And so much for the *Shorter Oxford Dictionary*.

I have not consulted the long one, which runs to an incredible number of volumes, but I doubt if it supplies much more information on this head, and I am quite sure that it fails to mention that Memory (mine, at all events) is a chancy thing with a mind of its own. It picks and chooses at random, rejecting any number of names, dates and incidents of (possibly) world-wide importance, which you would have thought it might have had the sense to retain, while preserving instead a whole rag-bag of odds and ends: a few lines of verse read long ago in an old pre-war copy of an American magazine, an almond tree in bloom in the garden of a shabby little Dâk-bungalow above the Kashmir road, and a full moon rising behind the enormous lateen sails of a fleet of Chinese junks setting out at dusk to fish in the Yellow Sea . . .

I am not criticizing my memory for its quirkiness in this matter of choice, because I have come to realize that, as memories go, it is Grade A and I am very fortunate in possessing it, since a majority of my friends (and both my daughters) seem unable to remember in any detail anything that happened more than a few years ago. I, on the other hand, have the pleasing illusion that I remember *everything*. Though I know very well that this cannot possibly be true, and that a great deal must have fallen through the net and been washed away by time; some of it, I suspect, of some importance — or historical importance, anyway. Yet, as I look back along the long road of my life, which in retrospect seems so astonishingly short, I don't regret the choices my memory has made. For even if I remember nothing else, that almond tree, and the autumn moon lighting the fishing junks out into the Yellow Sea, will surely serve as acceptable coin to pay the Ferryman for taking me across that last river. While as for those few lines of verse, they should furnish me with a password on the other side.

But, while I am 'yet in memorie and alyve', I find that remembering stands so high in my list of favourite things that I am astonished by the number of people who say, 'Oh, I *never* look back! The past is over and done with, and since it can't be altered one should throw it out with the bathwater and forget it. "Always look forward" is my motto!'

Well, all right. But why not do *both*? What's wrong with looking back? Apart from anything else, I should have thought that some of our more truculent nations and their governments, and/or dictators, might even begin to learn a thing or two by doing so. (Such as, for instance, that taking over Afghanistan isn't really quite as easy as you may think.)

There have been black patches, of course, some very harrowing ones. But we all get those, and, personally, I look back on most of my life with the greatest delight. In particular, on the joyful day of my return to the lovely land of my birth after almost nine years of exile in a boarding-school in England.

� I had been so afraid that I would never see it again, and on every day of those interminable years I had badgered God in my nightly prayers to please, *please* do something about it. But although my brother Bill had managed to return there and was now serving as a gunner in a mountain battery on the North West Frontier,* there seemed to be no chance at all of my ever getting back to the lovely land in which I had been born and spent the first ten years of my life. And then, out of a dingy sky in which I could detect no trace of blue, appeared a miracle in the form of an elderly British postman, who bore a letter from the Government of India asking my father, who had retired a few years previously, if he

* Yes, I know it is part of Pakistan now, but it wasn't then!

would please undertake the revision of Aitchison's Treaties,* a task that would necessitate his return to India for a limited time — probably a year at most.

My father, whom, as I have had occasion to point out before, we always called 'Tacklow'† (though we truly hadn't any idea why), accepted. But since he had seen almost nothing of his children during their school-years — in Bill's case a mere ten days between the ages of six and sixteen! — he decided that enough was enough, and that whatever it cost he would take Mother, my sister Bets and me out with him. The miracle that I had prayed for — and I still think of it as one — had actually been granted me and I was going back. It seemed too good to be true.

In September of 1927 the four of us boarded the SS *City of London*, and now, at last, after three weeks at sea, here was India again. And as I stepped off the police launch that our host in Calcutta, Sir Charles Tegart, Bengal's Chief-of-Police, had sent to take us off the ship, I was sorely tempted to do something that might not seem too over-the-top in these days, since the present Pope has made a habit of it whenever he visits a foreign country. Tempted to fall on my knees and kiss the ground because it was India's soil that my feet were standing on once again.

However, the first Polish Pope can barely have been born then, and since at that time I was far too young and self-conscious (and, thanks to that English boarding-school, far too British) to indulge in such continental gestures, I could only stand there like a dummy, struggling to swallow the lump in my throat and pretending that I had a bit of grit in my eye, while my parents greeted the Tegarts and shook hands with or embraced the large number of people who had come down to the docks to welcome them back again.

All of these, with one joyful exception, were strangers to me. The exception was Abdul Karim, our ex-*abdar*-cum-*khitmatgar*, who, back in that sad, traumatic spring of 1919 when Bets and I had been taken down to Bombay to board the SS *Ormond* and begin the long years of exile, boarding-school, and separation from our parents, had stood in for

---

* Treaties between the British and the rulers of the semi-independent princely states.

† After the publication of *The Sun in the Morning* a great many readers wrote in giving suggestions as to why Tacklow should have acquired that name. One (who did his National Service in the 7th Gurkha Rifles) wrote to say that not long ago in Bombay he heard a bald-headed man referred to as *Tacklo*, which it seems is Hindi for 'bald'. Since my Tacklow-Sahib was bald by the age of twenty-three, I bet that's the answer. Thank you, Mr MacLeod.

Tacklow's old bearer, dear Alum Din of fond memory, who had been absent on sick-leave and whose portrait I included over half a century later in one of my India novels, *The Far Pavilions*.

Alum Din had died and Abdul Karim had stepped into his shoes. But when Tacklow retired, Abdul had decided that he too would take his pension and return to end his days in his home village, giving as his reason that he had grown old in Kaye-Sahib's service; too old to learn another sahib's ways or face the prospect of working for anyone else. It was, he said, high time that his sons and grandsons shouldered the responsibility of looking after him and let him sit back and take his ease in the shade. But although he and my father had corresponded fairly regularly since then and had been punctilious in the matter of exchanging greetings on feast days and festivals, Tacklow had not written to say that he would shortly be returning. This was largely because he had found himself overwhelmed with an avalanche of chores, but also because Tacklow was afraid that if he wrote to tell Abdul of his return, the old man might regard it as a hint that he should return to work and consider it his duty to do so, even though advancing years, and a long spell of idleness, might well have made this beyond him.

'I'll write to him later on, when we're more settled and know where we are likely to be, and for how long,' said Tacklow. But he had reckoned without India's superbly efficient grapevine. For there, on the dock at Calcutta's Garden Reach, waiting to take us under his wing and boss us around as firmly as ever, stood Abdul Karim.

I am ashamed to say that I didn't recognize him immediately, because he had dyed his beard a ferocious and improbable scarlet, and when I had said goodbye to him all those years ago in Bombay it had been grey. Then, too, he seemed so much smaller than the tall, burly Punjabi I remembered; as though he had shrunk in the passing years. Or was it only because I myself had grown upward — and outward! — during that time, and so no longer had to look up so far when he spoke to me? A bit of both, probably. I recognized him suddenly when he stooped quickly to touch Tacklow's feet, and the two embraced as old friends.

Long ago, a man who had been a friend of Abdul's, Kashmera, Sir Charles Cleveland's *shikari* and one of the most admired friends of my childhood, had told me that I must not cry in public; it was *shurram* (shame), and *Angrezi-log* (English people) never did so! But it seemed that this spartan rule did not apply to men of his own race, for there were tears trickling down Abdul Karim's leathery old cheeks as he took a firm grip of the reins which he had relinquished on the day when Tacklow and Mother had left India for what they, and he, had believed would be the last time.

Now here they were, back again; and in the charming tradition of that most charming of lands, their Indian friends crowded round to garland them with necklaces of flowers or tinsel, which they hung about my parents' necks in such numbers that if Tacklow — who was a small man — had not been wearing the topi he had bought at Simon Artz shop in Port Said, we would not have been able to see the top of his head.

One of his friends, a tubby little Bengali who was a High Court judge, had been thoughtful enough to bring two splendid garlands of jasmine buds and silver tinsel for Bets and me, so that we should not feel left out. I could have kissed that man! Bets and I made *namaste* and, thus honoured and decorated, we stepped into a second car, together with the overnight suitcases, and set off in the wake of the one that carried our parents and the Tegarts, Abdul Karim following grandly behind in a third, in charge of the heavy luggage.

Calcutta was not part of 'my India',* for I had been born some 2,000 miles to the north-west of that great port, in the little hill town of Simla, which lies among the foothills of the Himalayas within sight of the uncharted snows. Here, in the days of the Raj, the Government of India, together with the Viceroy, the Commander-in-Chief, the Governor of the Punjab, and the whole of Army Headquarters — plus innumerable wives, families and holiday-makers — used to spend the months of the hot weather, escaping the intolerable heat of the plains. In autumn, with the coming of the cold weather, we would all descend, bag and baggage, 'Uncle Tom Cobley and all', to those same plains; most of us to Delhi, which by then would be no more than pleasantly warm and no longer sweltering in temperatures of between 115° and 125° in the shade.

By 'Delhi', I mean Old Delhi, for when I was a child New Delhi — the latest (and possibly last) of the cities of Delhi — had yet to be built. My Delhi was the wonderful walled city that the Mogul Emperor Shah Jehan, self-styled 'Ruler of the World', built for himself on the banks of

* Apologies to my Indian friends for the use of that possessive pronoun. Having been born there (it was all one country then), I feel it is mine by affection, as one of my dear friends is my sister-by-affection.

the Jumna river among the ruins of the six previous Delhis that had been built and fallen into ruins on those plains. That was my Delhi, and I loved every stick and stone of it.

Calcutta, on the Hoogly, not only lay a long, dusty, two and a half days' train journey to the south-east (no aeroplanes in those days) but was the capital city of Bengal. And there are a good many differences between Bengalis and the Himalayan hill folk; or, come to that, between the people of the UP — the United Provinces.* But I couldn't have cared less, as the car whisked us away from Garden Reach to the city that was once no more than a slimy mudflat, almost covered with water at every tide — for the Hoogly is a tidal river.

As far back as 1690 the mudflat had been given, in no kindly spirit (the gift had, in fact, been intended as a deliberate insult), by the local overlord, one Nawab Ibrahim Khan, to a Mr Job Charnock of the East India Company, in response to a petition for a site on which to build a small trading-post. Charnock had swallowed the insult and, having accepted the mudflat with every appearance of gratitude, landed on it at low tide accompanied by thirty of the Company's soldiers, whom he set to work raising an enclosing wall, inside which they then built strong fortifications which Job named Fort William for the then King of England, William of Orange.

That erstwhile mudflat was destined to become the great city of Calcutta — which to this day can often carry a distinct smell of sewage; as it must have done on the day that Mr Charnock and his long-suffering thirty began shovelling up the mud and the mudworms and banking up the stuff against the returning tide.

Perhaps because of its beginnings, Calcutta has the reputation of being one of India's more insalubrious cities, and nowadays, despite the almost fanatical loyalty and affection in which a majority of its citizens hold it, there is no denying that much of it is a major eyesore. But as we drove through its streets on that memorable evening it seemed, to my infatuated gaze, the most beautiful city in the world, populated by the most colourful and enchanting people and smelling of everything that I had missed for so long: sandalwood, incense and spices; masala, mustard oil, garlic and ghee; the heady smell of smoke from dung fires and the never-to-be-forgotten one of water sprinkled on sun-scorched ground. And, under-

* Now known as Uttar Pradesh.

8

neath it all, that faint, pervasive odour of sewage and rotting vegetable matter which is apt to haunt the bazaars and the poorer quarters of any Indian city, but which that afternoon was subdued by the sweet scent of fresh flowers — roses and marigolds and frangipani, and the jasmine blossoms in the garlands about my neck.

✳ The Tegarts' house was a tall three-storey mansion that must have dated back to the latter days of the East India Company. It stood among trees in a quiet road well out of earshot of the roar and bustle of Chowringhi, Calcutta's main street, where the European shops and big hotels stand looking out across a stream of traffic to the wide spaces of the *maidan* and the massive white marble Victoria Memorial, that pretentious would-be Taj Mahal housing a museum that is — or was — very well worth visiting.

One of the Tegarts' house servants took Bets and me up to our bedrooms, which were on the top storey, and I shall never forget the feeling of pure rapture with which I looked around that room, knowing that I had come home again . . . No more cluttered British bedrooms with their heavily lined curtains and hideous Axminster carpets. No more frilled or flounced pelmets and cumbersome mahogany furniture, squashy, eiderdowned beds, or fireplaces. No more patterned wallpaper liberally adorned with gilt-framed pictures. They were all in the past — over and done with. This was what the bedrooms of my childhood had looked like, and here once more were those familiar boltless doors, 'and the high ceiled rooms that the Trade blows through' that Kipling had written of, and remembered to the end of his life . . .

This room was high and very spacious, with whitewashed walls that were innocent of pictures, and in the centre of it, directly underneath the large, white-painted ceiling-fan, stood a single iron bedstead fitted with poles and a mosquito-net. The polished *chunam** floor was covered with matting and the furniture consisted of an *almirah* (a cupboard made from cretonne and criss-crossed slats of wood), a marble-topped dressing-table, a *morah* (a stool made of reeds), a cheval-glass and a couple of cane chairs. That, apart from a small bedside table, was all. But I wouldn't have added to it or altered it for anything in the world. This was what a *proper* bedroom ought to look like. It was heaven!

---

* A white plaster made from crushed shells that can be polished until it looks like marble.

Bets's room opened off it and was slightly smaller than mine. She came running back to me shouting, 'Mouse, *do* come and look!' and dragged me into her bathroom (there was one to each room). Despite the fact that we were on the top floor, and that there was actually a cold water tap, the bathrooms too were of the old, familiar pattern. The tin tub stood in a stone-paved section ringed off by a brick rim a few inches high, so that when the bath was emptied by being tipped up, the water did not flood the entire floor but drained away through an outlet pipe in one of the corners of the enclosed space. There was a wooden towel-horse and an old-fashioned washstand complete with china fittings, a box-commode, and, standing beside the tin tub, an enormous earthenware *chatti* (jar) full of cold water, and a tin dipper for ladling it out; the only modern innovation in the room being that single cold tap, from which the *chatti* was filled. There were wooden jalousies over the windows, and through them we could see the dense green foliage of the trees that towered up outside and filled the high-ceilinged room with a shimmering, watery light, flecked with blobs and ripples of gold as the leaves stirred in the evening breeze.

Bets and I looked around us with a rapture too deep for words, and I remember that we hugged each other before going back into my bedroom and out through the french windows on to the balcony outside my room, to look down at the small enclosed garden below and out towards the great, sprawling city whose rooftops lay spread out all around us in the last of the sunset. It was the hour of the evening meal, when the dust of the hot day merges with the smoke of innumerable cooking-fires to draw an opal haze over the city. The sky above us was dotted with kites; paper ones flown by children, and feathered birds of prey — 'Cheil the Kite', who swoops and hovers all day in the enormous Indian skies, searching for food.

We leaned side by side on the balcony rail, drinking in the sight and the sounds and the smell of Calcutta, as though we were a pair of parched travellers in a desert, who had stumbled at long last on an oasis and were slaking our thirst at a pool of cool water. The voice of the city drifted up to us like the sound of a vast orchestra tuning up before a concert: a joyous, muted medley of sounds made up of *tonga*-bells, the cries of street-vendors, horses' hooves and the horns of motor cars, buses and lorries, trams and train whistles; the blare of conchs from a score of temples and the remembered beat of tom-toms; the distant strains of a *fu-fu* band accompanying some bridegroom to his wedding; the cawing of crows, the shouts of children, and the nearer racket and chatter of birds coming home to roost in the nearby trees.

The familiar sounds, backed by the continuous muffled roar of traffic on Chowringhi, blended together into a purring hum like the drone of bees among heather-bloom on a hot summer afternoon, or the crash and drag of waves on a pebble beach. And as the swift green twilight fell and the city began to sparkle with lights, the garden below us awoke to a shimmer of fireflies, while overhead, legions of the fruit-bats which hang up to sleep all day among the trees awoke and flapped silently away to conduct their nightly raids on the orchards that lie beyond the outskirts of the city. And presently the moon rose, its size impossibly exaggerated by the veils of dust and the smoke from cooking-fires. That familiar moon of other days, rising in the dusk to welcome me back . . .

It was a wonderful homecoming. Better than anything I had pictured. For I have to admit that there were times when I had been afraid that, if I *should* ever have the luck to get back to the land of my birth and childhood, I might find that memory had cheated me and it wasn't in the least as I had pictured it. Or that Time had changed it out of all recognition. I don't think it had occurred to me that what children want most of loved and familiar people and places is that they should remain unchanged.

Most people who have had happy childhoods are afraid of change, and I was no exception. But I was also one of the lucky ones, for I had returned home after nine long years to find — against all the odds — that the happy highways of my recollection had not changed. They were still there. Just as I remembered them. Which is why I can truly say that among so many cherished memories, I count the memory of that particular day among the very best; because it was a dream come true, and therefore touched with authentic magic. A magic, moreover, that did not vanish with the morning; though as I lay listening to all the well-remembered sounds of an Indian dawn — sounds that I had awakened to daily for the first ten years of my life — I began to panic about how I was going to make out as a grown-up.

Judging from my performance on the *City of London*, I was doomed to be an outstanding social flop. For there was an aspect of my return which, in the euphoria of finding that the miracle I had prayed for so long had actually been granted me, I had not given sufficient thought to. If any. The fact that I was bringing back with me something that I had certainly not possessed when I left Bombay as a skinny ten-year-old. An inferiority complex.

I have told in *The Sun in the Morning* how, on arrival at my first boarding-school, I was pronounced by a mid-Victorian doctor and an equally bigoted and outdated Matron to be *much* too thin: unhealthily so. I needed 'fattening up'. (Shades of Hansel and Gretel!) And fattened up I was. Systematically stuffed like some hapless Strasburg goose, and dosed three times a day with large spoonfuls of some sickly-sweet goo that was a mixture of malt and cod-liver oil.

Since this regime was approved by our guardian, Aunt Bee,* it was continued throughout the holidays, with the result that I soon put on weight. And then too much weight. So much that my brother Bill, after the manner of brothers, took to calling me 'Fatty' or 'Old Piano Legs'. This in an epoch when for the first time in recorded history, women had cut down on petticoats, shortened their previously long skirts to above the knee, chopped off their hair and shingled it, and, disowning such curves as hips, waists and bosoms, endeavoured to look as much as possible like skinny schoolboys in drag.

The 1920s were the heyday of the thin-to-scrawny woman, and although, thanks to the fact that I had been seasick almost non-stop from the day that the *City of London* entered the Bay of Biscay, I could no longer be classed as a 'fatty', I was still painfully conscious of being an unsophisticated podge who had never yet attended a dance (no discos in those days). This feeling had been strongly reinforced by my failure to attract so much as a speculative glance from any of the many young men on the *City of London*, though every other girl on board seemed to have managed it with ease.

But in the event I need not have panicked, for the week we spent in Calcutta turned out to be one long, glorious party. The Tegarts were a deservedly popular couple and Lady Tegart, 'Thomas' to her friends, was a notable hostess who could not help giving her guests a good time.

She took us to the races, and to dine at Firpos and the Saturday Club. To swim and have breakfast at Tollygunj, and for an all-day picnic on the Hoogly in a police launch, from which we returned by moonlight to the romantic strains of a portable wind-up gramophone playing records

* Miss Beatrice Lewis, 'Aunt Bee', a friend of Mother's who took charge of us when Mother went back to India.

by such contemporary heart-throbs as Rudy Vallee and 'Whispering Jack Smith'. I remember that one of the songs was, inevitably, 'Moonlight and Roses', an old favourite that, to this day, still crops up on radio programmes featuring dance tunes from the long-ago twenties. Also that one of the young men in the party held my hand for most of the return journey, an attention that thrilled me to the core until I discovered that he had fallen asleep. Well, at least he had been awake when he took it, so someone had actually made a tentative pass at me, and landing from that launch I walked on air.

Among a multitude of new faces I can only put a name to two of the young men who had been roped in by Thomas Tegart to partner us at dinners and dances, and the only reason I remember those two was because they happened to be look-alike twins, although they bore different surnames: 'Ike', the elder by a short head, being at that time a Viscount, while his twin was merely an 'Hon', later to marry Barbara Jacomb-Hood, the child who had danced the Egyptian dance in the 'Pageant', an amateur entertainment in Simla that I wrote about at some length in *The Sun in the Morning*. All the other names have escaped me. Yet I can still remember in great detail the dress I wore for my first dance at the Saturday Club . . .

Like all our dresses, this one had been made up by one of those invaluable 'little women round the corner' who used to support themselves by dressmaking and were the prop and stay of all of us who could not afford to buy ready-made clothes — let alone *couturier*-designed dresses! I had designed it myself and actually succeeded, after prolonged pleading, in persuading Mother to allow me to have it made up in black net and taffeta. It had been no easy victory, since Mother (strongly supported by Aunt Bee) held the view that black was an 'unsuitable' colour for a young girl. Only married women and middle-aged-to-old ones should wear it. The young should wear white, or pale colours. The paler the better.

Undeterred, I stuck to my guns, pointing out that since black was known to be unkind to a poor or an ageing skin, but complimentary to a young one, why wait until I reached an age where it made me older and sallower instead of using it now to show off one of my few really good points, which was a pretty good line in complexions? Besides, black was also considered to be slimming, an invaluable plus in my opinion, since I was well aware that I veered towards podginess; and pale pink and baby blue merely emphasized that unfortunate fact. All of which, in my opinion, added up to the conviction that now was the time to wear black and look good in it.

These arguments eventually prevailed, and the dress was made up in a daring new design: short in front (an inch or two above the knee was still obligatory at that time, which was bad luck for those with unattractive legs), but dipping down on each side to reach, with the assistance of a wide hem of black net, ankle length at the sides and the back. It also boasted a tight-fitting bodice, with the thinnest of thin shoulder-straps and a sweetheart neckline edged with a frill of the same net. It was a resounding success. Mother was still doubtful — *black* . . . and while I was still in my teens! I might well (horrors!) get a reputation for being *fast*! But Thomas, bless her for ever, gave it her enthusiastic approval, and in it I felt gloriously grown-up and sophisticated and, in some odd way, almost as if I had put on a different identity and was as successfully disguised as someone wearing fancy dress at a masked ball.

I needed something like that to get me through the evening, because in those days I did not possess so much as a shred of self-confidence, and was painfully and humiliatingly gauche. It does not seem to have occurred to my unworldly parents that since they presumably hoped that Bets and I would find husbands for ourselves in the shortest possible time, it would have been a good idea to see that we were taught a few elementary social graces — such as how to dance, for instance. Our dancing lessons at school had been of a fairly high standard, but they had not included ballroom dancing, although that would have proved a far more useful accomplishment to most of us (certainly to me!) than ballet classes. As it was, I hadn't a *clue* how to dance the Charleston, let alone a foxtrot, two-step or tango, and the only reason why I had a vague idea of how to waltz was because that particular dance had featured in an end-of-term school play set in Victorian days, in which I had taken part.

I had to learn all these things the hard way: by practical demonstration, pushed or propelled by young men, most of whom didn't know much more about it than I did. Bets, a born dancer, fared better, and my partners were all kind enough to apologize each time I stumbled or trod on their toes, as if it was their fault and not mine. I could have *hit* them! However, buoyed up by the sight of my reflection in that flattering and sophisticated dress, and by the attention that it received, I thoroughly enjoyed the evening.

This was an India I had only caught glimpses of before and with which I had hitherto had nothing whatever to do — the India of the Raj at play. Mother's India, for which she had dressed in those pretty silks and satins, *crêpes de Chine* and marocaines I used to admire so much when she kissed Bets and me goodnight in the nursery, or waved goodbye from the rickshaw that was taking her to a garden party or a luncheon or a race meeting at Annandale. No wonder she had been so delighted at the prospect of returning to it! I had no idea one could have so much fun. Or that it was so heavenly to be grown-up.

That dance at the Saturday Club was the first grown-up one I had ever attended — if one discounts the occasional 'gramophone-hops' on the deck of the *City of London* (very few of which I had been able to attend because of seasickness) — and because I had enjoyed it, the weight of that terrifying inferiority complex that I had acquired at Portpool, the first of my two English boarding-schools, and had never been able to shed, began to lighten a trifle. In consequence, I had a lovely time in Calcutta.

There were, however, several flies in my delicious pot of honey. One, a mere gnat, was the slightly disturbing fact that Mother had once again (as she had done almost nightly on board ship) gone back on her decision that Bets would not be allowed to attend any dinners or dances until she was seventeen. Instead, she had wavered and said, 'Well — just this *once*!' Which was lovely for Bets, but to me an ominous repetition of the 'bra and high-heels syndrome' that had soured my school days. I had begged to be allowed to wear these and other status symbols of approaching young-ladyhood (such as make-up and flesh-coloured silk stockings) but had been firmly told that I was still *far* too young and must 'wait until I was older'. Yet no sooner had I achieved that necessary age limit than Bets, a full two years my junior, was immediately accorded them too. Now here it was again, and I have to confess that it made me uneasy, for I foresaw complications ahead.

A more obtrusive fly was a justifiable fear of putting on weight. For my parents had a great many Indian friends in Calcutta with whom we lunched or dined or attended receptions, and in their homes we ate once more the spicy food that I had missed so sorely during my years of exile in England.

The gulf between the delicious, spicy food of Asia and the bland diet of mashed or baked potatoes, over-boiled vegetables and tasteless stews, followed by tapioca, rice, suet or bread puddings, which British boarding-schools (and Aunt Bee) considered just the thing for 'growing girls', was ocean-wide, and one of the chief joys of being back in India again was being able to eat *Raan* and *Shahjahanibiriani* again, not to mention *balushahi* and other *halwas* (sweets). But I feared the effect they might have on my vital statistics, improved out of all knowledge by that abominable seasickness which, by the time we landed, had succeeded in removing well over a stone off my weight, so that for the first time in years I was no longer a fatty but the proud possessor of a comparatively slim figure. This, assisted by the flattering hemline of that black taffeta outfit (which was, at that date, revolutionary enough to make heads turn), plus the joyful fact that Mother had had to take the bodice in by inches, gave me the illusion of being fashionably shaped as well as fashionably dressed and did wonders for my exceedingly fragile morale.

The third, and by far the largest fly in my ointment — an outsized bluebottle of a fly — was the devastating discovery that I had forgotten nearly all the Hindustani that I had once spoken with far more fluency than my mother tongue.

Why it had never occurred to me before that I might have done so, I don't know. Presumably, I took it for granted that speaking a language was like riding a bicycle — once learned never forgotten — so that it must all still be there, stored up in some secure compartment in my brain and ready to bounce out as soon as I wanted it. I do remember thinking that if, by some miracle, I was able to get back to India one day, even if my pronunciation were a bit rusty, the moment I heard people speaking Hindustani again it would all come flooding back to me. This confident assumption was probably based on the fact that whenever I groped for a word in French, it invariably presented itself to me in Hindustani, something that I suspect happened to very many of us 'children of the Raj', for I well remember a young ex-Indian Army friend of mine, who had assured me that he could speak French fluently, entering a shop in Marseilles in search of a hat and announcing to a bewildered saleslady that, '*Hum eck* chapeau *mungta*' ('I one hat want').

To find myself in the same situation with regard to Hindustani was a nasty shock. And I am ashamed to say that, try as I would, I never again learned to speak it so that I could have passed as a native of the country, but remained at best a speaker of '*memsahib's Hindustani-bhat*', the result, I presume, of having a poor musical ear. I could always understand a great deal more than I could speak though, and I remember Mother, whose vocabulary was considerably larger than mine, being incensed when, many years later, her bearer, Kaderalone,* who, like all our servants, spoke no English, complained that he did not understand something she had told him, and that he proposed to get '*Mollie-missahib*' to translate it for him, because she spoke much better Hindustani. I didn't, of course: I merely attacked it at a gallop, gabbling it at twice the speed and far more colloquially. I have always spoken too fast (and too much) but it sounded OK to him.

Nowadays, few people will admit to speaking Hindustani, and the very name of that useful language is becoming forgotten. Those who remember it like to pretend that it was merely a bastardized form of Kitchen-Urdu, the invention of memsahibs who could not be bothered to learn the languages of the country. In fact, it came into being with the conquest of India by the Moguls — Tartars, Mongolians and Pathans who spoke a mixture of Arabic, Pushtu and Farsee (Persian). This mixture of Urdu and Hindi became in time the lingua franca of the land, and to this day, whenever I return to that great subcontinent that was all 'India' in my time, if I happen to be in the section that is still India today, old friends in the bazaars say, 'Ah! I see that the memsahib has not forgotten her Hindi!' and when I cross the border into what is now Pakistan they say, 'It is good that you still speak Urdu!' I don't, of course. What I am actually speaking — and badly — is Hindustani.

* Car-der-er-*lone* (accent on *lone*), *Card*erah for short — '*Car*-der-ah'. (Now try to pronounce it!)

Chapter 2

~✕✕✕✕~

From Calcutta we went on, up-country to Lucknow, leaving by train from Howra Station in the dusty evening, as twilight was falling and lamps were being lit.

The line ran through suburbs where the rich merchants of the East India Company had once lived in pillared and porticoed Georgian houses, shaded by lush green gardens full of banyan, palm and gold-mohur trees, mango groves and bananas and tall thickets of bamboo. These stately mansions had long since fallen into decay and were now little more than slum dwellings, divided into innumerable flatlets or bedsitting-rooms occupied by colonies of Indians and Eurasians who worked in the city as clerks, typists, shop assistants or waiters in one or other of the many hotels.*

By daylight one could have seen the shabbiness and decay that the years had inflicted on these once gracious houses, the discoloured stucco and flaking plaster, the fallen pillars; the lines of washing hung up between the over-grown trees; the *charpoys* on the flat rooftops where many residents slept out under the night skies while the weather remained hot, and the scuffed grass where hens, goats and cattle scratched and grazed on what had once been wide lawns and scented flowerbeds. But in the kindly dusk the scars became invisible, and stateliness returned to the tall white buildings whose pillared porticoes and wide verandahs one could glimpse through the crowding palm trunks, making them appear beautiful again; as beautiful and romantic as the castle of Hans Andersen's sleeping princess seen through the encroaching briar roses. Dusk hid the dirt and decay, and the bamboo branches shimmered with fireflies.

* For a wonderful description of this part of Calcutta, read *The Lady and the Unicorn* by Rumer Godden.

I watched, enchanted, as the train rattled through these once opulent suburbs, for it was as if I were seeing the city as it was in the days of Warren Hastings and Wellesley, William Hickey and Rose Aylmer — poor, pretty Rose who lies buried in Calcutta's Park Street Cemetery, and will always be remembered because Walter Savage Landor wrote two short verses that were engraved upon her tombstone:

> *Ah, what avails the sceptred race,*
> *Ah, what the form divine,*
> *When every virtue, every grace,*
> *Rose Aylmer, all were thine.*
>
> *Rose Aylmer, whom these wakeful eyes*
> *May weep, but never see,*
> *A night of memories and of sighs*
> *I consecrate to thee!*

In Lucknow we stayed for four days in Government House as guests of Sir William Marris, an old friend of Tacklow's who was at that time the Governor of the United Provinces. I remember that Bets and I were awestruck at seeing our names in two daily newspapers, the *Pioneer* and the *Civil and Military Gazette*. They figured in a couple of identical paragraphs in columns headed 'The Viceregal Court', which announced briefly that 'Sir Cecil and Lady Kaye, Miss Kaye and Miss Betty Kaye arrived at Government House, Lucknow on Tuesday afternoon.'

Years later, after Tacklow was dead, I was to stay for some time in this same house with a later Governor, who was also a friend of his, and my recollection of that second visit is a good deal clearer than that of the first one — which remains in my memory as a period of acute embarrassment. This was because Sir William's ADCs appeared to consider it their duty to entertain us by endless games of tennis. (Not for nothing was 'Anyone for tennis?' a favourite catchphrase of the Roaring Twenties.) They simply would not believe that I, for one, wasn't. Of *course* I played tennis. *Everyone* played tennis! Well, if they did, I was obviously the exception that proved the rule. For one thing, I have never been able to hit or catch anything that is thrown at me. I believe this is because I have one shutter missing in my range of sight, and I was once given a technical description of this, plus the Latin name of the condition, but did not really grasp what it was all about, except that I lose sight of the ball, or any object moving towards me, for a fraction of a second, and, as a result, I haven't a clue where it is going to land.

However, this did not let me off the hook, and those tennis sessions proved a blood-curdling embarrassment to me — made all the worse by whichever ADC had been unlucky enough to draw me as a partner apologizing to me for what were plainly my mistakes . . . 'Sorry, partner — I should have taken that one — not your fault,' etc., etc. Oh dear! His Excellency's ADCs gallantly took it in turns to partner me; and Bets (no Helen Wills, but a more than adequate player) and her partner invariably defeated me and mine.

The only redeeming features of the visit were, as far as I was concerned, the obligatory sightseeing tours that were laid on for guests at Government House. For this was beautiful, garish, decadent Lucknow, the city that Kipling described as being 'the centre of all idleness, intrigue and luxury'. Here, memories of the Indian Mutiny of 1857 were still green — so much so that there was still an old retired soldier attached to the staff in charge of the ruins of the old Residency, a white-whiskered veteran who seventy years previously had, as a drummer-boy, actually served there during the famous siege; while among the caretakers was an ancient, white-bearded Indian who had been a mere *chokra* (boy) in the service of the *Sahib-log* during that fateful summer, and who remembered the arrival of General Havelock's relief force — the one that had been meant to raise the siege, but which had ended up joining the beleaguered garrison and standing siege themselves.

The years had been kind to these ancient gentlemen, both the English one and the Indian. The one-time drummer-boy (who could not have been more than ten years old at the time of the Mutiny) still wore the scarlet coat of Victoria's army with, proudly pinned upon it, the campaign medals of a past century. His particular charge was the cemetery in which so many of the besieged British, including Sir Henry Lawrence, were buried, and he told me, in a hoarse aside, that in fact the cemetery, in addition to being heavily shelled during the siege, was subsequently dug up and desecrated after the remnants of the original garrison, together with the force that had hoped to relieve them, were forced to withdraw from Lucknow under cover of darkness and retreat to Cawnpore. This meant that when, almost a year later, Lucknow was finally retaken by the British, no one really had the least idea who had been buried where, or to whom the scattered bones and skulls had once belonged. So most of the Mutiny gravestones I had seen were no more than guesswork, and highly unlikely to match the remains of the men and women who were buried under them; a gruesome detail that I was to verify a good many years later when I was doing the research for *Shadow of the Moon*.

I had been told tales of the 'Black Year' ever since I was a small child in Old Delhi, so I was fascinated to come across relics of it here. Although by this time I had of course read Sir John Kaye's account of that rising, *The History of the Sepoy War*, it did not include the full story of Lucknow because he had got no further than the relief of Delhi when he died, leaving his readers with the fate of the besieged Residency in Lucknow still unknown.* I wandered all over the ruined Residency, trying to picture it as it must have looked when the old man with the white beard, who had elected to stay within the defences and continue to serve the *Sahib-log*, had been young, and the ex-drummer-boy, now acting as custodian of the cemetery, had been a ten-year-old fighting alongside other schoolboys inside these bullet-riddled and shell-shattered ruins. For the pupils of La Martinière, the only school (it survives today) that can boast of a battle honour, had taken refuge in the Residency and stood siege there, fighting and dying beside their house and form masters.

Ten years earlier there had been many citizens of Delhi who could remember the Mutiny, and when I was a child a large number of them had told me enthralling stories about those days. But it was more than exciting to find that here in Lucknow, and guarding the ruins of a building that had once been the British Residency in the final days of the East India Company, there were two people who had actually seen it all happen and could describe it to me: men who had seen Sir Henry Lawrence, Lady Inglis of the diaries, the irascible Mr Gubbins, and young Second-Lieutenant Bonham of the Artillery, who was wounded four times and whose son would one day marry my husband's Aunt Lily.

I could not hear enough. But H. E.'s Private Secretary and the ADCs, who had accompanied us, had taken too many visitors around the Mutiny sights and were, by this time, plainly bored stiff by the whole business. And since I was much too shy to stick my toes in and keep them waiting, we were hurried away far too soon and it was not until thirteen years

---

* This history was completed by a Colonel Mallenson, who married the only sister of the 'ten fighting Batteys', three of whom served in the Corps of Guides and appear as real-life characters in *The Far Pavilions*. The work was published as *Kaye and Mallenson's Indian Mutiny*.

later that, staying once more at Government House, this time with another Governor, I was presented with a piece of information, in the form of an unpublished letter that must still, I imagine, be preserved among the Government House archives, which was to result, after another long interval, in my writing the first of my three historical novels, *Shadow of the Moon*.

Strangely enough, my memory-bank has recorded two quite separate Government Houses, neither of them bearing the slightest resemblance to the other, despite the fact that there had apparently been no alteration to either house or garden — give or take a few trees that had fallen or been cut down in the interval between that first visit and the next. Odd. I wish I could account for this, but I can't.

✼ From Lucknow we went to Cawnpore, the *Pioneer* duly reporting that Sir Cecil and Lady Kaye, Miss Kaye and Miss Dorothy (*sic*) Kaye had left Government House. (My sister was christened Dorothy Elizabeth, but no one has ever called her by either of those names. She has always been 'Bets', just as I have always been known to my nearest and dearest as 'Mouse', which I would have said was a most unsuitable name. But then there is no accounting for nicknames: one is given them in an idle moment, and they stick.)

In Cawnpore we stayed with yet another family friend, Charlie Allen, — 'C. T.' Allen — whose father, Sir George, owned, among other things, the *Pioneer* newspaper, and had given a young cub reporter named Rudyard Kipling a job on its staff back in 1887. We had stayed with the Allens before; but in England. Freechase, their beautiful house in Sussex, contained something that I would have given almost anything in the world to possess, the original plaster relief of 'The Jat' — one of the illustrations that Lockwood Kipling had done for his son Rudyard's famous novel, *Kim*. Rudyard had given it to Charlie's brother George, who had become a great friend of his, and I used to sit and stare at it enviously.

These two brothers had a fascinating history, and I have always hoped that someone — preferably C. T.'s grandson, another Charles Allen* — would start work on one. Their grandfather had gone out to India in the heyday of the East India Company in the hope of making his fortune there. His first step in this direction was to hawk beer and soft drinks off

* Author of *Plain Tales from the Raj*, *The Princes*, etc.

a barrow to the British and Indian Army troops who were besieging Delhi in the summer of the Black Year. This enterprise obviously paid off handsomely, and he eventually ended up a millionaire tycoon, owning a tannery and a handful of cotton mills and this and that. He had two sons, and Tacklow always said that it was an indictment of the public school system that when he died his eldest son, George — who, having been born before he made his pile, was educated at a board school* — had taken over and built up his father's holding into a thriving empire that included a couple of major newspapers.

This remarkable character — the original 'rough diamond' — was, it seems, not only successful but also an exceptionally likeable man. Everyone liked him. And Kipling was no exception. I don't know whether he married or not, but if he did there were no children, for when he died he handed on the Allen empire to his much younger brother Charlie, who, born after their father had struck it rich, had been sent to Eton. C. T. (who, like that well-known television tycoon 'J. R.', was seldom, if ever, referred to except by his initials) had loads of charm but not a grain of business sense, and he managed to blue the Allen fortune in record time. But he was still riding high when he entertained us in Cawnpore in the autumn of 1927.

The Allen house, the Retreat, was one of the most attractive houses I have ever stayed in, a huge, rambling, East-India-Company-style bungalow with a thatched roof and wide verandahs from which flights of stone steps led down to a garden of sloping lawns and colourful, scented flowerbeds, and a vast, meandering lake full of shadowy creeks and shady backwaters where herons and wild duck nested. The banks were thick with palms and flowering trees, and the lake was patched with lotus and water-lilies and alive with butterflies and birds, and there was a graceful, Indian-style pavilion on a small green island. It was a beautiful, peaceful and enchanted place which we spent hours exploring, drifting around in a punt.

Mornings at the Retreat began with a clamour of birdsong; doves and pigeons, hoopoes and parrots, crows, mynahs, blue-jays and *sat-bhai*, saluting the day in joyful chorus. At around seven o'clock a bearer would appear with *chota-hazri* — literally 'small breakfast' — without which no Indian day would be complete. This consisted of tea and toast and

* A school run by an appointed Board; predecessor of today's state schools.

23

whatever fruits were in season: papaya when available, bananas (of which there were always at least half a dozen varieties to choose from), oranges, lychees and mangoes. After that, bathed in a tin tub and having dressed, one went out into the cool, glittering morning to walk through the gardens and along the lakeside, sniffing the flowers and watching the birds and squirrels.

Sometimes we would be taken out shopping in the bazaars, but always we were back again at the bungalow by eleven o'clock for 'brunch', the main meal of the day. This was a curious mixture of breakfast and lunch that was served on the verandah, and consisted of porridge for those who fancied it, and Grape-nuts or Shredded Wheat for those who didn't; fruit juice and coffee, bacon and eggs, and at least one Indian dish, such as curry and rice, *jhal-frazi* or chicken *pilau*, plus some pudding or other to end with. The earlier part of the afternoon was generally occupied by a siesta, and after tea on the lawn we would go out, as in Lucknow, to see the sights of the city.

And here, once again, we were back in the Mutiny; for Cawnpore was the scene of one of the great tragedies of that terrible period, a crime that shocked India almost as deeply as it shocked the British. For almost sixty years later, when I was a child in Delhi, listening pop-eyed and riveted to tales of the 'Black Year', I was told by a Muslim resident of that walled city a tale that had been current there for many years. How the head *maulvi* of the *Jumma Masjid* had nailed a manifesto on to the main door of that great mosque, denouncing the massacre of the captive *Angrezi* women and their children in the *Bibi-ghur*, and calling upon the Faithful to lay down their arms and return to their homes, since God could no longer be on their side because of the 'Sin of Cawnpore'. I used that tale when I wrote *Shadow of the Moon*.

Chapter 3

The story of Cawnpore would have differed very little from half a dozen other Mutiny stories, had it not been for the fact that the victims of the final horror of that terrible summer were all women and young children. Over 200 of them — all that were left of the 'more than 1,000' Europeans who had survived a horrendous twenty-one-day siege, followed by an even more horrific massacre in the shallows of the Ganges.

When I see and hear some of the anti-British tump that is being dished out today by *son-et-lumière* shows at Delhi's Red Fort, or in pamphlets sold in her bazaars, written by agitators still whipping that long dead horse, the Raj, and inciting racial hatred by retelling the tale of 'Hodson's brutal and unnecessary shooting of the unarmed sons of the King of Delhi',* I am reminded that no mention is ever made of another hapless fifty or so non-combatants, of whom all but six were women and children whose menfolk had been killed on that fateful June day when Delhi rose against 'John Company's' rule; and who, after being held captive for nearly three weeks in the fetid darkness of a stifling dungeon below the palace in that same Red Fort, were eventually dragged up into the glaring sunlight, to be butchered in an open courtyard by men armed with swords, bayonets and sabres, for the entertainment of a gaping, jostling crowd of onlookers . . .

The bodies were left there all day to provide the citizens of Delhi with a free raree show. And in the evening they were piled on carts by men of the lowest caste, untouchables who are the disposers of rubbish and filth, and taken to the river-bank to be flung one by one into the placid Jumna. 'Food for the crocodiles and the mud-turtles, the jackals and the scavenger birds: and a sign and a warning to a hundred villages as the

---

* The pamphleteers make them out to be children. In fact, anyone who cares to check will find out they were grown men.

bodies drifted with the slow stream, to be stranded on sandbars and burning-*ghats* and fish-traps, or caught in the eddies that washed the walls of fortified towns.'*

That story is *not* popular with the pamphleteers. Nor (though we still hear a lot about Amritsar and General Dyer) do we hear much about the fate of the Cawnpore garrison, whose numbers were roughly estimated as 'well above a thousand souls' (a figure that included their families, but not the scores of panic-stricken civilians who had flocked in from outlying stations to take refuge in General Wheeler's pitifully inadequate entrenchments). Incredibly, the garrison stood siege there for twenty-one days, under continual fire and appalling daily losses, until eventually, driven by lack of food and almost no water, they were forced to accept the terms of surrender offered by the 'Nana Sahib' — Dundu Pant, Rajah of Bithor — now being written up as a heroic freedom fighter. The terms had included a solemn promise to send the remnants of the garrison in *budgerows* (large eight-oared river-boats with thatched roofs) down-river to Allahabad, and the ragged, starving survivors gave up their weapons, ammunition and treasure and, carrying their wounded on mattresses, managed to drag themselves down to the mile-distant river and on to the waiting boats. But it had been a trap.

No sooner were they all aboard than a signal was blown by a bugler and immediately the boatmen set fire to the thatched roofs and, jumping into the river, waded ashore, allowing Dundu Pant's soldiery to open fire from either bank on the helpless passengers. The wounded and too weak burned to death, and of those who were not drowned or shot in the river but managed to struggle ashore, the men were immediately killed and the women and children herded into carts and taken away to be imprisoned in the *Bibi-ghur* (women's house),† where they were later joined by other wretched captives, of whom it is said that 'only four or five' were men.

As for the 200 or so women and children who had survived the horrors of the siege and the massacre of the boats, they had just fifteen more

---

* Well over eighty years later, while staying in one of the Rajputana states, I managed to make friends with an ancient, autocratic and notoriously anti-British dowager who, when she felt she knew me well enough, confided in me that the first members of my race she had ever seen were the bodies of the prisoners who had been massacred in a courtyard of the Red Fort in Delhi. She had been a small child lying on the wall of her father's fort, and had watched them circulating in the eddy under the main bastion.

† *Bee Bee-ghar* pronounced *garr*, single syllable.

days to live. For when, barely more than a fortnight later, Dundu Pant heard the guns of the relief force firing within earshot of Cawnpore, he turned like a mad dog on the helpless prisoners and ordered his sepoys to open fire on them. When, to their eternal credit and the fury of the Nana Sahib, they refused, he ordered butchers to be brought in from the town's abattoirs; men who, armed with sharpened swords and the knives and cleavers of their trade, set about butchering the close-packed mass of dazed and starving women and children.

It had taken all day to kill them; and according to the onlookers, when the butchers' weapons became blunted they were handed out through the windows to be re-sharpened or replaced by fresh ones. With the morning the avid crowds were back again in force, this time to watch the mangled bodies dragged out and thrown into a nearby well. Not all of them were dead, and one small boy who had lain all night, frozen with terror under the bodies of the dead, ran screaming round the well until one of the onlookers caught him by the legs and, swinging him against the rim, so that his head cracked on the stone, tossed him in. That savage mass-murder successfully accomplished, Dundu Pant marshalled 5,000 of his fighting men and marched out to meet the Company's army . . .

They were only narrowly defeated. But when their leader realized that the battle was lost, he took to his heels and fled into the *Terai*,* leaving his followers to face the music. His parting act before he fled was to order his guards to kill a Mrs Carter and her new-born infant. Which was done, despite the frantic protests of his wives and women, who had taken in and given refuge to the pregnant mother, whose baby had recently been born in the women's quarters of his palace. Not a man to look back upon with pride as a national hero, I would have thought.

By now the thunder of Havelock's guns could be heard firing on the outskirts of the city. So when the last corpse was flung into the well, onlookers and perpetrators alike took to their heels without making the slightest effort to cap the well or to clear away the gruesome evidence of the butchery that had taken place in the *Bibi-ghur*.

The stench of that charnel-house, and the sight of those appalling wounds and silent gaping mouths and sightless eyes that stared up from the well at the men who had arrived too late, provoked an explosion of

* The long belt of jungle and grassland that used to spread for many miles along the foothills of the Himalayas.

rage and hatred among Havelock's men, and marked an ugly turning-point in the campaign. For from that day forward men of the British regiments, who had felt no particular animosity to the mutineers and had always got on well with the sepoys, turned into vicious killers intent on revenge. They went into battle shouting as their war-cry: '*Remember Cawnpore! Remember Cawnpore!*' And they remembered Cawnpore and killed without mercy and hanged without mercy, condemning a man as often as not for the colour of his skin as from any proof of guilt.

The atrocities committed in revenge for those who were so brutally slaughtered at Cawnpore were as unforgivable as the deeds which prompted it. And, as ever, it was the innocent who suffered most. Countless Indians, many of them blameless, died violent deaths at the hands of infuriated soldiers who, blinded by the red fog of rage, forgot that they were, technically at least, Christians whose Bible states categorically that '"Vengeance is mine," saith the Lord, "I will repay."' They preferred to take the matter into their own hands — and did so. The results have been collected in detail in a book entitled *The Other Side of the Medal*, which does not make pretty reading.

❊ A little over sixty years later, in a last echo of those terrible days, the terrified, bloodstained little ghosts of those who died in the *Bibi-ghur* at Cawnpore crept out from the blackness of the well into which their bodies had been thrown, to haunt a man by the name of Dyer, who, though born seven years after their deaths, had been brought up by people to whom the Mutiny and its horror-stories were part of current history and their day-to-day lives.

He had joined the army and done well there, and shortly after the end of the First World War (by which time he had reached the rank of General) he was called upon to cope with a savage explosion of violence, anarchy and rioting that had broken out in the Punjab, whipped up by agitators demanding immediate independence. The burning and looting inevitably led to bloodshed, and in Amritsar, a centre of the violence, the mob killed five Europeans, three of them, Scott, Stewart and Thompson, bank managers whom they beat up with *lathis** before dragging them up to the flat rooftops of their respective banks and throwing them down on

* A long, stout staff of bamboo, bound with iron, used by all and sundry in place of a walking stick, and carried as a weapon by the police.

to the pavements below, where the mob doused them with kerosene oil and set them alight. Mr Robinson, a railway guard, was also beaten to death by the *lathis* of another 'unarmed' mob, while Sergeant Rowlands, an electrician peacefully on his way to work at the Municipal Power House and unaware of any trouble, was attacked and had his hands hacked off before being battered to death.

There was very nearly a sixth victim, a Miss Sherwood, whom the mob beat and left for dead. Poor Marcella Sherwood, a woman doctor who for fifteen years had worked selflessly for the Zenana Mission Society and the women of Amritsar, heard of the rioting and, though warned of the danger, sped off on her bicycle to make sure that all her pupils got safely back to their homes. She was well known and liked by the citizens. But by now the mob had embarked on an orgy of blood and violence, and seeing her appear a group of youths began yelling, 'She's English! Kill her! She's English!' A man in the crowd shouted back that she was a good woman, a healer and a teacher; but the crowds were drunk on destruction and one of the youths pulled her off her bicycle by her hair and pushed her to the ground. She managed to scramble up and run, only to be brought down again; and at that the frenzied mob closed in like hounds at a kill, snarling, ripping and kicking the defenceless woman until they reduced her to a bloodstained pulp. Shouting exultantly that she was dead, they left her lying in the gutter and rushed away in search of further entertainment; yelling, of *all* things, 'Victory to Gandhi!'

For it was Gandhi's tragedy (and India's even more so) that this Mahatma who preached peace and non-violence understood the mind of the British so much better than the mind of his own people, and never seems to have realized that any gathering of the latter must, when whipped up by inflammatory speeches by an agitator, inevitably lead to violence. It is only too possible that this revered and world-famous apostle may, after all, have been personally responsible for more deaths than Stalin. Though not, as it happened, for Marcella's, who by some miracle survived — her battered and unrecognizable body having been retrieved and cared for, at the risk of their lives, by a bazaar shopkeeper and his wife. But this savage attack on a harmless woman, and the brutal murders of the five non-combatant Europeans for no better reason than their nationality, served to convince many more people than Dyer that what they were seeing was a rerun of the opening days of the Mutiny.

Murderers like Dundu Pant are extolled as heroic freedom fighters, while men like Dyer are execrated in films,* books and newspaper articles, though Dyer acted as he did for one reason only: he firmly believed that he was preventing another Mutiny and a second Cawnpore. For the repercussions of that brutal Massacre of the Innocents, like a stone flung into a stagnant pool, had sent ripples out across India, driving men to acts of savagery that they chose to term 'reprisals'. And sixty-two years later the last of those ripples was to lap against the walls of the Jallianwala Bagh in Amritsar, when a man who had seen the smashed and mangled, near-dead body of Marcella Sherwood,† and feared a repetition of that appalling slaughter, ordered his troops‡ to fire on an 'unarmed' (if you don't count *lathis* and clubs as arms) mob of thousands, who had already tasted blood and were being urged by a series of well-known rabble-rousers to march on the Cantonments and kill all the '*Angrezi* monkeys'.

There is a postscript to all this.

Many years later, long after India had achieved her independence and become two separate countries, while on a visit to Indian friends in Calcutta I had an interesting conversation with one of that city's lively and cynical young writers. We had been commenting on his country's rewriting of British–Indian history, with special reference to such matters as the bricking-up, post Independence, of a narrow alleyway leading out of the Jallianwala Bagh, with a view to impressing on foreign tourists the extreme brutality of the British (it makes that terrible episode look even nastier if there was no other way out of it — and nowadays there isn't).

Then there was also the recent removal by the Calcutta City Council of a monument to all those who died from suffocation in a single night in the notorious Black Hole of Calcutta — a gruesome incident that occurred over a century before the massacre of Cawnpore — and the fact that, in addition to abolishing the monument (no loss; it was not a thing of beauty), the Council had pronounced the entire incident to have

* See Sir Richard Attenborough's film *Gandhi*.

† While still barely alive she had been smuggled out of the shop by night and taken to the fort, where Dyer had seen her.

‡ Incidentally, there were no British troops involved in the shooting in the Bagh. Dyer's force was entirely Indian. It consisted of twenty-five rifles of the Ninth Gurkhas; twenty-five rifles of the 54th Sikhs FF (Frontier Force) and the 59th Rifles FF, and forty Gurkhas armed with *kukris* (Gurkha knives). Plus two armed cars. Not that it makes any difference to the appalling fact of the shooting. But it's interesting that the anti-British lot should never mention it.

been a malicious invention; a lying piece of British propaganda without a grain of truth in it, fabricated for the sole purpose of discrediting that heroic freedom fighter, and the local Nawab, one Suraj-ud-daula (in those days the larger part of India was ruled by Muslim potentates).

I said that this seemed a pretty silly thing to do, considering the amount of evidence that existed, including letters from the only two survivors, and that I was surprised — if this type of Orwellian '*1984*' Newspeak was becoming so popular in India — that while they were about it they hadn't decided to repudiate the Cawnpore massacre as well. At which my chatty acquaintance laughed and said: 'Don't worry. We will! Just give us time. It's early days yet, and Cawnpore isn't nearly as easy to dismiss as the Black Hole was, because the evidence is still all there.'

When I asked what evidence, he said: 'The bodies, of course. They're still down there, and if we began to say that the whole affair was only a propaganda horror-story cooked up by your lot, someone has only got to take the top off that well and there they all are. Bones last for thousands of years and it's easy to find out how the owners died and what sex they were. And to date them. Besides, there must be a lot of other things down there. Hooks and eyes. Buttons. Whalebone from stays. Hairpins — any number of things besides a couple of hundred skeletons. But the bodies from the Black Hole were thrown into the Hoogly, which is a tidal river. See?'

I said I saw. And I did.

'I daresay that one of these days,' mused Young India, 'when the ground has been cleared and people have forgotten where that well was, or what happened here, some business corporation will build a whopping great housing estate on the site, all concrete beehive flats. And if anyone remembers the *Bibi-ghur* affair, we shall say that it was just a story that was put about to discredit us — another "lying bit of *Angrezi* propaganda".'

He laughed again, and I said it was quite a thought. But that nothing would induce me to live in one of those flats. Would he?

'*The gods forbid!*' agreed my cynical acquaintance with unexpected fervour; and shuddered as he said it.

✗ The little temple on the river-bank, from where Tantia Topi, the general in command of the Nana Sahib's forces, watched the massacre at the boats, was still there when Charlie Allen took us to see the sites in the autumn of 1927. But as soon as the Mutiny was over, the *Bibi-ghur* was destroyed and a garden planted on and around the place where it had stood. The well was properly capped and sealed and a sorrowing angel in white marble was placed on top of it, and the whole enclosed in a circular screen of ornately pierced and carved red sandstone. I gather that after Independence all this was swept away and the angel removed to the nearest Christian church. Which is no loss, since she was a singularly stodgy-looking Victorian angel in the worst tradition of British funerary sculpture.

Presumably the red sandstone enclosure has gone too; and if so the prophecy of my cynical young Calcutta acquaintance may well come true even sooner than he imagined. Although, as we agreed, one would not fancy living in any building that was erected on or even near that unchancy spot, for though it might be all right by daylight, it would not be by night — by no means at night. Back in the thirties I met, in New Delhi, a middle-aged Englishwoman who claimed to be psychic, and who had been invited out to spend a cold weather with relatives stationed in Cawnpore. She had looked forward to spending two or three months with them, but had left after less than ten days, and was in Delhi arranging for a return passage because, she said, she could not endure the ghosts that haunted the garden of her host's bungalow.

They were not there during the daytime, she said, but she had seen them again and again at dusk, and once or twice by moonlight — running distractedly across the open lawns to hide among the bushes and the tree shadows. Some appeared to be carrying babies in their arms, while others dragged older children by the hand; and when the moon was up she could see that their trailing skirts were tattered and stained with ugly blotches and that their eyes and their gaping mouths were dark pools of terror in their pallid faces. She had thought at first that they were gypsies.

I remember a sceptical listener suggesting that she had obviously allowed a surfeit of Mutiny horror-stories to prey on her mind until they gave her hallucinations; an explanation that the lady rejected with considerable indignation, insisting that prior to this visit all she had ever known about the Indian Mutiny was that there had been one! She had never been interested in colonial history, and as for her hosts, they had been far more interested in having a good time than in local folk tales, and it had not occurred to them to tell her grisly stories of a time they plainly regarded as being in the remote past. It was only when she inquired at breakfast one day about the groups of oddly dressed gypsy-women she had seen every evening, running across their lawn, that she realized that what she had seen were not living people, but the silent re-enactment of something that had happened back in the middle of the previous century.

Do I believe in ghosts? Yes, I certainly do. You cannot be born and spend your formative years in a country like India without accepting the truth of that famous statement that Shakespeare put into the mouth of Hamlet: 'There are more things in Heaven and Earth, Horatio, than are dreamt of in your philosophy.' There are indeed.

There are also more predators, one species of which I was to encounter for the first time within a few days of our arrival in Cawnpore.

❊ 2 ❊

'Me and my shadow'

Chapter 4

❧✦❧

In most hot countries it is customary to take a siesta during the afternoon, and since the habit had been adopted by the British in India, I was disappointed to discover that the 'grown-ups' (of whom I was now one, though I still found that difficult to accept) were apt to take to their beds during the hottest part of the day; a practice that seemed to me a terrible waste of time. However, I dutifully followed their example, and one afternoon, not long after our arrival in Cawnpore, I was jerked out of this post-prandial catnap by a terrific uproar from outside the house.

I could hear C. T. Allen's voice bellowing unintelligible instructions above a deafening clamour that sounded like a hundred tin cans being banged together, and my mind being full of the horrors that had befallen the British in Cawnpore barely seventy years ago, I thought for one wild moment that history was repeating itself and that we were being attacked by a hostile mob.

Leaping off my bed and into a cotton frock, I ran out into the verandah, to discover my parents and the Allens, and what appeared to be the entire indoor and outdoor staff of the Retreat plus their families, rushing across the lawns, yelling and banging anything made of metal that they could lay their hands on: cooking-pots, *dekchi* lids, tin trays, buckets, empty cans, and the dinner gong had all been pressed into service, and the din was indescribable. I could see no sign of an enemy, until C. T. yelled at me to fetch something and bang on it and pointed up at the sky above the lake. It was only then that I noticed for the first time that the sun was no longer shining and the brilliant afternoon had clouded over. There was a storm coming up; a dust-storm by the look of it. '*Lo*custs!' yelled C. T., and ran on towards the lake.

A curious dry, whirring sound became audible even above the frenzied clamour of shouting and banging, and I realized suddenly that the dingy,

37

dun-coloured clouds that had blotted out the sun were not clouds at all but millions and billions of winged insects, a blanket of outsize grasshoppers darkening the sky in the manner of an approaching storm.

Strangely, considering the noise that they themselves were making, they didn't like the pandemonium we were raising, so the vast majority of them flew on, passing over our heads to settle on and decimate the croplands and orchards of some other, and less fortunate, cultivator who had failed to notice their approach and muster sufficient helpers to drive them off. But although the terrifying brown blanket, disliking the din we were raising, flew on, a small proportion of locusts, lured by C. T.'s green lawns, flowerbeds and well-stocked kitchen garden, broke ranks and alighted. And judging from the damage they did, the devastation that an entire swarm can cause must be horrific. They could not have been more than a tiny percentage of the awesome whole — possibly one in every thousand. Yet every tree, shrub and plant seemed to be covered with great armour-plated grasshoppers whose jaws crunched so noisily that you could hear them munching.

The servants stopped banging on their makeshift gongs and concentrated instead on killing the creatures with sticks, ably assisted by flocks of crows, kites, shrikes and other carrion birds who hovered and swooped overhead, gorging themselves on this rich banquet. Baskets and sacks were filled with corpses and carted away in the direction of the servants' quarters, presumably to be burned or buried, for though the Chinese consider roast locusts to be a delicacy, I don't think India really fancies them as food.

This was the first locust swarm I had ever seen, and it was a truly alarming sight — made even more alarming for me by C. T. casually describing it as a 'small one'! What a really large one must be like I daren't think, for if our efforts to discourage it from landing had failed, there would not have been a leaf or a flower-petal, or a single ear of corn, in all C. T.'s green and flourishing acres. I have always believed that we ought not to meddle with the balance of nature, because every time we do we discover (invariably too late) that we have ended up with a worse problem on our plates, but I admit I can't see that the world would be worse off without locusts. Or, for that matter, muggers — not the human ones, but the hideous, blunt-nosed, armour-plated crocodiles of the Indian rivers. Both give me the grue; and though I'm sure Sir David Attenborough could find something nice to say about them, me, I could do fine wanting them, for I cannot see that either species has ever been of the slightest use to anyone.

�֍ We had several other friends in Cawnpore, among them the parents of a small girl, now grown-up. This was Gerry Ross, with whom Bets and I had acted in the children's plays which, during the First World War, had been staged at Simla's Gaiety Theatre by a Mrs Strettle, now Lady Strettle, who used to run the children's dancing classes.

Gerry had played the Rainbow King in a two-act dance-mime, *The Lost Colour*, and taken the part of Peter in *Peter Pan*, but we remembered her best for the fact that after having her head shaved in order to help her survive a severe attack of enteric fever — a treatment that seems to have been popular in those distant days — her beautiful, red-gold hair, hitherto straight, grew back in a riot of short, copper-coloured curls which were the envy of every little girl in Simla. Few of us will ever forget that dashing Rainbow King, clad in glittering gold leggings and short, belted tunic which exactly matched those glinting curls, and flourishing a sword upon the little stage of the Gaiety Theatre. Here she was once more, a decade later, a tall, slim and dashing young woman with a curly bronze head and enough poise and sophistication for six.

Gerry had spent a day with us at the Retreat, boating and picnicking on the lake, and when the time came for us to leave Cawnpore, her parents suggested that ours should let Bets and me stay on for a few days in their bungalow while Tacklow and Mother went on ahead to look for accommodation for us in Delhi. Their offer was gratefully accepted by my parents, and Bets and I found ourselves spending another week in Cawnpore, this time in a brick-built bungalow not unlike an official Rest House, which stood in an almost treeless compound on a flat, dusty and featureless plain; an unattractive place after the green and picturesque charms of the Retreat. But the starkness of the Rosses' bungalow somehow managed to fit the situation, for I remember living through the week that we spent there in a state of continuous embarrassment, from which I could not wait to escape. I had never had a very high opinion of my charms (brother Bill had seen to that!), but never before had I felt so gauche, plain and socially inadequate.

Gerry, who like my beautiful and beloved 'best friend' from my childhood days in Simla, Marjorie ('Bargie') Slater, was a few years my senior, had blossomed into an outstandingly attractive and sophisticated young woman, though she lacked Bargie's sweetness. Enviably sure of herself, she was the very model of a Raj débutante, a 'Week Queen' — which was a term given to girls who were invited as though by right to the many 'weeks' of the cold weather season. Lahore Week, Meerut Week, Horse Show Week in Delhi, and the many other 'weeks' that featured racing, polo and point-to-points and included a plethora of dinners and dances as well as the usual complement of white-tie and fancy-dress balls that were graced by all the prettiest and most popular girls in India: the 'Week Queens', in fact.

Gerry's poise and confidence made me feel appallingly gauche by contrast, while my sense of my own inferiority was considerably increased by the fact that each evening of my stay, though I was graciously invited to help her choose which of her many ravishing evening dresses she would wear that night, and to watch her do her hair and make up her face prior to being fetched by one or other of an enviably large number of admiring young men, it was never once suggested that, as a house guest, I might be asked to accompany her. Gerry explained that the various parties had been arranged, and invitations to them accepted, long ago, and that no hostess (or host either) could be expected to welcome an extra and partnerless girl at the last moment. I saw her point. But all the same, I felt a bit like Cinderella minus a fairy godmother.

Someone with a better figure and more self-confidence might have written this off as fear of a rival. But as one who possessed neither, I knew only too well that far from regarding me as a possible rival, Gerry considered me much too dull to inflict on her lively friends. Still, I did think she might have *tried* to include me in just one party, and I remember that week as long, dull, and sadly deflating.

But our Miss Ross had obviously decided that left to myself I would be a non-starter in the social stakes; and possibly for the sake of old times, she took it upon herself to give me a few pointers for my own good. Which considering the circumstances was very kind of her. In a lengthy lecture, delivered in the course of a long afternoon spent lying under the mosquito-net in her bedroom, she went to a lot of trouble to 'put me in the picture'; warning me what to expect when I reached Delhi, and telling me how I should behave.

According to Gerry, India was no longer the happy hunting-ground for spinsters in search of a mate that it had once been. The 1914–18 war had killed hundreds of thousands of young men, leaving an estimated

3 million 'surplus' British women who would never find husbands; and the annual trickle of Fishing Fleet girls had, in consequence, swelled to a flood. Each year every India-bound passenger ship brought more and more unmarried young women out eastward, and where men had once outnumbered women by at least five to one, the figures were now reversed. It was, therefore, up to any girl who wanted to have a good time, let alone find a husband, to keep her wits about her.

First and foremost it was essential that she acquire a beau to partner her at dances — any beau (I gathered that almost anything in trousers would do) — because unattached girls were always a liability. This meant that one had to corral a male who could dance. And one need not, to begin with, be too fussy — unless, of course, one was outstandingly pretty or the daughter of a well-heeled father who held an important post in the Government, in which case one could pick and choose, since ambitious young men would be only too anxious to take one out and about. However, since that plainly did not apply to me, Gerry advised me to keep my sights low and start by ensnaring some Indian Infantry subaltern, or even a junior *box-wallah* (a term for those in trade, who, according to Gerry, came at the bottom of the social scale except in places like Calcutta and Bombay).

Once you had managed to corral a steady beau you would be invited to all sorts of parties that you would never have been asked to as an unattached spinster; for although hostesses considered a spare man to be an asset to any party, they regarded an extra girl as a disaster. But once safely in circulation you could, with luck, pick up something better — graduate from a *box-wallah* or an Indian Foot subaltern to someone in a British regiment or in the Indian Cavalry; and from there, who knows? ... To the British Cavalry or one of the Viceroy's ADCs, or even to a member of the ICS — the Heaven-born, no less! It was up to you. The world of Jane Austen and Becky Sharpe had not, as I had supposed, disappeared along with Queen Victoria and her beloved Albert, but was still with us; very much alive and flourishing like the green bay tree in this outpost of Empire.

Gerry was kind enough to give me endless tips on how to outsmart other girls and ensure that my dance-programme* was filled. All this would, I feel sure, have proved invaluable to me if only I hadn't lacked

* Yes, we still had dance-programmes — and kept on doing so to the very end of the Raj.

41

the nerve to put them into practice. The lecture ended with a solemn warning: I must never, but *never!* emphasized Gerry, neglect to discard the early and socially less important admirers who had acted as stepping-stones to higher things, once their usefulness was over and I had 'made the grade'.

'I can see that sounds pretty shocking to you,' said Gerry, 'and that you think I'm being horridly hard-hearted. But believe me, it's the only sensible thing to do. If you mean to get on, you simply *cannot* afford to lumber yourself with useless and unimportant friends. Just harden your heart and drop them as soon as possible. If you've played your cards right, you'll find it easy enough to drop the riff-raff. One *has* to be ruthless!'

I can still see myself on that hot afternoon, wearing the regulation 'siesta dress' of bra and camiknickers (who remembers those?) and sitting hunched up and pop-eyed with horror on Gerry's bed under the misty folds of her mosquito-net; being instructed on how to attract men and become a social success by this enchanting and wildly successful 'Week Queen'. And I remember, too, how my heart sank down and down as I listened, because I knew only too well that I lacked the nerve to do or say any of the things that Gerry insisted were vitally necessary and *must* be done. I was, after all, the granddaughter of a devout Scottish missionary, and I was shocked to the core of my ignorant, innocent and prudish 'play-up-and-play-the-game' soul, by almost everything that Gerry had said. I had never dreamed that the search for 'love and laughter and happy-ever-after' could turn out to be such a harshly competitive affair; or that the pursuit of happiness entailed quite so much quick thinking and sharp practice. I knew I wasn't up to it and that I had better face the bleak fact that I was destined to be a wallflower at dances and end up unwed and unwanted in some home for destitute spinsters.

All in all, it was a profoundly depressing visit. Despite the efforts of Mrs Pankhurst and her valiant crew of suffragettes, we were still in the dear, dead days when marriage was not only fashionable, but also romantic; and we were great ones for Romance — 'Happiness, and I guess, all those things we've always pined for.' How else could one live happily ever after unless one married (see Cinderella & Co.), when boy-meets-girl or vice versa was the theme of almost every novel, play and pop-song ever written? *Of course* I wanted to get married! But not if it entailed setting my cap at some pimply-faced and presumably gullible youth, for the purpose of using him as a first step towards getting invited to parties where I might meet someone more worthwhile — who would in turn introduce me to something even better; and so on, up the ladder, towards the Prince Charming class, ruthlessly kicking away each rung as I mounted to the next.

The result of Gerry's pep-talk was that I left Cawnpore in a distinctly subdued frame of mind, and with my morale once more in flinders. But one look at Delhi Central as the train drew in did wonders for my drooping spirits, for it looked exactly the same as it had on the sad day when I had last seen it. And suddenly it was as though all those grey, intervening years of exile were no more than a brief dream from which I had just awoken. Nothing had changed!

Here once again were the same sounds and smells and sights. The familiar grey-headed crows, the jostling, shouting luggage coolies, the same vendors of food and drink, fruit and toys; the same milling and vociferous crowds of passengers, some, like ourselves, with their journey done, descending from the train, while others scrambled aboard it, bound for towns and cities in the north. I had last seen this station through a haze of tears, afraid that I might never see dear Delhi again. And now, once more, I found that my eyes were swimming because I was so happy to see it again and to know that I had come back to a loved and familiar place, even though there was something missing: of all the many friends that had crowded the platform to wish us 'bon voyage' on that long ago day of our leaving, none were there to welcome us back, and I was suddenly aware of the gap between ten and nineteen . . . the enormous gap.

Bets and I had travelled up in the care of a Major and Mrs Something-or-other who were bound for somewhere further north, and only our parents and Abdul Karim were on the platform to meet us. And presently we were driving out of the station yard through the ranks of *tongas* and *tikka-gharies*, along familiar streets and past familiar places. But this time, alas, we did not, as in the old days, turn left towards Old Delhi and the Kashmir Gate, but right — towards New Delhi, a place that had consisted of little more than the foundations of buildings when we had last seen it. Now it was the capital city of India and most of its buildings were not only completed but occupied. I thought it looked raw and ugly and barren, and found it difficult to believe that the thousands of small, struggling saplings that had been planted on either side of the wide avenues, each one surrounded by a zariba of chicken-wire or iron stakes to protect them from the depredations of wandering goats and cattle or the destructive attentions of vandals, would ever live to become tall and green. Or that the barren wastes of parched ground would ever be covered with grass and shrubs and flowerbeds.

The whole place looked as hot and bleak and colourless as the Thar, the great Indian desert that lies between Jodhpur and the Indus, while the grandiose buildings that Sir Edwin Lutyens and Sir Richard Baker had designed to lend splendour and dignity to the latest and (it was hoped) last and greatest city of Delhi, were, in my opinion, the ugliest things I had ever seen. In those early days the aggressively new red and white sandstone of which they were built had not even begun to weather, and at first sight the red lower third of the two huge Secretariat buildings that faced each other from opposite sides of the wide, rising slope of what was then known as the Kingsway (and is now known as the Rajpath, which means the same thing) was, to my mind, distressingly reminiscent of a tiled splashback in a bathroom, while the top section glared as blindingly white as though coated with fresh whitewash. I thought the whole thing was hideous, and a poor exchange for the leafy gardens and beautiful, mellowed buildings of Shah Jehan's Old Delhi.

We spent our first week in New Delhi in one of the houses designed by Sir Herbert Baker for the use of senior officials of the Government of India, and which had the appearance of being mass-produced. Each one stood on its own ample square of stony earth that would one day — nature and the monsoons permitting — be a green and shady garden; and each one faced in a slightly different direction to give an illusion of individuality. All these buildings were whitewashed, and the architect had striven to give them a slightly Eastern look by the addition of an ornate brickwork lattice here and there in place of a window. This may have helped to keep the rooms cooler during the hot weather, but certainly made them very stuffy during the winter and early spring, and earned them the title of 'Baker's Ovens'.

Our particular oven was shared by two senior bachelor friends of my parents, who had invited them to stay until Tacklow had made arrangements to house his family for the season, and they insisted that Bets and I, whom they had known practically from our cradle days, should stay with them until our 'camp' had been set up. For Tacklow, finding it difficult to get rooms in New Delhi (and impossible to rent even the smallest bungalow there), had arranged with the Committee of the Gymkhana Club to house all four of us in the tented camp that was in the process of being set up in the grounds behind the club-house, for the use of members with families, who would sleep under canvas and have their meals in the Club's dining-room. This scheme enthralled Bets and me, for we had many old friends — Buckie* among them — who not only used to spend their cold weathers in a luxurious tented camp on the far side of Old Delhi, originally set up for VIPs attending the great Durbar of 1911, but continued to do so.

Tents had always held an enormous fascination for us, particularly the semi-permanent variety, for India really went to town on those. They had wooden floors, raised high enough to keep them clear of flooding during the months of the monsoon or the short-lived winter rains, on which carpets or *durries* were laid. The canvas walls were double, with enough space between them to keep the interior of the tent cool in summer and warm in winter, while the furniture was much the same as you would expect to find in a house, and leading off each bedroom tent was a small India-style bathroom.

The tents were part of the dear, remembered days of our childhood, and when we moved into them it was with delight. The Club itself was at that time only standing in for the real Club, which was still unfinished; and when, in the following year, it was finally completed, the temporary one was bought by His Highness the Maharajah of Kashmir and renamed Kashmir House, while the new one became known as the 'IDG' — the Imperial Delhi Gymkhana Club.

We had barely got settled in our tents before we acquired the usual cat who, like all Kaye cats, was immediately named 'Chips'. I have no idea how we managed to collect it, and can only suppose that it had attached itself to Tacklow, who attracted cats like jam at a picnic attracts wasps. All I remember about this one is that he was a ginger kitten, presumably a stray and, at the time we acquired him, about six inches long and exceedingly talkative. Fortunately, since Tacklow was away so much and we would accompany him on his tours whenever we could, 'Club' Chips soon transferred his allegiance to the Club's cook, who used to feed him for us whenever we were away. Preferring a static owner to ones perpetually on the move, 'Club' Chips very sensibly decided to move in where the

* Sir Edward Buck, head of Reuter's in India for many years, and author of *Simla Past and Present*.

food was, and since the cook became quite fond of him, we lost him to the kitchen department some time during one of our Rajputana trips. This was lucky, since shortly after his defection, the Club *mali* (gardener) presented us with 'Pozlo'* — a tiny, naked hideosity, all eyes and beak and about the size of a somewhat battered golf ball. An unalluring object that, given the chance, should grow up to be a purple-headed parakeet.

Pozlo's parents, for reasons best known to themselves, had pushed him out of the hole in a silk cotton tree in which they had made their nest, and the *mali* had found him cheeping forlornly on the ground and had put him back. But an hour later he had been pushed out again. The same thing happened when we took over and returned him to his nest — twice. Nature is ruthless in these matters, and presumably there was something wrong with the poor fellow that was imperilling the rest of the fledgelings.

Since it was obvious that if we did not take him into care a cat or a snake would make a meal of him, we decided to keep him, even though he hadn't a single feather to fly with, being still only skin and quills, and we had no idea what to feed him on. However, he was far more afraid of falling than he was of us, and regarding a finger as a lifebelt, he would cling to it for all he was worth. It obviously spelled safety in a harsh world, and from then on we were friends and allies. I think I am right in saying that we started him on a cannibalistic diet of chopped hard-boiled egg, before abandoning it in favour of mashed banana and any other available fruit, on which he flourished and grew feathered. And, as with all our pets, he ended up by attaching himself firmly to Tacklow.

Purple-headed parakeets are small birds that look larger than they are because their blue tail-feathers are at least three times the length of their stumpy little bodies. But since Pozlo had not acquired a tail, he fitted very nicely into the palm of one's hand. Tacklow bought him the biggest cage he could find in the bazaars and Pozlo loved it. He learned very soon how to open and shut the door and it was a treat to see him turning to latch his front door carefully behind him. I daresay if we had provided him with a notice saying 'Do Not Disturb' he would have learned to hang it out when he felt like it.

It was in the ballroom of the future Kashmir House that I attended what was to be my very first ball, as opposed to a mere dance. A 'Blue

* Kaye-language for 'Polly'.

46

Cross Ball' in aid of the RSPCA, it was a best-dress, sixteen-button glove* affair, since it was attended by an assortment of the Great, including His Excellency the Governor of This, That and the Other Province, as well as the Viceroy and his wife, a glitter of Indian royalties, a shimmer of Indian Civil Servants, a froth of Foreign-and-Politicals, and any number of full-dress uniforms — the Raj in splendour!

Fortunately, we had been invited to join a large party, and since it was the custom for every male guest to dance at least once with every female one, I cannot have had to sit out too many dances. Anyway, it stays fixed in my memory as a wonderful and exciting occasion — which it certainly would not have done had I spent it being a wallflower. But although I can't remember the colour of the dress I wore, or who I danced with or talked to, I still remember very clearly one particular item of the amateur cabaret show that was almost an obligatory accompaniment to any charity ball.

The lights in the ballroom were all switched off, except for a single spotlight focused on a lone woman who danced and sang in the centre of the darkened floor. A thin little woman who wore a blouse, tights, and one of those flat, peaked caps in midnight blue, and sang a song that I had never heard before. It was called 'Me and My Shadow', and is, by now, a very old song, but it was new then, and I have never forgotten the words or the tune, or how the singer's shadow followed her every movement until the spotlight blinked out on the last note.

To this day, whenever I hear that tune played on some 'golden oldies' programme on the TV or the radio, I am once again the young Mollie that I was, sitting enthralled in that darkened ballroom in New Delhi and watching a spotlight in which someone is dancing with their shadow . . . It can even bring back the strong mixture of odours that permeated the ballroom. Coty's 'Mon Boudoir' and 'L'Aimant', cooked food and cigarette smoke, and the strong scent of orange-blossom, sweet peas and roses that drifted in from the garden and brought with it the strange and wholly individual smells of the dusty roads and raw-new buildings of this latest Delhi.

* Sixteen-button gloves were the very long, white kid gloves which custom decreed should be worn by all memsahibs of the Raj when attending any Viceregal function.

Chapter 5

~~☆≪✕≫☆~~

Tacklow, when not away visiting princely states, was busy for most of the day in an office in the Secretariat building, and Mother, Bets and I spent a lot of time looking up old friends. But, for me, a lot of the old magic had gone.

The Khan-Sahib had been dead for several years, and his children and grandchildren had moved away from Delhi long ago. And though we often visited his widow, the Begum, who still lived in their house in the old walled city, spoke no English and had always kept strict purdah, bereavement had turned her into a sad, prematurely old woman who preferred to moan to Mother about the misery of widowhood and the difficulty of getting really trustworthy servants in these degenerate days, or attempting to talk to Bets and me in our now halting Hindustani.

The Diwan-Sahib had returned to his home in Rajputana, and I remember seeing him only once, when he called in to see Tacklow on his way north to visit relatives who lived somewhere near Karnal. The fathers of most of the Indian children with whom I used to play in the old days had either been promoted or left to take up senior appointments in other provinces or districts, or, like Tacklow, retired after years of service in the Government of the country and gone back with their wives to spend their old age in their own home towns or villages. Their families were scattered: the daughters married and gone to their husband's homes, and their sons studying in universities in Bombay, Calcutta or England, if not already in jobs in one or other of India's great cities.

Vika* had married the son of some merchant prince and now lived in great splendour in, I think, Madras, while the house off the Rajpore Road in which lovely Lakshmi and her parents had lived had changed hands several times during the last nine years, and the only person who

---

* See *The Sun in the Morning.*

remembered them was an old *mali* who said he thought they had been transferred to Lucknow. Of the rest, very few still lived in Delhi, and since all of them had, like myself, spent a large part of the intervening years in school, their English had improved out of all knowledge and they no longer spoke to me in their own tongue, but in mine.

When we were young it had been different. Because they knew that I could speak and understand their language we used that as a matter of course and without thinking. But now that they were grown-ups and it had become fashionable to speak English, they were not going to slip back into the old ways. This was all right by me, because I'd forgotten far too much of theirs — and was ashamed of having done so. But there was one change that I should have been prepared for, since Tacklow had spoken of it often enough, it having been the reason why he had meant to retire after his job of Deputy Chief Censor came to an end.

He had wanted to go while he still had many Indian friends, and before those friendships soured. Like many Anglo-Indians,* he had supposed that the invaluable help that India had given the Allies during nearly five murderous years of war must, with victory, be rewarded by an immediate move toward Dominion Status, at the very least. When that did not happen he foresaw serious trouble ahead, and the breaking of many old ties.

He was right. For as the prospect of self-government and freedom from Imperial rule receded, hostility toward the Raj increased. I became aware of its effect among many of my one-time friends. Not among the ordinary people, the servants and shopkeepers, villagers, artisans and the poor, or among the princes, the hereditary rulers of semi-independent states; but among Indians of our own social level, the well-educated middle and upper-middle classes who sent their children to convent schools and colleges, and who stood to gain the most from Independence. Or thought that they would. The ordinary people were as friendly as ever, and the royals continued to be as regally pleasant as they had always been. But with several of the families I had known, the ease and companionship which I had enjoyed as a child, and had confidently expected to find waiting for me, had become tinged with reserve, and I became conscious

* I use that term in its old meaning: whites who spent their working lives in India, but returned to their home country on retirement.

of a barrier that had not been there before: an almost undetectable one, for Indians have beautiful manners. But a barrier just the same.

They were as charming as ever, but I was no longer one of them; it was as though I had once been 'family' and was now only a guest. To all appearances a welcome one — except in only one case, where the family concerned, having joined the Congress Party, made it woundingly plain that they no longer wished to have any close contacts with 'the enemy'. In particular, not with the daughter of a one-time Director of Central Intelligence.

'You can't blame them, you know,' said Tacklow, comforting me. 'If they are seen to be too friendly with you, their fellow Congressmen might suspect them of double-dealing. You have to put yourself in their place.'

He did his best to explain away that hurtful unhappy episode. Without much success, for I have never really got over it, and although it happened so very many years ago, the scar is still there. Even now, looking back on it, I can still remember the pain and shock — and the shaming embarrassment. We had all been such friends! I suppose part of the trouble was the inferiority complex I have already referred to.

It made me notice, too, and become painfully conscious of the fact that although the mothers of various Indian girls I had known seemed happy enough to let me remain on friendly terms with their daughters, it was a different matter when it came to their sons. Friendship between their darling boys and *Angrezi* girls, with whom they had played and laughed and squabbled in childhood, was not to be encouraged. Not now that they had left childhood behind them and become young men and women. Politics, religion and caste had become important, and the old careless, casteless, happy-go-lucky relationships were not to be recovered. It was not possible to be unaware of this; or unhurt by it.

Nowadays, when I read books about the Raj written by people who were not even born in those days, yet who like to make out that the British memsahibs despised Indian women and either patronized or snubbed them, I remember the times when I was made acutely aware that the boot was on the other foot, and that it was *I* who was not considered to be the equal of some well-bred and high-caste lady who not only would not socialize with the British, but would not allow her menfolk to enter the living-rooms of her house wearing western clothes, insisting that before doing so they must change into traditional Hindu dress, and who, if she could not avoid taking the hand of a European, would first cover her own with a fold of her sari.

These were the exceptions rather than the rule. But there were still enough of them to make me tread very carefully. And everyone was aware that among the ranks of the ruling princes there was at least one Maharajah, the ruler of no small state, who on any occasion on which *Angrezis* might be present, made a point of wearing specially made thin silk gloves, for fear that he might have to shake hands with one. I cannot think of any *Angrezi* who would have wished to take that particular hand, since his reputation for cruelty was of the blackest, and rumour credited him with several murders, including that of a wife or two; the law that prevented a ruling prince being prosecuted in any public court saved him again and again from being hauled before a judge. It was only when he flew into a rage with one of his horses which had either failed to win a race, or performed unsatisfactorily on a polo field — I forget which — and, calling for a can of petrol, flung the contents over the unfortunate animal and set a match to it, that the Government of India, which had been reluctant to prosecute him when it was a human life that was in question, suddenly came over all British, decided that His Highness had gone too far, and had him deposed.

There may have been a time when I was unaware of the existence and the rules of caste (one could hardly have been a child in India and *not* known them). But, if so, I don't remember it, and I suppose I can't have been much affected by them because, when last there, I had been regarded as being below the age of caste. But now it was different. Now I was a grown-up. And far from feeling myself superior to the natives of the country — as every trendy author from Forster onwards insists was the almost universal *Sahib-log*'s attitude — I realized that it was I, as an *Angrezi*, who was the second-class citizen; and I was, and still am, deeply grateful for the kindness and good manners of the many Indians of all faiths, castes and classes who never made me feel an interloper. For their sakes I can forgive the very few who did. But because of the disproportionate pain and embarrassment inflicted by those few, I withdrew into my shell and became wary of making overtures for fear of being snubbed. And lost, in consequence, that carefree feeling of ease and belonging and comradeship that had pervaded the years of my childhood.

I felt that loss keenly. But it was only with Indians of my own class that I felt I must now watch my step. With the servants, bazaar-folk and villagers — the 'populace' — the old ease was still there, probably because the masses were still sublimely uninterested in politics and, unlike the middle and upper-middle classes, had not yet (outside his home patch) heard much, if anything, about Gandhi. If only I had not forgotten how to speak fluent Hindustani, I think that with them I could have picked up the threads of my life exactly where I had been forced to drop them when, over nine years before, I sailed tearfully away from Bombay.

As it was, my command of the language was now practically nil. It was a grave disadvantage, for although the majority of the Indian friends who came from the same social stratum as myself spoke fluent English, the ordinary working-class folk in the bazaars and villages did not. And I was soon to discover that I could no longer chatter freely with them, even though there were still so many of them in Shah Jehan's Delhi and its outskirts whom I remembered with affection, and who had not forgotten either me or my sister Bets. Although I learned soon enough to translate what they were saying and to make myself understood, it was never again with the ease and familiarity of those early years, when I could gossip and crack jokes with them. That comfortable degree of familiarity never returned, for the gift of tongues that Tacklow possessed, and which I had once hoped that I had inherited, was denied me. Nor have I transmitted it to my grandchildren. It has been left to Bets to hand it on, by way of her younger son, to no fewer than three of her granddaughters.

For the reasons that I have given, my memories of my first season as a grown-up in Imperial Delhi are not entirely happy ones. Many of the British companions of my childhood, who had left India similarly bound for boarding-schools when the 'Great War' ended, had not returned. Some never would; and of those who did, only one or two had been close friends. As for the very few Indian ones who still lived in Delhi, and with whom I could no longer talk without thinking in their own tongue, I felt, for the first time, as though I did not belong in their country by right. Yet the land itself, particularly Old Delhi, was kind to me and never let me down. It had changed very little, and just to walk around it again and visit all our old haunts was a deep and satisfying delight.

Curzon House, which had been home to me for so many cold weather seasons during my childhood, had now become the Swiss Hotel. But its old name remained on the wrought iron of the gates, while the gardens, and the Kaye Battery marking the site of the siege battery commanded by my kinsman, Edward Kaye of the Bengal Artillery, during the attack on Delhi in the early autumn of the Black Year, were still as I remembered them — as was our favourite playground, the Kudsia Bagh. But our secret hideaway on the ruined gateway had been unkindly exposed. The bamboos and the flowering creepers which had previously concealed it had been ruthlessly uprooted, or else equally ruthlessly pruned, and the magic had gone. So, too, had the gap in the hedge through which Bets and I used to crawl in order to play with the Indian children who lived in those beautiful 'John Company' style houses between Maiden's Hotel and the Kudsia Bagh. As for our old friend and ally, the *chowkidar* who used to occupy one of the ground rooms in the ruined gateway that was once the main entrance to the Begum Kudsia's palace, there was no sign of him and no one could tell us where he had gone; or when. There had been no *chowkidar* for many monsoons, they said; who could tell how many? When we asked if he were still alive, they only shrugged and gave India's time-honoured reply: 'Who knows?' Yet superficially, at least, very little had changed.

The Old Delhi Club still functioned, and the band still played dance music on the lawn of an evening; only now it was: 'Avalon', 'Always' and 'Miss Annabelle Lee' instead of 'Long, Long Trail' and the 'Merry Widow Waltz'. As many butterflies as ever still lilted through the hot, sun-chequered shadows of the old cemetery, and the peacocks still cried at dusk and dawn. And though our old *chowkidar* had gone, the parrots and the blue-jays and hoopoes had not, while the *galaries* — the little striped-back Indian chipmunks that we used to call 'tree-rats' and for whom we used to save up our toast crusts and cake crumbs when we were children — still whisked up and down the trunks of the peepul trees exactly as their great-great-grandparents used to do in the days when Punj-ayah would take us for our morning walks through the Kudsia Bagh to feed the birds and squirrels.

Best of all, that first year, one of my parents' old friends, Monty Ashley-Phillips, who, while Bets and I were in boarding-school in England, had shared their bungalow in Rajpore Road, had arranged to take us all out to a shooting-camp over the Christmas holidays. So once again we donned the familiar camp uniform of khaki shirt, breeches and topi that were obligatory wear for such occasions, drove for miles along the Grand Trunk Road, crossed the Jumna by country-boat, and then jolted and bumped for more miles along a rutted cart-track towards the little village of Hassanpore, on the outskirts of which our camp had been pitched in the shade of a mango tope.

There must have been other guests, for as far as I remember the party numbered four or five guns in addition to Mother, Bets and myself, who did not shoot and were merely spectators. Everything that was shot went into the pot. Duck, teal, partridge, quail and snipe, an occasional black-buck and, understudying for the traditional Christmas turkey, a plump peahen. The camp's *khansama* (cook) would look over the day's bag to take his pick, and anything that was left over would be distributed among the local villagers.

Game was plentiful and the days were blue and gold and windless, and it would have been a halcyon period if it had not been for the temperature. But the starry nights were bitterly cold, and I still remember, with a shudder, our first night under canvas, and the way the cold struck upwards from the ground through the thin mattress of my camp-bed, making me feel as though I were lying on a block of ice. It took me quite a time to realize that some of the blankets, *resais* (padded quilts) and coats that I had piled on top of me would do a lot more good if I put them underneath me instead; and it was only after I had crawled out, shivering, into the darkness to grope for and light a hurricane-lamp and reorganize my bedding that I unfroze enough to get some sleep. But, apart from that, every day was magic, and it was as if I had never been away.

Chapter 6

~✕✕✕~

Tacklow's work was concerned with the princely states of Rajputana; that vast expanse of sun-scorched country that Kipling called 'the Cockpit of India', and which nowadays is once again known by its own name of Rajasthan — the Country of the Kings — though technically there are no more kings, for twenty-four years after Independence, Mrs Gandhi abolished them and only the afterglow of their glory and their legendary deeds remain. But back in the twenties, as rulers of semi-independent sovereign states, they still wielded a good deal of power, and one of the first states on Tacklow's agenda was Gwalior, whose late Maharajah, old Madhav Rao Scindia, had been a personal friend of his — as was its then Resident, Mr Crump, who had invited Tacklow to stay with him and to 'bring Daisy and the girls'.

The Residency at Gwalior must have been one of the most splendid in India, second only to the absurdly grandiose one in Hyderabad, Deccan, and possessing, in a land where water is precious, that luxury of Indian luxuries, a swimming-pool. Mr Crump was the nicest of hosts, and we were wined and dined at the palace and taken to see all the sights of the state, which included riding up to Gwalior Fort on one of His Highness's elephants. The fort is everything that a medieval fort should be: it dominates the country for miles around, for it is built on the crest of a soaring outcrop of rock that juts up out of the plain to tower above Gwalior city, lying close-packed in its shadow below.

Mother, who dabbled in watercolours and would, during the succeeding years, paint the fort again and again, made her first attempts to capture it on Cox's paper,* standing sentinel above the flat-topped roofs of the city, dark against a clean expanse of clear, turquoise sky; while Tacklow

---

* The two best papers for watercolourists, used by major artists and gifted amateurs for well over a century, were Cox's and Whatman's Rough — both, alas, now unobtainable.

told me an intriguing story about it that the old Maharajah had told him long ago. I have never forgotten that tale. It still fascinates me, so if you are sitting comfortably (or even if you aren't) I now propose to tell it to you . . .

It concerns the old Maharajah — Scindia of Gwalior — and a fabulous treasure that according to local legend was buried centuries ago somewhere within the fort. This, according to the Maharajah, had been searched for by several generations of the ruling house, including himself. He had, he said, searched for it again and again in his youth, until there was hardly a foot of ground within the circumference of that enormous fort that had not been probed and dug over, or examined for signs of a secret chamber. In the end he had decided that there was no truth in the story. But one day an aged man appeared at one of his public *durbahs* (councils) and asked for a private audience, saying that he was an astrologer who had some very important information to impart that was for the ear of His Highness alone . . .

Well, it was not Scindia's custom (so His Highness assured Tacklow) to grant private audiences to strangers. But something about this particular petitioner aroused his curiosity. And since the man looked far too old and frail to be planning any rough stuff (and even if he had, he, Scindia, felt himself to be more than capable of dealing with anything in that department), he consented, and the two withdrew to the *Diwani-i-Khas*, the Hall of Private Audience.

Only when he was certain that everyone else had been excluded did the old man, lowering his voice to a hoarse whisper, confide that he knew the secret hiding-place of the treasure. He had, he claimed, seen it himself and was prepared to show His Highness the hiding-place. But only on one condition: if, on the night of the next full moon — then only a few days ahead — His Highness would come alone and unarmed to the main gate at the foot of the rock upon which the fort was built, he would meet him there and lead him to where the treasure lay. Was the Maharajah-Sahib prepared to take the risk?

His Highness thought the matter over and inquired if the old man too would come alone and unarmed? 'Certainly,' replied the stranger; moreover, should the Maharajah-Sahib wish, he could come to the assignation with as large an armed guard as he desired. But they must stay outside the outer gate and he must go the rest of the way alone. 'Done!' said H. H., and when the old man had gone he took certain precautions.

For two days before the night of the full moon, the fort was closed to the public and exhaustively searched to ensure that the stranger did not have a gang hidden there among the ancient ruins, or in one of the empty palaces — the beautiful Chit Mahal or the Jahangeri Mahal, or any of the old disused buildings that had once been used as gaols, and whose foundations were pitted with underground cells. In addition, on the night of the full moon the foot of the entire rock was ringed by troops — 'So that not even a mongoose could have slipped out unseen.'

True to his word, the old astrologer was waiting outside the first of the outer gates, alone and unarmed, carrying nothing but a hurricane-lamp. After he was searched the two were admitted, and together they climbed the long, steep road in the bright moonlight. Once through the gateway on the summit the old man stopped, and turning to Scindia said that from now on the Maharajah-Sahib must go blindfold. When Scindia jibbed at this he was told that in that case they would have to call the whole thing off and go back, and since he obviously meant it, H. H. gave in. Whereupon his guide blindfolded him very efficiently and led him forward.

Thereafter the two walked and walked for what seemed like hours, twisting and turning, climbing up and down stairways and in and out of empty buildings, so that in no time at all Scindia had lost all sense of direction and hadn't the least idea where he was or in which direction he was facing. Then at long last they began to descend a narrow stone stairway that wound down and down into cold, airless blackness . . .

The old Maharajah — who had been a young man then — told Tacklow that he could just make out a faint gleam of light from the hurricane-lamp at the edge of the bandage across his eyes. But that was all. Then all at once, after they had groped their way down for a long time, he thought he heard the sound of soft footsteps creeping down behind him. He strained his ears to listen, and soon became certain that there *was* a third person on the stair. Stout-hearted as he was, he panicked, believing that despite all his precautions he had let himself be lured into a trap and that he was being led to his death.

He had not brought a gun or a knife with him, but had taken the precaution of hiding a weapon in the shape of a short length of lead among his clothing. Now, bringing this out, he snatched his hand from the clasp of his guide's elderly, claw-like hand and, ripping the bandage from his eyes, hit the old man as hard as he could at the base of his skull.

He said he heard the bone crack and as the old man fell forward the lamp, released, crashed to the ground, flared up and went out. Scindia was left in pitch darkness. Gripped by panic, and armed only with the lead truncheon, he turned and fled back up the stairs, guiding himself with one hand against the cold, slimy stone of the curving wall, and, he confessed, in deadly fear of running straight on to the knife of an armed assassin above him. But he met no one.

He told Tacklow that the narrow stairway seemed to wind up for ever, and that when he reached the top, gasping and breathless, he made for the first gleam of moonlight he could see. After groping his way through a maze of dark rooms, and gaping doorways that seemed to lead nowhere, he found himself in the open at last and rushed out into the night, yelling for his guards, and with no idea where he was because, by that time, the moon was well down in the sky and all the shadows were far longer and lying at a different angle. He had, he confessed, worked himself into such a state of terror that he rushed to and fro, screaming and shouting like a lunatic, and when at last he found himself on the slope below one of the inner gates, he pelted down it and collapsed into the arms of the anxious guard with barely enough breath to order that no one must be allowed to leave the rock until further orders.

It was only when he awoke next day that he realized that the footsteps he had heard behind him were probably no more than an echo of his own and his guide's, resounding hollowly in the tunnel-like walls of that winding stair, and that he had almost certainly killed the old astrologer who had been leading him down it. Well, that was too bad. But at least he now knew where to look for the treasure, even though he hadn't the remotest idea in which building or what part of the fort that staircase lay. For now they only had to search for a dead man and a broken kerosene lamp; and neither were insignificant objects that would escape the eye.

No? Well, he was wrong there, admitted old Scindia. They went through the fort with a fine-tooth comb, every foot of it, over and over and over again. Yet they never found a trace of either. No corpse, no broken glass, and no trace of spilled kerosene — or of any stairway that corresponded with the one he had been led down, blindfold, and escaped from in pitch darkness and a state of blind panic. Which could only mean that the entrance to it must have been hidden by a slab of stone that the old man must have been at pains to lift earlier in the evening. Yet if that were so, how had it been closed? And by whom? 'For I tell you, my friend,' insisted old Scindia, 'I heard his skull crack! — on my head and my life, I heard it! Who then let down the stone? Or closed it, if it stands in a wall? Tell me that.'

There is no answer to that one: unless you choose to visit the great fort at Gwalior and see for yourself how easy it would have been for a single accomplice (or even half-a-dozen!) to lie hidden in one of those huge, half-ruined buildings, wait for the moon to rise, and, when the self-styled astrologer appeared with the blindfolded Maharajah in tow, follow the two into that final building, wait for them to emerge from the hidden stairway and — when only one, the panic-stricken ruler — rushed out and fled screaming into the night, cover up the entrance before making his, or her or their own escape.

There is also, of course, another explanation. That His Highness Sir Madhav Rao Scindia of Gwalior was pulling my beloved parent's leg. He was, let's face it, well known for his fondness for practical jokes, and also for being no ordinary character. In his younger days he had managed to blarney himself into accompanying the British Expeditionary Force which, in the opening years of the twentieth century, was sent to China to help put down the Boxer Rising (which was probably the reason for his fondness for my father, since Tacklow, too, as a Captain in the 21st Punjabis, had seen service in North China at that time).

Nevertheless, Tacklow himself was firmly convinced that in this case Scindia had spoken nothing but the truth. This was mainly because H. H. admitted that he had always been haunted by the conviction that if only he had kept his nerve and not given way to panic — if only he had had just a *little* more courage — he would have realized that the footsteps that he thought he heard following him were only echoes, and gone on to find that the fabulous hoard of gold and jewels was no legend, but his for the taking. It was, he insisted, the one great regret that he would take with him to the grave.

If he *had* invented the whole story, said Tacklow (who knew him well), then he had certainly ended by persuading himself that it was all true.

I like to believe that too. India has always been in the habit of salting away gold and jewels in the earth, and I have myself seen a fabulous hoard of gold coins, hidden centuries ago and unearthed by chance in another Rajputana state in the 1940s. In fact, the habit of burying treasure

in times of war, or as an insurance against a rainy day, was so prevalent*
that few Indian palaces or forts would be worthy of the name without a
treasure trove having been hidden somewhere at some time under or in
it. And what treasures they are! While at Gwalior we were taken to see
the State Jewel House, which I had expected to be in some underground
dungeon, but turned out to be a small, square, unpretentious and very
modern-looking building with whitewashed walls and an armed guard
standing outside the door.

The guard, and the fact that the walls of the building looked to be a
good six feet thick, while the windows were mere slits protected by solid
slabs of glass and further reinforced by iron bars, gave it a forbidding
look. But the interior of this modern Aladdin's cave was, at first sight, a
distinct anticlimax. It looked far more like a kitchen or a larder than a
jewel house, for down the middle of it ran a long, plain wooden kitchen
table, while against the whitewashed walls stood what appeared to be an
unending line of kitchen dressers, with narrow shelves and row upon row
of cheap brass hooks. But laid out on that table, propped on those shelves
or hanging from those hooks, were some of the most incredible jewels
you could possibly imagine, and I cannot begin to think what they must
have been worth in that day — let alone in this one!

Necklaces, rings and brooches, swords and sword-belts, nose-rings and
bracelets, anklets and pendants, set with emeralds, rubies, sapphires and
diamonds, turquoises, tourmalines, fire opals, amethysts and aquamarines,
plus any other jewel you can think of; strings of enormous pearls, the
size of pigeons' eggs, hung casually from the brass hooks, side by side
with glittering ropes of uncut emeralds, peardrop diamonds and balas
rubies.

Some of the diamonds had obviously been sent to Europe, probably
to Amsterdam, to be recut, and very splendid they looked. But many of
them were table-cut in the old way, and I remember one fabulous
sword-belt that was fashioned from wide links of solid gold, each one
measuring at least three inches by six, and of a gold so pure that the rows
of large diamonds that had been set into it had been hammered into holes
gouged out of the soft metal, before being sliced level with the flat surface
of the links. Every diamond was roughly the size of my thumbnail, but

* See Rudyard Kipling's wonderful description of one such hoard in 'The King's Ankus', in
The Second Jungle Book.

though the thing must have been very nearly priceless, the stones, in that setting, lost most of their brilliance and might just as well have been pieces of glass.

It was the sheer casualness with which they were treated that impressed me more than the beauty or value of the jewels. The matter-of-fact manner in which incalculable riches and beauty were carelessly laid out on that unstained and unpolished kitchen table or casually slung on cheap brass hooks. Yet they would have made even the Crown Jewels in the Tower of London look unimportant by contrast.*

Oh, the jewels that were once the glory of India! Where are they now, I wonder? — now that the princes have been deprived of their titles and revenues, and many have been left penniless? So many great names have become no more than the names of towns to which the package tours dispatch their streams of camera-carrying tourists. 'Where has all the splendour gone? Gone to tourists, every one! Oh will we never learn . . .'

No, of course we won't. We never do; until it's too late!

✂ One evening we were invited to Jai Vilas, the Maharajah's city palace, to see a famous conjuror who was visiting Gwalior, and I was bitterly disappointed to find that the palace was not in the least like the ones I had seen in Jaipur and Agra, and in the Lal Khila at Delhi. It was a curious western-style mock-up that suggested an over-decorated wedding cake, and was full of European furniture and fittings which included a huge cut-glass fountain, exactly like an immense cruet, in one of the white marble entrance halls.

The palace had, in fact, been built in a tearing hurry in the seventies of the previous century, in anticipation of a visit by Queen Victoria's eldest son, the future King Edward VII, then Prince of Wales. It was designed by an amateur architect, one Lieutenant-Colonel Sir Michael Filose, a one-time British-Indian Army officer who had left the army to enter the service of the state. The Colonel, whose family roots were Italian, obviously had grand ideas; though unfortunately, European rather than Indian ones. But the interior of the palace could not have been more impressive. Cinderella and her prince would have felt truly at home in that vast expanse of shimmering gold. Gold-leaf, gold brocade, gold-plated

* Trevelyan says in his fascinating book *The India We Left* that the pearls in the jewel house were 'coils and coils of dead pearls'. They didn't look dead in 1927. They were wonderful!

this and that, and glittering crystal chandeliers as far as the eye could see. It took your breath away. As for the conjuror, he, too, was out of this world.

Tacklow's pal, the eccentric old Scindia of Gwalior, had died in 1925, and our host that evening was the Regent, since the heir, H. H. George Jeewaji Rao Scindia Bahadur, was still not of age, though he and his sister, Mary (they had been named after George V and Queen Mary), came in to shake hands with us and to watch the show. They were as charming a pair of children as you could wish to see, and so plainly dressed that they might have been the offspring of any commoner, if it had not been for the fact that each was wearing a short necklace of the largest and most lustrous pearls that I had ever seen; each pearl quite literally the size of a pigeon's egg and, unbelievably, casually strung on the type of cheap tinsel ribbon that could be bought in almost any bazaar for considerably less than an anna a yard. Only an Indian royal, I reflected with awe, could have treated such fabulous jewels so carelessly.

Except for Mother, Bets and me, and the little princess who was below the age of caste, the party was a strictly masculine one, since in those days the majority of royal ladies kept strict purdah and, apart from Mr Crump and my family, all the other guests were Indian. None of them seemed to be particularly impressed by the conjuror's performance. I suppose they had seen this sort of thing since they were knee-high to a tiger-cub and so accepted it as a matter of course. But to me it was pure magic.

The conjuror, an unremarkable middle-aged man in white, began with a few spectacular tricks of the kind that all conjurors do, and then, moving towards the guests, whom the Regent had seated in a half-circle, he did a trick for each one of us in turn and in close-up. I don't remember any of the turns except the one he did for me, and the one he did for Tacklow, who was sitting on my left. Tacklow's was the old trick of a length of rope that is cut again and again, but always ends up in one unbroken piece. But this time there was a difference, because it was performed by a man standing immediately in front of him and less than ten inches away. A man whose hands and wrists were in clear view throughout, and who, instead of cutting the rope himself, gave it to Tacklow to cut with a razor-sharp knife and then took the two ends from him, one in each hand, merely crossed his hands under Tacklow's nose (and mine!) and in the same unhurried movement handed it back in one piece. What's more, he repeated the trick in several different ways; sometimes cutting it himself while Tacklow held it, sometimes letting Tacklow do the cutting; but always ending up with the same unblemished piece of rope.

The trick he did for me was far more exciting. He asked for a tall glass, which he told me to hold, and while I was holding it he filled it about half full of water and beckoned to one of his assistants, who stepped forward with a silver shovel on which there were several lumps of coal. This, after I had examined it (getting coal-dust all over my fingers in the process), he proceeded to smash up with a hammer until it was reduced to a pile of black dust and small fragments of coal which he added to the water in my glass. He then took it from me and, putting his other hand on top of it, shook the glass briskly and threw it all over me. I remember shrieking as the contents hit me and that was the only moment that I took my eyes off him; because I had flinched back instinctively, expecting a shower of wet, black slosh and bits of coal all over my party dress. Something damp did deluge me; I felt it on my face and hair and arms. But when I opened my eyes I found I had been showered not with coal but with dewy rose petals, and the glass in the conjuror's hand was as clean as a whistle. I kept some of those petals for years, since clearly they were magic ones. But alas, as things do, they got lost.

Nothing so special happened at any of the other princely states we visited. We arrived. We were greeted kindly — in Tacklow's case almost as though he had been a valued and much-loved relative returning home after a long absence: they all seemed to know him well. We were housed in magnificent rooms that looked out on to lakes and glorious gardens. We breakfasted on marble verandahs or *bara-durris* screened by curtains of flowering bougainvillaea, jasmine, climbing roses and trumpet-flowers. And while Tacklow went off to talk to the rulers and their *diwans* and councils, our hosts' wives and their ladies made us welcome in the women's quarters, and took us for drives and picnics in their purdah cars, whose tinted windows did not prevent us from seeing out, but prevented anyone from seeing those inside.

Since the royal women were gay and charming and, to my shame and dismay, *far* better educated than I was, we had a wonderful time in the company of these beautiful, laughing creatures, who showed us their jewels, their shimmering saris and their adorable babies, and gossiped about mutual acquaintances. There was only one awkward occasion.

In one of the princely states, while Tacklow was being dined by the ruler at an all-male party, the senior Maharani gave a splendid all-girls banquet in the women's quarters for Mother, Bets and me. It was held in an immensely long and magnificent room, lined on one side by looking-glass that faced and reflected the long row of arched windows on the opposite side, so that whichever way you faced you could see treetops, flowering creepers and sky. Since the room was on the second floor, it was too high up for anyone at ground level to see into it, and the open windows were screened by very fine wire gauze that kept out the moths and beetles and other night-flying insects.

There must have been a good twenty or thirty of us seated at that enormously long table, below shimmering cut-crystal chandeliers that made a tinkling music overhead as their dangling crystals swayed gently to every breath of breeze that came in from the gardens outside. And though I wore my very best evening dress for the occasion, I still remember how dreadfully dowdy I felt among all those slender, glamorous Indian beauties in their wonderful saris and astonishing jewels. Even the stout and elderly ones — of whom, thank goodness, there were a reasonable number — managed to look graceful and gorgeous, for the sari is surely the most becoming dress that was ever invented.

Below us on the lawn the Maharajah's brass band played western dance music. Tunes such as 'Tea for Two', 'Always', 'Mountain Greenery' and other pop-songs of the day, all of them rendered *fortissimo*, which did not appear to worry the royal ladies at all. They merely raised their voices a couple of octaves, and shrieked blithely above the volume of brass drifting up from below. And since thirty or more women all shrieking together can make a considerable din, we drowned out that twenty-strong brass band without even trying.

I had a junior Highness on my left and a cosy little visiting Rani on my right, and both of them screamed cheerfully at me throughout the meal, jerking me out of my shyness and keeping me as well as themselves in gales of laughter. It was a hilarious evening. But Oh, that meal . . . !

Judging from the enormous menus, each one emblazoned on the cover with the Maharani's coat-of-arms, and printed in Hindi on the right-hand side and English on the left, we were going to be faced with an incredibly large number of courses. I remember studying the menu in front of me with some apprehension, and noting, with disappointment, that not a single Indian dish figured on that long list, presumably in compliment to Mother and for the benefit of European guests. I thought this a pity, as

I had been looking forward to sampling some really good Indian cooking. And while appreciating Her Highness's thoughtfulness, I wondered how on earth I was going to deal with all those courses without offending my hostess by refusing at least half of them. In the event I decided to take a very modest helping of every dish that was offered to me, spreading it out on my plate to make it look more.

But, alas for good intentions! What I did not know was that Her Highness employed an extremely expensive European chef to cook all western meals, and every dish was so delicious that I ended up eating far more of them than I meant to. Even then, I barely managed to get through the final course. Only to discover, with horror, that what I had taken to be a translation into Hindi on the right-hand page of the menu was, in fact, a list of Indian dishes which, having toiled through the western ones, we were now being offered! What's more, they were the very best of Indian dishes. Wonderful stuff. And *how* I would have appreciated them if only they had come first . . .

Mutaujua and *jinga pulao*. *Badshaki*, *kitcheree* and *kutchi biryani*, *moghli koftas*, *shami kebab*, *kandi gosht* and *murgi tikka*. *Unda dopiaza*, which is spiced spinach with boiled eggs. *Pora* (baked eggs with shrimp), and stuffed peppers — *mirchi bharwan*. And to end with, *jellabis* and *halwa sharin*, the 'Sweet Sweet' of Persia, and half a dozen other delights. How I wished I had taken the trouble to learn how to write the language I had once talked so fluently. Or at least had the sense to ask one or other of the Highnesses seated on either side of me to translate the Hindi script for me!

But it was too late for regrets, for by then I could barely swallow another mouthful of *anything*, however ambrosial, and bad manners or no, I was incapable of doing more than help myself to the smallest possible quantity of the delightful, spicy dishes that followed one after another during the best part of another hour — and to push that about my plate so that it looked as though I had at least eaten some of it. Neither of the bejewelled ladies on either side of me was deceived; both of them regretting that I did not care for Indian food, and clearly disbelieving me when I assured them that I did, but had no more room, having over-eaten during the first half of the banquet. I could see that after that they wrote me off as just another die-hard *Angrezi* visitor.

�֍ Among the many semi-independent states in the Country of the Kings that we visited that cold weather was beautiful Jaipur, where we stayed at the Residency, a building that had once been a royal palace, the 'Raj Mahal', and has now become the Raj Mahal Hotel, but will always be linked in my mind with one of Noel Coward's best-loved melodies: a song from 'Bitter Sweet'. Because, as we arrived, a gramophone in one of the rooms off the hall was playing 'I'll see you again'.

It was the first time I had ever heard it, and even after all these years whenever I chance to hear it I am walking up the porch steps and into that cool shadowy hall that smelt of flowers and furniture polish, and it is all there again, tied up with ribbon and rosemary. Youth and the haunting beauty of springtime and romance. Jai Sing's wonderful rose-red city in the sunlit years between two World Wars.

There are two rather creepy ghost stories attached to the Residency in Jaipur, and so far no one has come up with anything that might account for them. The first concerned a small locked room off the right-hand side of the hall as one entered the building. No one used it. This was because (or so the Resident told us) someone, many years ago, in the early days of the East India Company, was found dead in it in very suspicious circumstances. The victim appeared to have been strangled, though both the doors and the windows leading into the room had been securely fastened on the inside, and a window had to be broken when he did not answer to knocking and shouting. There was a fireplace in the room, but the chimney was too narrow to allow anyone human to enter that way, and anyway, there were no traces of entry. The thing remained a mystery, and in time was forgotten, until once again it was used as a temporary bedroom for some unexpected visitor, who was found dead next morning in precisely the same circumstances.

Since the Indian servants insisted, unanimously, that it was the work of some evil spirit, and refused to enter the room, it was cleared of all furniture and locked and barred. And it remained so until well into the twentieth century, when a foolhardy guest, hearing the story and pooh-poohing it, insisted on spending a night in the room and bet his host 100 rupees, or a case of champagne or something of the sort, that he would be found alive and well in the morning. His host was reluctant to accept the wager, and with one voice every Indian in the service of the Residency implored him not to take the chance. But he remained adamant. Ghosts? *Pooh!* Evil spirits? *Bah!* Finally a bed was provided for him, and, having barred the windows, he locked himself in. And that was the last time he was ever seen alive, for when the door was eventually battered in the next morning they found that he, too, had been strangled . . .

The second ghost story is even stranger, though a lot simpler. Because the Residency was once a royal palace it had, in place of staircases, long, sloping passageways that led up to the purdah quarters where the royal ladies and their waiting women lived, for the convenience of the bearers of palanquins in which the women were carried. These passages were said to be haunted by the ghost of a headless *chupprassi* — a red-coated messenger, such as those who squat by the door of any Burra-Sahib's office to this day, ready to usher in or forbid entry to a caller, or run with messages. There was no story attached to this haunting either. Though from what I know of India, I am willing to bet that every native-born Jaipuri knows the true tale that lies behind it, but chooses not to tell. As far as I know, the headless *chupprassi* never caused any harm; the poor fellow merely confined himself to running up those sloping passageways on bare, terrified feet, forever pursued by the nameless enemy who had decapitated him — or, possibly, in frantic search of his missing head?

The room in which at least three people were mysteriously strangled has been swept away in its entirety and become part of a large open hall and another far longer and wider room, which was, for some months in the spring of 1983, taken over, together with the entire building, by the television company who were filming my *Far Pavilions*. It was all very tarted-up, modern and efficient, and devoid of any hint of ghostliness or ancient evil. Whoever or whatever evil spirits had once haunted it had packed up and gone, beating a hasty retreat in the face of electric typewriters, computers and modern technology. The old, sloping passages had gone, too, swept away in rebuilding and redecorating of the old Residency and the older palace, to be replaced by a magnificent white marble staircase. No painted and gilded palanquins containing a slender, dark-eyed 'Ornament of the Harem' could negotiate those stairs. But the headless *chupprassi* makes light of them, for he is still there, as I was one day to discover. But that story will have to wait its turn. It does not come within the scope of this book.

Chapter 7

One of the most nerve-racking social engagements of the Delhi season turned out to be my first Viceregal dinner party. This daunting function must have been among the last to take place in the original Viceregal Lodge in Old Delhi, for by the beginning of the next season the grandiose Viceroy's House, which Sir Edwin Lutyens had intended to be the focal point of New Delhi, would at last be ready for occupation by the then Viceroy, Lord Irwin, and his family.

Any chance of the evening being an enjoyable one was wrecked at the start by the combination of a dim-witted taxi-driver and my first pair of white kid sixteen-button-length gloves. The pair I had borrowed from Mother for that Blue Cross Ball had not been a success, for her hands were a good deal larger than mine and the unused space at the end of each finger was distinctly inelegant. A pair in the right size had duly been bought for me at Rago Mull's, and I carried them carefully on my lap, wrapped in tissue paper — intending to put them on in the ladies' room where we would shed our evening cloaks, rather than risk getting them grubby *en route*.

Tacklow had hired a taxi for the occasion, to save Mother from having to cope with parking problems. But, alas, this turned out to be a disaster. The 'experienced driver' whom we had been promised (and who had confidently assured us that the way to the Burra Lat Sahib's house was well known to him) not only grossly underestimated the time it would take him to get us there, but took several wrong turnings in an effort to find an imaginary short-cut. We arrived late, to find several frantic ADCs and an assortment of Viceregal servants waiting for us on the porch steps, literally dancing with agitation.

There was no time for any powdering of noses in the cloakroom, and amid urgent White Rabbit-like cries of 'You're late! You're late!', our cloaks, and Tacklow's overcoat and scarf, were snatched from us and I found myself being rushed down interminable corridors between a couple of panting ADCs, each of whom was endeavouring to help me put on a brand-new elbow-length kid glove, which should by rights have been slowly and carefully eased on after being properly stretched. The Viceregal servants must have seen some peculiar sights in their day, but even their normally impassive faces registered several degrees of shock, ranging from raised eyebrows to grins, as we fled past. My parents preceded us at the double, accompanied by an appalled minor official, while I, in full and unfamiliar evening dress and high-heeled shoes, scuttled behind them, both arms at full stretch, with a frantic ADC on each, tugging at that malignant and unyielding white kid. The end, of course, was inevitable. Just as we reached the anteroom in which our fellow guests were already assembled, the left-hand glove split from top to bottom, above the first button. *Disaster!*

My parents were whisked away to stand in line among the more senior guests, and the two ADCs, having hustled me in among the lowly ones, thankfully abandoned me, beetroot-faced from embarrassment and on the verge of tears, with a long strip of white kid hanging limply from my wrist. In the same moment the doors at the far end of the room were thrown open to admit their Excellencies and their house guests and various members of the Household. And had the devil himself been passing, I know that I would willingly have sold my soul in exchange for invisibility — or just to be allowed to sink through the Viceregal carpet.

Fortunately, Mephistopheles was not present, and I was saved by an angelic elderly woman with a heart of twenty-eight-carat gold who wore a long chiffon scarf. Taking in my situation at a glance, she whipped off the scarf, wound one end round my left arm, enclosing and hiding the split glove, draped the other round my shoulders and whispered encouragingly: 'Don't worry, they'll never notice!' And they didn't — bless her for ever. I hope she has been given a specially nice room in the heavenly mansions in recognition of that kindly deed.

The rest of the evening is a blur. As the most junior person present, I was seated at the far end of the long table, among the ADCs, of whom I was scared silly because they were said to be chosen for their social standing, good looks and ability on the dance floor. They also had the reputation of being abominably conceited; for to annex a Viceregal ADC as your beau appeared to be the height of every girl's ambition (the next best thing being an ADC to the Commander-in-Chief, or the Governor of a Province). It was not only the Fishing Fleet lovelies who made a dead set at them. Elderly members of the Viceroy's Council, the Civil Service, the armed forces, and their wives, were not above treating them as favourite sons — calling them by their Christian names and inviting them to dinner parties and dances as partners for their daughters and nieces. The competition for the attention of these gilded youths was intense, and I am sure that they were charming to the damsels on whom they bestowed their approval. But sadly, I was never one of that elect line-up so, as far as I and the rest of the Sour Grapes Brigade were concerned, the average ADC was an ornamental, superior and mannerless young so-and-so who could not be bothered with anyone whom he did not consider of sufficient importance, or pretty enough, to attract his attention.

There were, of course, exceptions to this rule; and it was my good fortune to be taken in to my first Viceregal dinner by one of them, a sprig of the nobility who could not have been nicer. Within minutes I had lost my heart to him. Not because he listened sympathetically to the saga of those gloves, but because it struck him as wildly funny and he laughed so much that I had to laugh with him, and stopped feeling that I had disgraced myself and my parents.

�֍ A few nights later we were all invited to a far more modest, but equally memorable dinner party and dance at Maiden's Hotel in Old Delhi. It was quite a small party, given by that old friend of Tacklow's, Sir Edwin Lutyens, the main architect of New Delhi. Sir Edwin proved to be a most enchanting host. He drew pictures on the tablecloth for Bets, and booked me for two or three of the dances, explaining, to my relief, that he did not dance but hoped I would not mind sitting them out with him. *Mind!* I was delighted to do so, for he was not only a world-famous man, but a most entertaining conversationalist. Moreover, he kept me enthralled by covering my dance-programme and a few of the nearest menus with fascinating drawings. I can't think why I hadn't the sense to cherish them for posterity, but I suppose, because he was a friend of Tacklow's, I took him too much for granted, and those charming scribbles soon went the way of so many valuable trifles, cherished for a season and then lost.

Yet an echo of them was to follow into the future, for although at the time I had not the faintest idea that I would one day take to writing books, the seeds of authorship must have already been there — manifesting themselves in a collector's instinct that makes writers stash away certain incidents in their memory just in case they may come in handy some day. Nearly a quarter of a century later I was to use Lutyens's method of entertaining me in one of my whodunnits, when I made my artist-hero amuse a group of Cypriot children by doing quick crayon sketches of dragons, pirates and witches, and sailors dancing the hornpipe, on his drawing block. Paul Scott once told me never to waste anything, and I don't think I ever wasted much.

A day or two later Sir Edwin took us on a personally conducted tour of his still unfinished Viceroy's House, and complained that he had planned it as the focal point of New Delhi. It was, he said, meant to stand on the highest bit of land, with everything else leading the eye up to it. But owing to some miscalculation on the part of his co-architect, Sir Richard Baker (he of the Baker's Ovens), and the fact that he, Lutyens, had not been in India at the time when work on the twin Baker-designed Secretariat buildings had been begun, the two buildings, which had been intended to lead the eye up to Viceroy's House had been placed just too high up on the slope of the Kingsway — now the Rajpath — to allow the Viceroy's House to be built on the highest point of the rise. By the time Lutyens arrived out in India, work on the two Secretariat buildings was too far advanced to be scrapped, and there was nothing for it but to build the Viceroy's House a good deal further back, at a spot from which it was barely visible, and redraw the dome, in a belated and not too successful attempt to make it stand up much higher. It looks squat to this day — rather like a toad squatting in a dip of ground, that has puffed itself out sideways and is staring out crossly above the ridge of earth in front of it. Which is a pity, because it really is a rather splendid building.

Sir Edwin did not say so, but I got the distinct impression that he thought Baker had moved his Secretariat buildings higher up the slope on purpose — knowing perfectly well that by doing so he would force his rival to build the 'focal point of New Delhi' much further back, and deprive him of the high ground. It certainly worked. Baker's Secretariat buildings, with their twin towers and their lavish use of decorative pavilions which (whether intentionally or not) exactly mimic those white pith helmets, topped by a metal spike, which were habitually worn on all state occasions by members of the 'Heaven-born' and the British officers of certain Indian Army regiments, certainly hog the view in New Delhi, and have successfully up-staged Viceroy's House — see any tourist's snapshots!

I couldn't help feeling a bit sorry for Sir Edwin, whose ace had been so neatly trumped, but it was obvious that he had had the greatest fun designing his 'focal point', even if it had missed out. He had a strong sense of humour and had given it a field-day when it came to designing this vast Viceregal palace. The house was crammed with jokes, not all of which came off.

There is the tale concerning the wonderful marble grand staircase, which was open to the sky, and what happened to the surrounding rooms and passageways shortly after the last of the furniture and fixings had been moved in and arranged, and the whole gorgeous, fairy-tale palace was ready to be occupied. Legend says that no sooner had this happened than the father and mother of a rainstorm drove in from the south, and the clouds emptied themselves on to the eighth and last city of Delhi, paying particular attention to Viceroy's House. The staircase had been built to cope with the yearly monsoon, and there were numerous marble gutters intended to catch and channel the rainwater and direct it out into the gardens. But though these may have worked in theory, they proved to be inadequate in practice. The gutters flooded, and a huge piece of canvas the size of a couple of tennis courts was hastily rigged up to close off the pouring sky above the stairway. For a brief while, all was well. But as the downpour continued the canvas ceiling began to sag ominously, and eventually, unable to stand the strain of hundreds of tons of water that had collected in it, it broke, depositing a Niagara-like flood on to the stairway below, which swept, foaming, into the side rooms and passages, soaking carpets and sofas, chairs and curtains, and toppling innumerable occasional tables.

Well, it certainly makes a good story, and the embroideries on it were many and various, and always accompanied by shrieks of mirth from whoever happened to be telling me about it. The only thing that makes the whole story suspect is the fact that the main structure of the house, including that staircase, was, as far as I can remember, complete except for furniture and decoration when Tacklow and I were taken over it by Sir Edwin during the cold weather season of 1927–8, which means that it must have come through at least two monsoons by the time Lord Irwin and family moved into it. In which case, why did nobody ever notice what would happen to the staircase and the ground-floor rooms when the rains came? I can well believe that no one thought about it until then. But I do not believe that the rooms were carpeted and decorated before anyone drove up to it.

However, I don't suppose either Lutyens or Baker was in India except during the cold weather, and no Indian would have dreamed of pointing out an error of judgement on the part of the boss. It's rude to criticize. Let them find out the hard way.

Many years later I was to come across exactly the same attitude when I arrived in Jaipur to watch part of my novel *The Far Pavilions* being filmed, and found that almost every Indian word, and all the place names and given names, were being pronounced wrongly. 'Ashōk', for instance, was being pronounced '*Ash*-shock', though it is a popular name in India, and every single Indian on the set must have winced whenever they heard it mispronounced. But when I inquired why the heck no one had spoken up and corrected it, they looked shocked and replied that it was 'not their place' to speak out, and I spent my first week in the country apologizing to the various Ashoks whom I know. Oh well, that's India, that was. And I bet it still is and always will be.

That open-to-the-sky staircase wasn't the only piece of nonsense-work that Lutyens put into his Viceregal extravaganza. He had many more jokes up his sleeve. There was a tower room, for instance, that had the effect of being entirely surrounded by windows, which looked out on every side on to the gardens and distant views of the plain. It was 'all done by mirrors', of course; the outer ones showed the view, while the inner rooms merely mirrored it in looking-glass, an effect that could be distinctly disconcerting: once you had closed the door behind you, you were not sure for a moment or two which way you were facing, or how to get out again . . .

Then there was the Viceroy's bedroom, where the main feature was a single, giant-sized bed set against a high and equally vast piece of carving designed, explained Sir Edwin, to be useful as well as ornamental. He demonstrated by seating himself in a recumbent position in the centre of the bed and pressing a button, whereupon the outer section of the carving instantly detached itself from the main block and descended unnervingly on to the bed, capturing its occupant in an open space surrounded by a waste of polished wood. 'Neat, isn't it?' demanded its designer proudly, obviously expecting applause.

'Very,' agreed Tacklow. 'But what's the point?'

Sir Edwin requested him not to be silly. Surely *anyone* could see that it provided the Viceroy with an instant surface to support his *chota-hazri* or his breakfast tray, as well as a work-table if he should happen to be bed-bound? And what, inquired Tacklow, would happen if His Excellency should, in a careless moment, neglect to return to a position of dead centre after pressing the button? A bonk on the head from that ton-and-a-half of elaborately carved teak, and the Council would either be indenting for a new Viceroy or laying on a State funeral for his wife — should the poor woman happen to be sharing his bed and board that morning.

Sir Edwin looked a bit taken aback, and admitted that he hadn't thought of that, adding that it had looked all right on paper: apparently this was the first time he had seen it in action. He replaced it and brought it down again several times, and finally remarked cheerfully that at least it would teach the occupant to be careful. I believe (though I cannot vouch for the truth of the story) that a subsequent occupant, awaking with a hang-over which made him less than careful, missed being whanged on the head by the narrowest of margins. After which the movable section of the carving was firmly nailed to the wall and the early-morning tea-tray-cum-work-surface was no more.

The 'Lutyens conducted tour' of the still unfinished Viceroy's House stays in my memory as one of the landmarks of my first cold weather season as an adult in New Delhi. As does my introduction to a girl called Audrey Wrench, who was to become a lifelong friend.

Aud's father, Sir Evelyn Wrench, as the head of India's railways, had been allotted one of the larger and more attractive of New Delhi's Baker's Ovens, number 12 King George's Avenue, and I painted a large pastel-coloured mural on the wall above the fireplace in Aud's bedroom, a decorative affair of Harlequin serenading Columbine, painted directly on to the whitewashed wall in poster paint. Mother took a snapshot of it, and many years later I did a copy of it on another whitewashed wall, this time in a bedroom in the British Consulate at Khorramshar in Persia.* This copy survived into the 1950s, only to be blown to bits when Khorramshar was reduced to rubble during the ferocious battles between Iran and Iraq. Some time during the Second World War years, the house on King George's Avenue was briefly occupied by the Mountbattens,

* Or, if you prefer, Iran.

and I was told that when the officials of the Public Works Department, or whatever, gave orders for the entire house to be repainted before the 'Supremo' moved in, Lady Louis had asked that the mural should not be touched. So, for all I know, it may still be there.

Aud designed me a spectacular evening dress and helped me choose the material at the Tree-Shop, which still flourished in the Chandri Chowk in the shadow of the Clock Tower. She also stood over our verandah *darzi* (tailor), who made it up, and when it was finished to her satisfaction she embroidered the cunningly draped top with a spatter of small square, cerise-coloured sequins. The end result was a triumph that would not have disgraced the great Stiebel* himself and I fancied myself in it no end.

With the bazaars and shopping centres of New and Old Delhi crammed with fantastically beautiful materials that cost only a few annas a yard, plus the astonishing skill of the verandah *darzis* who, it seemed, could copy *anything* — you only had to show them a picture — it was no wonder that one of the most popular pastimes of the Raj years was the fancy-dress dance. The Horse Show Ball was always a fancy-dress affair and so was the Bachelors' Ball which by tradition wound up the season. I attended the first dressed as the young Queen Victoria, wearing a black velvet crinoline that I bought for the enormous sum of ten rupees from a friend of the Wrenches who had had it made by some purveyor of fancy dresses in London. I kept it for years. With additions or subtractions and with or without the crinoline (which was a real one, constructed out of grey alpaca and whalebone), it did yeoman service at any number of fancy-dress dances. It featured again at that year's Bachelors' Ball (this time minus its black velvet sleeves, which had been removed and replaced by long medieval ones of lilac satin sewn with large artificial pearls). On this occasion, I seized the chance of showing off my hair, which by now reached below my waist. And very fetching it looked, flowing down my back from under a cap made from a network of pearls. The chaps loved it, and it created quite a sensation: the 'shingle' had been all the rage throughout the Roaring Twenties, and by now people were beginning to forget what long hair looked like. Well, it looked pretty good on me, and I regret to say that I traded on its novelty-value shamelessly, letting it down on every possible occasion from fancy-dress affairs to bathing

---

* Victor Stiebel, a famous London *couturier*, whose style I admired enormously.

picnics, until a year or so later a girl called Leila Apcar appeared upon the scene and trumped my modest ace with a Rapunzel-like supply of the most gorgeous pale gold hair you ever saw.

Since Leila was also an outstandingly pretty girl, I gave up appearing at fancy-dress dances as Queen Guinevere or Jeannie with the Light Brown Hair or whoever, and a year later succeeded in badgering my reluctant parents into letting me join the ranks of the shingle-brigade: a great improvement on those two hideous coils of tightly plaited hair exactly like a pair of earphones, that gave me the appearance of a school-marm. There were not all *that* many fancy-dress revels and bathing picnics!

Mother still had a great many friends in Delhi, among them the parents of Aunt Bee's niece, Maxine Mitchell, the small girl who had spent a summer holiday with us in a rented house in the Isle of Wight and used to drive us nuts by following us around wherever we went, like an adoring puppy. Mrs Mitchell was a particular friend of Mother's, and I admired her enormously. She was not only very pretty, but she dressed beautifully and in the sort of clothes that even at that age I realized, with awe and admiration, no verandah *darzi*, however skilful, could possibly have copied. Here at last was someone who wore models designed, cut and sewn by experts, the sort of dresses that ordinary women could never aspire to and that would for ever be out of my reach. So you can imagine my rapture when, one afternoon, she presented me with one of those fabulous outfits — the only Paris model I have ever owned, and certainly one of the most exciting presents I have ever received.

It had been designed to be worn at cocktail parties and consisted of a slip of a dress in pale, pinky-beige *crêpe de Chine*, short and sleeveless, and worn under a finger-length, satin-lined coat of the same material, embroidered all over with a shimmering web of matching pearls, beads and sequins.

Mrs Mitchell had apologized for the fact that the outfit would soon be terribly dated, since hems were already beginning to descend while waists, which had vanished a decade earlier, were returning to favour. She was, she said, afraid that every line of the enchanting confection she had just given me would soon be old hat. As if I cared! The mere possession of that glamorous outfit was enough to lift my spirits into the stratosphere, although Mrs Mitchell was right about the changing fashion; for in no time at all out went the boyish flat-as-a-board figure, and bosoms were in again. And with them, after an absence of many years, were waists.

Belts and sashes returned there after a prolonged sojourn around the hip, and down went hems once more, so that the skimpy dress of my lovely Chanel model was soon to look as dated as an Edwardian bustle.

The dampness and humidity of another monsoon (added to the fact that it was too tight for me) helped to split the material, and I was forced to abandon it. But the Tree-Shop provided me with *crêpe de Chine*, and the skill of the India dyers, who, for a modest sum, will match the exact tone and colour of any pattern you choose to give them, meant that I was able to have a new *darzi*-made dress to go under that beautiful coat. I wore the coat for years, and would probably still have it if only the material had been able to stand up to the climate. It got frailer and frailer; the silk frayed and split and began to shed its beads and sequins and develop bald patches, and I was forced to abandon it, though I can't remember how or when it passed out of my life.

I still possess a fragment of another dress that I acquired that year. This one, too, was worn until it disintegrated, but I cut a piece off the remains and kept it as a souvenir. (I have these silly ideas about some inanimate objects.) It is now in one of our many scrapbook-cum-photograph albums, and I hope to be able to include myself wearing it in this book.

Chapter 8

~%&%~

Back once more in our tents behind the Club, I discovered that more of our childhood friends and acquaintances had returned to Delhi — among them Peggy Spence, Sybil Roberts and Phyllis Moncrieff-Smith, plus their parents. I also made a new friend, one Olive Targett, the occupant of a tent just behind my own. Olive, who was a few years older than me, had come out to India to spend a season in Delhi under the chaperonage of her bachelor brother, Robert, who was one of the Club's resident members and had a fairly senior job in the Stores Department.

Olive told me in strict confidence that she was unofficially engaged to a young man in England, and that these few months in India were in the nature of a final fling before settling down to be a model wife and mother. But since she did not wear an engagement ring, and was pretty and very popular, none of the swains whose hearts she collected that season were aware that they were wasting their time on a girl who was already 'bespoke'.

There was never an evening when Olive was not booked to go out dining or dancing (usually both), and I still remember the shock I received on discovering, between awe and admiration, that, except for a minute pair of 'bafflers' (twenties slang for panties), she wore nothing under her dress. I remember sitting in her tent one evening, chatting while she got ready to go out to a dance and watching her put on a pair of silk stockings, ensuring that they stayed up above the knee by rolling them and tucking in a *pi*, that smallest of Indian coins, as an anchor. (Your grandmother can probably show you how this was done.) I knew that she had nothing else on under the loose silk kimono she was wearing, so when my eye fell on the clock as she dealt with her hair and her make-up, I said anxiously, 'For goodness sake, Olive. Do you know what the time is? You're being called for in exactly two minutes.'

'That's all I need,' said Olive, blithely. And, flinging off the kimono, she donned the obligatory pair of *crêpe de Chine* bafflers, wriggled into a tube of something gold and sparkly that was supported by the thinnest of shoulder-straps, stepped into a pair of matching high-heeled shoes, and, picking up a beaded bag and her evening cloak, announced that she was ready — 'On the dot! And here comes Reggie,' or Tom or Dick or Harry, or whoever was taking her out that night. 'Goodnight, darling.' And she was off and away.

I was astounded. The idea that a girl could go gaily off to a party wearing practically nothing under one of the skimpy dance dresses of the twenties struck me as incredibly daring, and more than a little shocking. Even if I had had a dress like hers I would still have considered myself undressed unless I put on layers of underclothes: a vest, a bra, silk stockings and a suspender-belt to keep them up, a pair of camiknickers that combined wide-legged panties and a camisole top, and finally a petticoat. All this before I topped it off with a dress! Olive's evening dresses were exquisite, and not one of them could possibly have been run up by some 'little woman around the corner', let alone a verandah *darzi*. I admired everything about her, her assurance most of all — probably because I myself had none. This circumstance was not improved, on the social side, by the fact that Tacklow's pension, now gravely reduced due to his commuting some of it in order to pay for our passages out to India, was not sufficient, even with the payment he received for the work that he had returned to do, to pay for parties for us that better-off parents, who lived in style in the Baker-built houses of New Delhi, gave for their daughters prior to every dance at Maiden's Hotel or at the Club, or a ball at Viceroy's House.

Poor Tacklow simply could not afford to entertain for us, except on a very modest scale, and I was soon to discover that Gerry's disclosures as to the prevailing social pitfalls were correct. Unattached men, who were very much in the minority, had become so spoilt that like the 'Deb's Delights' of the London season, they would never accept the first invitation they received, but would wait until they received several, and then choose the one that offered the best prospect of a good dinner before the dance and the most lavish supply of drinks during the evening. And as if this situation by itself was not guaranteed to give a bad headache to any mother of two unmarried daughters and a very lean purse, mine made it even more difficult for herself by doing her best to see that if I were invited to a party, Bets would go too. Yes, she *had* promised once that

Bets would not 'come out' until she was seventeen. But as she told her friends, she couldn't *bear* to see 'poor little Bets' left out of anything. It was soon known to every hostess in Delhi that if you invited Daisy Kaye's elder daughter to a party you had to have the younger one as well. And that meant another two men instead of one: four guests straight off! So as you can imagine, I didn't get many invitations. I decided, sadly, that this was due to my lack of charm and social small-talk, allied to the fact that I didn't play bridge, couldn't talk 'horse', did not ride or play golf, was a useless partner at tennis and a pretty indifferent one on a ballroom floor. In short, I had nothing whatever to offer by way of 'singing for my supper'. I have seldom felt so inadequate, and it was not until Gerry Ross arrived in Delhi that I learned from that seasoned campaigner the real reason for the sudden dearth of Invitations to the Ball.

This information, which might have been expected to add to my depression, in fact cheered me up considerably; it was only Mother being dotingly maternal about her 'baby', and not, as I had feared, me being hopelessly dull and boring. The relief that this information brought was enormous and considerably increased by the discovery that even so dashing and popular a 'Week Queen' as Gerry could have her setbacks. For I had learned in Cawnpore that she (in company with any number of other women, both young and not so young) had fallen for the charms of one of Delhi's most attractive bachelors, a Flying Officer Stephens, whom everyone knew as 'Steve', and who during the previous season had apparently given Gerry reason to believe that he was one of her conquests — in fact practically her personal property.

However, that was last year; and now, arriving in Delhi expecting to carry on where they had left off, she was outraged to discover that she had been cut out by a grass widow — and one who was several years her senior at that! 'She's twenty-five if she's a day!' I remember her rushing into my tent like an infuriated whirlwind to tell me all about it: 'And they are going to the dance here tonight — together,' finished Gerry through gritted teeth. 'Well, if she thinks she's going to get him away from me, she's wrong — *lend me a pair of gunmetal stockings!*'

Sadly, I can't remember if the gunmetal stockings were a success or not. But I have never forgotten Steve, for he was, in addition to his other talents, an excellent dancer, and one of the very few men I was ever to dance with (and that was only once!) who gave me the illusion that I too was an expert. Had he given me the *faintest* encouragement I am quite sure that I too would have fallen hopelessly in love with him. But apart from that single dance, he was never more than pleasantly polite to me. So I fell in love instead with Olive's brother, Bob Targett, who was nothing much to look at, but possessed more than his fair share of charm.

Bob must have been pushing forty (roughly the same age as Tacklow had been when he fell in love with my mother, whom he still quite obviously adored), and he was not what you would call 'handsome'. But it was an attractive face, and in spite of the fact that he wore hornrimmed spectacles he had the reputation of being a 'ladies' man'; though to date, his liaisons had always been with married women. He was strictly a bachelor type, who had no intention of getting involved in matrimony if he could help it.

I don't know what he saw in me, for I wasn't his type at all. He preferred married women, who knew the rules of the game and didn't embarrass him by making claims on him; and his favourite pastime was bridge, a game at which he was in the championship class. When Lord Willingdon took over as Viceroy, Bob became the Vicereine's favourite partner — she being a notable bridge-addict with a well-known fondness for winning. In fact it was rumoured that when Bob was eventually knighted, the honour was more for his skill at cards than for any particularly good work in the Stores Department! I, however, have always detested bridge or any form of card games: they bore me rigid and Bob knew it. Luckily for me, though, it amused him to take me to dances and parties, so that for the duration of that season we became a recognized 'twosome' and were invited to parties together, though I always lost out when bridge was the alternative. His partiality for my company saved my first season in Delhi from being a dire disappointment, for as an eligible bachelor who had become an experienced avoider of matrimony, it had amused him to flirt with me, and I decided that here at last must be True Love.

The remainder of that season was, in consequence, a magic time for me. I floated on air — all ten stone of me — and envied no one, not even the 'Week Queens' with their troops of admirers. I had never wanted half-a-dozen rivals for my affections. I only wanted one.

✳ The most memorable event of that Delhi season, though for all the wrong reasons, was the last Viceregal garden party to be held in the grounds of Viceregal Lodge in Old Delhi, since next cold weather, Lord and Lady Irwin would move into Lutyens's magnificent marble and sandstone palace, which, for only a brief spell — less than twenty years (and what are twenty years to India?) — would be known as 'Viceroy's House' before becoming the official residence of future Presidents of India.

The occasion was made truly memorable by the sudden death on the brink of the garden party of the Queen of somewhere-or-other — I think she must have been a Scandinavian crowned head connected in some way with the British royal family (which, via Victoria, most crowned heads were). I don't imagine that more than twenty people in Delhi had ever heard of her, but a cable from London announced to the Viceroy that Court Mourning would be observed for a stated number of days. Well, you would have thought that in the circumstances the easiest thing to do would be to cancel the garden party, wouldn't you? But no. Someone in authority decided that it was far too late for that; either because there was no way of ensuring that every guest was warned of the cancellation in time to prevent a good many of them turning up on the dot, or because of the more obvious 'What on earth are we going to do with about a million assorted buns, sandwiches and all the rest of the food and drink and flowers that have been clogging up the kitchens for the past week?' (No fridges in those days) Or perhaps it was just the good old showbiz motto, 'The show must go on' that carried the day. Whatever it was, the verdict went out that the party was on — *but* that 'mourning would be worn'.

Well, that was fine by the men, since most of the civilian British possessed a dark suit, while the Indians, who wear white for mourning, could wear either that or black. But not many memsahibs possessed black dresses that were suitable for a garden party. All those who didn't tried borrowing from those who did, or, if that failed, hastily dyed something of their own. Every *dhobi* and dyer in both Delhis was pressed into service, and the place reeked with the smell of freshly dyed dresses — most of which were a total disaster, for in those days garden party dresses were for the most part ankle-length, frilly, pretty and floating confections, in pale-coloured chiffons and muslins, worn with wide-brimmed matching hats.

But though many tried it, dyeing those wretched hats proved impracticable; while as for that frivolous, ruffled dress in apple-green voile, in which you thought you were going to look so charming, it proved to be incredibly dreary when dyed a rusty black and worn with the only black hat you possessed, which happened to be a felt pudding-basin.

NOVEMBER, 1927.   NOVEMBER, 1927.

ate.	Hour.	Remarks.	Date.	Hour.	Remarks.
esday 1st	10 a.m. 10.45 „	Chief Secy. Babu Krishna Pratap Singh Sahib. Legislative Council meeting.	Thursday 10th	5.30 p.m.	H. E. attends 25th anniversary of the Ewin Christian college and lays the foundati stone of the Turner hostel.
	3.50 p.m.	Sir Cecil and Lady Kaye, and the Misses Kaye arrive.			
	4 „	Tennis.	Friday 11th	5.30 a.m.	English mail despatched. Armistice day. H. E. attends commemorati service.
ednesday 2nd	10 a.m. 10.45 „	Judl. Secy. Dr. M. B. Cameron. Legislative Council meeting.		11 „ 11.30 „	H. M. I. & A. H. M. L. S.-G.
	4 p.m.	H. E. plays golf with Captair			
ursday		Legislative Council meeting.			

According to this, we never left! (Perhaps we're still there??)

Right: The SS *City of London*, which brought us out to Calcutta – one of the many passenger ships that plied between England and the Far East in the days of Empire.

Left: We stayed with the Taggarts in Calcutta. *From top left*: ?, Lady 'Thomas' Taggart, Tacklow, Bets, Sir Charles Taggart (pulling faces as usual!), self holding the Taggart dog, Tim, on my lap.

Below: The ruins of the British Residency in Lucknow with the flag flying, the only Union Jack that is never hauled down, night or day, in memory of the men who lost their lives keeping it flying during the siege of the Residency in 1857, in which Sir Henry Lawrence was one of the many who died.

Above: The Sati-Chowra Ghat, Cawnpore. This is where Tantia Topi, the Nana-Sahib's general, sat to watch the massacre of the survivors of the British garrison. They had accepted his terms of surrender and had embarked in the fleet of river boats that would, they had been promised, take them down-river to safety. When the last of the survivors had crawled aboard he gave the signal for the boats to be set alight and for his troops to open fire on them from both banks. It is curious to think that both that tree and the little temple saw it all happen and were still there when I last saw them, well over 100 years later.

Above: Mother in one of C.T. Allen's punts on the lake at his Cawnpore house, the Retreat.

Right: An afternoon on the lake with an old friend, Gerry Ross.

Above: Monty Ashley-Phillips laid on a Christmas camp to welcome us home. Christmas camps were always part of the festivities in the old days. There were at least another four or five people at this one, but I can't remember who they were. It was a lovely 'homecoming'. *Left to right*: Monty, Mother, Tacklow.

Above: A street scene in Rajputana.

Above: The gateway to Gwalior Fort. This is where Scindia met the old man who said he would show the Maharajah where the treasure was hidden.

Right: Mother and Tacklow and an unknown district officer, having their photographs taken after having been profusely garlanded. Mother has not given the name of the state – she only wrote 'Rajputana', as a heading to several pages of snapshots.

Left: A. I. R. Riley took Mother up for a flight over New Delhi and she took several snapshots. This is one. Our tents lie behind the temporary Gymkhana Club – see in the centre. This building was later bought by His Highness the Maharajah of Kashmir and became Kashmir House. The photograph shows a raw, unfinished and almost treeless New Delhi.

Right: All dressed up as Juliet for the Bachelors' Ball at the Old Delhi Club.

Left: Steve. By the time this photograph was taken, he had become Air Vice-Marshal Stevens, CB, CBE, MC.

Right: Delhi. Part of a palace in the old Lodi period ruins, later the Willingdon Gardens. This was the Golf Club which we hired for the cowboy party for the Horse Show fancy dress ball.

Above left: Sitting on the steps of the Gymkhana Club. Mother, self, lovely 'Ooloo' Riley, Bets and Ooloo's hou

Above right: One of the Lodi tombs as it was before a Vicereine, Lady Willingdon, had most of the grounds where the Lodi ruins stood turned into a park. Beautifully tidy and flowery but not so romantic.

Above: The Secretariat, New Delhi.

Right: The Grand Trunk Road somewhere between Delhi and Agra.

Below: Agra revisited.

Bob Targett.

Above: Viceroy House, New Delhi in the late 1920s. There are still hardly any trees or nearby building

Left: Bedr, Hyderabad State. The banyan tree and some of our unwelcome visitors, the *bandar-log*.

Below: The walnut-seller's daughter

Left: A gateway in Rajputana – 'Country of the Kings'.

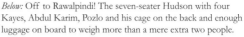

Left: Tacklow with his good companion Pozlo.

Below: Off to Rawalpindi! The seven-seater Hudson with four Kayes, Abdul Karim, Pozlo and his cage on the back and enough luggage on board to weigh more than a mere extra two people.

Above: Tacklow with someone on the left whose name I can't remember, and Cherub – at that time Mrs 'Cherub' Shakespeare and later the Duchess of Sutherland.

Right: The sisters Kaye, hastily dressed up for a pirate party at the Ambala Club, Ambala.

Above: Rawalpindi, where we stayed with General Sir Claude Auchinleck (the Auk) and his wife, Jessie, who were old friends of my parents. *Left to right:* My brother, Bill, the Auk, someone whose name I've forgotten and Jessie.

Right: A charming Buddha with attendant saints, excavated at Taxila by Sir John Marshall.

Right: Torkham: the borders of Afghanistan on the North West Frontier Province of what was then India and is now Pakistan.

Above: Bill.

Below: A typical Raj-period bungalow. This is, broadly speaking, the bungalow that everyone lived in, in the plains. (Houses in the hills and the Retreat were built of wood and were much lighter and easier to keep warm.) But though the rooms of the plains bungalow were apt to be dark, they were very high and those verandahs kept them comparatively cool, while the small windows near the ceiling could be opened to let the hot air out.

Above: Damaged railway lines, due to flood damage in the monsoon.

You have no idea — unless you happen to be one of those who were there yourself — how *incredibly* dowdy we Brits looked. Like a vast flock of bedraggled crows. By contrast, all the wives of the Indian guests who, lucky things, did not have to wear hats, looked elegant and enchanting in black, white or grey saris, shimmering with touches of embroidery. As did a solitary English girl who had refused to toe the line and join the crows.

It was the custom in those days for the bachelor 'chummeries' in Delhi to host parties for Horse Show Week and invite their girlfriends, suitably chaperoned, to stay. And since Eileen Clinton-Thomas was one of the prettiest and most popular of the Raj girls, you could be sure of meeting her at almost every 'Week' in India. Arriving in Delhi on the day before the Viceregal garden party, she had been informed by her hosts of the Court Mourning bombshell, but had refused to believe it, being firmly convinced that her high-spirited admirers were pulling her leg and probably had a bet on whether they could con her into making an exhibition of herself by turning up at a Viceregal garden party wearing hastily dyed black.

Still convinced that the whole thing was a hoax, she turned up at the party in a ravishing primrose yellow confection with matching gloves and shoes, and a cartwheel hat composed of layers of pale yellow organdie. The total effect was stunning. Particularly when contrasted with a sea of disgruntled memsahibs wearing extremely tatty black dresses.

Among other visiting VIPs in Delhi that year was — unless I have got my dates mixed — a temporarily deposed monarch, George of Greece. An attractive man, he was one of those convivial, party-loving types who can be found dancing on a table at around three o'clock in the morning on almost any night of the week, and during his prolonged stay in India's capital city he managed to steal the affections of a Mrs Britten-Jones,* whose husband (also a well-known charmer) was at that time acting as Controller of the Viceroy's Household — or something equally impressive.

I rather think that he was himself more than slightly embroiled in a clandestine love affair with a great friend of mine at the time, so perhaps, what with that and managing Lord Irwin's household, he was too occupied with his own affairs of the heart to realize what his wife was up to. Either that or he thought that as the ex-King was a married man there was

* I don't know how they spelt the 'Britten'.

nothing to worry about. But in the event his wife ran away with the ex-King, and when, shortly afterwards, he managed to regain his throne, she became his *maîtresse-en-titre* and later still accompanied him into exile in Portugal when he succeeded in losing it for a second time. As one of my friends remarked cheerfully: 'Well, we don't have much money, but we *do* see life!'

✴ In the days when Bets and I were children, we would not have considered any cold weather season in Delhi to be complete without at least two visits to Agra and the Taj, and one to our friends the Perrins at Narora, the head of the Ganges Canal. But though the Perrins had left some years ago, and the new Canal Officer was a stranger to us, we still revisited Agra whenever we could, travelling there by car along the Grand Trunk Road, instead of in a sleeper on the night-train as we used to do when I was a child. The Age of the Car, as far as India was concerned, was still in its infancy, and the 120-odd miles of road that separated Delhi from Agra had not changed very much since the days of the Great Moguls. It ran for the most part between a double avenue of shade trees and the open countryside that stretched away on either side of it, sparsely dotted by palms and kikar-trees, feathery clumps of pampas and the occasional field of sugar cane, and seemingly largely untenanted, since of the five towns that one drove through — Mahrauli, Faridabad, little Palwal, Hodal and Muttra — only the last could be classed as a city.

The branches of the trees that lined the unmetalled road met overhead to make a tunnel of shade that was pleasant relief from the blazing sunlight, but had one major drawback: it was impossible for a car or lorry to drive through it without raising a dense, choking cloud of dust through which, as you passed (and for a full minute afterwards) you must drive blind. Fortunately, in those days most of the traffic to be met with on that particular stretch of the Grand Trunk was (when not pedestrian or cyclist) either bullock-drawn carts or horse-drawn vehicles such as *tongas*, and when one saw another car, or worse still, a bus or lorry approaching, one slowed down, frantically wound up the windows, and burying one's face in a scarf or handkerchief, kept handy for that purpose, plunged into the inevitable wall of white dust, hoping not to hit anything or anybody while engulfed in the blinding smother.

But dust or no dust, I loved that Agra road, and the favoured places, where we used to stop *en route* and picnic, still stay in my mind as leafy and enchanting, even though the last time I was driven along part of it, well over thirty years after India had become independent, I did not recognize anything at all. The long, quiet, tree-shaded road and the vast, sun-baked and seemingly empty countryside through which it had run had vanished completely, victims of a population explosion that had forced the hasty construction of thousands upon thousands of jerry-built houses, ranging from high-rise concrete office blocks to the mud-and-wattle *bustees* of the poor.

�֍ In the first year of our return to India and during subsequent cold weather seasons there, we visited Agra whenever we could; and despite the many occasions on which I saw the Taj, it never failed to make me catch my breath and feel my heart contract. Every time it was as though it was the first time. The shock of surprise and delight, and the sense of wonder, were always there, always fresh. And once again, as when Bets and I were children, the Taj became our own special and private possession.

By chance, our first return visit had coincided with a full moon, and we had been afraid that we would find the place crowded with fellow sightseers. But apparently the tourist trade was still reeling from the First World War, for despite the fact that the moon was at the full, there was no one there but ourselves. The silent, scented gardens were ours to wander through, and so also was every part of the Taj itself. For in those long-ago days you were allowed to climb the inner stairway leading up to the flat square of roof that supports the four graceful pavilions and the great central dome, and to sit, if you so wished, high atop the enormous cliff of marble above the great arch which gives entrance to the tomb. From this dizzying vantage-point you could look down on the wide, white marble platform below, with its four slender minarets, one at each corner; on the lawns and on the dark, sentinel avenue of cypresses that lines the fountain-filled water-channels. Or, from the *chattris* on the opposite side, on the silver sandbanks and the gleaming levels of the Jumna, which flows past the outer wall of the river terrace towards the distant line of Agra's fort, and the Jasmine Tower, in which the Emperor Shah Jehan, who built the Taj as a tomb for his beloved wife, Mumtaz Mahal, was imprisoned by his son Aurangzeb for the last seven years of his life.

At no time during many visits to the Taj did I ever see anyone forbidden from entering. There used to be a solitary individual in a shabby khaki coat — presumably an old soldier or a retired police constable — who dozed among the shadows of the great marble and red granite entrance gate, or leant against one of the doorposts, chewing *paan* and brooding on life. Plus the odd *mali* or two and an elderly white-robed, white-turbaned character who presided over a small stall on which were displayed postcards and guidebooks for sale. No one else. No tickets. No charge for entering. No rows of shops and stalls selling souvenirs, or gangs of clamorous guides, full of inaccurate information, to badger the occasional visitor. No whining beggars either. And, astonishingly, almost no Indian sightseers.

The Taj is, of course, a monument raised by a Muslim Emperor to the memory of his Muslim Queen; and I have heard that it reminds some Hindus of the Muslim conquest, and revolts the bigoted among them.* But I will not believe that even the most intolerant Hindu can be so petty and small-minded. It belongs, after all, to all Asia.

India obviously took the Taj for granted, and could not be bothered to visit it. Her people had never shown much interest in their ancient cities and monuments, especially those that were deserted or ruined. To them the past was the past and they saw no reason to be sentimental about it, let alone take steps to preserve it. An attitude that, but for tourism, would, I suspect, still prevail today: since except for the really spectacular relics of her magnificent past — the 'money-spinners' which lure millions of tourists to India, where they yearly spend incredibly large sums of money on accommodation, entrance fees, and souvenirs (in addition to providing employment to many more millions of the populace) — many other fabulous palaces and forts that lie off the beaten track have been allowed to crumble into ruins and become the home of squatters, dacoits and beggars, and the haunt of bats, owls, pigeons and the monkey-folk.

Agra retained all its old magic for us. But after spending a long weekend at Sikandar, in the walled park which surrounds the tomb of the Emperor Akbar, I was never quite sure which tomb I loved best: the Taj, or Akbar's tomb at Sikandar. This was largely because the Archaeological Department owned a small bungalow† inside the park, and that year they lent it to Tacklow for a weekend. It was an enchanting little house, built on a wide platform of red sandstone and shaded by the branches of a tree that grew out of a hole in its thatched roof. Flights of stone steps led up to it from

* See James Cameron, *Indian Summer*, Penguin, 1987.
† Sadly, it was destroyed by a fire in the early 1980s.

each side, and the carved stone balustrades that edged the platform dripped with flowering creepers.

We had been careful to pick a weekend when the moon was full for our visit to Sikandar, and accompanied by Abdul Karim, with Mother driving the Hudson, we had arrived there on a Friday evening, intending to spend the best part of that night at the Taj, and the following one in the Dâk-bungalow at Fatehpur-Sîkrî — the wonderful, deserted city that Akbar built on a ridge of high ground to the west of Agra and which he was eventually forced to abandon when several successive monsoons failed, the tanks and wells dried up and there was not enough water for the people's needs.

But in the event we spent both nights at Sikandar, because we had not realized that the four great gates in the massive battlemented wall enclosing the tomb and its surrounding park were closed each day at sunset and would not be opened again until nine o'clock on the following morning. This put paid to any idea of visiting the Taj and getting back before the gates were shut. But it also meant that while they remained closed we could make-believe that we were the undisputed Lords of Sikandar. It was an alluring prospect, and as we had arrived there a good hour and a half before sunset, we were able to do a good deal of sightseeing by daylight.

The tomb of the greatest of the Great Moguls was not in the least like any of the other famous tombs that I had seen, and if I had not known whose it was, I would have taken it to be a memorial *chattri* raised above the spot on which some Hindu ruler had been cremated. But then Akbar's views on religion were surprisingly liberal, so perhaps his mausoleum — on which work had begun during his lifetime — had been intended to convey this. Built of red sandstone and white marble, it is made up of four decorative pavilions set one above the other, and the topmost, which is mostly of white marble, consists of a great marble-paved floor as big as a ballroom, left open to the sky and surrounded by a pillared cloister, the outer arches of which are filled in by exquisite marble filigree, so fine that you can see through them as easily as if they had been made from lace instead of carved from slabs of polished stone. In the centre of the courtyard, standing on a raised platform and cut from a single block of white marble, stands a copy of the true tomb, which can be found in a dark vault below ground level. The mock tomb is decorated with carved flowers and texts and, in addition to Akbar's name, the ninety-nine names of God — the hundredth, according to legend, is known only to the camels, which accounts for those animals' haughtily held heads and insufferably superior expressions.

We lingered on the top storey that first evening at Sikandar, watching the other visitors leaving as the sun sank down towards the horizon and the sky above us turned from blue to a duck-egg green scribbled all over by the innumerable dark dots and thin, wavering lines of birds flying home from the city to roost in the park. As the light faded, leaving the tomb and the park in shadow, and bats flittered out to meet the night, we heard the great doors in the main gate clang shut and saw the full moon rise in the last wash of the sunset; and by the time we reached the garden the shrubs and flowerbeds were spangled with fireflies.

The raised platform on which the Archaeological bungalow stood formed a wide stone terrace on which we dined under the stars, and afterwards we explored the great tomb again and wandered about the gardens and the park and along the dry stone water-courses along which once — but no longer — lines of fountains had played. The moon was so bright that you could have read a newspaper, and there was a ring round it. I had heard of such a thing, but this was the first time I had ever seen it — and to this day, I have never seen anything quite like it again. For this was no hazy or rainbow-like halo, but an enormous circle, as thin and sharp as though it had been drawn on that cloudless sky by a gigantic mapping-pen dipped in gold ink.

Even Tacklow, who had given me my first lesson in astronomy (thereby hooking me on it for life) could not remember ever having seen anything quite like that before, though he added that a ring around the moon was supposed to warn of bad weather to come. But, looking at this one, I refused to believe that anything so beautiful could be ill-omened. For me, it added an extra touch of magic to a magical night, and writing about it after all these years I can remember it as clearly as though I was back again at Sikandar, standing once more by Akbar's mock tomb with the heady scent of *Rhat-ki-Rani* drifting up from the garden below, and that incredible gold-ringed moon in the sky overhead.

The night had been so quiet that in order not to disturb that silence, we had taken off our shoes and walked up the dark stone stairways and across the marble floors in our stockinged feet. Perhaps because of this, when we left the building and were on our way back to the bungalow, we suddenly became aware that there was a herd of black-buck in the park. We never saw them by day. But by night they emerged by ones and twos to graze on the lawns and flowerbeds of the formal garden surrounding the tomb, and if you stood quite still in a patch of shadow they would come close enough for you to catch the glint of their eyes and see the moonlight gleam on their long, twisted, backward-sloping horns. To watch them, and to walk shoeless across the lawn and along the stone pavements that bordered the ornamental water-courses, listening to all the many small noises which added together make up the sum total of silence, was so fascinating that it was difficult to tear ourselves away and go tamely to bed, even after the ghostly black-buck had vanished and the shadow of the tomb had begun to stretch out across the moon-flooded spaces. Yet Sikandar in the early morning turned out to be even more entrancing than it had been by the light of that haloed full moon.

✵ The sun was still well below the horizon and the sky a pale lemon yellow, as clear as glass, when we were woken by what sounded like every bird in India saluting the dawn. Dew spangled and glittered on every leaf and blade of grass, a light belt of mist lay like a gauzy scarf above the awakening land and everywhere one looked there were birds twittering, screeching, chirruping, warbling. Abdul Karim and the *chowkidar* served us with *chota-hazri* on the verandah, and afterwards, since the gates would not be opened for another two hours and the park was still ours alone, we walked across the lawns and around the tomb in our dressing-gowns, smelling the morning and listening to the birds. Every dome, every pillar and every carved screen of the four-storeyed tomb was alive with parakeets, gossiping to each other and peering down at us with bright inquisitive eyes. The gardens were full of butterflies and from behind the high surrounding walls we could hear the sounds of India waking: the creaking of well-wheels and bullock-carts, a donkey braying, the twanging bell of a passing *tonga*, and the occasional toot of a car-horn or rumble of a lorry as traffic began to flow along the Muttra road. But inside there were only the birds and squirrels and ourselves — and the memory of a great Emperor.

It was many years later that I heard for the first time the hymn 'Morning has Broken', written by novelist Eleanor Farjeon, and was instantly reminded of that long-ago morning at Sikandar. I have often heard it since then, but whenever I do I am always back in that glittering morning. And at the beginning of my days, not the end.

Chapter 9

~❄~

By the time we returned again to Delhi, the cold weather season was drawing to a close and the tents were becoming uncomfortably hot. Olive Targett was already packing up to leave for Bombay and England, to be married and become Lady Something-or-other to do with biscuits, and since she had not yet seen the Taj, Bob arranged a Last Weekend Visit to Agra as a farewell party for her.

I've forgotten which of her many swains she chose to accompany her, but I remember that there were four car-loads of us, one driven by Mother, who had been asked to chaperon the party, and that we all put up at Lowry's Hotel. Our visit coincided with the last full moon before the annual exodus to the hills began, and in addition to doing the rounds of all the obligatory Agra sights, such as the Fort, Akbar's tomb at Sikandar, the tomb of Itima-ud-Daula and the deserted city of Fatehpur-Sîkrî, we spent an entire night, from sunset to sunrise, in the garden of the Taj. After wandering hand-in-hand with Bob through those romantic flower-scented and moon-drenched spaces, I received, in the shadow of the great dome, what I was to discover later was a remarkably chaste kiss (it was in fact the first I had received as a 'grown-up') and, somewhat naturally, I leapt to the conclusion that this must be Love.

I returned to Delhi in a state of total euphoria in Bob's car, with our luggage and Pete, Bob's bull terrier, on the back seat. We had been the last of our party to leave, but as Bob's car was capable of a lot more speed than my parents' seven-seater Hudson, or the car driven by Olive's swain, we had expected to catch up with the others on the road. But we were held up by level crossing gates that had been prematurely closed on the orders of an extremely pompous little Punjabi, a small, tubby and very minor railway official who, backed by an escort of two uniformed members of the railway police, and intent on showing his zeal for the *'Kaiser-i-Hind'* (the Viceroy), had insisted on closing the crossing because the Viceregal train was timed to pass that way at four o'clock precisely. The fact that it was not yet three made no difference to his decision. He did not seem to think it in the least important, and though Bob argued, pleaded, ordered and finally (I suspect) resorted to bribery, the little man refused to budge.

Compared with the flood-tide of traffic that pours down the Grand Trunk Road in these degenerate days, there were remarkably few travellers on the road that day, and most of those were pedestrians who simply ducked below the barrier and walked across, no man saying them nay. Nevertheless, as the minutes crawled by, the road on either side of the track filled up inexorably into an impressive traffic-block consisting of bullock-carts, *tongas*, country carts, assorted *gharis*, cars and lorries, a smattering of bicycles, several camels and a solitary elephant, all of which served to block us in. Indians are, in general, a patient race. They have never been averse to squatting down to wait for a train or a bus, or merely permission to move, and now they hunkered down happily to await the passing of the Burra Lat Sahib's train and (it was to be hoped) the subsequent lifting of the barrier.

Immersed in the idiotic throes of first love, I should have been only too pleased to be delayed for an extra hour or two with the object of my affections. And I would have been, if there had been even an inch of shade. But though the Grand Trunk Road was lined for most of its length with a double row of shade trees, this particular stretch of road happened to be treeless; probably because the constructors of the signal-box and the two small brick buildings had cut down the surrounding trees and used them for fuel.

For a good half-mile in either direction the landscape was treeless, and the sun beat down fiercely out of a cloudless sky. The heat shimmered and danced on the rails and the cinder-strewn track, the parched earth and brittle grass and the patient ranks of waiting traffic. And, as we waited, the bullocks, ponies and camels, the elephant and some humans answered the call of nature, and strewed the ground with droppings and urine. The temperature must have been well above a hundred, and the thin canvas roof of Bob's car — for very few cars in those days had solid, built-in roofs — provided little protection from the scorching heat and none at all from the tormenting swarms of flies that accompanied the assembled livestock. The white dust of the Grand Trunk Road rose in choking clouds from under the many restless, fidgeting hooves, and Pete, whose tongue had been lolling out as he panted distressfully in the back seat, began to express his displeasure with the heat and the smell by whining and scrabbling at the sides of the car, and finally being sick all over the luggage.

The stench had been bad enough without that, and Pete's contribution was the last straw; but hemmed in as we were there was nothing we could do about it. We had no water, and no hope of clearing up the mess until the Viceregal train had passed. And, judging from the obstinacy of the crossing-keeper, he might well keep us all waiting for a further ten or fifteen minutes after that, just to be on the safe side. I think I rather expected Bob to be galvanized by Pete's unsocial behaviour into taking up cudgels again with our jailer. But he, like Kipling, had obviously been out in India long enough to realize the futility of 'trying to hustle the East', and, resignedly accepting the situation as part of the White Man's Burden, he merely glanced back reproachfully at his faithful hound and said sadly: 'Oh, Pete, you bunch of violets, you!' Whereupon the wretched animal was sick again.

The half-hour that followed had nothing to recommend it. But it passed at last, and so did the Viceroy's train, by which time the traffic jam had turned into such a complicated piece of knitting that it took the various components an age to unravel themselves. Wheels had become entangled with other wheels, bullocks had become bad-tempered and backed their carts instead of pulling them forward; camels squealed and bit; car drivers honked on their horns; men shouted abuse at their animals and one another, and the hot, white dust 'stood up like a tree above the smother' . . . But in the end, of course, it all sorted itself out and we reached Delhi a good two hours late and smelling like a sewage farm.

It was not really an auspicious beginning to my first grown-up love affair, but the next night there was a big farewell party for Olive at the Club, where, buoyed up and made suddenly confident by the conviction that this was Love at last, I danced for the first time as though my feet were at least two inches above ground, instead of stumbling or treading on my partner's toes.

Almost every memorable occasion in my life seems to have had a tune attached to it — nearly always some popular dance tune. The two that recall Bob Targett are 'Lantern of Love', to which I danced with him that night, and 'Your Tiny Hand is Frozen' from the first act of *La Bohème*, which he sang to me (in English, not Italian) as we strolled hand-in-hand in the intervals, between dances, among the tree shadows of the moonlit gardens of New Delhi's first Gymkhana Club. I had never heard that tune before, and though I have heard it sung any number of times since then — often by some of the great singers of the world, Gigli among them — always it is Bob in the moonlight that I hear singing it, though by now he must have been dead for many years.

It was Olive's farewell party, coming on the heels of our late return from that weekend at Agra, that first alerted my parents to my interest in Robert Targett. Until then they had, I think, regarded him only as 'Olive's older brother'; a pleasant, thoroughly reliable man, verging on middle-age and given to wearing hornrimmed spectacles. Not at all the type of man to attract a girl in her teens. (I presume they had forgotten their own courting days.) As for me, though it had not, at that date, occurred to me to regard myself as a member of the Fishing Fleet (for was I not one of the India-born, and therefore one of the elect, coming home?), I had recently begun to have daydreams about how pleased my parents were going to be if all went well and I was to end this, my very first season in India, engaged to be married and live-happily-ever-after.

My parents' reaction to their belated discovery that their elder daughter looked like becoming seriously interested in 'dear Olive's' brother, was anything but enthusiastic. Yes, of *course* they both hoped that I would get married one day. The sooner the better, in fact. But only to the right man. And neither of them, it seemed, thought that Robert Targett was the right one for me. Mother's reasons, surprisingly enough, were (a) that he was too old for me, and (b) that he was only in the Stores Department, which, strictly speaking, ranked slightly lower on the snob-scale than the *box-wallahs*.

When, affronted, I pointed out that she herself had married someone exactly double her age, and that her in-laws had originally been very sniffy about her on the grounds that she had been the penniless daughter of 'some missionary or other', all I got was the age-old retort that, in a similar situation, every generation in turn gets from its elders: 'That was *quite* different!'

Poor Mother. She wasn't usually given to the slightest form of snobbery, but I suspect that the fact that I had been invited to a reasonable number of parties during the season in Delhi had raised her hopes, and that she had been cherishing dreams that I might attract the attention of some dashing man in the ICS or the Foreign and Political; or — at the very least — in a cavalry regiment. A mere employee in the department that Raj Society generally referred to as 'the Sausage and Tum-tum' was not in the same league at all, and though until then she had been untainted by such considerations, the interview had ended with her remarking, as though it must be the deciding factor in her case against Bob, that although she had begun by thinking that he was a reasonably nice man, she had come to the conclusion that there was something 'I don't quite like about his face'.

Oh, the times we were to hear that fatal phrase in the future, after some light-hearted love affair that might have ended differently if Mother, at first enthusiastic, had not suddenly decided that there was something that she 'didn't quite like' about some possible suitor's face. In the end it became a family joke which Bets and I greeted by collapsing in gales of helpless giggling.

Tacklow dealt with the situation quite differently. He pointed out that while I still had control of my head as well as my emotions, it would be wise to remember that I would be taking on a life as well as a man: his life, not mine. For this, you must realize, was long before the strident days of Women's Lib and bra-burning, and Tacklow was still essentially a Victorian in his thinking. Bob Targett, for instance, played cards and was known to be one of the best bridge players in Delhi, possibly in the whole Punjab. And bachelors of a certain age and seniority — Bob must be nearing the end of his thirties — were fixed in their ways and unlikely to change. It would be his wife who would have to change if he married a non-card-playing one, just as any girl who took on, say, a dedicated golfer, yachtsman or racing man would in the end have to learn to share her husband's pastime if she expected to have a happy and successful marriage.

That mention of bridge gave me pause. I knew all about Bob's reputation as a first-class bridge player. And both Bets and I had long ago vowed that we would never, never be lured into taking any interest in cards. This was because so many of our elders and betters in the days of our childhood in Delhi appeared to be hooked on them — particularly on bridge.

I did not realize that my beloved Tacklow had once been one of the best bridge players in the Punjab, but had suddenly given it up. Buckie, himself a bridge addict, eventually told me this, and when I asked Tacklow why he had stopped playing, he said that after Bets was born, and he found himself with a wife and three children to support, he could no longer afford to play; it was too risky. He had played a good game of whist, bridge and poker in his bachelor days and had made quite a bit of money. But cards were something you could not play for counters — it had to be for money; and since even the best of players could not always win, he did not feel he could risk running into debt now that four people were dependent on him. So he cut out card-playing in the same way that he had stopped collecting stamps. He made a lot of sacrifices for us, did dear Tacklow. And now he had made another one — he had given up Three Trees* and brought us back to India.

He was right about Bob, of course. There were very few things, if any, that Bob and I had in common; and I knew that nothing would have *induced* me to take up bridge, or any other form of cards. For watching that long-vanished 'Curzon House bridge-set' had given me a horror of the game — I had felt as though all those adults were slaves to something as potent as a drug or drink; something that had caught them and would not let them go. Well, it wasn't going to catch *me* — so there!

The fact was, of course, that I was still only playing at being in love. Bob had not proposed; nor, when I came to think of it, had he shown any serious signs of doing so. And if he did, I hadn't the least idea what my reaction would be. I was excited at having attracted the attention of someone so much older than I was, and who — judging from report — was known to be what the twenties called a 'lady-killer'. The whole thing went to my head, and I have to confess that it never *occurred* to me to apply the Gerald du Maurier test — 'What would you say if I asked you to marry me?' *'I'd be ready in five minutes . . . No — make it three!'* I could not really bring myself to believe that Bob could possibly be serious about me. I thought he was merely an accomplished flirt, who was keeping his hand in, and I enjoyed the whole thing enormously. Tacklow could have saved his breath.

* The house in England that he had hoped to buy one day.

✳ 3 ✳

'My blue heaven'

～✿✿✿～

Chapter 10

~XXXX~

The majority of India's princely states lay in the plains, where, in the hot weather, the temperatures can soar to unbelievable heights, but one notable one, Kashmir, lay well above sea level among the mountains of the Karakorams and the Hindu Kush. So it was for Kashmir that we made when our tents in the Club gardens became too stiflingly hot to be borne.

Kashmir enjoys a pleasantly cool climate throughout the summer and plenty of snow in winter, and had in consequence become a favourite hot-weather resort for those who could not afford the more expensive and social hill resorts, such as Simla. Living was cheap in Kashmir, for since no European was permitted to buy or own land there, the British had taken to renting furnished houseboats on the shores of one of its many lakes, or, if they preferred golf and cooler air, log-huts in the holiday resort of Gulmarg, which was in effect one enormous golf course. Others took rooms in hotels or guest-houses, or went camping under canvas among the pines and deodars, fishing for trout in the rivers and side-streams of that delectable country.

Bob Targett gave a farewell party for us at the Club, and in early March, while the weather was still cool enough to make travelling pleasant, we made for Kashmir.

Why is it that the things that happen to us in our youth remain so clear in our memory? Why, of all the many times that I was to journey to that valley in the future, was this the one that remains so indelibly printed on my mind that it could easily have happened yesterday? By now, I have reached the age when I cannot remember, without a considerable effort of concentration, what I had for lunch yesterday, or if this is the right day on which to put out the milk order. Yet I can remember every incident on that first momentous drive to Kashmir as though it had happened last week, and almost see every mile of the road.

March is a cold, grey month in the hills, but a lovely one in the plains. The ground glittered with dew and the early morning air was fresh and cool as we left New Delhi behind us and drove through Old Delhi, the red walled city that Shah Jehan had built in the days of Elizabeth Tudor — the city that Bets and I had known so well as children that we both still have the pleasing illusion that we knew, at least by sight, almost every one of its citizens. It seemed to have changed very little since those days. The same shade trees, the same shops, the church that 'Sikandar Sahib' — Skinner of Skinner's Horse — had built just within the Kashmir Gate, back in the early years of the nineteenth century, and where we used to walk to morning service every Sunday. The battered gateway itself looked no different, but the dry moat that circled the city had been filled in, so that the road now ran straight through it instead of crossing the bridge on which there had been one of the fiercest battles of the Mutiny year. Curzon House, where we had lived during the cold weathers, had received a coat of yellow colour-wash and was now the Swiss Hotel. But otherwise little had altered, and as we swept past the Kudsia Bagh and Ludlow Castle (the latter still a club, though no longer the 'Delhi Club' but the 'Old Delhi Club'), Imre Schwaiger's shop, Maiden's Hotel and Metcalf House, I felt as though I had stepped back in time and could have been sitting in the back of Buckie's old pantechnicon, on my way to one of Mrs Strettle's children's dancing classes.

In those careless days many stretches of the Grand Trunk Road were still very much as Kipling described it in *Kim*, and no one has ever described it better. He called it a broad, smiling river of life, 'built on an embankment to guard against winter floods from the foothills, so that one walked, as it were, a little above the country, along a stately corridor * seeing all India spread out to left and right'. So it was on that glittering March morning in the late twenties of a century that is now almost over. One passed an occasional motor vehicle, but in the main the traffic consisted of *tongas*, bullock-carts and pedestrians — thin-legged villagers striding along in the dust, followed by little groups of their women in gaily coloured saris and chinking silver anklets; sepoys on leave; *powindahs* with their camels and ponies, making for the hills; wedding parties complete with bands and guests, and occasional flocks of sheep or goats

---

* The Grand Trunk runs between an avenue of trees whose roots serve to buttress the embankment and whose leaves provide shade for travellers.

being herded along by their owners. Tinkers, tailors, soldiers, sailors . . . and for long stretches no one at all. Only the busy crows and the monotonous creaking of well-wheels that is, or was (I suspect that it still is) the day-time song of India.

I remember stopping for lunch on that first day at the Dâk-bungalow at Karnal, where my father, having first done a careful reconnaissance of the garden to make sure there were no cats, pi-dogs or kites around, took Pozlo for a walk in the grounds, and where we all ate a picnic meal on the verandah in the sun-freckled shade of a bougainvillaea and an orange trumpet-flower that had climbed to roof level and then spilled over to make a bright, sweet-scented curtain. In those days, and perhaps in these, it stood back from the road in a compound so full of trees that one could only catch glimpses of the passing traffic. Among them, growing to one side of the bungalow, was a single date palm which, that morning, was full of gossiping parrots nibbling at the dates. Parrots are almost my favourite Indian bird — the ordinary large green parrots with a red and white ring about their necks which are, correctly speaking, parakeets and not parrots at all. I have always had a great fondness for these amiable and gregarious chatterers, possibly because I myself have always talked far too much. Parrots in flight shriek for joy, but once a flock of them have settled in a tree they chat to each other non-stop, and if you care to listen you will be convinced that they are gossiping together in confidential undertones that suggest that they are talking scandal. ('My dear — did you *see* her! . . . There she was, making the most *shocking* advances to Nutee's husband, while poor Nutee was wearing her wings to the quills feeding those chicks — no wonder her own eggs are always addled!') Pozlo, our baby purple-headed parakeet, whom we let out to wander around the outside of his cage, though belonging to a different branch of the family, listened delightedly, and put in an occasional excited screech. Presumably they speak the same dialect.

Karnal is not far from Ambala, so we took our time over lunch and arrived at the Circuit House in the cool of the evening — to find it occupied, entirely illegally, by squatters in the form of the Commanding Officer of one of the units stationed in Ambala, complete with wife and a family that included at least two daughters in their late teens and, I rather think, a couple of schoolroom-age children as well. None of this lot were in the least pleased to see us, and the whole situation was deeply embarrassing. The authorities in Delhi, who had imagined the house to be empty, had sent word to the caretaker that Sir Cecil and Lady Kaye and family would be arriving on Friday evening, and would require food and proper attention for a period of three days, and the caretaker (who had presumably come to some unofficial arrangement with the CO that allowed him to occupy the place without permission) had panicked and put off informing the illegal occupants of our arrival until the eleventh hour; presumably in the hope that in the interim we should be smitten with smallpox or cholera or involved in a fatal car crash and fail to turn up.

Unfortunately for him, no dire accident had befallen us, with the result that the CO and family hadn't had time to remove themselves hastily to the local Dâk-bungalow or some hotel, and were all *in situ* when we arrived. Luckily, the Circuit Houses were intended to put up such exotic birds-of-passage as Viceroys and Governors of Provinces with their gilded staffs, so there were plenty of spare rooms; the best were already occupied by the CO and his brood, who had not even had time to shift their personal belongings into the less attractive guest-rooms, and who made an embarrassing situation a good deal more embarrassing by being simply furious at our arrival and showing it all too plainly. Having established squatters' rights in this strictly VIP accommodation at the beginning of the cold weather season, and got away with it, they had begun to look on it as their rightful home, and, but for our un-expected arrival, their illegal occupation of it would never have been found out.

The CO (whose name is one of the few I have never forgotten — perhaps because his predicament embarrassed me far more than it embarrassed him!) was plainly torn between fury at being caught out, fear that Tacklow would report the matter to Delhi so that he would be hauled up before his superiors and given the rocket of a lifetime, and rage at having to feed and put up no fewer than four unwanted guests, and look as if he liked it. Well, he didn't, and it showed. He was too angry to make any serious attempt to hide it, or even to be polite. His wife was even angrier, for a reason that soon became plain. We could not have arrived at a worse moment.

One of the drawbacks to life in India is that it is impossible to keep a secret from one's servants, and through them half the bazaar invariably knows all that there is to know about one's private affairs. For instance, any bearer or *abdar* worth his salt will know exactly where and when his

Sahib is being posted next, several days before the Sahib himself hears of it.

According to the local gossips, the CO was on the verge of retirement and this was the family's last season in India. They would be packing up and leaving for good in the near future, and it was their earnest hope that before that happened one, if not both, of their two grown-up daughters would be engaged to be married. One daughter, at least, was plainly on the verge of getting engaged, and they had invited the young man, as well as three or four other young officers and a couple of girls, to dine at the Circuit House on the very next evening, prior to the whole party attending the last big special event of the season, a fancy-dress ball at the Club, at which everyone had been asked to come dressed as a pirate.

Quite apart from the fact that great hopes had been placed on the outcome of that particular fancy-dress ball, it must have been infuriating, both as a mother and as a hostess, to find four extra and most unwelcome guests unloaded upon her just before a carefully planned party. Particularly since two of them were girls of about the same age as her daughters, whom she would not only have to wine and dine, but take to the ball and provide partners for. It was a horrid predicament, and I couldn't help sympathizing with her, though I would have been a lot sorrier for her if she hadn't shown her annoyance so clearly.

Left to ourselves, we would have turned tail and made for the Dâk-bungalow and put up there instead, provided there were not too many travellers doing so already. But when Tacklow suggested this, the squatter and his wife refused to hear of it; insisting that there was *plenty* of room for all of us in the Circuit House, and if we did not mind taking 'pot luck' they would be only too pleased to entertain us. They did not look in the least pleased. But our last few days in Delhi had been hectic ones, what with packing and farewell parties, and apart from that lunch-break at the Kurnal Dâk-bungalow, Mother had been driving since eight o'clock that morning and was (like all of us) feeling hot, dusty and tired. She had been looking forward to a peaceful weekend in that very pleasant and comfortably furnished Circuit House in which she and Tacklow had often stayed, during the years when he had been the Director of Central Intelligence and she had gone on tour with him. The thought of driving on instead to the Dâk-bungalow, and probably finding that it was already full and that we must move on and try the hotels (which in those days let their rooms for the season and seldom had more than one or two rooms available for those who were just passing through) was a most unwelcome one. So although it was plain to her that the only thing that prevented our being requested to find rooms elsewhere was fear of the scandalous tale our servants and the staff of the Circuit House would be bound to spread through the bungalows and bazaars of Ambala, she accepted the offer at its face value, and we moved in.

A further complication on that first evening was Bill, who turned up at the Circuit House half an hour later, making a fifth unwanted guest at supper that evening; fortunately he had long ago been booked to attend the pirate dance with a group of friends. But the meal was hardly a cheerful one, and everyone turned in early.

I can't think why my parents did not refuse the invitation for us to join the pirate party. I can only suppose that they were too annoyed to feel inclined to make things any easier for the CO and his family. But it came a bit hard on us. The costumes were easy enough. Slacks and a shirt, a brightly coloured sash round the waist and another round the head, brass curtain-rings for earrings, and that was that. (See snapshot.) But apart from Bill we knew no one at the dance, and the two extra young men who had been invited at the eleventh hour to partner us had obviously only been available because no one else had asked them. All I remember about them is that they couldn't dance for toffee, and, after the first amateur attempt, faded into the crowd and were seen no more. Our reluctant hosts made no attempt to introduce us to anyone, so apart from a dance or two with friends of Bill's, we sat out most of the evening, sipping lukewarm squashes and staring moodily at the mob of strangers whooping it up on the ballroom floor.

However, Nemesis decided to avenge us, for on the following night, driving back late after dining with friends of my parents, we were startled to see something black and circular bounding wildly ahead of us down the white, empty, moonlit Mall. A moment later the Hudson crashed heavily down on one side, and we came to a grinding halt. The left-hand front wheel of the car had come off and hurtled into the blue.

We picked up a *tonga*, which took us to the nearest garage, and, leaving matters in their hands, we went back to the Circuit House, where the following morning we had to break it to our unfortunate hosts that they were going to have to put up with us for another two days. The squatters were naturally horrified, but they had to lump it. We really felt quite sorry for them by the time we were able to leave.

Our next stop was with friends who lived in an ancient fort on the outskirts of a little village lying a mile or two off the Grand Trunk Road. I have no recollection of how they came to be living there, but I still have a clear picture of the Grand Trunk as we drove along it in the brief Indian twilight, just before we turned off it ... The sun has only just slipped below the horizon, and the quiet sky is darkening to a deep, duck-egg green streaked with high wisps of lemon and apricot clouds against which, in sharp black relief, are long, wavering lines of crows flying home to roost: thousands of them, cawing as they return from the croplands where they have been feeding all day, to the belts of shade trees that line the Grand Trunk or the mango topes on the outskirts of little towns and villages.

I couldn't possibly count the times that I have watched birds flying home to roost at dusk, but this particular evening is still the clearest in my memory, though I don't know why. Writing about it, I am seeing it again as though I was looking at it now.

We set off the next day in the cool of the morning, when all rural India wakes to the sound of the squeaking, creaking well-wheels, screaming flights of parrots and the cry of peacocks, to stop for several days with the Commissioner of Jullundar, Mr Sheepshanks — known to his many friends as 'Sheeper'. I remember him taking us to see the Golden Temple at Amritsar, where he could have been an honorary Sikh, for the guardian of the temple treated him as a blood-brother. There are only two things I remember about this visit, the first being some advice that Sheeper gave Bill (who was returning north with us to rejoin his battery). It was a piece of advice that had proved, in the course of a long and distinguished career, to be invaluable.

According to Sheeper, all senior officers and VIPs feel it their duty to ask intelligent questions, and do so, *ad nauseam*. The thing to remember, said Sheeper, is that they don't really want to know the answer, they only wish to show an interest; all that is required is a prompt reply. 'Ers' and 'ums' were fatal to advancement, and he illustrated this with a tale of his younger days in Rawalpindi, when it had been his task to act as escort to no less a personage than the Governor of the Province on tour.

His Excellency, trundled round the station in a staff car, observed a large and obviously new structure (probably another cinema) in the course of construction, and asked what it was. Sheeper (who had no idea) instantly replied: 'That, sir? Oh, that's the new town incinerator.' 'Indeed?' said

His Excellency, satisfied. And let it go at that. Some years later Bill, recalling our stay in Jullundar, admitted that he had found Sheeper's advice most useful, and had used it frequently. 'He was quite right,' said Bill, 'they don't really want to know, and provided you give them a brisk answer they're perfectly happy. But if you don't know, and admit it, it's a black mark against you.'

Leaving Jullundar and Sheeper with regret, we drove on through the Salt ranges to the garrison town of Rawalpindi, where we spent a further few days in Flagstaff House as guests of the GOC. I have no idea who he was, but I do remember that Bill, who was stationed in 'Pindi and so would be going no further, introduced us to his friends and fellow subalterns and that our stay there was very social.

Rawalpindi was a cantonment town and, in those days, a very pretty one; gay in the old meaning of that hijacked word, and set on the open, rock-strewn and for the most part treeless plains, within easy reach of the Himalayan foothills and the long, dusty highway that winds upwards to the hill-station of Murree and onward to the independent princely state of Kashmir. Its wide, straight, tree-shaded roads were flanked by whitewashed bungalows and boarding-houses, along with all the extras that went with the word 'cantonments'. Barracks, parade and polo grounds, tennis courts, a golf course, churches and hospitals and a sprawling bazaar.

Our fellow guests were the Auchinlecks, who were friends of my parents, and though my memory retains no trace of my first meeting with that future Field Marshal, Lord Auchinleck — 'the Auk' — I remember his pretty, flighty wife, Jessie, whom I mentally placed in the same age group as Mother because they obviously enjoyed each other's company and seemed to spend a lot of their time with their heads together alternately chatting in undertones or shrieking with laughter.

I was to see 'Pindi and the GOC's house on several occasions during the next decade, and find it unchanged. Well over half a century later and more than thirty years after the territory it stood in had become Pakistan, I was invited to lunch there by the then President of that country, General Zia-ul-Haq, and though there had been a number of alterations, the entrance porch and the long verandah, even the masses of bougainvillaea, were so familiar that for a moment I was back in the past, still in my teens and being greeted by a couple of smiling young ADCs and a gorgeously uniformed *chupprassi*, who opened the door of the Hudson with a flourish . . . '*Time, you old gipsy man / Will you not stay . . . ?*'

Apart from those fragments of memory, only one other thing remains to remind me of that first stay in Rawalpindi, a song that still crops up with reasonable frequency on radio programmes. It was new then, and we heard it for the first time in Jenners, a European-owned music shop that sold everything from pianos and sheet music to gramophones and the latest 78s. We already owned a gramophone, one of the portable, wind-up variety that were popular in those days. But if either Bets or I had wanted a new record we would have had to buy it ourselves out of our excessively modest allowances and I doubt very much if we could have run to even a few gramophone needles. Bill, however, was at the time sentimentally interested in one of the Jenn sisters, which probably accounted for the amount of money he spent on records. Vera and Dolly Jenn were pretty young things who counted their admirers by the dozen, and half the young bloods of 'Pindi used to drop into Jenners on the chance of catching a glimpse of one or other of them stocking up the latest 78s.

One of them, at least, was there that morning, and though I don't remember if she was the one Bill had his eye on, I do remember that we stayed in the shop for the best part of an hour, listening to the latest batch of records, and that among them was 'My Blue Heaven' — a charming melody that made such an impression on Tacklow that he bought it on the spot.

I like to think that a reference in the lyric to 'just Mollie and me' had something to do with his fondness for this particular tune, which eventually became 'my' tune in the same way that over thirty years previously 'Daisy, Daisy, give me your answer, do' had been Mother's. All her beaux including Tacklow, had in the past sung that song to her and during the next few years most of mine were to sing 'My Blue Heaven' to me. In the meantime, we played that record, or sang the song, so often during the rest of our journey that to this day when some popular singer of 'old time' songs on radio or television embarks on it, I am instantly back again in that long-ago morning in Rawalpindi, listening to it for the first time.

Chapter 11

~✿✿✿~

The majority of travellers bound for Kashmir turn off the Grand Trunk
Road at Rawalpindi and make for the mountains and the little hill-station
of Murree, from where, on a clear day, you can see the Kashmir snows.
But we went forward on the Grand Trunk, for we had been invited to
stay for a few days with an admired friend of Tacklow's, the archaeologist
Sir John Marshal, who was engaged in excavating the ruins of one of
India's most historic cities, Taxila, once the capital city of a small kingdom
whose territory covered an area of land between the Indus and the river
that is now called the Jhelum, but that was once known as the Hydaspes
— a name that was to go down in history as one of the great battles that
were fought and won by the superb generalship of that 'young god of
the world's morning', Alexander of Macedon.

I knew very little about Taxila beyond the fact that its king had played
host to Alexander, and that it rated a mention in one of the Buddhist
scriptures, the *Jatakas* — the 'Birth Tales', which the Lama, that charming
character in Rudyard Kipling's novel *Kim*, tells to Kim and the priests of
the Temple of the Thirthankas in Benares. But I knew a good deal
about Alexander, since both Tacklow and Alum Din, who had been a
Pathan and Tacklow's bearer, had told me stories about him. All Pathans
have a fund of stories about the legendary 'Sikandar Dulkan', and to
this day there are tribes who claim that their fair skins and pale eyes
are a legacy of the Greek governors Alexander the Great left behind
him to govern his Empire. Not surprisingly, Alexander had become
one of my childhood heroes — along with such dashing characters
as Rupert of the Rhine, Robin Hood and the hero of the *Ramayana* —
and I wanted to see Taxila because of its associations with those early
tales.

Now that carbon-dating has arrived on the scene I suppose we know
when Taxila was first built. But all we knew about it in the 1920s was

that 326 years before the birth of Christ it was there, and flourishing, when Alexander and his Greeks appeared before its gates and were given an enthusiastic welcome by its King — who seems to have been on bad terms with the rulers of several neighbouring states. I imagine he hoped this all-powerful invader and his army would, if treated kindly, be willing to eliminate them for him by way of thanks.

The upshot was the Battle of Hydaspes, which has gone down in history as one of the finest examples of Alexander's generalship. Both Tacklow's and Alum Din's descriptions of it, though differing here and there in detail, agreed in principle; and my interest in Taxila was enormously heightened by the fact that these narrow trenches cut into the dry, dusty earth, along which Sir John guided us, were roads and lanes along which Alexander and his men must have walked, and these mudbrick walls were the actual walls of rooms and banqueting halls in which he and his Greeks would have slept or eaten, listened to speeches or planned future conquests.

I don't remember the name of Taxila's ruler, but I do remember the name of his enemy, because it reminded me of 'porous plasters' — the old-fashioned kind that doctors used to prescribe when I had a bad cough: strong-smelling grey sludge, heated and then spread on a square of lint and clapped on my shrinking chest. His name was Porus, but though Tacklow pronounced that as Poh-rus, I could read by then, so I knew how porous plasters should be pronounced. And also that a 'po' was an unmentionable object.

Tacklow and Alum Din could both tell a story so well that you felt you could actually *see* what they were describing; which is why I can still visualize the opening scene of the Battle of Hydaspes.

Porus's long front line consisted of at least 200 war-elephants, and at first it seemed as though he was going to win a bloodless victory. For when Alexander's cavalry attempted to cross the ford, their horses refused to face the elephants lined up on the other side, and the initial assault ended in a wild confusion of furious shouting men, trumpeting elephants, flashing hooves and rearing, splashing, screaming horses.

But Alexander was more than a leader of men, he was a brilliant tactician. Undeterred by that first rebuff, he pulled back his army and set about finding another place where he could cross the Jhelum — or the Hydaspes if you insist. He found one after several weeks, some sixteen miles upstream of the ford, and, with the aid of a small island in a sharp bend of the river, got his army across, attacked Porus's flank and won a resounding victory after a fiercely fought battle with appalling loss of life — only a fraction of them Greek — and the capture or destruction of all those unfortunate elephants. Porus, who had reportedly fought like a tiger and sustained any number of wounds, was taken prisoner, but treated with such generosity that he became an ally of his ex-enemy; when, later, Alexander's army, grown homesick and battle-weary, refused to move any further into the unknown land and he was forced to turn back, he appointed Porus to be his Viceroy over that part of his conquests which lay between the Jhelum and the northern bank of the Hyphasis — the river that we now know as the Beas.

Nowadays the excavations at Taxila cover so much ground that it is hard to believe that there can be anything left to look for, but in the closing years of the 1920s there was comparatively little to see, for the digging had presumably stopped during the war years and, as far as I can remember, the museum consisted of only one or at the most two small and rather poky rooms in the modest house where the Marshal family lived, instead of the spacious building that has replaced it. But buried treasure has always held a potent spell, and I remember being fascinated by the necklaces and brooches fashioned from beads or beaten gold and copper wire, the coins, seals and fragments of pottery, displayed in glass cases, and the maze of narrow streets and roofless rooms that Sir John guided us through, explaining as he went so that the city seemed to come alive again as he talked.

It was a memorable two days. We left with regret after an early breakfast and drove on in the sparkling, dew-washed morning up the straight white corridor of the Grand Trunk Road; the newly risen sun at our backs and the shadows of the sal trees and the scarlet-blossomed silk-cotton trees stretching long and blue ahead of us. There can have been few more pleasant things to do in that post-war world, when the horror and destruction of the 'Great' War was less than ten years behind us, and the twentieth century was still young, than to drive along the more northerly stretch of the Grand Trunk on a spring morning. Even now, when it carries a river of petrol-driven traffic that fouls the air with fumes, it can be beautiful, for many years later — forty years after the land through which we were travelling had become Pakistan — a sad errand took me down that same road on another spring morning. But despite that sadness, and the racket and dust of the streams of traffic, the Grand Trunk was still beautiful, the flowering shrubs still starred with blossom and the dâk trees ablaze with scarlet.

The Moguls, too, had liked to spend the worst of the hot weathers by the lakes of Kashmir, on the shores of which they had built some of the most beautiful gardens in the world, and the route they preferred to take was the one that we were taking that year, by a side road which branches off the Grand Trunk at the little wayside town of Hasan Abdul and leads towards Abbottabad and the high hills. We stopped in Hasan Abdul to fill up with petrol — which, in those pre-petrol-pump days, was sloshed straight from a can into the car's petrol tank with the aid of a tin funnel — and while Mother and Abdul kept an eye on these proceedings, Bets, Tacklow and I went off to see the tomb of Lalla Rookh — the lovely lady whose name will always be linked with the Vale of Kashmir.

In those days her modest tomb stood on a bare hillside, well outside the town and in a little walled garden in which there were a few jasmine and rose bushes — the small, sweetly scented roses that Omar Khayyam wrote of — several fruit trees and a single dark cypress. I have an original watercolour sketch of that little walled garden, painted by a Major Edward Molyneux over ninety years ago and reproduced in a book on Kashmir by Francis Younghusband.* That little sketch shows that except for the height of the trees in the garden, Lalla Rookh's tomb cannot have altered very much since it was first built; for on that spring morning in 1928 it looked exactly as it had to Molyneux when he painted it in the closing years of the previous century.

But I would not advise any present-day tourist to go in search of it, because Hasan Abdul is no longer that small wayside town; even less is it like the quiet little village where Ash-Ashok, the hero of one of my India novels, riding across country from 'Pindi to Attock, stopped at twilight to let his horse rest and graze while he ate his evening meal on a grassy hillside overlooking Lalla Rookh's tomb.

The little town is now a thriving, bustling place, full of shops, garages and petrol pumps, that has spread out across the once open country at its back. The tomb itself is still there. But the garden wall with its beautifully proportioned gate and charming little domed corner towers has gone and the garden is now a mere matter of gravel paths and a few neat flowerbeds

* *Kashmir. Described by Sir Francis Younghusband and Illustrated by Major E. Molyneux DSO.* Published 1901 by A. C. Black Ltd, London.

thinly sown with marigolds and zinnias, strongly reminiscent of a public garden in one of the less attractive seaside towns in England. Both the charm and the romance have left it.

But both were present on that spring morning near the end of the twenties, and the road to Abbottabad was one of the prettiest in the Punjab. Even that sedate publication *Murray's Handbook for Travellers in India, Burma and Ceylon* said that although the road to Kashmir via Murree was the most important, the one via Abbottabad 'though 35 miles longer, is more picturesque and has easier gradients'. I don't remember the gradients being much better, but it was certainly more picturesque, and compared with the Grand Trunk there was very little traffic on it; less and less as the fruit blossom, mango groves, cane-brakes, banana palms and orchards of limes and oranges gave place to fir and pine. With every mile the air became noticeably cooler as we climbed up and up into the forest-clad foothills that smelt as Simla used to — of pine-needles, maidenhair fern and woodsmoke. For the thrifty plains do not burn wood; their fuel is dung-cakes made from the droppings of cattle, carefully collected and patted into large, flat pancakes that are pressed on to the walls of the houses to be dried by the sun. The scent of dung fires is as potent a reminder of the plains as woodsmoke is of the hills.

We must have stopped somewhere for lunch, probably in Abbottabad. But I don't remember anything about that small hill-station, which was then the headquarters of a brigade of Gurkhas and Mountain Artillery, and a popular summer resort for the wives and families of men stationed in that part of the Punjab. I was to know it well later on when Bill's battery was stationed there, but my mind is a blank as far as my first sight of it is concerned. Nothing about it left any impression at all, yet I can remember a large part of our journey there from Hasan Abdul, and almost every yard of the steep, zig-zag road through the bazaar at Mansehra, a hill village some twenty-five miles further on which we reached at about sunset, and in whose Dâk-bungalow we spent the night.

Down on the plains the late March weather had been warm verging on hot, and we had been wearing cotton dresses, but Mansehra (according to Mother's red guidebook) was just over 3,500 feet above sea-level and its Dâk-bungalow stood on the crest of a bare ridge strewn with enormous lichen-covered boulders, its back to the village and facing a long, unpopulated valley that stretched away below it, ringed by mountains whose peaks were still white with snow and, as the sun dipped behind the horizon, it was suddenly very cold.

Dusk does not linger in eastern countries as it does in the west, and twilight was barely a breath between daylight and the dark: one minute the snows glowed pink and gold and apricot, and almost the next minute they were coldly blue against a darkening sky in which the first stars twinkled like hoar-frost. The night wind arose and began to blow through the long verandah of the isolated bungalow, bringing with it a lovely fragrance — which surprised me because there were few trees on the ridge and those were still leafless, and what little grass there was on the bare hillside was brown and parched. It was plain that spring had still not reached Mansehra, yet the night wind smelled of flowers. It was a small puzzle, and Bets and I abandoned it and went inside to hunt out a few winter woollies from the suitcases that Abdul Karim had directed the Dâk-bungalow servants to unload and stack in our bedroom.

In those days there was no electricity in such places, but there were hurricane '*butties*' a-plenty, and by their light we bathed in tin tubs filled with piping-hot water, heated in kerosene tins over pine-log fires which made the water smell deliciously of woodsmoke. Later we ate the usual four-course Dâk-bungalow dinner of soup (Brown Windsor or Mulliga-tawny), *murgi* (chicken, curried or roast), followed by something that the *khansama* called '*broon custel*' and finishing up with a savoury that was usually sardines on toast, or cheese straws. This menu seldom varied, though 'mutton cutlet' (invariably goat) was sometimes substituted for chicken — and for my part, much preferred, as I never really grew resigned to seeing, and worse still, hearing, some unfortunate hen being chased shrieking around the back premises to be caught and killed, vocal to the last; to appear on the menu a scant hour and a half later, either over-cooked or curried. At least the portions of stewed or roast goat were purchased in the bazaar and not noisily slain on the premises.

I still have, in one of my many photograph albums, kept as a cherished memento of countless Dâk-bungalow style meals, the menu of the very last meal I was to eat on Indian soil as the curtain fell on the Raj and we sailed away from a city that was about to become the major port of a brand-new country, Pakistan. The menu is hand-written by the *khansama* and, either in honour of the occasion or as an affectionate gesture towards the departing *Sahib-log*, it was a strictly British meal, starting with onion soup and including such colonial favourites as 'Cottage Pie and Cabbag', followed, for the pudding course, by: 'Blanc Monge and Mallon'. The only thing absent on this one is that popular vegetable usually rendered in English by a majority of *khansamas* as 'russel-pups', which the initiated will instantly recognize as brussels sprouts. Dear Dâk-bungalows — how I miss you!

After breakfast next morning, while Abdul Karim and his platoon of helpers were loading up the cars, Bets and I went for a walk down the hillside below the house. The sunshine of yesterday had vanished, and it was one of those cold, colourless days when the sky looks like polished pewter and even though there are no shadows, everything, near or far, appears in sharp focus. The mountains that ringed the valley seemed much further away than they had seemed in the sunset, and as decoratively artificial as a stage-setting, as though they had been cut from cardboard in several shades of grey and pasted, layer by layer, on the flat pewter sky, then carefully embellished in poster-paint with chalk-white snow-peaks.

I can still see that view as if it was a picture, one like Hobbema's *Avenue* or Constable's *Haywain* that you can instantly visualize if someone speaks of it. I cannot explain why it fascinates me so — except that it still means spring to me. True, there were no colours in it; only endless shades of grey, the odd touch of black, that startling white and, under the huge wind- and water-worn boulders that littered the hillside, small splashes of green. For I had been wrong in thinking that spring had not yet reached Mansehra, and I knew now why the night wind had smelled so sweet. Sheltering under every boulder, protected from the wind and the wintry gales, were patches of white violets, hundreds and hundreds of them, smelling of paradise.

I imagine that everyone will know how it is when something suddenly lifts your heart, and for no explained reason makes life seem lovely and the world a nicer place — the sight of something, or someone; a waft of scent or a bar of music; a line from a poem; a 'rainbow and a cuckoo's song'. It must happen to everyone at some time or another, and the white violets on the black hillside at Mansehra did it for me. I picked a bunch of them for Mother, and I pressed one or two in my sketchbook, where they turned brown and eventually disintegrated. But they, and Mansehra, are fixed in my memory for good.

The thing I chiefly remember about our drive next day was that the weather turned nasty on us, and so did the road, which twisted and turned with such wild abandon that I became horridly carsick (shades of my youth and my first car ride down the hill road from Simla to Kalka!) and we had to stop while I decanted my breakfast over the edge of the road. I was filled up with brandy and changed places with Tacklow, who always sat in the front seat by Mother. I'm not sure which of these two prescriptions did the trick; perhaps it was a combination of the two. But I can recommend it to the carsick. By the time we arrived at Domel, where the two main routes to Kashmir, the one from Rawalpindi and the other from Abbottabad, meet, and the Kishenganga river merges with the Jhelum, I was feeling a bit hollow but otherwise OK.

There is a toll to pay before one crosses the bridge at Domel, and a customs post where all travellers must have their baggage checked — and on occasions searched. There is also, we belatedly discovered, a toll on animals and birds, and when a whispered warning of this was hurriedly conveyed to me by Abdul Karim, I took the precaution of transferring Pozlo from his travelling cage to the small, flannel-lined Lipton's Tea tin which he treated as a nest when the weather was chilly, and successfully smuggled him past the customs — thus saving a toll of annas four — or it may have been eight. Not a gigantic sum, but as we had failed to look up the rules relating to birds, we did not care to risk having him confiscated.

The *khansama* at Mansehra had provided us with a picnic lunch we had meant to eat by the roadside, but as the day had turned wet and cold we ate it instead on the verandah of the Dâk-bungalow at Garie, before driving on to arrive late in the wet darkness of a rainy evening at the little Dâk-bungalow that stands on a steep hillside above the Kashmir road at Uri. Here, after dining by the light of a couple of flickering oil-lamps, we fell asleep lulled by the muted roar of the Jhelum river racing high and furious through the narrow gorge below, and awoke in the thin sunshine of a March morning to find that here, as under the gaunt boulders that littered the bleak ridge at Mansehra, spring had arrived before us; for the window of our bedroom looked out across a verandah on to a blaze of pink blossom, an almond tree in full bloom in the narrow strip of garden above the Domel–Srinagar road.

That almond tree was as lovely and as unforgettable a sight as the white violets, and it has always remained in my memory as a fitting introduction to the valley of Kashmir. Perhaps because, like the violets, it was so unexpected — coming as it did after the previous day's driving through non-stop drizzle and clinging mists that blotted out everything beyond a range of fifty yards, the ghastly carsickness and that unappetizing picnic eaten on the verandah of the least attractive of Kashmir's Dâk-bungalows. But whatever the reason, it still stands out in my memory, together with the violets at Mansehra and the frangipani tree seen by moonlight on the Kalka–Simla road,* as something very special — like one of the Seven Wonders of the World. That almond tree is not there any more; nor, I gather, is the Dâk-bungalow, and perhaps Uri, too, has been blown out of existence. In the fighting that followed Independence and the partition of India into two separate countries, Pakistani and Indian troops fought each other among the Kashmir mountains, and, according to various newspaper accounts at the time, Uri was shelled and the fighting around it was particularly fierce.

It is sad to think of that charming little village reduced to rubble and the almond tree smashed by shell-fire; but as far as I am concerned it is still there, exactly as it was when I first saw it, its blossoms looking like a milky way of rose-pink stars in the early morning sunlight. Only when I am dead will it cease to be real.

The sunlight of the early morning did not last. We left it behind us when we drove away from Uri, singing 'My Blue Heaven' and 'I've Fallen in Love with a Voice', and the steep sides of the gorge closed in on us; the enormous rock-faces soaring upwards on either hand, their tops lost in the mists, bare as the back of one's hand or spiked here and there with tall deodars, pine and fir trees and dripping with maidenhair fern and a thousand little waterfalls. Here and there the water washed across the winding road to pour out of gaps in the low stone walls that edged it, and plummet down the steep hillsides to join the raging mill-race of the Jhelum as it rampaged down the narrow gorge several hundred feet below, whirling down thousands of baulks of timber, thrown into it by logging camps many miles up-stream, to stock timber-yards in the Punjab. Mother kept on pointing out bits of scenery that she assured me were really spectacular if only the mist would lift and the drizzle stop; but it didn't, so I had to take her word for it. Even the gorge at Rampur, which I was sure of recognizing from Molyneux's painting in Younghusband's *Kashmir*, was shrouded in mist, and there was nothing visible of the famous limestone cliffs, and only the occasional glimpse of the deodar forests. About the only thing we could see clearly was the power station, where

* See *The Sun in the Morning*.

the Jhelum has been harnessed to generate electrical power for houses, houseboats and hotels throughout the valley, as well as for the irrigation of millions of acres in the plains of the Punjab. Useful, admittedly. Very useful. But hardly lovely to look at.

The mountains dwindled in size and became hills, and the hills in turn drew back from the road, taking the mist with them, the valley opened out in front of us, and soon we were driving through the streets of Barramulla, the town that stands sentinel at the entrance to the valley.

I have described in *The Sun in the Morning* the culture shock that the sight of my native land dealt me on the day when, as a dismayed and deeply apprehensive ten-year-old, I followed Mother and Bets down the gang-plank of the passenger ship that had brought us from Bombay — then one of the most beautiful cities in India — into the depressing squalor of London's Tilbury Docks and the miles of mean streets, grimy commercial buildings and sea of smoky chimneys that stretched between the docks and Charing Cross station. And this was the country that my parents called 'Home'! It had been a traumatic experience, and here it was repeating itself all over again. *This* was the fabled 'Vale of Kashmir'!

I had read Moore's *Lalla Rookh* and Younghusband's *Kashmir*, admired Molyneux's delightful watercolours and Mother's amateur efforts at copying them, seen endless snapshots in other people's albums as well as the ones Mother kept so carefully, and in general heard a great deal about the spectacular beauties of that favoured country — starting with the famous tale of the Mogul Emperor Jehangir, son of Akbar, greatest of the Great Moguls, who built the most beautiful of the Kashmir gardens, Nishat Bagh, and so loved the country that when he lay dying and those who watched around his bed asked if there was anything he desired, he is reported to have said 'Kashmir . . . only Kashmir!'

Well, here I was in this fabled valley and, save for the day of my arrival at Tilbury Docks, I have never been more disappointed. Frankly, I thought the place was perfectly hideous. Here there was no trace of spring, only the leavings of winter — gaunt, leafless trees, great patches of dirty snow that had slid off the roofs of houses, or been shovelled to one side to clear a pathway, and now lay blackened with mud and soot and pitted with small dark holes where icicles which had formed at the edges of overhanging roofs had dripped on it from above. The houses themselves were built on the same pattern as Swiss chalets, though here there was none of the decoration and spick-and-spanness of the Swiss prototypes, or of the colour. There was, in fact, no colour anywhere, unless one counts mud as a colour. There was plenty of that — muddy streets, muddy fields and mud-coloured houses. The river which had raged through the gorges behind us was placid here, a wide, sluggish stream reflecting the overcast sky and leafless willows, and the wet thatch of the country-boats that were tied up to the muddy banks. Even the people appeared mud-coloured: their clothes in drab shades of brown to dingy black, men, women and children alike wearing the knee-length smock-like garment which is known as a *phiran* over Isabella-coloured *shalwa* — the loose, full cotton Mohammedan trousers that are worn with a drawstring. None of them looked as though they or their clothes had had a wash in months. It would have been difficult to tell which were men and which women if it had not been for their headgear, the women covering their heads with shawls and the men with a turban, and, in general, only the men wearing shoes.

I remember feeling my own cold toes curl in sympathy for those brown bare feet walking casually through that icy mud and those patches of frozen snow. The majority of them appeared to be pregnant, if female, and outstandingly pot-bellied if male, and it was only later that I learned that it was the custom of the Kashmiris to ward off the cold by carrying a basket-like arrangement containing a small earthenware pot filled with live charcoal underneath their voluminous *phirans* to keep themselves warm. All too often this led to bad burns and, on occasions, setting their clothing alight. It does not make the wearer look particularly attractive.

There is a legend in the valley to account for this. The story goes that long and long ago Akbar the Great was denied entrance to the valley by a small body of its citizens. He was surprised, for the Kashmiris have always been a peaceful and artistic people; those who are not farmers or shepherds are craftsmen — weavers of cloth and carpets, embroidered shawls and carvers of wood. Their gesture did not amount to much, for they broke and fled before Akbar's seasoned fighting men, and his small army met no real resistance until it reached Srinagar,* where the Fortress of Hari Parbet was found to be strongly held and well stocked with guns and ammunition. When Akbar's demands for its surrender were treated

* S'rin-*ugger*. The tourists started calling it 'Shri-na-garr' for reasons of their own. In my day, and my father's and grandfather's, it was pronounced by the Kashmiris as S'rin-*ugger* (accent on the second-to-last syllable).

with scorn, his troops settled down to besiege it, to discover, as the weeks went by, that the garrison at the fort appeared only too happy to sit it out until the coming of the cold weather forced the Mogul court and its soldiery back to the plains.

There was nothing for it but to take the fort by assault, and this was done, though not without a good many casualties among the attackers. But when at last it fell, the garrison was found to consist entirely of women, whose menfolk had run away at the first sight of the advancing troops. Fortunately for them, Akbar is reported to have regarded this as a hilarious joke, and to have issued an edict that as the women of the valley were plainly far braver than their men, in future the men would wear the same dress as their women; which they do to this day, save in the matter of headgear.

The story is probably apocryphal, for I have never found any historical evidence for it, though the history books credit Akbar with 'conquering the territory' at the end of the sixteenth century. He evidently visited it at least three times and there are two separate bridges in Srinagar, one in a lakeside village on the way to Nagim and another one on the lake, facing the Nishat Bagh, both of which are known as 'Akbar's Bridge'. Nevertheless, the legend persists, mainly among the women. I never heard a man admit that it was true. I heard it first from the wife of our *manji* (boatman), a beautiful creature whom I used as the model in a series of paintings that I did for the *Illustrated Times of India Weekly*, illustrating Lawrence Hope's *Kashmiri Songs*: 'Pale Hands I Loved Beside the Shalimar' and 'Ashoo at Her Lattice' and all those. I still have two of the originals, 'The Bride's Song' and 'Kingfisher Blue'. I suppose I must have sold the others.

Chapter 12

꒷꒦꒰ꕥ꒱꒦꒷

We left Barramulla behind us, and drove along the long straight road that leads through an avenue of Lombardy poplars and is raised several feet above the level of the valley to protect it from floods and buttressed on either side by the stout silver trunks of those tall, straight trees. There are mountains all round the valley, walling it in, their lower slopes dark with forest trees and their crests white with snow. But that day the rain-clouds lay so low on them that all we could see between the poplars were wet, level fields with here and there a huddle of houses and a clump of leafless willows, and an occasional glimpse of forest as the cloud-banks shifted uneasily to a sullen wind.

Thirty-four miles of this brought us to Srinagar, which was a larger and more dismal and even wetter version of Barramulla, since its main street, like Venice's, was a river — the Jhelum, of course. And though up to now there had been surprisingly little traffic, suddenly we were joining a traffic-jam of buses, lorries and cars — the first two hooting their horns like crazy — *tongas* and cyclists ringing their bells, and hordes of very vocal pedestrians, as we all crawled cautiously forward over a long wooden bridge and into what appeared to be the main bazaar. I have a dim recollection of stopping somewhere to sign bits of paper — customs or immigration, or another toll? Or were we merely asking directions? I remember checking to see that Pozlo was still safely back in his Lipton's Tea tin, so perhaps it was a toll. Anyway, the stop was a brief one, but it gave me the chance to take a look at Srinagar city. I didn't think much of it. The wooden-built houses were just as hugger-mugger, rickety and drab as the ones in Barramulla and Parten (the only town of any size that we had passed through on the road between Barramulla and Srinagar), the people as chilled and drab, and the same dirty patches of pockmarked snow lying piled by the roadside and between the houses.

We drove on in the gathering dusk up to the Gupkar road, to one of the modern houses built on the hillside above the road. I have forgotten the number and the name of the house, and with it the name of its Kashmiri owner, a doctor and a long-time friend of my parents, who had offered to lend us his house for a few weeks while we looked around for somewhere to live for the next eight or nine months. Mother wanted a furnished house (instead of the usual houseboat that most people settled for) but wasn't sure whether she preferred to try for a house in Srinagar or a hut in Gulmarg — a resort in a green cup in the mountains, roughly twenty-five miles from Srinagar and a good 3,000 feet higher up, and consisting of little more than a series of pleasant golf courses encircled by a liberal scattering of wooden bungalows that were known as 'huts' and strongly resembled those in any of the cowboy films set in frontier towns in the American Wild West.

Bets and I were all for a houseboat, and Tacklow remained strictly neutral; his tastes were simple and he had never bothered much about his creature comforts, or been fussy about food. He would, I think, have been perfectly content to spend the rest of his life in a Dâk-bungalow — preferably near some river in which he could fish, and always provided, of course, that there was plenty of room for his books! Meanwhile, until the question was decided, we could stay in the house in Gupkar Road.

Bets and I hoped that this would not be too long, for though grateful for the doctor's kindness, we took an instant dislike to his house. It was a modern two-storeyed house built in the Colonial hill-station style, from wood with a tin roof and, as far as I remember, with echoes of Victorian Balmoral in a pointed turret, and furnished in a manner that matched its architecture. It was also deadly cold, for it was normally kept locked and shuttered from mid-October to the end of April, and had only been opened up as early as this for our sakes. The doctor had written to the middle-aged gentlemen who went with the house (one acting as *chowkidar* and the other as a sort of cook-housekeeper) to warn them of our arrival, but had given them insufficient time to get the place shipshape before we turned up. This was patently not his fault, but was mainly due to bad weather and the consequent delays to the mail caused by late snowfalls and a series of landslides on the main road through the mountains. These permanent retainers had their own living quarters behind the house, but they had plainly not kept to them, preferring — somewhat naturally — to occupy the sitting-room and bedrooms of the main building.

A fire had been lit in the drawing-room but it smoked badly and gave out little heat, and though the house was lit by electricity, the light was both low and erratic, for the power station at Rampur, which provided the power for the whole valley, was not up to coping with the demands that were made on it after dark and in cold weather. All in all, it was a depressing introduction to Kashmir; and the bad impression that this so-called paradise had made on us was not improved when, after breakfast next morning, Bets and I put on our winter woollies and our thickest coats, mufflers and berets and set off to explore.

Gupkar Road runs up and along the lower slopes of the 'Throne of Solomon', the Takht-i-Suliman,* a rocky, isolated hill which in those days was almost treeless and which pilgrims would climb by a single stony pathway to reach the small, stone Shankahara temple, dedicated to Shiva, that crowns its rocky summit 1,000 feet above the city. This is said to be the 'new' temple, raised on the spot by one Raja Gopaditya (I always liked that name) in or around 400 BC to replace a much older shrine that was built over 2,000 years earlier — *two thousand*! No wonder they think of Raja Gopaditya's as the 'new' temple. The doctor's house had been built on the lower slopes of the hill, and Bets and I set off to climb up to the temple from the back of the house, using one of the many goat-tracks that twist and turn between the rocks and move on a slanting line up the hillside, rather than attempting to claw our way straight up it.

The line we took eventually brought us out half-way up a sharp ridge and through a little wood of pine trees that, except for a single ancient chenar tree that grew by the temple, were, in those days, the only trees on the Takht. It took us quite a time to climb above them, and we still had some way to go before we reached the temple when we ran out of breath and stopped at a point from where we could turn and look down on the city and the lakes and the low, fort-crowned bulk of Hari-Parbat, which sits like a crouching lioness watching over the city.

We sat and stared down at it in silent disbelief. True, it was a dingy day. There was a hint of sleet in the cold wind that whinged complaining around the rocks and through the pine trees, and a blanket of cloud like a sodden layer of grubby cotton-wool concealed the tops of the amphitheatre of hills that throw a protective arm about Srinagar and its famous lakes. But it was hard to believe that even if the day had been clear and the sun shining, there could be anything much to admire in the

* Takht — pronounced 'tucked', as in 'tucked up in bed'.

unalluring scene that lay stretched out below us; for the clouds were not low enough to disguise the fact that the hills surrounding the lake were completely bare, while as for the Dāl lake, which we had expected to be an enormous stretch of water reflecting forest-clad mountains and glittering snow-peaks, like a glorified Lake Geneva — it looked like nothing so much as a derelict flooded fenland, a shallow sheet of water cut into sections by bunds that were prickly with leafless poplars and willows, and innumerable quantities of what looked like dead rushes.

It was only later that we learned that those masses of dead rushes were, in fact, floating islands, a familiar sight on Kashmir's lakes. There is such a shortage of arable land around Srinagar that the Kashmiris manufacture more by the simple expedient of collecting a mass of dead rushes, which they lash together and then plant with live rushes which grow downwards to the mud, thus anchoring the original bundle to the lake floor. Once that is done the living reeds are cut back and more and more water weeds are collected by thrusting a long pole into the lake, twiddling it round and round, and hoisting out the resulting dripping spool of weed, which is then slapped on top of the reed islands, where they look exactly like a swan's nest. This in turn can then be planted with any crop that likes plenty of water and a rich compost of rotting vegetation — such as melons, marrows, cucumbers and tomatoes. Towards the end of autumn, when the air turns chilly and the summer visitors have gone, these floating allotments are towed out and anchored firmly in deeper water, from where, in early spring, they will be cut loose again and towed away by their owners to be anchored in more accessible positions. What Bets and I had seen that gloomy morning were these islands, still in position, or being towed away to their summer moorings. No wonder the lake looked like floods in the Midlands!

We never got as far as the temple that morning, for not only had our first sight of the view from the Takht put a damper on our spirits, but the hint of rain changed from a hint to a threat, and we decided to get back to the house. When we did, we found that the resident care-takers had had a turn-up with Abdul Karim, who had accused them (rightly, I may say — the crime had been patently obvious from the moment of our arrival!) of moving themselves and their families into the house during the winter months, instead of keeping to their own quarters behind it.

The row had reached major proportions and, in the heat of combat, no one had remembered to produce any lunch, while the fire in the drawing-room had been allowed to go out. Mother re-lit it, and we huddled round it and ate something out of a tin — probably sardines. It was not an auspicious start to our first visit to Kashmir; Bets's and mine I should say, since Mother and Tacklow had been there before, and apparently enjoyed every minute of it.

There is a theory that first impressions are very important and can make or mar our opinions of people and places. But I have reason to know that this is not always true, since no one could *possibly* have had a worse introduction — or received a lousier first impression of Kashmir — than Bets and I. It was dire. There is no other word for it. Yet in spite of this, we both ended up regarding the place as the most beautiful we had ever seen, and it became the yardstick by which I judge true beauty. To this day, when in any really beautiful or charming place, I think to myself: 'It is almost as beautiful as Kashmir.'

The beauty of the place did not hit me all at once, but crept up on me gradually, while I wasn't looking. The weather improved and the wind lost its cutting edge, and one day the clouds lifted and we looked out from the verandah of that damp, unfriendly house, across a sea of almond trees that were fast breaking into blossom, to the bright ribbon of the Jhelum river curving through the valley, and behind it, against a cloudless sky the colour of an aquamarine, the long line of the mountains on the far side of the valley, the opal tints of the foothills merging into the dazzling white of snow-peaks and snow-fields, glittering like a long, crumpled swathe of the best white satin.

Months later, sitting on the roof of a houseboat anchored on the shores of the Dāl, watching the daily magic of the sunset on those treeless hills that I had thought so dauntingly stark and barren, and seeing them catch the dying light and glow apricot and gold, rose-pink and rose-madder, crimson and lilac and purple, streaked and shadowed with pure ultramarine in the gullies and crevasses, I remember saying: 'I can't think how the same thing that I'm looking at now could possibly have looked so ugly to me when I first saw it.'

'I *did* tell you,' said Tacklow, mildly.

'You told me to wait and see. You didn't explain,' I retorted.

'You probably wouldn't have believed me,' said Tacklow. 'It's always better to see for yourself.'

I could have replied that I would always believe anything he told me, and perhaps, in view of what was to happen soon, it would be better if I had, because I have an idea that he would have put me straight on the ramifications of that one and the advisability of making up one's own mind.

✵ One result of Abdul Karim's difference of opinion with the two resident retainers was that his decision to retire and hand over to a younger man was reinforced. He had no intention of staying on any longer than was absolutely necessary in a household where he was not the boss. And here we were guests and not owners. The upshot of this was that Tacklow and Mother went off one morning to Nedou's Hotel, Abdul Karim having insisted that candidates for the post should not be interviewed at the house, where they could be got at by the doctor's two servants (who would, he said, demand a cut of the nominee's wages and 'make trouble for him').

At the hotel, with the permission of old Willy Nedou, the Swiss proprietor, whom my parents already knew from their previous visit, they interviewed a number of candidates, with the advice of Abdul Karim who, it transpired, had previously whittled the hopeful candidates down from a dozen or so to two or three, for the look of the thing, but had quite obviously chosen the winner in advance.

His favourite nominee turned out to be a mere youth, a tall, gangling young Kashmiri named Kaderalone, who cannot have been much older than seventeen or eighteen and was not, at first sight, in the least prepossessing, for he was as thin as a rake and his hollow-cheeked face was pitted all over by the marks left by smallpox. He had no previous experience of service with the *Sahib-log*, and no references except Abdul's recommendation.

But since that alone was worth a dozen laudatory 'chits', he was taken on the strength of it. For although few, if any, employers would have engaged an emaciated, shabbily dressed and totally untrained Kashmiri, with no knowledge of English, Tacklow, like Abdul, did not judge by externals, and both saw something in the young man that went deeper than his mere outward appearance. And rightly; for Kadera was one of the best things that ever happened to us. He was like my introduction to his country all over again, for I remember being horrified by my first sight of this shabby, gaunt and appallingly pockmarked young scarecrow. I thought he had one of the most off-putting faces imaginable; yet I think

125

of it now as one of the nicest and kindest faces I ever knew. Dear Kadera — what a lot we owed you!

Abdul packed his scanty baggage, which consisted of the inevitable *bistra*, a tin trunk and bundle containing foodstuff for his journey, and after enjoying a last invigorating set-to with the house-owner's staff (a contest which his command of invective enabled him to win easily) he bade us an emotional farewell and, commending us to the mercy of Allah, left to resume his temporarily interrupted 'retirement'. We all piled into the car and, with Mother at the wheel, drove the old man to the bus station in the city to see him off, and to wave goodbye, assuring him, more for our own comfort than his, that we would surely meet again — to which the old man had replied, philosophically: '*Inshallah*' (God willing). Abdul was obviously not sorry to see the last of Kashmir. But it was a sad moment for Bets and me, because he was the very last of our old servants, and the one who had travelled with us to Bombay when as children we left India bound for England and boarding-school. Now he had gone too, and we both realized that this time it really *was* 'goodbye'.

Those early days in Kashmir remain in my mind as a whirl of activity and an explosion of beauty. Spring arrived in the valley with unbelievable swiftness and in the manner which is described in that much-loved children's book, *The Secret Garden* — with an almost audible flourish of silver trumpets. Suddenly the almond orchards were ablaze with blossom and the fields were yellow with mustard, while every inch of common-land was carpeted with millions and millions of tiny Japanese dwarf irises, a carpet of fragile flowers on which you could not take a single step without crushing at least half a dozen. The whole valley was sweet with their scent.

✄ My memory is like the title of Christopher Isherwood's tale of Berlin, *I Am a Camera*, for it works almost entirely by sight. If I remember something, I can see it as though it was film being run again before my mind's eye. And not a silent film in black and white either, but a top-quality video in sound and colour. It is obviously something I was born with, which I have always taken for granted and imagined that everyone must have. That everyone hasn't is something that I have discovered only recently, which makes me even more grateful for this wonderful bonus. Yet the fact that I can visualize clearly and in great detail anything that I can remember does not mean that there are not scores of things that I must have forgotten. Well, it stands to reason, doesn't it, that there must be a limit to what one's brain can hold; and unfortunately mine is far from being an outsize one. But that first spring in Kashmir is something that no one could possibly forget. It was like watching a series of spectacular transformation scenes played out on a stage in some fabulous pantomime, as day by day — almost hour by hour — that ugly duckling of a valley turned into a glorious swan.

Perhaps it had something to do with the light and the fact that the air is — or was then — so clear and pure, like cut crystal compared to the dusty atmosphere of the plains. The light is reflected not only off the wide curves of the river and the many lakes, but off the hundreds of unseen miles of snow on the mountain ranges that ring the valley. Whatever the reason, it is the colour of Kashmir that makes it so special, and which causes countless prosaic visitors to rush out and buy a paintbox and sketchbook and try their hand at getting it on to paper. And can you blame them?

It wasn't just the acres of almond blossom, a froth of pink against that dazzling backdrop of snow-peaks, or the soft green haze that was creeping across the mud-coloured valley as the leaf buds of a dozen different shades of green began to unfurl on poplars, willows, larch trees, Persian lilac and chenar, but the new grass and the new green things that sprang up to cover every inch of earth. The bedraggled floating islands were towed away and new reeds, rushes and water-lily pads transformed the placid levels of the lakes.

In those days, and for almost a decade after the beautiful little country was annexed by India and ceased to be an independent princely state, it was the custom in the valley to roof a house with shell-shaped tiles, each one hand-cut from pine-wood and overlapping the one below. These wooden tiles lasted for years, weathering to a pale, warm grey and in time collecting dust and grass seeds, which sprouted into green coverlets. These, in turn, eventually became solid enough to provide a root-hold for other seeds, deposited there in bird droppings, so that in spring many of the houses wore a roof of scarlet or pink-and-white striped tulips or mauve irises.

There was, I remember, somewhere on the right-hand side of the road to Bijbehara, a little whitewashed and somewhat ramshackle wooden temple, vaguely reminiscent of Thailand, whose roof in the springtime was a gorgeous splash of mauve from the dwarf irises that grew so thickly upon it that one could scarcely see any green leaves. It stood on the edge of a vast expanse of rice-fields, which at that season mirrored the snow-peaks and the sky (for the rice was not yet more than a few inches high), and when its roof was in flower it made such a charming picture that no would-be painter who passed that way in spring could possibly resist trying to capture it in paint.

Mother did so most successfully on several occasions. But none of her watercolours of it are still in the family; she sold them all, which was lovely for her but sad for us. I only painted it once, in poster-colour on a very small piece of black paper. And because there was no colour photography in those days, and I wanted to keep a reminder of it, I never put it into an exhibition — not even when I was really strapped for money — which is why I still have it to this day. It hangs on the wall of my bedroom as a reminder of how beautiful Kashmir was, 'once upon a time'.

The bare, rocky slope of the Takht acquired an overdress of emerald green grass, violets and the little striped wild tulips that Western garden centres call 'Kaufmannia' and sell for exorbitant sums per bulb, and every tree seemed to be alive with nesting bulbuls and golden orioles. Gupkar Road ran up towards a gap where the lower slope of the Takht dwindled down to meet the road, and rose again, on the far side, to become part of the mountain barrier that ended at the Dāl lake. At the mouth of the gap, standing high above the road and overlooking it from a ledge of rock that had been made into a garden, stood a large, modern house where a Mr and Mrs Wakefield lived. I don't remember exactly what Mr Wakefield's job was, but he was in the service of H. H. the Maharajah, not the Raj — Personal Adviser to His Highness, or something like that. His wife was Helen Keelan's* aunt, whose two sons, Alan and John, I had met on and off in the days when we were all at school and who by now were both, like my brother Bill, subalterns in the Indian Army. There was also a daughter, Ruth, who was one of the prettiest girls I have ever met — like a Raphael Madonna, or one of Michelangelo's angels.

The view from their house was out of this world, for, standing as it did on a low spur of the Takht, it could see both ways — across the fruit orchards and the Jhelum river to the snow-peaks of the Pir Panjal. Or, from the other side, to the Dāl lake and the lakes beyond it, across a wide

* My best friend at school. See *The Sun in the Morning*.

sweep of orchards and gardens and the scattered roofs of one or two houses, to where, high up along the flank of a mountain, lay the ruins of what is known as the Peri-Mahal, the Fairies' Palace, with behind it the massed chenar trees that hide the gardens of Nishat Bagh and Shalimar. Most of the houses — what little you could see of them between the blossoming fruit trees — were of the usual Kashmiri pattern and roofed with wooden tiles. But one had verandahs and a corrugated tin roof that had once been painted pillar-box red, but had faded to a deep rose colour. And it was from the Wakefields' garden that, looking down at it, we first saw the house that we named the 'Red House', and eventually rented.

There was, in those days, an *Octroi*-post at the gap, and though as far as I can remember pedestrians paid no charge, all wheeled traffic and various dutiable goods — livestock among them — paid some small charge, or should have paid it. Pozlo did not, because although we always took him out for a walk with us, he passed the *Octroi*-post sitting snugly in my coat pocket and was only let out once we were out of sight in the almond avenue, after which he rode on someone's shoulder, Tacklow's for choice.

That almond avenue had to be seen to be believed, and should by rights have been listed as one of the Seven Wonders of the World. In those days the metalled road stopped at the gap, and after that it was just an unmade road that skirted the foot of the mountains and led on round the lake to Harwan and the trout hatchery, through several small villages and past the famous Mogul gardens. This was an area of smallholdings, cornfields and orchards, and to one side of the road — the right if one approached it from the Gupkar Road — someone, very long ago, had planted a double avenue of almond trees. I imagine that once it had been intended to lead to a house. But if so the house had vanished long ago, for the avenue led nowhere. It merely ran parallel to the road for a couple of hundred yards and then stopped.

To walk through it was a marvellous experience, especially when the petals began to fall and lay thickly underfoot, for then one was literally walking through a scented tunnel of pink blossom — overhead, on either side, and underfoot — and through the lattice-work of flowers one caught glimpses of blue lakes and white snow-peaks. It was magical, and while it lasted we used to walk through it and back again at least once every day. But 'Beauty vanishes; beauty passes; however rare — rare it be.' And, like all beautiful things, it passed. There would come a night of wind and rain, and next day the trees were stripped of blossom and there was a brown carpet underfoot in place of the pink one that had been there only a day before. A year or two later the ancient trees were hacked down to widen the road; for His Highness had decided to build a new palace within a mile of the gap, a large, modern, and not particularly attractive building which is now, sad to say, a tourist hotel.

But back in 1928 we had no time to mourn the almond blossom, because though it is always the first to flower and the first to fall, hard on its heels came the paler pink of pear and apple and the white of plum and cherry, until half the valley was awash with blossom and the whole place was so extravagantly beautiful that about the only things missing were a Drury Lane orchestra and some popular musical-comedy star of that era such as Jack Buchanan or Dorothy Dickson, backed by a chorus line of lovelies, to burst into song. Off-stage, for preference. Somehow, you would not have been surprised to see it happen.

Chapter 13

The spectacular Springtime Special being put on by Mother Nature did not do all that much to lighten my spirits, which were, during that first month, suffering from the fact that I fancied myself in love with Bob Targett and, knowing that my parents disapproved of the whole affair, felt compelled to hide the fact that we were corresponding.

I would watch from a top window for the arrival of the postman at the next-door house, and the minute he appeared I would rush downstairs and, sneaking out by a side door, manage to waylay him before he turned in at our gate, so that if there was a letter from Bob I could extract it before sending the postman on to our own front door. There was also the problem of my letters to Bob. My pocket-money (now grandly termed an 'allowance') was still exceedingly meagre, and the price of writing-paper, envelopes, stamps and ink put a considerable strain on it. In addition, there were the problems of not being seen buying these items, and of posting the end result without being caught doing so. That last necessitated Bets and me creeping out of the house and down the drive with all the caution of stage conspirators, and, once out of sight of its windows, racing down the length of the Gupkar Road to post an almost daily letter in the pillar-box that stood at the bottom end of it.

Looking back from this distance on my first grown-up romance, I can't bring myself to believe that either of my parents would have bothered very much if they had realized that I was receiving approximately two letters a week from Bob Targett, or that he was getting at least four from me. They would have known very well that active opposition was only going to fan the flames, while as for waylaying the incoming post and confiscating Bob's letters, such an idea might have been possible in their own youth, but certainly not in the Roaring Twenties. The days of Victorian parents were over, and it was no longer possible to lock up one's daughters. I am quite sure that there was no reason for all that secrecy and sneaking out of back doors. But, let's face it, it was tremendous fun while it lasted. And it didn't last long.

A day came when I received a letter from Bob in which he said that he could not make up his mind whether to come up to Kashmir for his holidays or not, because if he did, it would be to ask me if I would marry him. He added a bit about worrying over the age gap between us, and how young and inexperienced I was, and how was I going to feel at some time far in the future when I suddenly realized that I was married to a white-haired old dodderer — or words to that effect. There was a lot more, but none of it meant anything except that opening sentence. He 'couldn't make up his mind whether to come up to Kashmir or not, because if he did he was going to ask me to marry him'. '*If*' indeed! I was furious.

Oh dear, how *young* the young are. All the poor man's doubts and worries on my behalf went for nothing; I could only take in that he was wavering over coming up to see me, and presumably expected me to write and *urge* him to come up — thus accepting a proposal that he hadn't yet made (and for all I knew, might decide not to make!), and also that he had no doubt at all about the answer he would get. *If* he came, I was going to say 'Yes!' The conceit of it! How dared he? I sat down and wrote a snarky letter telling him that it was a matter of *supreme* indifference to me whether he came up or not. (So there!)

Poor Bob. He fully realized that apart from the few tips on Life that I had received from the sophisticated Gerry, I still had no idea how many beans make five, and he was honestly worried for fear that the gap between us in the matter of worldly wisdom, as well as age, was too great, and that he could be accused of taking advantage of my 'youth and inexperience'. (I was rising *twenty*, damn it!) But he was right about one thing: I was still deplorably callow and ignorant. Even worse, I still suffered from an outsize inferiority complex, and it was this that drove me to fasten on that 'if' as an insult.

Suddenly, I saw myself as chasing after him during those months in Delhi, clearly showing him (and everyone else) that he only had to say the word and I'd leap into his arms with a shriek of joy, while all the time he, on his side, was unable to make up his mind whether he really wanted me or not, and was so sure of me that he could keep me hanging about in Kashmir, biting my fingernails and wondering if the verdict would be a telegram to say 'Arriving Srinagar first week in June. Writing,' or 'Decided cannot manage Kashmir this year, sorry, Targett.' In the event I received neither. Bob did not write again, and nor did I.

We were to meet again, of course, in Delhi. That we should do so was hardly avoidable in India. And the complications of love being out of the way, we became great friends. Bob was to marry twice, the first time a few years later. Later still, after the first marriage ended in divorce and he had been knighted, he eventually married again — and this time, as far as I know, lived happily ever after. He only once referred to our brief romance, and that was a full ten years later during a Viceregal Ball in New Delhi, when his first marriage was over, and when I had turned thirty and was still unmarried. We had been dancing together, and afterwards we walked out into the lantern-lit garden to sit out the next dance and talk, and he said unexpectedly that he'd been a fool not to marry me, and that he believed that we would have made a great success of it, and that I had taken his letter in quite the wrong way and my reply to it had given his *amour propre* such a staggering kick in the teeth that his immediate reaction had been to make straight for Kashmir, demand to know what the hell I thought I was up to, and shake me until my teeth rattled. Which was, he said, exactly what he should have done if he'd any sense, because it might have shaken some sense into me, and he should have refused to leave until I'd agreed to get engaged to him and set a date for an autumn wedding in Delhi.

'What a mess some of us make of our lives,' said Bob. I remember pointing out rather tartly that, apart from the failure of his first marriage, he seemed to be doing all right! He agreed — and then startled me by asking what I'd say now, if he were to ask me the question that he would have asked years ago, if I hadn't effectively stopped him by handing out that resounding smack in the face. Well, there was only one way to deal with that one, so I said soulfully: '*Darling* Bob! Don't tempt me — here I am, with a foot in the thirties, and according to Mother firmly on the shelf. What do you *suppose* I'd say?'

For a moment he looked so terrified that I burst out laughing, and presently he began to laugh too, and we sat there in the Mogul garden, shrieking our heads off. Because, of course, he hadn't meant a word of it; he'd enjoyed half a dozen hectic affairs and one disastrous marriage since then, and had only been raking over dead coals for fun, in the firm conviction that there wasn't a single spark left and that the answer would be a hasty: 'Good heavens, no! Are you off your head?' But reminded of my years and my spinster state, it had suddenly occurred to him that I might take up his offer in the spirit in which it had definitely not been meant, and then he really would be in the soup.

As for me, it had not taken me long, after posting that snubbing letter, to realize that he was not going to reply to it, and that I had effectually put an end to my first adult love affair — or to decide that it couldn't have been the real thing after all, because if it had been, *surely* I would have taken longer than a couple of weeks to get over it? I remember being rather ashamed of myself for not losing more sleep over the loss of Bob, and confiding in Bets that falling in love was a lot more complicated than one would think. How did one tell if it was the real thing or not? It was humiliating to discover that the thing I missed most during the weeks that followed the end of my first romance was the excitement of looking out for the postman and intercepting letters, and the writing and posting of replies in secret.

Life was a lot more boring now that there was no undercover stuff of that sort, and thinking it over, I realized that if I had applied the du Maurier test I couldn't possibly have said, 'Make it three' to Bob, and that in fact I had never paused to give that aspect of it a single thought. Odd. I decided that the next time I would remember to do so. If there was a next time, I remember wondering gloomily. It seemed unlikely, after the painful experience of the Residency Ball . . .

Even now, after all these years, I cannot think of that occasion without cringing, and if it had been possible to have erased it from my memory I would have done so long ago and with alacrity. But alas! one's memory (mine, anyway) decides for itself what it will retain or discard, and it has etched that hideous evening indelibly on the tablets of my mind.

It must have been towards the end of April, because I remember that the trees in the gardens were wreathed in fairy-lights and the ground was dotted all over with little tables and sofas and chairs so that the hardier guests could sit out between dances — those who did needed a fur cape or a warm evening cloak. There was also a *shamiama* (marquee) somewhere or other in the grounds. The ball was, in effect, an opening shot that signalled the start of Kashmir's social season, and everyone who had signed the Residency book was automatically invited. I don't remember why Bets was not among them, and nor does she — (she thinks she must have been considered too young, or had a bad cold). But Mother and Tacklow and I attended: with disastrous results.

I was new to Kashmir and its 'regulars' — the wives, families and girlfriends of men serving in India, who came up every year from all over the plains to escape the discomforts of the hot weather, and the influx of men on leave from the armed forces, the ICS or one of the big trading companies such as Burmah Shell, Ralli Brothers and Dunlop's. And though I had attended a dance or two in Calcutta and several in Delhi, it had always been as one of a party that had dined together beforehand. Never once as a lone girl on my own, for my parents were no substitutes for partners. Tacklow, anyway, was a non-dancer. So I had no idea what I was in for until I arrived at the Residency, and found the hall and the ladies' cloakroom and main staircase crowded with total strangers, all of whom seemed to be on Christian-name terms with each other. It was a daunting moment, and worse was to come.

I had already met one or two girls of my own age during the past few weeks — the bank manager's daughter, Meg Macnamara, the Jenn sisters, who were spending the summer in Kashmir, two ex-schoolfriends — Noreen Bott and Pat Mills — Leela Apcar and several others. But I could spot no face I knew among the chattering crowd of women in the cloakroom, where I left my imitation white mink cape (shaved rabbit) and was presented with a dance-programme before edging my way back to the equally crowded hall.

Tacklow had been scooped in by Sir Evelyn Howell, the Resident, to play bridge, and I could see no sign of Mother, or anyone I knew, so I hung about, shifting uneasily from one foot to another and apologizing nervously whenever some hurrying fellow guest, burrowing through the crowd *en route* to the ballroom, happened to bump into me. Eventually, following the herd, I too found myself in the ballroom, where I spotted Mother foxtrotting gaily in the arms of our host, and looking as though she was having the time of her life.

I did not, as yet, know any of the young men who attended that dance; and since all the older men were either playing bridge or dancing with their wives or the wives of their contemporaries, not a single name sullied the pristine surface of the little white and gold dance-programme that dangled from my wrist. However, there were still some vacant spaces on the window-seats and the sofas and chairs where the older women — mothers and non-dancing chaperones — could sit and gossip and watch the dancing; and, seeing an empty one next to an old family friend, Lady Maggie Skeen, I edged around the floor and sat down beside her, resigned to spending the rest of the evening wedged in among the dowagers. But it was not to be. Unfortunately, I was spotted by my hostess, who sailed across and demanded to know why I wasn't dancing and where the rest of my party were. She looked horrified when I said I didn't know anyone and hadn't come with a party — only my father and mother — and, clasping my arm, said comfortingly: 'Oh, you *poor* child! Well, we must introduce you at once to some nice young men! Now let me see — '

The next ten to fifteen minutes were among the most shame-making in my life. I stood there, unable to leave because of that grip on my arm, while my well-meaning hostess used her free hand to grab every young man within reach and, having demanded his name if she didn't happen to know it already, introduce him to me. And one after another each one of these hapless youths mumbled a polite acknowledgement, added hastily that they were so sorry that they couldn't ask me for a dance but unfortunately their programmes were already full, and backed away, melting thankfully into the crowd. Not one of them was free to ask me for a dance, not even if they had wanted to! Well, what does a girl say in answer to that? I thought of so many things afterwards, but none occurred to me at the time, for my brain seemed to stop functioning. Why, I thought next day, hadn't I sweetly said to those young men who claimed their programmes were full, 'Oh, really? So's mine! What a pity — well, some other day perhaps.' Or made a joke of it and said something like 'Lucky you!' But all that was later. At the time I was too paralysed with shame and embarrassment to do anything but stand there with a sickly smile glued to my face, feeling like some unattractive slave on the block as a series of unwilling bidders, hauled relentlessly forward by Lady Howell, parroted the same phrases before backing thankfully away to join one of their girlfriends on the floor.

I do not know how long that purgatory went on for. Probably not more than fifteen minutes at most, but to me it seemed like hours, and I remember literally praying God to let something — anything! — happen that would put a stop to this ghastly party; for a bad storm to blow up so that everyone who lived on a houseboat would have to rush back in case it got too rough on the lake for the *shikarras** to paddle them home; or for a bolt of lightning to strike the Residency and set it on fire, so that we'd all have to leave; or for me to trip over my feet and break an ankle

* The flat-bottomed, punt-like little boats that are the taxis of that Eastern Venice, Srinagar.

(or even a *leg* if necessary). Anything that would let me get back to my own bed, pull the blankets over my head and hide from the whole lot of them.

But God was obviously not prepared to bother His head over such matters that night. When one thinks of what He has to deal with, what with wars, rebellion, persecution and natural disasters cropping up all over the globe like measles every day, it surprises me that any prayers concerned with such very trivial and derisory matters — even such really frantic pleas as mine were that night — ever get answered at all. The truly astonishing thing is how many of them actually do.

They didn't that night. At long last my harassed hostess gave up the unequal struggle. The band started up again, immediately the floor was invaded by dancers, and, releasing my arm, she took a last hunted look around the fringes of the packed ballroom and, seeing no unattached male that she could unload me on to, shouted a few kind words above the music to the effect that she was sure that I'd soon find some partners, and left me to it.

By now someone else had taken the chair next to Lady Maggie, and I could see no other vacant ones in the ballroom (which on a normal occasion was the dining-room), so I slid back into the hall and made a tour of the public rooms — walking briskly as though I was on some errand, in case anyone should guess that I had no one to dance with or talk to, and was hoping that someone would call out to me and ask me over to join their party. No one did, and I came back, with one of those awful, artificially carefree smiles fixed to my face. Finding that those couples who were not dancing were sitting in pairs, holding hands on the staircase, I beat a hasty retreat to the cloakroom, where I lurked for as long as I dared, under the sympathetic and far too knowing gaze of the ayah, who obviously did not believe a word of my headache story, and kept on patting my shoulder and telling me that it would pass — it would pass. She couldn't have been kinder if she had been my own Punj-ayah, who had said the same thing to me so often in my childhood, and I would have given a good deal to have been able to weep on her comfortable shoulder, as I used to weep on Punj-ayah's when things went wrong. But I did not dare to do so, because there were constant interruptions from other women guests, and for fear of smearing my newly acquired mascara all over my face.

I have heard very young men complaining of the horrors of turning up at dances where everyone else appeared to know each other and they knew no one. But no male, of whatever age, can begin to understand the true horror of being a wallflower — particularly at a dance in the days when there were dance-programmes and it would have been social death to dance with another woman or go on to the floor and jig about by oneself. Any man, however young, has only himself to blame if he won't ask a girl to dance merely because he doesn't know her and she doesn't appear to have a partner. But in my day no girl could go up to a boy and ask him to dance with her. She had to sit there and wait until some Lord of Creation condescended to come and ask her to dance with him. A partnerless male could always stand with his hands in his pockets, looking on at the dancers, and it would not occur to anyone to think, 'Poor chap — he can't get anyone to dance with him!' On the contrary (if anyone thought about it at all), they would think he was hard to please, or was merely assessing the local talent to see if there was anyone there who looked worth getting to know. And in the last resort, the single male could always prop up the bar, without making any attempt to earn his keep as a guest, or attracting the least attention by doing so.

But a partnerless girl in the same situation had no escape. She must sit, silent and upright among the dowagers and chaperones, pretending an interest in the couples gyrating past her on the dance floor, or retire at intervals to the ladies' cloakroom where one could waste a certain amount of time pretending to repair one's make-up or inventing a head-ache. I must have taken refuge in the cloakroom at least three or four times that night, and eventually, driven out by the embarrassment of being found lurking there yet *again* by an acquaintance who remembered seeing me there half an hour earlier, and exclaimed, 'Hallo, you still here? Aren't you feeling well? Oh, bad luck. Ask the ayah to get you some aspirin — Gosh, there's the next dance starting, I must rush . . .', I went out by a back door into the garden. Here, finding that one of the groups of chairs under the chenar trees on the front lawn was unoccupied, I huddled down in one and sat there in the moonlight, invisible in the speckled shadows of the chenar leaves, and wishing I was dead.

The dances at Tollygunj and the Saturday Club, and all the picnics and parties in Calcutta, had done wonders for my self-esteem; and so had Bob Targett's attentions in Delhi. But the experience of finding myself a wallflower and a social flop at my very first dance in Srinagar destroyed my newly acquired and still very fragile confidence in about fifteen minutes.

I felt like a hermit crab who, having successfully crawled out of his original shell, can't find another one in which to hide his extremely vulnerable self.

For a time I huddled in my chair in the garden, listening to the music and laughter and the chattering voices, and soaking in self-pity. But eventually the cold drove me indoors, and once again I took refuge in the ladies' cloakroom. I was there, pretending to powder my nose or touch up my lipstick, when the heavenly intervention I had been praying for arrived in the unlikely person of Mrs Wakefield, who came in to collect her evening cloak, explaining that her husband had to be getting home as they were due to make an early start for somewhere or other next morning. I grabbed at this lifebelt with feverish gratitude (knowing that her car would have to pass the gate of our house in order to get back to her own) and implored her to give me a lift home and drop me at our gates because I had a cracking headache — which by then was only too true — but did not want to drag my parents away, for Tacklow was pinned down in a bridge four, and Mother was enjoying herself.

Mrs Wakefield said yes, of course she would, and as Mother was dancing with one of her old flames I scribbled a hasty note which I asked the *abdar* (butler) to deliver, saying that the Wakefields were taking me home, and left with enormous relief, vowing that I would never allow myself to be trapped into a similar position again. Never, never, *never.* Even if it meant never attending another dance. Back once more in my bedroom I burst into tears and wept my way into bed, convinced that I had reached life's lowest ebb and that nothing that could happen to me in the future could be as bad as this. In which I was speedily proved wrong. For I was still awake and snivelling when shortly after midnight my parents returned. I had purposely left my light on so that they would know that I was awake and in dire need of sympathy and encouragement. I was so sorry for myself that I was sure that they would be even more sorry, and I confidently expected Mother to come running upstairs to inquire after the headache that had been my excuse for cadging a lift home from the Wakefields. I couldn't wait to pour out my woes and weep on her sympathetic shoulder, and be petted and hugged and comforted, and assured that I would never have to endure such an ordeal again.

Well, I was wrong. The worst part of that nightmare evening was to come, since far from being sympathetic, Mother was furious, and I found myself being given the talking-to of a lifetime. Worse still, Tacklow agreed with every word of it. I had behaved like a spoilt brat, shown no gratitude for my hostess's kind efforts to find partners for me — she had done her best to do so, and it wasn't her fault that we had arrived late and found all the available young men already booked for every dance. I had given her *no* help, but thrown up the sponge at once and spent the next couple of hours hiding in the cloakroom or the garden, instead of behaving sensibly and talking to the several people I *did* know — no, of *course* not the young ones, if they were on the dance floor. But there were plenty of older people whom I knew besides Lady Maggie and the Wakefields, and I could easily have sat down with them and made myself pleasant; and then perhaps one of the older men would have asked me to dance. I couldn't expect to go to a party of this type and spend the whole evening within my own age group, and it had been cowardly and silly, and very rude to my kind host and hostess, to cut and run in this childish fashion. The tirade ended with Mother snapping off the light and slamming the door shut behind her. Leaving me to pick up the pieces in the dark.

I remember sitting there, stunned and shivering, with shock more than cold, though the fire in the archaic wood-burning stove in my bedroom had burned out long ago. It had never occurred to me that my parents could possibly see the whole horrible affair from any side but mine. Or even that there could be another side! I felt as though the bottom had fallen out of my world.

Neither Bets nor I can remember where she was that night. We don't think she can have been in the house, for surely I should have gone straight in to tell her the whole sad story as soon as I arrived back, and I know I didn't. She could have been asleep and I might have decided against waking her. But I don't remember Mother exactly lowering her voice during that distressing telling off. All I do know is that I didn't tell Bets anything that night, but that she got the whole sad story next morning and gave me the hundred per cent support and sympathy that I had signally failed to get from my parents.

Tacklow, though he had let Mother do all the talking that night, supported her view of my behaviour next morning, and it was the first and only time he ever failed me. I thought that he at least would sympathize with me; not that he would 'take my part' against Mother, but that he would *know*, because it was me, exactly how I had felt during that humiliating evening and therefore understand how unbearable it had been and why I *had* to leave at the first opportunity. But he didn't. He agreed with Mother, though he wasn't angry about it, as she was, merely disappointed at my hysterical behaviour; he had expected me to have more sense, and more social poise, and I hadn't shown either.

Bets and I retreated to a point half-way up the Takht, from where we could look down on the roofs of the Gupkar Road houses and out across the valley to the snows, and, discussing the whole affair, agreed with the conclusion that I had come to in the small hours of the previous night: that any girl, however sensible and insensitive, would feel just as I had done if trapped in a similar situation, but that it was impossible for either of our parents to understand what an appalling ordeal it had been for me. Tacklow, apart from being a man, wouldn't have a clue, because it was something he could never have experienced; he never went to dances if he could help it. He merely escorted Mother to them, waited until her programme was full, arranged with someone to bring her home and went happily back to bed. And on those occasions, such as a ball at Viceregal Lodge, which was practically a command performance, or some official piece of entertaining such as the Residency Ball, he would dance once with Mother and spend the rest of the evening either playing bridge or wandering around talking to friends or watching the dancers. He simply could not understand why women could not be content to do the same.

Mother, on the other hand, who as a woman should have sympathized with the horror of my position, was in fact as ignorant as Tacklow on such matters — probably even more so, since she had less imagination. She was never very good at seeing another person's point of view or putting herself in their shoes, and so she, even less than Tacklow, had no idea why I should have worked myself into such a state over something so trivial.

All I had had to do was sit down somewhere in full view, and some young man would have rushed up and asked me to dance with him. It never failed. Well, it hadn't for her. Mother had been collecting beaux since she was fourteen — and she was only sixteen when Tacklow first saw her on the platform of a railway station in North China and fell instantly in love with her. He courted her for the next three years and, having at last won her father's consent, married her a few days after her nineteenth birthday and took her back to India when his regiment returned there after completing a three-year term of duty in China. She enjoyed her first taste of army life under the Raj, and she was barely twenty-one when Tacklow was posted to Simla, where she was an instant success.

So one couldn't really blame her for not having a clue as to what it felt like to be a wallflower at a dance. Other girls (and later, other women) might lack partners and have to sit against the wall for hour after hour, trying to look as though they were enjoying themselves, talking to women twenty or thirty years older than themselves, and wishing that the floor would open and swallow them up. But since this was something that she herself had never had to do, I don't suppose she even *noticed* them — she would have been too busy dancing, laughing and flirting light-heartedly with some bedazzled male. And as it is never easy to understand and sympathize fully with an emotion you yourself have never experienced — and are never likely to! — it was not surprising that she should have failed to realize what a nightmare that dance had been for me.

Bets and I, sitting in judgement, decided that taking all that into consideration she could not be blamed: and oddly enough, I didn't blame her, not after talking it over with Bets. We decided that as Mother really didn't understand, there was no point in trying to make her, while as for Tacklow, the same went for him.

I was to dine and dance at the Residency on many other occasions, and Bets would be married from there and hold her wedding reception in its garden. But the memory of that first dance remains in my mind as a small black stain on the green and gold and the almond and apple-blossom pink of that first spring in Kashmir, and it is one of the things that makes me doubt if I would really like to live the whole of my life over again, given the chance. 'If we could have it all again, would we? Could we?' Well, yes. I would, of course. For though the black patches were bad enough in all conscience, they were very far outweighed by the good ones.

Chapter 14

~❄︎⟡❄︎~

We made a good many friends in Kashmir, among them Ken Hadow, whose father (or perhaps his grandfather) had, back in the nineteenth century, been so impressed by the artistry and industry of the Kashmiris that he had decided to settle there and set up a carpet factory. The charm of the Hadows' hand-woven carpets had made them a great success, and as far as I remember the Hadows also had something to do with the lumber trade and the making and carving of beautiful furniture. Ken had introduced us to one of the state's forest officers, Bruce Bakewell, and his wife, Edna, who spent most of their time in a forest bungalow in the Lolab Valley but would come in occasionally to spend a few days in Srinagar. That year Ken would often drive us out to the Lolab for an all-day picnic, or for a long weekend with the Bakewells.

The Hadows owned a large, two-storeyed house on the outskirts of Srinagar, and another one in Gulmarg, to which they would retreat in the summer months when the weather in the valley grew uncomfortably hot and muggy. And since Mother rather fancied the idea of renting a hut in Gulmarg, Ken drove us up for our first sight of that glorified golf-course-cum-American-western-cow-town, which is what Gulmarg looked like at first sight — great sweeps of close-cropped grassy meadowland (*marg** means meadow, and Gulmarg, meadow of roses) lying in a green cup in the hills, with scattered all around and across it huts built of pine-logs and roofed with the same shell-shaped pine-wood tiles as the houses throughout the valley. Some of them were out in the open, others half hidden by the forest trees that clothed the sides of the bowl and swept steeply up behind it, to meet the snow-line on the slopes of Apharwat, the long ridge of mountain that overlooked it.

I was enchanted by the place, largely because it reminded me of Simla,

---

* Pronounced *merg*. Gul rhymes with 'pull'. The accent is on *merg*.

the town in which I had been born and spent the first ten summers of my childhood. It smelled the same, of woodsmoke and pine-needles and moss; and there were the same forests and the same enormous panorama of mountains and snow-peaks. Patches of snow still lingered between the great tree-trunks and alongside the little streams that wandered across the *marg*, and though here there were no lilies of the valley there was something even more spectacular: primulas. Thousands and thousands of them, *Primula reticulata*, spreading pale pinky-mauve carpets across the Meadow of Roses. It was one of the most beautiful sights you could wish to see, and to the non-resident visitor one of the rarest, because they evidently need exactly the right conditions before they flower. If spring is too late or too early or too cold, or the snow lies for too long — or the previous summer's rains have been too scanty — they either stay underground and sulk or there is nothing to see but acres of withering leaves and dead flower-heads. They are, or were (for I am told that like other endangered species they have vanished from modern Gulmarg) very difficult to catch at just the right time; and the many times I visited Kashmir, I was only to see them once again.

Nowadays one can, unfortunately, drive up to Gulmarg, and most people do. But in those days, and certainly as late as the early sixties, the road would only take you as far as Tangmarg, a little village at the foot of the hills, and from there one rode up to Gulmarg on one of the hill ponies known as *tats*. I have always taken a dim view of horses, and the creatures obviously know this and treat me accordingly. But since the only alternative to riding one of the wretched animals was to walk, I chose the lesser of two evils and, selecting the smallest and least dashing-looking *tat* of the scores that were on offer — their owners all extolling the merits of their nominee at the tops of their voices — I managed to ride up the steep hill track without falling off, or allowing my mount to break into a gallop wherever there was a flattish bit of ground.

The Hadow hut was still closed and shuttered for the winter, but we ate a picnic lunch on the verandah and spent most of the day looking at the few huts that had not already been booked for the season. There were not many of these, but we soon realized that we could not possibly afford any of them. And certainly could not afford to take rooms in any of the hotels or boarding-houses. So it would have to be Srinagar. A decision that I, for one, received with some relief, partly because to me Kashmir was lakes and lotuses and not forests and golf, and largely because *tats* were the only form of locomotion in Gulmarg apart from one's own two feet, and summer visitors, other than those who took rooms in Nedou's Hotel,* would ride across the *marg* to attend dances in Nedou's ballroom, wearing wellington boots under evening dresses that were kilted up over the knees and shrouded by dust-coats or mackintoshes, and — if it was raining — carrying an umbrella, their high-heeled slippers accompanying them in paper bags carried by an attendant *tat-wallah*. All in all, a daunting prospect for someone who, apart from having a deep-seated distrust of horses, found it difficult enough to remain seated on one even when suitably dressed and shod, and able to use both hands.

Mother had set her heart on a house. And a house she got. Ken Hadow put her in touch with a Kashmiri agent, Ahamdoo Siraj, who was to prove a tower of strength and a personal friend during the many years that she would spend in Kashmir. It was Ahamdoo who found us the Red House and persuaded its owner to let us rent it, furnished, for the season, with an option to take it on again for the following year.

The Red House was a large, comfortable two-storeyed building with wide verandahs, that stood in an orchard on the sloping ground beyond the gap, where Gupkar Road stopped and became that unnamed and unmetalled road that continued on, through a froth of blossoming trees, to circle the lake. Unlike the old Kashmiri houses, its roof was of red-painted corrugated tin — hence the name that we gave it. For until we moved in it had no name; merely going by the name of its owner, a merchant who had another house in the city in which he apparently preferred to live, leaving this one empty.

Ahamdoo, who had made all the arrangements, also made himself responsible for engaging a *masalchi* (dish-washer and kitchen assistant), a sweeper, a *mali* (gardener), a competent verandah *darzi*, and last, but most important of all, a *khansama* (cook) named Mahdoo, who turned out to be the find of a lifetime. He was a tiny little man, a Kashmiri, who had once been cook to a Frenchman who had spent several years in Kashmir, apparently studying the fauna and flora of the valley with a view to writing a book. Since, like the majority of his countrymen, he was interested in what he ate, he had taken the young Mahdoo in hand and turned him into a superb cook; hence Mahdoo's claim to being a 'Flench cook'. He himself never ate the dishes he made so superbly, preferring the food of

* The Nedous owned two hotels, one in Srinagar and one in Gulmarg.

his own land — chapattis and the red-hot curries and dishes made from green chillies and lentils. So how was it that he knew so exactly how some complicated *cordon bleu* dish should taste? I suppose his 'Flench Sahib' had taught him to keep the details of ingredients, mixing and timing so clear in his head that he could not go wrong. Like Karen Blixen's Kenyan cook in *Out of Africa*, he was a superlative cook in any language.

In appearance, Mahdoo and Kadera could not have been less like each other, Kadera being tall and thin and clean-shaven and Mahdoo small and dumpy, with a neat round beard that was already showing traces of grey. But they took to each other on sight, remaining friends for life, and were a part of Mother's life for almost forty years. When, sixty-two years later, she was beginning to fail, and was still hankering to get back to Kashmir, I used to think that if only I could take her back there and install her on a houseboat on the Dāl, with Mahdoo and Kadera to look after her, I would do so without hesitation; in the sure knowledge that those two old gentlemen would see that she was safe, and care for her like a couple of Norland nannies. But, alas, by that time both of them were dead. Kadera has appeared in several of my books, and I put Mahdoo into *The Far Pavilions* by name, just exactly as he was. In the words of the *Du'a*, 'May the mercy of God be fixed upon them for ever'.

Ahamdoo must have mentioned the name of the merchant who owned the Red House, but if so I forgot it long ago. We certainly never met him, and did not realize until after our first night in the house that during the winter months it was occupied, five or six to a room, by a horde of his relatives and friends who made their living out of the tourist industry and the summer visitors to Gulmarg, Pahlgam* and Sonamarg, and other more distant parts of the state that were snowbound and deserted during the winter months.

Mother was the first to discover this. The master bedroom boasted an enormous double bedstead decorated with beautifully carved swags of flowers, fruit and ribbons *à la* Gibbons, in some pale-coloured wood. Mother had a brand-new mattress made to her own specification to fit it (the one provided being a gaily coloured and somewhat lumpy *resai* — the thin, cotton-padded coverlet that normally does duty for either a blanket or a mattress, from one end of India to another). The new mattress proved very comfortable, and though her own double-bed-sized sheets

* Pronounced pile-*garm*.

and blankets were barely large enough to tuck in, she turned out the light on that first night, happily convinced that she was in for a good night's rest. It was not to be.

Tacklow, tired out by all the activity, had, after his usual fashion, fallen asleep at once, though his duties had not been exactly arduous. He had outlined them as: 'Your Mother can decide where the furniture is to go, you and Bets can carry all the lighter pieces between you, Kadera and his henchman can cope with heavier ones, and I shall exercise a general supervision.' But Mother had lain awake for a while, and presently she began to scratch.

Five minutes later she was still scratching. And five minutes later still Tacklow woke up and inquired, a shade testily, how she expected him to get to sleep if she kept fidgeting. Mother said she was not fidgeting, she was scratching, and that it felt as though she had come out in a rash, and when Tacklow suggested that she try dabbing on some witch-hazel or calamine lotion, she turned on the bedside light, turned back the sheets — and with a shriek that woke Bets and myself, in our bedrooms at the far side of the landing, so suddenly that we nearly bit our tongues in half, she leapt out of bed. Followed, with an equally loud yell, by Tacklow.

The sheets were literally alive with bed-bugs. Dozens of them, crawling all over the place. Mother tore off her nightgown and rushed, starkers, into the bathroom for her dressing-gown; frantically brushing herself all over with her hands as though she could still feel the insects crawling over her. They hadn't touched Tacklow — I suppose he didn't taste so nice, or else his skin was tougher. But they had certainly made a meal of Mother. By the time Bets and I arrived, panting, to help repel or capture a burglar, Tacklow had ripped off his pyjamas and was wearing a towel tied round his waist, the sheets had been stripped back and, apart from a couple of corpses that Mother must have squashed as she scratched, there wasn't a single bed-bug to be seen anywhere. They had vanished like the morning dew, leaving nothing but a nasty smell of squashed bed-bug from the two casualties.

We spent the next twenty minutes or so laying out two of the *bistras* that in those days no one ever travelled without — long canvas holdalls on which one's bedding was laid out as though on a bed, plus pillows and night-wear, and then rolled up in a tight roll and fastened with straps, ready to be unrolled and slept upon when needed, laid out either on the seat of a railway carriage, or on the floor, or on the bare ground if necessary. They made very adequate beds, and Mother and Tacklow took them downstairs to the drawing-room, where Mother's was spread out on a sofa and Tacklow's on the floor.

Bets and I, whose beds were ordinary country-style *narwar* ones, were untroubled by bugs, but a very apologetic Ahamdoo explained to us next morning that the magnificent double bed had been slept in that winter by an entire Kashmiri family, father, mother, grandmother, at least half a dozen small children — and probably an aunt or two as well — all huddled together in order to keep warm. The bugs had obviously moved in with them, and spent a happy and well-fed cold weather, being fruitful and multiplying like crazy.

The bed was carried out to the front drive, where Kadera and Ahamdoo took it to pieces; it was beautifully made and solid enough to have held up under a platoon of soldiery, let alone a family of Kashmiris. It was in excellent shape, but literally *crammed* with bed-bugs. Wherever one could squash itself in and raise a family, it had done so, and though we massacred as many as we could reach, there always seemed to be more of them. We tried flushing them out with Jeyes fluid, which seemed to work fairly well on the more active bugs, but Tacklow doubted that it would have any effect on their eggs, of which there were a horrifying number, promising a population explosion capable of taking over the entire house.

'It's no good,' said Mother, almost in tears. 'We'll never get rid of them unless we burn it — no, we can't do that. It doesn't belong to us. We'll have to send it back and hire a couple of *narwar* ones. I wouldn't mind so much if it wasn't so pretty — and I hadn't wasted all that money on a mattress made to fit it. But we can't possibly keep it, or those horrible things will spread to every room in the house as soon as their eggs hatch. Ahamdoo, *merabhanise'wapis layjao — Arj!* (Please take it back — today!)'

But in the event Kadera rose nobly to the occasion, as he was to do in any crisis, major or minor, during the next thirty to forty years. He might be young and with no previous experience of being anyone's bearer, but he had already stepped so comfortably into old Abdul Karim's shoes that we had begun to wonder how we had ever managed to get on without him. 'There is no need for the Memsahib to lose her beautiful bed,' announced Kadera, soothingly, in the vernacular, 'for since a hard-boiled egg (*sakht khaulna unda*) cannot hatch, we have only to pour boiling water on the wood and the eggs will be cooked.' So we did, and it worked. Not only on the eggs (which, as Kadera said, were all hard-boiled), but on any hapless *kutwa* who had managed to survive the initial assault. Though, even then, Mother took no chances, but left the bed in sections — and initially steaming from the cans and pails and saucepans of boiling water that had been poured over it — out in the middle of the lawn for the remainder of that week, while she and Tacklow dossed down temporarily on a pair of *narwar* beds that I presume had been borrowed from some houseboat-owning friend of Ahamdoo's.

There was no more trouble with bed-bugs, and for the remainder of that season my parents slept comfortably on the reassembled bed. But we had not finished with plagues. The Red House still had something up its sleeve. Mice.

Well, I don't mind mice. (My nickname in the family has always been 'Mouse', because the first of many animals that I pretended to be for the amusement of Bets when she was small was a mouse. An unsuitable choice for someone of my size, I can't help thinking.) But not a plague of mice; and certainly not when tangled in your hair.

I woke up one night to feel something tugging wildly at my hair, which in those days fell below my waist, and which I used to brush out and leave loose for the night. Something was pulling at it — which is not a nice way of being woken up in the small hours. I sat bolt upright and realized in the same instant that something alive and frantic was caught up in my hair. With a shriek of panic I groped wildly for the switch of my bedside light, and pressing it down, found a mouse inextricably tangled up in my hair — and a good deal more upset about it than I was.

It took me a good two minutes — shrieking all the while — to get rid of that wretched mouse. Bets and my parents all erupted into my room, demanding loudly what on earth I was yelling about. I was not pleased that they all three fell about laughing when they discovered that my assailant was a minute rodent who, complete with quite a lot of my hair which I had torn out with it, escaped and fled out of the room like a streak of light.

I took a dim view of the whole affair, and refused to go to sleep again without every light in the room being left burning which, of course, meant shutting the windows, as the light attracted a horde of night-flying moths, beetles and creatures of every size and description, including a bat or two. Next morning, though it was too early in the year for mosquito nets,

Kadera unpacked one and put it up for me, and Tacklow went shopping and returned with a couple of mousetraps.

I don't remember why we were entertaining a large party of friends on that particular weekend. But as Bill was there, I presume he and a few friends of his had driven up from Rawalpindi for a weekend and we had decided to throw a party. All I can remember is that we were putting up so many of the guests for the night that the upper verandah was turned into a dormitory for the boys, who bedded down on a long row of *bistras*, while Bets's bedroom and mine, as well as the spare bedroom, were packed with camp-beds for the girls. We laid on a buffet supper on the lower verandah, and, having cleared the drawing-room of furniture, rolled back the carpet and danced to the gramophone until well after midnight.

It must have been at least two o'clock in the morning by the time the Srinagar-based guests left, and everyone was safely in bed with all the house-lights out and the first gentle snores beginning to break the night silence. Mine had been the last light to go out, because I have to read for a time before I can go to sleep, and for a few minutes afterwards, not more than three or four, I lay awake in the darkness wondering which of our guests was the one snoring. I was just beginning to get drowsy when from the other side of the room came a short, sharp *bang!* like the report of an airgun, and I shot up in bed, jerked out of sleepiness and suddenly wide awake again, realizing almost at once that the mousetrap Tacklow had set that evening had been sprung.

I switched on my bedside light again and confirmed this, but though the mouse had been killed instantly — it was one of those old-fashioned spring-traps that back in the twenties could be bought for ninepence and worked a treat provided you could set it without catching your fingers in it — I had no intention of letting the victim's body lie there all night. This was not, I'm afraid, because I quailed at the idea of spending the night with a dead mouse in the room. It wasn't a question of sensitivity, but plain sense. The place obviously swarmed with mice, and if we hoped to get rid of them with the aid of traps it seemed to me a mistake to let the intended victims have a good look at what had happened to their late comrade, and get the idea that it would be advisable to keep away from this peculiar bit of wire and wood, regardless of the alluring lump of cheese. After all, even mice must have some sense.

But I was not going to remove the corpse and re-set the trap myself, because I wasn't all that sure how it was done, though I had watched

Tacklow set it last evening, and noted the painful crack he got across his thumbnail when he set it off by mistake. I therefore rose and routed out my brother Bill — waking up most of the boys' dormitory in the process and pin-pointing the snorer as Tony Weldon. Bill was not particularly pleased at being roused to remove a dead mouse and re-set the mousetrap, but he did it all the same, and I gave him a minute or two to get back to his camp-bed before snapping off my light. Roughly ten seconds later, *bang!* went the trap again. We had caught another. Bill stumbled back, yawning, removed mouse and set trap, and he had barely made it back again when there was another bang and a third mouse had handed in its dinner-pail.

This time Bill was even less pleased at being called up to deal with the departed, but his friends from Rawalpindi chose to think it was hilarious, and by the time the fourth mouse met its end, they were rolling about with laughter and making such a noise that they succeeded in waking Tacklow and Mother, as well as Bets and the girls who were the inmates of the spare bedroom. A fifth mouse bit the dust in record time, but Tacklow, viewing the bodies, declared that this had gone on quite long enough, and would have confiscated the trap if he had not been implored by the verandah dormitory to let it be set for *one* more time — it seemed that there had been a bit of spirited betting as to whether the trap would make it half a dozen, and money had already changed hands. 'Oh, all right,' said Tacklow. 'But this is the last time tonight. If it catches a sixth, just let it lie there until morning. No more getting out of bed or turning the lights on, or none of us will ever get any sleep. That's an order!' With which he stumped off, turning off lights as he went, and we all went back to bed.

This time there was a long interval of silence, long enough for most people to start drifting off into sleep. Either we had caught the lot, or all the lights and the talk and laughter, and the arrival of my parents, had scared the remaining mice back to their holes. I, for one, had definitely dropped off to sleep when the now familiar *bang!* of the trap woke me. But this time it was followed by an appalling racket that woke everyone; a banging and a clattering that sounded as though a collection of tin cans was being kicked around the floor. Lights sprang up again, and Tacklow and everyone else in the house came charging in to see who had fallen over what, while I stood up on my bed and yelled — adding to the general clamour.

For it wasn't a mouse. It was a rat that had been lured by the smell of cheese and, having somehow managed to get its tail caught by the trap, was tearing frantically round the room, leaping into the air, squeaking and throwing itself about in a frenzied manner as it tried to shake off this horrible thing that was holding on to its tail like grim death. This time the racket reached the servants' quarters, and Kadera arrived at the double carrying a *lathi*, with which he killed the rat with speed and efficiency. We did not set the trap again that night, and I don't remember how we eventually dealt with the showers of mice; no more traps were set in my room but I refused to sleep without my mosquito-net.

Kadera suggested that the problem would best be solved by acquiring a cat, but though this would have been the obvious thing to do, there was Pozlo to be considered. He was still no bigger than a ping-pong ball, and we kept his wings clipped so that he could flutter up from the floor to the back of an armchair, or down from a chimney-piece, but would never have escaped from a cat. We also turned down the idea of poison for the same reason. Pozlo might pick it up. And we would rather put up with any number of mice than risk losing Pozlo, who really was a most endearing creature. He and I used to spend a lot of time in the morning-room at the back of the house, where there was a window-seat from which I could look out down the slopes of the apple orchard to Gagribel Point and the lake, and write letters, or draw, or read without constant interruptions.

I must have spent hours there, either writing long, frivolous letters to Helen or Bargie, or curled up with an apple and a novel. Or, when the fit took me, with a drawing-board propped up against my knees supporting a sketchbook or a painting block, industriously working away at some picture that, with luck, would prove saleable at the Srinagar Club's next art exhibition. And while I wrote, read or drew, Pozlo would push into the neck of my dress and, taking a firm hold on one of the straps on my bra, fluff up his feathers and go to sleep; I think he preferred to sleep in the dark, and felt safer under cover. He did not always keep silent in there; sometimes, safely hidden inside my dress, he would feel chatty and we would carry on a long conversation — Pozlo in exactly the same low, gossipy, confidential tones that his fellow purple-headed parakeets used when discussing life with each other in a tree. Sleeping or waking, he hated to be disturbed, and should anyone come into the room while he was taking a nap or talking, he would start growling. It was a very small growl, but totally un-birdlike; a low, cross sound that was definitely a warning, and if the intruder stayed too long he would unhook himself from the bra strap and stick his head out to see who it was. If it was only a member of the family, or Kadera or Mahdoo, he would withdraw again. But if it was a stranger he would stay staring at them in a marked manner and continuing to growl until they left.

He really was the most intelligent and endearing bird, and a constant source of entertainment. And I still cherish the memory of his reaction on seeing me walk into my bedroom with my head tied up in a towel, having just been washing my hair. He had been promenading among the photographs and knick-knacks on the chimney-piece, and not recognizing me with this vast white turban on my head, he uttered a startled shriek and fell off backwards on to the floor.

But he was not really my bird, for like every other creature that we had ever possessed, furred or feathered, his 'heart belonged to Daddy'. Tacklow was another Dr Doolittle where the animal kingdom was concerned, and all our pets fell for him on sight. Pozlo adored him, and if Tacklow happened to be around, he was the one whom Pozlo would go to. If you put him on the ground in a room full of people he would stand there, looking around him until he spotted Tacklow, and would then make a beeline for him and climb up him, beak-over-claw, until he reached his shoulder, where he would nibble gently at Tacklow's ear and murmur a few loving remarks into it before fluffing himself up and settling down to stay there until removed.

No one could have resisted such enchanting declarations of affection, and Tacklow returned it in such full measure that we soon found that we could hardly ever persuade him to accept any invitation that would prevent him from taking Pozlo out for his evening constitutional, a daily outing that never varied. Tacklow, with Pozlo riding on his shoulder, would walk down to the far end of the big lawn, which ended in a grassy bank that sloped sharply down to the orchard. There was a huge and very old apple tree that grew near the top of the bank, its lower branches leaning down over the slope, and when they got there Tacklow would reach up until his fingers touched a branch and Pozlo would scuttle up his arm and on to the tree, climbing up it, in places with the aid of his stumpy wings and in others with his beak, until he reached the very top of the very highest bough, where, clinging on with those scratchy little claws, he would flap his wings madly, as though he were about to take off, and shout and cheer at the top of his voice, in the hope — so Tacklow insisted — that some of his own kind would hear him and answer. But, sadly for him, there are no parakeets in Kashmir.

Having finished his exercises, Pozlo would spend a happy half-hour exploring; fluttering from bough to bough, nibbling at fruit buds and, later on, apples, keeping up a long conversation with himself or calling down to Tacklow, who sat on the bank below and smoked his pipe. When he thought that the evening's outing had lasted long enough, he would whistle to Pozlo, who would come tearing down at top speed, jump into Tacklow's raised hand and so down his arm to his shoulder, where, as always, he would give a loving nibble to Tacklow's ear as the two of them went back to the house. This performance was repeated daily, and it never varied.

Chapter 15

❦❦❦

That first season in Kashmir was a lot of fun. Bets got co-opted to perform in a charity song-and-dance show at Nedou's Hotel, as a member of the chorus in several numbers and solo in another two. Nedou's was equipped with a proper stage, complete with footlights and spotlights, heavy crimson curtains and dressing-rooms (normally the ladies' cloak-room). The Srinagar season always included a number of cabarets and revues, and this particular song-and-dance show was put on by Helen Don, an ex-schoolmate of ours who as a child had been one of the shining lights of our dancing classes at the Lawn, with ambitions to become a professional. She had evidently not thought much of my efforts as a high kicker, or else she considered that my legs were not up to standard, for I was not invited to join her six-girl chorus-line consisting of herself and Bets, the Jenn sisters, Meg Macnamara and a girl called Noreen Bott,* all in the shortest of short skirts and wearing tap shoes (see photograph, if I can find it). The talented Miss Don designed their costumes, and Bets and I designed the ones for Bets's solo dances.

In the days of the Raj the *Sahib-log* who served in India had to make their own amusements, and since there were only a handful of theatres for touring companies to appear in — and even fewer companies who were prepared to face the hazards and discomforts of touring in the East — amateur theatricals flourished like bay trees. Almost every hall in every British Club was provided with a small stage and a pair of curtains, and there was always a pool of amateur talent to call upon. Everyone seemed to think they could act, and one or two of them actually could; Sylvia Coleridge among them. We designed our own costumes, which our *darzis* made up for us out of the materials bought in the bazaar for the most modest of sums. Who can ever forget those piled bales of Bokhara silk?

* Another ex-schoolmate.

155

Lovely, shimmering stuff like heavy taffeta, in every conceivable shade of every colour you can think of, 'shot' or plain, and selling for eight annas a yard. That's about sixpence, and I well remember the shock and lamentation when somewhere around the early thirties it rose to one rupee! I don't know if it's even made now; it was very much a 'fancy-dress dance' type of material, for if you spilt water or any liquid on it, all the colour came out, leaving you with a whitish blot surrounded by a dark ring. You couldn't wash it, and dry-cleaning, which was in its infancy then, did it no good at all. But for anything in the nature of theatricals it was spectacular.

Simla, when Tacklow first went there in Edwardian days, had topped the list of social hill-stations in India — but, as some latter-day Mrs Hauksbee was to remark acidly, it was a place where you 'couldn't sleep at night for the grinding of axes'. To the British, Kashmir, as a semi-independent native state, owned and ruled by its Maharajah, was a holiday playground where you could go camping or trekking, dance every night, play tennis, golf or polo, go fishing for trout in its rivers, shoot *chikor* on the hillsides and bear in the forests, stalk *markor* in the high mountains, and ski in the winter. If you were a painter, you could sit down almost anywhere and be sure of at least four wonderful views to paint — the one in front of you, the one on your left and the one on your right, and, by turning round, the one behind you. And for the benefit of would-be artists, the Srinagar Club held two art exhibitions a year, and up in Gulmarg, the Club there held another one. British and Indians alike flocked up in their hundreds.

Mother had always dabbled in watercolours, and since the art exhibitions consisted entirely of paintings by amateurs, she decided that she, Bets and I should all send in a few pictures to one of the exhibitions that year and try our luck.

I don't remember what my family's entries were, or if they sold any of them, but I remember what mine were. Realizing that ninety-nine per cent of the entries would be sketches of Kashmir, I decided to try something different and sent in a small line-and-wash drawing that I called 'Madonna of the Cherry Trees', and an illustrated verse for a child's bedroom or a guest-room, which incorporated a couple of guardian angels, neither of whom can have been keeping an eye on the job, since they were both sound asleep. The whole thing was very much in the style of Margaret Tarrant and the verse was by that well-known poet, Anon.

Even after all these years I still remember every line of it; and remember, too, that I sold both those pictures within minutes of the exhibition being declared open.

Since these were the first pictures I had ever sold, I was not so much thrilled as relieved: I was a wage-earner! And if I could sell my pictures, I could make my own pocket-money and earn my own keep, and so relieve poor, darling Tacklow of some of the burden of supporting his family; something that I was aware pressed heavily on him. It would soon press even more heavily, once he had completed the task that the Government of India had called him back to do and was again living on a very small pension — now smaller than ever because he had commuted a portion of it to bring Mother, Bets and myself out with him.

These reasons alone would have made that art exhibition stand out in my mind as a memorable occasion. But in the event it was to prove far more important to Mother than it was to me. For her it was a real gold-letter day, for among the scores of amateur efforts displayed on the rows of canvas screens which filled the Club's ballroom were three that stood out like diamonds on coal-dust.

The pictures were signed M. Molesworth and we were all riveted by them. I felt that I would have given almost anything to be able to paint like that, and Mother wasted no time in hunting up the exhibition's harassed Secretary and demanding to know if M. Molesworth gave painting lessons. The Secretary said she had no idea, but that she could give her the artist's address. This turned out to be a tent in a large camp pitched on about an acre of ground dotted with chenar trees, near the entrance to Gupkar Road; it had a name, 'Chenar Bagh', I think. The tents were usually hired out to impecunious subalterns who could not afford to take rooms in one of the hotels or guest-houses, or to hire a houseboat. But since Mother hadn't realized that, she had neglected to ask the Secretary whether M. Molesworth was male or female, and had made up her mind that whoever it was must be an established artist; she was expecting to see someone aged at least forty, and was very taken aback to discover that M. Molesworth was an eighteen-year-old girl.

The M. stood for Mollie, and she said she would be delighted to give Mother a few lessons at five rupees an hour since she needed the money, though she had never taught anyone before and hadn't a clue how to set about it. However, if Mother was willing to take the risk, she would certainly do her best. The deal was clinched and the two of them started on the first lesson that same week. And what a bargain it turned out to be. True, Mollie was no teacher. She couldn't put it into words. But she could do better than that: she could snatch the brush from you and demonstrate brilliantly.

The few lessons she gave Mother before she left Kashmir turned Mother from a painstaking amateur into a painter of real charm. Better still, a painter whose paintings sold — which was to prove a godsend to Mother in the lean years after Tacklow died and she found herself having to make ends meet on a widow's pension of £394 a year, a sum that was not increased until right into the early seventies. Her paintings saved her from penury, and today there must be hundreds of them scattered in homes all over India, in houses and bungalows and clubs and regimental messes that were once owned by the British. Not long before she died there was an article in the *Telegraph* on the dwindling numbers of British, nearly all of them widows, who had 'stayed on' in Ootacamund after India became independent, because they no longer wanted to return to England. The writer of the article included a description of the 'typical drawing-room' in any of the bungalows they inhabited, a decor dating back to the Raj — chintz-covered chairs and sofas, mantelpieces and occasional tables cluttered with faded, silver-framed photographs and snapshots of men and women long dead and children who by now must be grandparents, 'and watercolour paintings by Lady Kaye on the walls'.

I gave the article to Mother and told her that this was Fame! I wish I'd kept it, because I doubt if there are any of those who decided to stay on left in all India, let alone in 'Ooty'.

I can still remember, in detail, one of those paintings of Mollie's that we saw that morning, and I still regret, bitterly, that we could not afford to buy it — or any of her other pictures. Heaven knows they were cheap enough. But, knowing her worth, she had priced them a good deal higher than the average amateur exhibitor had dared to do. I only have two of her pictures: one of them a painting of a pine tree that she did to show Mother how it *should* be done, and which I was fortunate enough to see her do, having gone with them to watch.

The method, sureness and swiftness of the execution was a revelation to me, and I was dumb with admiration. It is the only one of her demonstrations that survived among Mother's papers. The other is a quick, unfinished and, alas, unsigned sketch of Vernag, the little colonnaded pool teeming with carp which are said to be the descendants of those put there by the Emperor Akbar. It was given to me by Mollie's husband in the 1980s, and from him I learned that she had, while still in her twenties, given a one-girl exhibition of her work in a London gallery that had been a sell-out. He showed me the press comments and a laudatory half-page article in, I am almost sure, the *Illustrated London News*.

She told us, that first day in Srinagar, that she had won a scholarship at one of the more prestigious London art schools — I can't remember which — but that they wouldn't take her until she was nineteen. As that left her with a year to fill in, she sailed for India, where she had an uncle who was a General, and having stayed with him for a week or two, left to do a working tour of India, paying her way by selling her pictures. We never met her again, but some time in the early thirties she married a young missionary doctor and they came up to Kashmir for their honeymoon. On the way back there was an accident; the taxi they had hired to take them down the mountain road to Rawalpindi went over the edge. Her husband, though injured, survived, and so I think did the driver. But Mollie was killed.

Some years after she died, an acquaintance of mine took me to have tea with a middle-aged lady who lived somewhere near Tunbridge Wells in Kent and who turned out to be a relative of Mollie's — an aunt, I think. She showed me an enchanting illustrated diary that Mollie had made on a trek to Tibet, and any number of sketches that she had done some years before her marriage, while she was spending a few months somewhere inside the Arctic Circle. Her sketches of snow-covered mountain ranges silhouetted against the fantastic patterns of the aurora borealis, or icebergs like crystal palaces moving slowly down green and blue channels of open water among the ice-floes, with the pale sun shining through them, were some of the strangest and most beautiful pictures I have ever seen.

I managed, in the 1980s, to trace Mollie's husband, but all he had, apart from a framed selection of her paintings, were a few unfinished and unsigned rough sketches (one of which, the one of Vernag, he gave to me) and an illustrated diary of a trek to Lhasa, which wasn't a patch on the one to Tibet. I don't even know how she managed to get there, for in those days Tibet was a closed country. But then she had fairly high-powered relations scattered around the world, of the type whose names do not get into print but who, behind the scenes and unobtrusively, can pull quite a few strings.

Among the 'regulars', the people who came up year after year to spend the hot weather in Kashmir, were many who had been friends of my parents for years and whom I had known in my childhood; among them Sir Micky and Lady Roberts, and 'Smiler' Muir. In the old days, when Smiler had been Personal Private Secretary to the Viceroy, or something of the sort, he had spent the summers in Simla, as had the Robertses, who used to lease a haunted house known as the Bower at Mashobra, some five or six miles outside the town. (I have told the tale of our encounter with the Bower ghost in the first volume of my autobiography.) Smiler Muir had officially retired some years ago, and now spent his summers in Kashmir with the Robertses on their houseboat on the Jhelum at Srinagar, where Micky, who was a doctor and still practising, would join them when on leave.

The Robertses' daughter, Sybil, who had been one of our childhood friends, was now grown-up and married, so for a large part of the season Lady Micky and Smiler were the only occupants of the houseboat, a fact that, despite their ages (Lady Micky was no chicken, while Smiler must have been at least sixty — and looked it!) had attracted the attention of a group of elderly regulars, who, having taken exception to the post-war (the 1914–18 one) influx of jazz-age visitors, whose standards, mores and morals were, they considered, getting laxer every year, had founded a Purity League.

A deputation from this august body requested an interview with the Resident, and when ushered into the Presence inquired sternly if he was aware that two well-known British visitors were 'letting the side down' by publicly living-in-sin on a houseboat not far from the Residency. If so, what did he propose to do about it? — or, for that matter, about the shocking 'goings-on' in *shikarras* and houseboats out at Gagribal Point and Nageem,* the details of which could not be described, but could be attested to by members of the League who, unable to believe the evidence of their eyes, had combined to buy a telescope, with the aid of which they had been able to confirm their worst fears. In the opinion of the League, a bit more of this and the Raj would fall.

The Resident asked for the names of the erring couple first mentioned,

* Pronounced *N'geem*; though later on, for some unknown reason, it began to be spelt (though never pronounced) 'Nagim'.

and on being told, exploded into laughter. Controlling himself with difficulty, he pointed out that, since that particular connection had been countenanced by at least three Viceroys, he thought it was a bit late in the day to start criticizing it. Smiler was a born bachelor, and his devotion to Lady Micky had been accepted for years by everyone (including Micky) as just that. As for the 'goings-on' at Nageem, he suggested that he might be willing to do something about that in exchange for a good long look through the telescope. The League, aware that they were being trifled with, were furious and stamped out without further words. Lady Micky and Smiler continued placidly to live on the same houseboat; the 'goings-on' at Nageem presumably continued uninterrupted, and the summer visitors laughed their heads off.

One of the visitors that year was the young Duke of Northumberland, a tall, thin-faced, lanky young man who was taking a look at the Empire under the wing of an elderly ex-Indian Army officer, Colonel Henslow, who was to become a great friend of ours. The two spent some time in Srinagar, as guests of the Resident, and I saw quite a lot of young George, who, I discovered, was enormously interested in ghosts. I remember spending an entire morning in the foyer of Nedou's Hotel discussing the subject, in the course of which I told him about the Bower ghost and the grateful one who used to put in an appearance in my grandfather's house in times of crisis. George was intrigued by both, especially by the latter, for he too had never heard of a grateful ghost before. But what really interested him about ghosts is why there should be any. What made a ghost decide to haunt a given spot? A favourite theory was that if someone died a violent or a terrible death, the sum of their terror and agony must leave an impression on the spot where they died — on the atmosphere and the very place itself, like a picture registering itself on photographic plate or a piece of film. This, however, according to George, couldn't possibly be true, because as far as he knew his own castle of Alnwick was not haunted, though once, in fairly recent times, doing a survey of the dungeons below the castle, a hitherto unknown one was discovered which, when opened, was found to contain the skeletons of prisoners taken after some Border raid, who had plainly been locked in there and forgotten. 'Just imagine what they went through before they died,' said George. 'If a terrible death could leave any impression on the atmosphere, then at least one of the poor brutes must have left behind his ghost to haunt the place. Yet they haven't. So *that* can't be the reason.'

Well, he had a point there. And I wasn't surprised at his fascination for ghosts, for his family name was Percy and throughout history almost any form of mayhem or conspiracy that cropped up seems to have ended with a Percy having his head chopped off on Tower Hill. George himself was destined to die on a battlefield early on in the Second World War.

❧ Several times that year, once for a long weekend but more often for the day, Ken Hadow would drive us all out to have a picnic with the Bakewells in the Lolab Valley, which is one of the most beautiful of the many side valleys in Kashmir. Ken had a passion for sea-shanties, and it became a habit with us to sing them with him in chorus as he drove. His favourite was 'Shenandoah' and, as with most of my clearest memories, there is an accompanying tune that immediately invokes those long drives through glittering sunlight and the lovely Kashmir scenery to the Lolab: 'Oh Shenandoah, I'm bound to leave you . . . away, you rolling river'.

Bruce and Edna Bakewell lived in an enchanting forest lodge, a log house on a hillside overlooking the valley and the Lolab river, a rushing mountain stream that was one of the tributaries of the Jhelum river. The deodar forest rose up protectively on three sides of it, dwarfing and sheltering it, while its front windows faced the level sweep of the valley with its orchards and walnut groves and the forests that swept up again on the far side. The air smelled deliciously of pine-needles, herbs and woodsmoke, of the little yellow climbing roses that grow wild in the Himalayas, and of the flowers that Edna Bakewell grew in the garden below the verandah. Bruce would tell us stories about his adventures as a forest officer, and he had a fund of tales about the wildlife in woods and forests and uplands.

He and Edna had twice played foster-parents to bear-cubs found abandoned and starving in the forest and brought in by one of his rangers. They made, he said, wonderfully entertaining and affectionate pets, but were very hard on the furniture, on which they liked to sharpen their claws. Both had eventually, and successfully, been returned to the wild. On bright, blazing summer days we would bathe in an arm of the little river just below the house, and ride the logs that were carried down from the logging camps higher up the valley. The logs floated majestically down, turning lazily to the current on their way to the Jhelum, and from there down the gorges to the great timber-yards on the plains. Even on the hottest day the water was ice-cold, for it came straight from the glaciers and the snow-peaks of the mountains. Sometimes we would walk up to one of the logging camps, or climb up through the shadowy forest by paths made by deer and bear and other forest creatures — to come out on bare, grassy uplands, where the deodars stopped and the only trees were silver birches and rhododendron scrub, and one could look back and down on the valley, and up towards belts of scree and a waste of rocks where patches of melting snow still lingered, with behind and above that a dazzle of snow-peaks.

I find it curious that although I lost my sense of smell almost thirty years ago, the *memory* of a scent can still come back to me, and I imagine I can smell the pines and the wild climbing roses, the special smell of the sun-baked grass on the uplands, and even — as happened once, when in a hollow on a bare ridge above the forest we came across the remains of a leopard's kill being disposed of by half-a-dozen hill crows — a scent that is not an unfamiliar one in the plains: the nauseating, sickly-sweet smell of corruption.

❊ 4 ❊

'Charmaine'

Chapter 16

~ЖৡৡৡৡЖ~

In those days, as a favourite holiday resort of innumerable carefree girls, grass widows and single men on leave, Kashmir must have been one of the most romantic places in the world. Coming on top of that enchanted spring, my sense of this was heightened by two weddings; one of them the wedding of Peggy Spence, a girl we had known in the days of our Simla childhood.

Peggy was marrying a handsome young man in the Foreign and Political Service,* and since her parents had been friends of ours for many years, her mother asked if Bets and I would make the bouquets for Peggy and her bridesmaids; though I can't think why we were selected for this task since neither of us had any skill in flower-arranging.

Possibly it was because we were reputed to be 'artistic', and 'If you can draw and paint then surely you can cope with bunching up a few flowers?' Anyway, we accepted gaily and Peggy's mother told us that she had arranged with an elderly and prominent member of the Kashmir Old Guard, one Mrs Hart, to provide the flowers for us. This ancient autocrat lived almost next door to us, in a large, ramshackle house surrounded by an equally large garden in which you could scarcely move for flowerbeds.

Peggy's mother took us over to meet her and Mrs Hart led us round, so that we could get an idea of what flowers were available (frankly, I'd never seen so many; the Chelsea Flower Show wasn't in it), and afterwards asked us in to tea. The interior of her house proved to be a riot of Reckitt's blue—blue walls, doors and paintwork—and as crammed with occasional tables loaded with assorted bric-à-brac as her garden was with flowers. The overall effect was dark and gloomy, and one hardly dared stir for fear of knocking over some dusty piece of Chelsea or Meissen china. Very unnerving.

* Normally known as the 'F and P'.

It was arranged that we should come over to pick what flowers we needed not earlier than five o'clock in the evening on the day before the wedding, so that we could carry them back to the Red House and stand them overnight up to their heads in water on our back verandah. White flowers for Peggy, roses, lilies, pinks and carnations, plus various silvery-grey foliage plants and sweet peas for the bridesmaids. The Kashmiri head *mali* (gardener) would be warned to expect us: 'He is going to be simply furious,' said Mrs Hart. 'He seems to think the garden is his, and always makes a terrible scene whenever I want flowers for the house. This is really going to upset him! Silly old fool!'

She tittered maliciously, and I remember smiling weakly because I thought she meant to be funny. Alas, no. It was no joke, and had I realized what we had let ourselves in for, I would have wriggled out of the assignment then and there, however unpopular the move. For though we had received fair warning about the *mali*, no one had thought of warning us that Mrs Hart, who was well known to be an outstandingly tough baby, was also the possessor of a totally unreliable memory. Or that her house guest, a companion or niece or whatever, who happened to be out that day, was equally quick on the draw and had the lowest flashpoint on record. These omissions were to let us in for one of the most embarrassing half-hours of our lives.

In the cool of the evening on the appointed day, Bets and I, armed with baskets, scissors and secateurs, trundled dutifully over to Mrs Hart's garden like a couple of lambs to the slaughter, and set about selecting sufficient flowers to kit out one bride and three attendant bridesmaids. But we had barely been at work for five minutes when a human typhoon came charging down between the flowerbeds, breathing fire and slaughter. It was the *mali*, and Mrs Hart had not exaggerated. He obviously regarded the garden as his personal property and every flower in it as a favourite son.

With yells of fury, he fell upon us, snatching away such flowers as we had already picked, and screaming that he would set the police on us and we were nothing more than common *badmashes* who had come sneaking into Hart Memsahib's garden to steal her flowers. At this point, alerted by the uproar, one of the nearest windows in the house was flung open and an unknown memsahib of uncertain age — the niece, or companion, or whatever — leant out and added a particularly carrying voice to the uproar, demanding to know what the hell we thought we were up to, trespassing on other people's property and stealing their flowers.

We stood there under her window endeavouring to explain, but she wouldn't let us get a word in edgeways. And when she paused to draw breath, the *mali* filled the gap with yells of rage. Eventually, dumbfounded by all the uproar, I turned on the *mali* and yelled in his own tongue a furious command, ordering him to shut up or else! — accompanied by several exceedingly crude epithets learned in childhood from bad little bazaar boys, which five minutes before I would have sworn that I'd forgotten. Sheer rage had dredged them up from me, and they worked wonders on the *mali*, who stopped in mid-flow and stood gaping at me open-mouthed. The harridan in the window, deprived of her back-up team, stopped shouting for just long enough for me to explain that Mrs Hart had given us permission to collect flowers for the Spence–Allington wedding, and told us when to come. It cut no ice. I was flatly disbelieved and we were ordered to leave immediately.

It was my first experience of outrageous and totally uncalled-for rudeness from a grown-up of my own kind, and of abuse and bad language from an Indian — or rather a Kashmiri. Nor had I ever been accused of lying and theft. It was all too much, and instead of marching off in search of the owner of this madhouse, I threw out the few flowers that the *mali* had not already snatched from me, and grabbing Bets — who by this time was in tears — by one arm, turned about and stormed out of the garden.

I think we were both in tears from shock and sheer fury by the time we got back to the Red House, and at first Mother had some difficulty in understanding what had occurred. When she did, she immediately got into the car and drove off to fetch the Hon. Mrs Spence, and the two of them went round to see Mrs Hart, who was not in. They seem to have interviewed the harridan while waiting for her and demanded — and got — an apology. Mrs Hart finally turned up. She was the kind of woman who boasts that they have never apologized for anything or to anyone in all their lives, and 'doesn't mean to start doing so now'.

Regardless of the fact that she had been out at the hour at which we had been told to turn up, she said that Bets and myself were at fault for not coming to see her first and ask her permission to start picking, and added that she had more important things to think of than warning her *mali* that we would be coming round to pick flowers, or remembering what day or hour we would be coming. Mother and the Hon. Mrs S. wasted no further time on her, or the old horror of a companion, but came back to fetch us, and we drove over at top speed to Ken Hadow's to ask him if he could let us have enough white flowers for Peggy's bouquet (he could — a lot of lilies) and then broke the speed limit to the Residency to ask them if we could raid their sweet peas. We could, and we did it by lantern light as by now it was dark. Judging from my snapshots our first and harrowing attempts at making up bouquets looked pretty good, though a bit untidy. Probably the effect of stress!

Apart from being guests, we had nothing to do with Molly and 'Bolshie' Tatham's wedding, except enjoy it and admire Molly's dress — handkerchief points were new to me and I liked the effect. At each of these weddings I remember sitting in the flower-decorated church in a daze of romance, smelling the orange-blossom and listening to the organ, and praying fervently that I would soon be able to trail up that aisle in yards of tulle and white satin to be married to the man of my dreams.

Both of these weddings — like practically all weddings in Kashmir — were followed by a reception in the gardens of the Residency. And at both an unseen band played, among other things, a dance-tune that was new in those days, but would appear again and for at least another quarter of a century — 'Charmaine'. I had never heard it before, and it still has the power to switch on that private video that I keep in my brain, and which can show me, in sound and colour and scent, three separate wedding receptions on the wide Residency lawn under the shade of four gigantic chenar trees: Peggy's, Molly Tatham's and Bets's. I can see them all, young and laughing and visibly glowing with hope and happiness. The air is full of scent from the long barrier of sweet peas that used to hide the kitchen gardens from the lawns and trees and formal flowerbeds, and from behind it Nedou's band is playing, softened by distance . . . 'Charmaine, Charmaine . . .' Ah me! Romance! Romance . . .

I acquired two new beaux that year, both of them, so far as I remember, friends of my brother Bill, through whom I met them. One of them, a high-spirited subaltern named Tony Weldon, was the proud possessor of an exceedingly noisy motorbike on which he roared around the town and which he relied on to get him up the 290-odd miles of hill road to Srinagar whenever he could manage to wangle a few days' leave, which he did at frequent intervals. The other was a Donald someone, whose surname escapes me (I hadn't remembered Tony's either but Bets came up with it; she says the motorbike was unforgettable and the name stuck with it!).

Donald was several years older than Tony, four or five at a guess, and he started by taking Bill and me out on the Dal in a minute sailing boat that he had hired for the duration of his leave. We took a picnic tea with us and the afternoon was a great success. It was the first time I'd ever been in a sailing boat, and I was not only enthralled but much impressed by the skill with which Donald handled it, and delighted when he invited me to go sailing with him again on the following day. This time Bill was not with us, though whether because he had not been invited, or because Donald had hinted that he'd be grateful if Bill made himself scarce, I don't know.

After that I saw quite a lot of him; enough to make Mother suggest to Bill that it was high time he asked this young man, who was monopolizing so much of Moll's time, to dinner so that she and Tacklow could meet him. Bill issued the invitation, Donald accepted, and presented himself at the Red House, looking very spruce in a dinner-jacket. The evening was a great success. Far too much so, I'm afraid, for when our guests departed, Donald was the last to go, and as we waved goodbye to him Tacklow said, 'That's a very pleasant and intelligent young man . . . I enjoyed talking to him.'

The comment was made quite lightly, but I took it seriously. Tacklow approved of him; QED he had passed a rigorous test with flying colours. I was already half in love with him, but slightly uncertain, for although I was fascinated there was something about him that I found a bit daunting, something that made me feel childish, gauche and immature, as if I was advancing too quickly into unknown and possibly dangerous territory. He made Bill and Tony and various other subalterns whom Bill brought to the house seem a lot of callow little boys; which was odd, for he wasn't nearly as old as Bob Targett, who had never had that effect on me, and had always been so easy to get on with. Admittedly, neither had passed the Gerald du Maurier test. But perhaps no one ever would, and if so . . . ?

I had been havering and wavering about Donald, excited at having captured such an attractive and sophisticated man, but not quite knowing what to do with him now that I had. To land him, or throw him back? That was the question. And then, while I teetered on the brink, Tacklow expressed approval and instantly the scales dipped. If Tacklow liked him, then I could safely take the plunge, for my father had always been both my touchstone and my private Oracle of Delphi. Everything was going to be all right . . . Everything was wonderful! Here comes the bride — !

You notice that it did not occur to me — and would not at that time have occurred to any girl of my age and class — that the next move was not marriage. There was even a song that dance bands belted out nightly in every country in Europe and America — 'Love and marriage, love and marriage, Go together like a horse and carriage' and ended firmly 'you can't have one without the other'. Too right. Nowadays, it would appear that love by no means leads to marriage; which to my mind is just wonderful for men, since nine times out of ten it merely means that they can acquire an unpaid housekeeper-cook-cum-mistress who not only pays up for half the expenses of a flat or whatever, but can, in a year or two — or five, or ten! — when lust grows cold and the novelty wears off, be discarded without a qualm.

Rampant women's-libbers will argue that women can do the same, and walk out on their men. Yes indeed; the real charmers will always be able to play the field; and should they discard a man, he and his friends will raise all hell about the appalling behaviour of 'that heartless bitch!' Which could be one reason why the 'faithlessness' of women gets so much publicity when one of them decides to discard a husband or a lover, men being permitted to yell the roof off when dumped in the ash-can. A woman in a similar position is, by tradition, expected by one and all (but in particular by men) to 'behave with dignity'. In other words, to sit down and shut up and do any howling she has to do in decent privacy.

Within two days of that dinner party, and while dancing cheek to cheek to the strains of the Club band, I became engaged to be married. Bill, who had taken his current flame to the same dance, was the first to be told, and his initial reception of the glad tidings was unflattering to say the least of it. He didn't believe a word of it and was convinced that his much admired friend had had 'one over the eight' and was merely pulling his leg. For like many another brother, he could see nothing alluring about a mere sister, and was convinced that someone as mature and worldly-wise as Donald could not possibly have fallen in love with 'Old Piano Legs'.

It took some little time to convince him that the whole thing wasn't an elaborate joke, and when he finally accepted that it wasn't, he offered his congratulations but took his prospective brother-in-law aside and assured him earnestly that anything he had said would not be held against him unless repeated on the following day.

Bill's reaction to the news cast a distinct shadow over what had until then been a glittering evening, and I began to wonder uneasily if perhaps Donald *had* been knocking back a few drinks too many, and if he really would come round to the house the next morning and repeat in the unflattering daylight all the charming things he had said into my ear on the dance floor to the accompaniment of the band playing 'I'll be loving you always, with a love that's true, always' — Would he . . . ? Yes, *of course* he would! But Bill's bucket of cold water was not to be the only setback I was to receive that evening. Leaving Bill and his current girlfriend to get on with the dancing, Donald had taken me for a stroll in the moonlight . . . For just to add to the romance of the occasion, there was a moon that night. There always seemed to be a moon in Kashmir when one needed it, and looking back on countless evenings in that delectable valley it is only the moonlit ones that I remember, so that when, many years later, I was to write a 'whodunit' set in Kashmir, my original title for it was *There's a Moon Tonight*. (Alas, the publishers wouldn't wear it — don't ask me why; I still think it was a good title.) It ended up with the unalluring one of *Death Walks in Kashmir*.* Well, it was a murder story anyway.

The Srinagar Club stands on the left bank of the Jhelum river, behind and just below the broad, high, manmade embankment known simply as the Bund and built to protect the land behind it from being inundated in flood years. The Bund is overhung by willows, poplars and great chenar trees, and it was along this romantic, tree-shadowed and moon-splashed walk that Donald and I went strolling arm-in-arm, while behind us the night was made hauntingly sweet by the distant strains of the dance band playing an old favourite of my school days: 'Avalon, Avalon, River of Dreams . . .'. Odd how a cheap melody and every word of its accompanying lyric can attach itself like a limpet to one's memory, when a name cannot.

There seemed to be no one else on the Bund at that hour, most of the courting couples who went strolling on it having turned up-stream, where there were fewer houses and more trees, instead of down-stream as we had done, towards the Post Office and the shops. Donald and I had the Bund to ourselves, and it was here, in the black shadow of a huge chenar tree, that he stopped, and, pulling me into his arms, gave me what I subsequently learned is known as a 'french kiss'.

* Republished as *Death in Kashmir*.

Well, I'd been kissed before, of course, and found it pretty exciting. But not in this way, and it gave me the shock of my life. Frankly, I thought it was disgusting, and I remember standing there, clutched in a close embrace, and thinking wildly: 'If this is how people kiss when they are married, I'm going to have to put up with it every day of my life from now on! How am I going to *bear* it? It's revolting! I'll *never* get used to it. But I'll have to, I'll *have* to — '

Bob had never kissed me like that, yet his kisses had given me a terrific kick, but the meal that Donald was making of me filled me with nothing but disgust and panic. Panic at the thought of having to endure this sort of thing every time he felt like kissing me, without letting him know that I wasn't enjoying it as much as he was. It didn't occur to me to think, 'I can't marry this man, and I'd better call it off at once,' and I hadn't even the guts to struggle or make any attempt to push him away. With hindsight, I suppose I imagined that all modern and sophisticated couples kissed like this once they were engaged, and I didn't want him to think I was a boring little ninny who knew nothing whatever about men — or making love. I merely thought that the sooner I learned the better; though the prospect of having to do so chilled me to the marrow, and I blamed myself for not having applied the du Maurier test earlier on, instead of saying 'yes' first and then beginning to wobble.

In view of this, it is hardly surprising that my first — and when I come to think of it, last — engagement did not last long. Whether Donald had sensed the shock and disgust with which I had received his first celebratory embrace on getting engaged, I don't know; but he presented himself next day at the Red House in the character of an accepted suitor, and was received as such. (Though a little warily I noticed, which I did not take in very good part since, after all, if it hadn't been for Tacklow's approval my very first 'official' love affair would probably never have got off the ground, so it was too late for him to be cagey about Donald now.)

Looking back at that period of my life, I realize that although Tacklow's main reason for returning to India in order to revise Aitchison's Treaties had almost certainly also been because he knew that it would delight Mother, for whom parties and dancing and gaiety were the breath of life, and who had endured the dullness and hard work, the non-stop cooking, ironing, housework and gardening of the past few years in England without complaint, there had been a strong secondary reason: the hope that if he brought his daughters out to India they might find husbands there. For with all his many perfections, my darling Tacklow was a true child of his time, and that time was the Age of Victoria, when well-bred young women did not go out to work but stayed demurely at home, occupying their empty hours with embroidery and good works until the glad day when some suitable knight-errant appeared on the horizon to rescue them from the dragon of boredom and bondage to ageing and autocratic parents, and allow them to escape into one of child-bearing and housekeeping instead.

Looking back to that period now, I wonder if Tacklow did not think that from what little he had seen of Donald, this young man might not turn out to be a far better bet as a husband for me than the only previous contender for that role — Bob Targett. He certainly did not refuse his consent, or anything of the sort, but allowed the situation to remain vague; there was little or no prospect of Donald being able to get married in the near future, so we would have plenty of time in which to get to know each other better. Well, that was all right by me. I didn't in the least mind having 'an understanding' rather than an official engagement and an announcement in the papers to the effect that 'A marriage has been arranged, etc, etc'. Nor did Donald or Tacklow, and I'm not sure how the affair would have ended if it had not been for Mother's long-time friend, Lady Maggie Skeen, taking a hand. To this day, I can't think why she should have bothered to do so. But interfere she did. Perhaps she thought Mother was too unworldly to handle the situation and needed help and advice.

Hearing of my engagement, she was apparently shocked to discover that the prospective bridegroom had not even troubled to get me an engagement ring. An omission, insisted Lady Maggie, that plainly showed that he had no intention of getting married and was merely using this 'understanding' as an excuse to monopolize my time and attention — while at the same time warning off other possible suitors — without committing himself in any way. Had he been serious, the purchase of a ring would have been the very *first* thing he would have done!

Whereupon Mother, who until then had been rather preening herself on having one of her daughters engaged to be married so soon after arriving back in India, was thrown into a fluster and began to nag me about the absence of that ring. Worse still, it was at this point that she produced, for the second time, the form of criticism that she had originally applied to Bob Targett and was to use with regrettable frequency in future years, and which never failed to be an ominous sign. She announced once again that although on first acquaintance he *seemed* nice enough, there was *something about his face that she didn't quite like* — 'I don't quite trust him . . .' Poor Donald! And poor Mother. She had always been so gay and friendly and uncritical and had made friends so easily. People fell for her by the score. But that first 'official' love affair of mine, and Lady Maggie's needling, had unearthed — or possibly even manufactured — a streak of suspicion in her hitherto blithe and happy-go-lucky nature which was to grow like ground-elder or some equally invasive weed, until it became in time a dreaded phrase.

I can't remember how I acquired my first engagement ring. I don't *think* I passed on Mother's criticisms on the subject to Donald, and I have a strong feeling that it was actually Lady Maggie herself who took the poor young man aside and gave him a lecture on the subject, though I may be maligning her. But whoever was responsible, it resulted in my getting a temporary engagement ring in the form of Donald's signet ring — there being no European-style jeweller's shop in Kashmir, and Donald refusing to buy one of the Indian-style rings on offer. The signet ring was too big and kept slipping off my finger. And not surprisingly, what with Mother finding that there was something that she didn't quite like about his face, and Lady Maggie putting her oar in, the brief affair culminated in tears and high words and the return of the signet ring to its owner, and that was that. 'Told you he'd think better of it,' said Bill briskly, adding, presumably by way of consolation, 'Bad luck, old girl. Don't take it too hard. There's plenty more fish in the sea.'

It might have been expected that Bill's pessimistic view of my chances of acquiring a husband, added to the fact that I had already succeeded in losing a couple of 'possibles', and endured the horrors of my first Residency dance and the shock of being loudly accused of theft and lying, would have cast a gloom over my first season in Kashmir. Yet I still look back on it with delight. The valley seemed to get more impossibly beautiful every day, and it was difficult to believe that I had ever thought it was ugly.

Lady Maggie, possibly suffering from a guilty conscience over the part she had played in putting paid to my brief engagement to Donald, invited me to stay with her and General Sir Andrew for a week on their houseboat at Ganderbal on the Jhelum, where His Highness the Maharajah had lent them one of his private *ghats* (moorings) for the summer. I think she may have expected me to be nursing a wounded heart, and that a change of scene would do me good. If so, she was wasting her sympathy, for I can't remember losing much sleep over the 'man who got away', and I had a lovely time at Ganderbal; going out painting with Lady Maggie — who like most visitors to Kashmir had become a keen amateur watercolourist — and meeting the many Indian officials of the state who came out to have lunch or tea with the Skeens. It was a nice, peaceful interlude; and since I sold every painting at the next Srinagar exhibition, a very lucrative one from my point of view.

Later on in the year, as Tacklow still had a certain amount of work to do relating to the group of twenty-one Rajputana states that included such fascinating names as Jaipur, Jodhpur, Udaipur, Bundi, Tonk and Jelawar, it had been arranged that he would spend a month or so in Tonk as the guest of a British couple who were in the service of the Nawab, from where he could pay a series of visits to the rulers of various other adjoining states; and since Mother wished to go with him but could not leave Bets and myself alone and unchaperoned at the Red House, the Howells very kindly stepped in and invited Bets and me to stay with them in the summertime Residency up in Gulmarg while our parents were away. Their offer was accepted with considerable gratitude by our parents, and delight from us, and Bets and I moved up there on the same day that our parents left — taking with them Kadera and Pozlo (from whom Tacklow refused to be parted), and leaving Mahdoo to keep an eye on the Red House.

The Gulmarg interlude was enormously enjoyable, and more than made up for that agonizing Residency dance. The Howells could not have been kinder, and the days passed at racing-car speed. Why, oh why do the days have to sweep past like a millrace when one is enjoying life, and crawl like a land tortoise when one is sad or unhappy? Every summer visitor in Gulmarg was on holiday and there was a dance or a dinner party every night, to which you rode on your *tat* (hill pony).

The place was a golfer's paradise, for the gently undulating *marg* was divided up into several different courses, and it was here that India's pros competed yearly for the 'Hill Vase'. Neither Bets nor I played golf, but there were wonderful walks and rides round the Outer Circular Road and up through the pine-woods to Khilanmarg and Apharwat — yearly playgrounds of the Ski Club of India — or down through the forest to Ferozpur Nullah, where the little river that is fed by the glaciers of

Ferozpur Peak cuts its way through the rocks and the steep hillsides to wind down past Tanmarg on its way to join the Jhelum.

Here, in a wide pool below the neck of the *nullah*, one could fish for snow-trout, which would go straight into the pan to be fried over a fire of fir-cones and fallen deodar branches, as the main course of picnic lunches eaten on the sun-baked boulders by the waterside. The sunshine and smell of the pines and the woodsmoke, and the rushing sound of snow-water, acted as a powerful soporific, and most picnics ended with everyone falling asleep for most of the afternoon. We would wake when the sun left the *nullah* and the shadows and the blue-green snow-water brought a chill to the air, and ride back up through the woods to the Gap.

Alternatively, one could ride or walk up to picnics on Khilanmarg, the 'Meadow of Goats', which is the long slope of open, grassy ground that marks the height at which the snow-line cuts off the forests as cleanly as with a sharp knife. From there you can look down on Gulmarg lying in its green, tree-fringed cup at your feet, or ahead at the whole sweep of the Kashmir valley, its shimmering lakes and the rampart of mountains that form its far wall. On a clear day, you can see the white cap of Haramokh, 16,900 feet above sea level, and the silver spear that is Kolahoi. Far to the right of both is the tiny white triangle that is K2, the second highest mountain in the world. And, if you are fortunate, high up in the sky above the snow-line, and eighty miles distant across the valley, something that at first glance appears to be a small white cloud floating in the blue, but that you suddenly realize is a mountain. One of the most beautiful mountains in the world — Nanga Parbat, the 'Naked Maiden'. She is only the eighth highest mountain in the world, being outranked, among others, by Everest, K2, Kinchingunga and Dhwalagiri (a mountain I had never even heard of). But when she condescends to show herself, which is something she can be maddeningly capricious about, you can understand why she would have won the golden apple every time if the gods had held a beauty contest for mountains. The secret of her charm is that she has no competition. She is not hemmed in, as Everest and that other Naked Goddess, Nanda-Devi, are by a squad of ladies-in-waiting who make it difficult to see which one among them is the Queen. Nanga Parbat stands alone, enthroned in the sky a good 10,000 feet above her nearest neighbours in that stretch of the Outer Himalayan Range that faces Gulmarg.

Tourists, climbers, and mountain-fanciers by the thousand have travelled half-way round the world just to see her, to paint or photograph her, and have had to leave without catching so much as a glimpse of her. But luck was with us, for the sky was cloudless for almost the whole of our stay with the Howells, and when it rained it only did so at night. Day after day, in a clean washed sky, we would look out across the valley from the windows or the verandah of the Summer Residency and see that adorable mountain floating serenely in the blue; seeming so close that we felt it must be possible to hit her with the catapult that one of the *mali*'s more junior assistants used to scare birds from robbing the kitchen gardens.

In those days, the *thé dansant* still flourished, and most evenings, riding back from some picnic among the woods or a walk across the *marg*, we would drop in at the Club — it was the original Club then, the old one near the polo ground — to drink tea and dance, before returning to bath and change and, on most evenings, ride out again either before or after dinner, depending on where we were dining, to dance until well after midnight at Nedou's Hotel or the Club, without a care in the world. That was a wonderful time; sun-soaked and pine-scented days, and moonlit or star-spangled nights, laughter and dancing, and a band playing hit tunes of the day — 'I can't give you anything but love, Baby', 'One alone', 'The Birth of the Blues', 'Me and My Shadow', and 'Charmaine' — How well I remember them.

✳ 5 ✳

'Tales of far Kashmir'

Chapter 17

Looking back, I find it very hard to realize that in the eyes of history all those dancing years were no more than a very brief 'half-time' between two devastating wars, and that so many of those light-hearted young men with whom I laughed and danced were fated to die in the jungles of Burma and Malaya, in Japanese prison camps or on the Death Railway; in North Africa and Greece and Italy; on the beaches of Dunkirk and Anzio, the Normandy landings and scores of other battlefields on land and sea and in the air. Perhaps it's just as well that we can't see into the future.

Mother returned from Rajputana and Bets and I from Gulmarg. Mother reporting that the Nawab of Tonk had set aside one of the official guest-houses for Tacklow's use, and that he and Pozlo had settled in very comfortably with a temporary staff. It was sad not to have them with us, but what with painting for the autumn art exhibition, taking part in yet another charity cabaret show, attending a resplendent ball thrown at the River Palace by H. H. of Kashmir, and Mother's chickens, we didn't have time to miss them over much.

The chickens were another of Mother's efforts to bolster up the Kaye bank balance, but they proved to be a disaster. Anxious to do her bit, she had been lured by one of her Kashmiri friends into buying a large number of day-old chicks, the idea being that she would in time be the owner of a thriving business, a sort of poultry-queen of Kashmir. Those enchanting balls of yellow fluff had indeed grown, in a remarkably short space of time, into a flock of boring chickens which had to be fed twice a day and needed a large number of wooden coops. But after ruining an outsize expanse of lawn, enclosed for their use and wrecked in what seemed a matter of minutes by their scratching up all the grass, the wretched creatures contracted a distressing malady peculiar to chickens, called 'the gapes', and died one by one in no time at all. The whole thing was reminiscent of the Black Death and the less said about it the better. Poor Mother! It had been an expensive venture and she wept buckets, both for the unfortunate chickens and the financial loss (she was sadly out of pocket), and blamed herself for not sticking to painting instead of trying her hand at poultry farming to jack up the family finances.

Watercolour sketching was not really in my line. I preferred children's book illustration, and found, to my pleased surprise, that the public bought the things — possibly because they were a change from endless pictures of 'Sunset on the Dāl Lake' and 'Apple-blossom-time in Kashmir'. That painfully twee painting of a couple of sleeping angels and a pear-tree in the moonlight, designed as a decoration for a verse entitled 'Sleep Sweetly', was a huge success. The original had sold within a minute or two of the exhibition being opened, and demands for copies from a sentimental public kept me busy for weeks.

Over half a century later I came across the original pencil drawing of this piece of marshmallow, and on impulse traced it on to a bit of hot-press, painted it — plus verse — and put it into the Bexhill Art Exhibition (where it only narrowly avoided being blackballed by the Chairman of the Selection Committee). Once again it was bought almost immediately, this time by a summer visitor from Holland, who wrote to me on his return to the Netherlands to tell me how charmed he was by both picture and verse. He had, he said, hung it in his guest-room, where it had 'drawn much admiration'.

I did, however, try my hand at sketching the Black Marble Pavilion in the Shalimar Gardens. Without much success. Mother and Bets were far better at this sort of thing than I was, and, recognizing that melancholy fact, I gave up trying to put Kashmir on paper and went back instead to book illustration, and to trying to describe it in long letters to friends back home. European writers, travellers, explorers and humble tourists by the thousand have attempted this ever since Marco Polo the Venetian lauded the beauty of Kashmir's women; when Thomas Moore wrote his potted drama *Lalla Rookh*, which caught the fancy of the early Victorians, he became one of the long procession of poets and writers who have written about that delectable country and will do so in the future, following in the footsteps of François Bernier, who visited the country in 1665 and was himself following Marco Polo.

Here are three more modern stories of the valley — the first one is dated 1925, only two years before I first saw it.

�֍ When the time came for the Old Maharajah — General His Highness Maharajah Sir Pratep Singh, ruler of Jammu and Kashmir since 1885 — to die, he did so in the Shergarhi Palace on the left bank of the Jhelum river and (as is customary with kings, who have little privacy), in the presence of a large number of ministers, relations, courtiers and priests. The windows of his room had been opened to help the dying man breathe, and a moment after he drew his last breath, a large moth that had been hiding somewhere in the draperies behind the royal bed fluttered out and flew through the open windows. The story goes that someone in the room said in an awed whisper: 'It is his soul,' and that those who leant from the windowsill to watch its progress as it dipped down to skim across the placid surface of the Jhelum saw a large fish rise with a swirl and a splash, and take it. Afterwards, an order was given that held in my day and for all I know still does, forbidding all fishing for a certain distance up-stream and down from the spot where the moth had met its end, for fear that someone might catch and eat the fish that had swallowed His Highness's soul.

I think, though I am not certain, that it was either this same Maharajah or his father, H. H. Ranbir Singh Sahib, who, wishing to marry a girl who for some reason was not considered by his Council of State to be of sufficiently high rank to be the Senior Maharani of Kashmir, got around this tricky social question of precedence by espousing a chenar tree, to which he was married with all the pomp and ceremony that attends an Indian wedding, and which was known thereafter as Her Highness the Senior Rani of Jummu and Kashmir. Protocol being satisfied, he then married the lady of his choice, who duly became the junior wife of the ruler.

The third tale, which is my favourite, once again concerned the 'Old Maharajah'. I heard it first from a member of the Council of State at one of the Skeens' luncheon parties at Ganderbal and again, many years later, on a BBC radio programme, told by an English judge, one Sir Grimwood Mears, who had recently married in his old age a dear friend of mine, Margaret Tempest, who must be well known to millions of children as the illustrator of the *Grey Rabbit* books.

Sir Grimwood had been sent out to India as a judge for a few years, in the course of which he had made the acquaintance of the old Maharajah. The two men had become great friends, so much so that when Grimwood's tour of duty overseas ended, he travelled up to Kashmir in order to say goodbye to his friend. The old man, who had ascended the *gudee* (throne) in 1885 and reigned for almost forty years, was nearing his eightieth birthday and appeared to be in excellent health. But when Grimwood said confidently that he looked forward to meeting him again in the future, His Highness shook his head and said, no, he did not think they would meet again, but that he had a request to make that he hoped Grimwood would grant: 'I do not think that it will be long now before you hear that I have died,' said His Highness, 'so now I would like you to do me a last favour.' Sir Grimwood told him that he had only to ask, and His Highness said, 'I would ask you, on the first anniversary of my death, to go to the Shalimar Gardens, where you and I have picnicked on many occasions, and sprinkle some rose-petals on the water in remembrance of me.* Will you do that?'

Grimwood protested that His Highness was still hale and hearty and would certainly live for many more years, but that of course he would promise. Whereupon the old man embraced him and they parted, Grimwood to return to England and continue his professional career. Not long afterwards, he heard the sad news that his old friend was dead, and a year later he arrived in Srinagar on the day before the anniversary — though it had not been easy, back in the 1920s, to arrange a sufficiently long holiday to allow for a return trip to India and back again for in those days one travelled by ship. An average voyage by P & O from London to Bombay took over two weeks, and from Bombay to Kashmir a further four days, and there had been times when Grimwood was tempted not to make the long and tedious journey. But a promise was a promise. So he had arranged it, telling no one but his wife and making arrangements for someone to stand in for him.

On the day following his arrival, allowing himself time to get to Shalimar at the hour the old Maharajah had mentioned, he took a taxi and was driven out around the lake. Once there, telling the taxi-driver to wait, he walked up the path alongside the water-channels where the fountains were playing and, reaching the spot where, in the old days, he had picnicked with the late ruler, he stopped and took off his hat and stood looking down at the water and thinking of the old man. It had been his intention to pick a handful of petals from one of the many rose trees but,

* I think he gave an exact hour, but if so I have forgotten it.

as he turned away to do so, a gorgeously uniformed palace official stepped out quietly from behind the shelter of a group of bushes and, coming up to him, bowed and proffered a silver bowl full of rose-petals ... 'His Highness knew that you would not fail him,' said the official.

Grimwood left Kashmir on the following day to begin the long journey back to England; and some forty years later, long after India had achieved Independence, he told that tale on the radio, as an illustration of the friendship, liking and trust that had existed between so many British and Indians in the days of Empire. This liking was what made possible the very existence of the Raj, since without it, the Raj could not have lasted a year, if that. The British have been accused again and again of following a policy of Divide and Rule. But those who squawk that parrot cry have not bothered to take a look at India's history and discover that until the coming of the Raj, that vast subcontinent, though technically under the rule of the Great Moguls, was divided into scores of independent sovereign states, all of which spent much of their time making war on each other.

Nor have they registered the fact that a good many of these states were Muslim, and that most of the Punjab was ruled over by Sikhs. It was the British who by conquering the country for their own ends — which were trade and profit! — welded it into a cohesive whole. But their task was only made possible because they liked the people of India and that liking was returned by many — perhaps because we are all, basically, Aryans. I don't know. But I do know that, for the vast majority, the liking was mutual, which was perhaps our tragedy. I have yet to meet an ex-Indian Army officer who was not deeply devoted to his regiment and to the men who served with him or under him, or who did not grow attached to the country and look back on his years of service there with deep affection.

Chapter 18

— Ulwar sabre and Tonk *jezail* —

Tonk. That name is still an ominous one to me. As for the *jezails* — those long-barrelled, muzzle-loading muskets that were in general use among the Frontier tribes when Tacklow was a young man (and which I last saw in use long after the partition and independence of India, carried slung across the shoulder of an elderly Pathan tribesman who was buying walnuts in Torkham bazaar, a scant fifty yards from the Afghan border), they were still in evidence in Tonk when we went to live there in the winter of 1928. For Tonk was in many ways a piece of the ancient India that was still living in the past.

Most of my seasons in Kashmir remain crystal clear in my memory. Yet for some reason I cannot remember how we came to spend that particular cold weather in Tonk. I know that Tacklow had made that antique state his headquarters for some months, so that from it he could more easily visit a number of neighbouring ones, and that in the course of his stay there he had come to know its aged ruler well. Moreover, the old Nawab (the ruling house of Tonk was Muslim) had taken a great fancy to him, and had requested permission from the Government of India to engage Sir Cecil Kaye as President of Tonk's Council of State as soon as the work that he had been called back to India to do had been completed. What I am not sure about is *when* that offer had been made to Tacklow. Or, I am ashamed to say, when his work on those treaties was completed.

All that I can remember is that by invitation of the Nawab, Tacklow was in residence in one of the guest-houses in Tonk, but not yet working for the state, when Mother, Bets and I, together with Sandy Napier (who was spending a short leave in our company) and accompanied by Mahdoo and Kadera, joined him in the winter of 1928.

At a guess, I imagine that the Nawab's offer of employment must have looked like a lifeline to Tacklow. The work he had come out to do would have been almost finished, and he would have had no desire to join the ranks of those who, having spent their working lives in India, found that they could not face the prospect of retiring on a small pension to end their days in the rain and cold of England, so opted instead for a bungalow in some hill-station, or a houseboat in Kashmir, in the land (and the climate) that from long association had become home to them. If he were to stay on in India it could only be because there was still work there for him to do. And now he had been offered it by an old man whom he had come to like and to respect. But would Daisy like being buried in a medieval state, well off the beaten track? Or the girls?

Tacklow was well aware that all three of his women-folk would rather live in India than anywhere else in the world, and were dreading having to return to England and housework and the search for paid employment, which it had not occurred to their parents to fit them for. At least they were all three doing well out here with their paintings. But his daughters were not going to find husbands in Tonk. Or much social life either, since the little-known state was not even on the railway or a made road. Nor was there any electricity, which meant, among other things, no electric lights, ceiling-fans, ice-boxes or artificial means of heating or cooling. No running water or telephones either, and very little in the way of entertainment. No Viceregal balls or garden parties. No race meetings, Club dances (no Club!) or European-style shops. And certainly no art exhibitions. He had asked for time to consider the Nawab's offer, and looking back on those days I have come to think that our first stay in Tonk was really only a sort of trial-run, a visit, at the Nawab's invitation, so that we could see what we would be letting ourselves in for if Tacklow took on a full-time job there. Whatever the truth, for my part I couldn't have been more delighted because it meant, among other things, that I would be seeing a new part of the beloved country.

When Tacklow had first gone there I had been interested enough to look up the history of the state, and been charmed to discover that it had been created by the ruler of one of the more powerful and war-like Hindu states who, in India's turbulent past, had presented it as a reward to one of his *condottiere* generals — a Muslim soldier-of-fortune who had won a number of spectacular battles for him, and ended up ruling over a by no means inconsiderable portion of Rajputana with the title of Nawab of Tonk.

The history of the princely states had fascinated me ever since Tacklow had introduced me, as a twelve-year-old, to the first volume of Kipling's *Letters of Marque*, which is an account of the young Kipling's rovings as a youthful newspaper reporter in the 'Country of the Kings'. And since both Rudyard and Tacklow had made mention of Todd's *Rajasthan*, I had managed to get all four volumes of that fascinating work out of a local library in the course of a school holiday and, having read all of them at breakneck speed, become hooked on Todd* for life. Though I took a poor view of his dedication to King George the Fourth — the one-time fat and scandalous 'Prinny'. Todd was obviously riveted by the history and annals of Mewar and the Maharajahs and Ranis of the fabulous Country of the Kings, and could no more resist chronicling their doings than I could resist reading his books.

If Todd could have come back from the grave he would have felt perfectly at home in Tonk, for it was the old Rajasthan, preserved like a fly in amber. A piece of the past, left behind by the receding tide of the Mogul Empire, rather in the manner of some ancient deep-sea shell that has been stranded on the shore by a neap tide. Very little of it spoke of the twentieth century and a great deal of the past. It lay well off the beaten track, and its nearest railway station was Sawai Madhopur, itself a small town where few trains stopped and you had to change trains to get any line that would take you to Delhi or Agra.

❊ The Nawab had sent a couple of cars to meet us at the station, though this was more a polite gesture of greeting than for transport, since Tacklow had informed him that Mother and Sandy would both be driving their own cars, which they had brought from Delhi on the same train. However, we were grateful for the gesture, since it helped lighten our loads and also acted as a guide — one of the Tonk cars going ahead while the other followed in case of accidents which, judging from the state of the *kutcha* (unmade) road, must have occurred only too frequently.

The road from Sawai Madhopur to Tonk wound through miles of barren, waterless and apparently largely uninhabited land, scored all over by dried-up river-beds and stony water-courses which, in the season of the monsoon, would become subject to flash floods and turn into raging

* Lt. Col. James Todd, East India Company. One-time Political Agent to the Western Rajput States, author of *Annals and Antiquities of Rajasthan*.

torrents. A land dotted with small, stony hills and sprinkled with camel-thorn, cactus and an occasional kikar-tree whose thin, prickly foliage cast little or no shade. It was not exactly a hospitable country, and I remember that the comments of Mahdoo and Kadera, hill-men both, were far from complimentary. Sandy, too, did not think much of it. But it did not seem hostile to me, for I had always had a particular fondness for the plains: the sense of space and enormous skies — and the silence . . .

When I think of Tonk, the things that I remember return in disconnected fragments. Sometimes it is a melody that comes back. A dance tune, 'Just Imagine', that I used to play over and over again on our wind-up gramophone. Sometimes my first sight of the little city, the palace and the bazaar, viewed from the *howdah* of an elephant that the Nawab sent on our very first morning to take us on an exploration of the town. Sometimes it's a new moon, the signal of the end of Ramadan, hanging like a thread of silver in the green of an evening sky; or a row of earthenware *gurrahs* — water-jars — suspended by their narrow necks in the full glare of the blazing sun, from a rope stretched between two kikar-trees. For people still used the old way of cooling their water: by evaporation.

Having a totally un-scientific brain myself, as well as a hopelessly un-mathematical one, I have never understood why this should have worked. I can only say that one of the first things I learned in Tonk is that it *does*. If you fill your water-jar with the available tepid water, and then hang it up somewhere in the open where there is no shade, sufficient water will seep through the porous earthenware to keep the surface damp, and the hot sunlight will do its best to dry that damp. The resulting evaporation does not, as one might suppose, help to warm up the water inside, but chills it. This still sounds pure spinach to me, but it works like a charm and the egghead in your family, aged seven, will almost certainly be able to explain to you *why* it does.

Our guest-house was on top of one of the many small, conical hills that abound in Rajputana, and above it, on a slightly higher one, was the No. 1 state guest-house, where VIPs on tour put up, and where the Nawab's senior wife, 'the Begum' (as opposed to 'So-and-so Begum') occasionally threw a *zenana* party for the inmates of the women's quarters in the palace. There was another and similar house, where a Major and Mrs Meade lived, and somewhere on the fringes memory suggests a couple called Ferguson — May Ferguson? But I don't remember where they fit in, or if Mr Ferguson was the AGG from Ajmer that winter. Anyway, that concluded the Raj's section of Tonk. All else was as it must have been in the days when the first Nawab was presented with the territory, built himself a palace and seated himself on the throne.

Our house was the usual flat-roofed, whitewashed bungalow surrounded by a wide verandah with steps leading down from it on to a path that was strewn with *kunkar* — a dark, reddish, sharp-edged species of charcoal that covered all the nearby paths and was said to discourage snakes from entering the bungalows. And so it should, for it was hard and harsh enough to make it very uncomfortable to walk on in anything but stout leather shoes. Not that it was entirely successful as a discourager of snakes: in the early days of Tacklow's tenancy there was a hot night when Tacklow, wearing, he told me, nothing but a towel tied sarong-fashion round his waist, entered his bathroom with the intention of taking a cold dip in the tin tub (modern sanitation had not yet reached Tonk) and found a snake there.

Afterwards he always insisted that it was the backwardness of Tonk and the fact that there was no electricity that saved his life. Because had he been able, by pressing a switch, to flood the room with light from a bulb near the ceiling, he would not have seen the cobra until it was too late. As it was, he was alerted to its presence by the fact that he was carrying an oil lamp — a 'hurricane *butti*' — and its flaring wick, shining from much lower down, threw the enormously enlarged shadow of the menacing cobra on the wall behind it, as it swayed ominously to and fro, preparing to strike. Tacklow says he stood very still and called softly to Abdul Karim (who in the absence of Kadera — left with us in Kashmir — had returned to serve him on the strict understanding that the service was only temporary), who loaded Tacklow's shotgun and, entering cautiously behind him through a crack of the door, shot the creature's head off.

There was only one way by which it could have entered the bathroom — through the sluice which carried the bathwater away. How it had managed to cross the *kunkar* was a mystery. Abdul Karim said that it had been 'put there by an enemy' — most probably, in his opinion, the caretaker who had been in charge of the bungalow before Tacklow's arrival and who, according to Abdul, had hoped to be offered a place as the Sahib's bearer himself. Tacklow said that personally he did not see how eliminating the Sahib would help to improve his prospects of becoming that Sahib's bearer. To which Abdul merely replied darkly that on any normal occasion it would have been he himself who would have entered the *gussel-khana* first.

I used the cobra incident many years later in *Shadow of the Moon*. The very next day Tacklow had a double layer of wire netting fixed over the outer ends of all the bathroom sluices, after which we never saw another snake. Though one day one of the junior Begums was bitten by a cobra, and was treated by the Nawab's senior *hakim* in a fashion that was purely medieval . . .

A rat was caught (did they, I wonder, keep a supply of them, just in case?) and, after a deep cut had been made on the unfortunate Begum's arm, just above the double puncture marks, the rat was cut open and tied over the wound. This, we were told, was a sovereign remedy for snake-bite. And certainly that Begum lived. Though she very nearly died — not from snake-bite but from blood-poisoning. For it was during the hot weather, when snakes like to slither into cool places like bathrooms, and the corpse of the rat had gone bad in the heat.

I remember being shocked to the core by the fact that such 'witch-doctor' forms of medicine could possibly have lasted into the enlightened twentieth century, but our doctor laughed and said that behind every instance of such treatments there was sound common sense. The freshly killed rat was the ancient equivalent of a poultice, and acted in the same way — the heat drew off poison. The theory was sound, but it had been left on long enough to go bad, the fault of the hot weather. Interesting.

The Meades offered to give Bets and me riding lessons; an offer which Bets accepted with enthusiasm and I with reluctance. Bets took to it like the proverbial duck to water. But I found that I was as allergic to horses as ever. Or possibly it was the horses that were allergic to me. I struggled with the wretched creatures for a while, probably in the hope that I might suddenly become a superb rider and thereby catch the eye of some dashing cavalry man. But it was no good: I could manage the plodding little hill-ponies — the Kashmiri *tats* — all right, but I was still afraid of proper horses; the animal provided for me sensed this immediately and, despising me as a poor specimen of humanity, treated me with the utmost disdain, refusing to move until it felt like doing so, and just standing insultingly stock-still with one hip negligently thrown out in the manner of a bored fashion model. If I wanted to turn left, it turned right, and if I wanted it to trot it either broke into a canter or took off for the horizon as though shot from a catapult. Bets continued to ride, but after a few days of this I gave up the whole idea once and for all.

However I did learn to drive a car. Tonk was a marvellous place to do that in, for there was hardly any traffic. The Nawab owned an enormous selection of cars — you could say he collected them — but they seldom left the royal garages. A few of the purdah cars could be seen towards sundown, taking the *zenana* ladies for a drive along the dusty, unmetalled roads to 'eat the evening air', or members of the court and the local nobility and gentry out to shoot duck and teal on the lake or the river, or partridge and black-buck in the open country. Sometimes one would meet a lorry or a rickety bus taking innumerable passengers and their goods and chattels to some market. But such petrol-propelled traffic as there was was only to be met with in or near Tonk City and its outskirts, and once beyond that the road stretched away to left and right across the empty land, to Sirohi on one side and Sawai Madhopur on the other. Any activity on the roads was apt to be confined to the early morning and the evening, when the air was cooler and the rocks and the little hills threw shadows on the plain; and that was mostly ox-carts or horse-drawn vehicles, *tongas* or *eccers*, the occasional cyclist, and now and again a plodding group of pedestrians from one or other of the small farming communities on the plain.

It was a perfect place to be a learner driver. No traffic, and long, straight roads that seemed to stretch out before one for miles and miles. If there was anyone on the road you could see them from about a mile away, and all you had to do was to start tooting your horn as loudly as possible, whereupon, in the time-honoured manner of India, anyone walking, riding or cycling on the right-hand side of the road would decide that the left-hand side was safer, and vice versa. There would be a rush to change sides, which frequently led to confusion and collision in the middle of the road. But by the time you arrived at the spot, they would have sorted themselves out again, and you tooted gratefully and trundled on.

Driving in such circumstances was a piece of cake. But I was never any good in built-up areas, where there were no rules of the road (there still aren't) and not only was it 'every man for himself and last across the road is a chicken' but the crowded streets contained swarms of livestock and children, playing or pecking around between the feet of pedestrians and the hooves of horses, as well as sacred Brahmini bulls and the occasional cows to be avoided. I stuck to the empty highways and avoided the town as much as possible, and was fortunate enough to escape running over anything — not even a pi-dog puppy or a hen.

The Nawab proved to be a charmer, and I was not surprised that Tacklow had become so fond of the old man. We, too, became fond of him. He had a curiously pear-shaped head, adorned with a neat turban, and was small, merry and stout, though his tubbiness was partly due to the fact that the *achans* that he habitually wore — those straight, three-quarter-length coats that button down the front and are almost a uniform for middle- and upper-class India — were made of padded silk. I imagine he wore thin white cotton ones during the hot weather, since if he didn't he would have died from heatstroke, but I don't remember ever seeing him in anything but padded silk ones, and I have a vivid recollection of the day on which he arrived at our house wearing a particularly attractive one in dove-coloured silk, scattered all over with a pattern of small flowers.

It was one of the prettiest materials I had seen for a long time, and Mother, forgetting years of experience in the customs of the East, exclaimed in involuntary admiration at the sight of it. Whereupon, despite the fact that it happened to be an unusually cold day, His Highness instantly stripped off the alluring coat — displaying the skimpiest of Aertex vests tucked into a regulation pair of white-cotton jodhpurs — and gallantly presented it to my deeply embarrassed parent. Nothing would induce him to take it back, and he was instructing one of his ADCs to return immediately to the palace and fetch a replacement when Tacklow saved the day by nipping into the bedroom and reappearing with one of Mother's hand-knitted cardigans in a fetching shade of green. This in turn was presented to His Highness, who was enchanted with it, and wore it frequently during the rest of the cold weather.

Mother was equally enchanted with the coat, which she wore for many years, either as a dressing-gown or as a housecoat. When the padded lining wore out, she relined it herself with silk; and I am not at all sure that it isn't still in existence somewhere, probably shut away in one of her many boxes that are sitting in the cellar and which Bets and I have still not got around to sorting through — and I suspect never will. In which case, since things last so much longer than people, it may well turn out to be one of the very last mementoes of a dear old man of whom we were all very fond. And the last, faint echo of something that happened very long ago on a sun-drenched morning in one of the one-time princely states of Rajasthan whose hereditary powers and revenues were stripped from them years ago by the daughter of a commoner.

At some time during the early days of Tacklow's stay in Tonk, the Nawab had unexpectedly turned up at the house in the cool of the early morning and, finding Tacklow at the breakfast table, had been invited to join him. This had proved a great success and the Nawab had fallen into the habit of coming to breakfast every Sunday morning. It had also become his practice to choose the menu, and by the time Mother, Bets and I arrived in Tonk, this meal had not only achieved banquet status, but had become just as formalized as the lavish Victorian breakfasts that my Kaye grandfather insisted on having served at Upton House.* The only difference was the weirdness of the old Nawab's selection. The meal consisted of no fewer than five courses, the first being porridge, which Tacklow had happened to be eating at that first breakfast, and which His Highness had taken a fancy to — though (like me) he preferred it with sugar instead of salt. Then came tinned salmon, followed by mutton chops, chicken pilau, fried eggs accompanied by tinned sausages (beef ones — pork being unclean food for both Muslims and Hindus), tinned apricots with blancmange made with tinned milk and, to wind up with, hot buttered toast and Oxford marmalade!

Both coffee and tea were served with this gargantuan meal — Mother and Bets preferred tea and Tacklow and I coffee. The Nawab, however, having tried Rose's Lime Juice Cordial with soda, and approved of it, stuck to that. There was not, as at breakfast in Upton House, any question of choice: the Nawab ate his way through every course with undiminished enthusiasm, and expected us to do the same. We had to have a bit of everything, and Sundays became a day on which we skipped lunch! But I look back on those breakfasts with great affection, because that old man was such very good company, and because the meals were always accompanied by a great deal of laughter. And because Mahdoo was a king of cooks whose inventive sauces could make even tinned beef sausages taste delicious. I remember the Nawab telling us once, in a conspiratorial whisper just as he was leaving, how much he looked forward to Sundays. We looked forward to them too. They were the high spot of our week.

* See *The Sun in the Morning*.

His Highness did not come unattended to these Sunday 'brunches', so we always laid for two or three extra guests. Sometimes it would be one of his sons or grandsons, and sometimes a member of his Council of State, but the one who came most often was his favourite son, the eleven-year-old 'Nanhi-Mirza'. The name was, I believe, a title given to the heir-apparent and indicated that if the heir, the Sahibzada Saadat Ali Khan, had no son, he would be succeeded by his youngest brother even though there would still be two older ones. The boy was always known as 'Nunni-Mir', or 'Nunni', and Mr Meade had been appointed his guardian and English tutor. He was a nice boy; the Meades were very fond of him and the old Nawab doted upon him. But I gathered from the Tonk gossips — notably the Tikka-Sahib who was, I think, from Bhopal — that should Nunni ever succeed out of his turn, the question of his legitimacy would certainly be raised. I never really sorted out the relationships between members of that enormous royal family, since the Nawab was said to have fathered 100 children. Or so his subjects boasted, and I have no doubt it was true. The old man himself professed not to be certain: he said he had lost count.

Tonk could be distinctly chilly in mid-winter, and I remember a day when the air was cold enough for Tacklow to have unearthed a suit of brown Harris tweed. It happened to be a Sunday and the Nawab, who as usual was having breakfast with us, was fascinated by the material; he kept on leaning across to sniff at it — I believe the smell of it pleased him even more than the texture — and he was charmed to hear that the material was said to be handwoven in the cottages of crofters in the Isle of Harris in the Hebrides, and that the natural dye and peat-smoke were supposed to give it that pleasant smell. He wanted to know if Tacklow could get him a bolt of the tweed in exactly the same colour as the suit he was wearing. Tacklow wrote off to the Scotch House in London, enclosing a pattern, and in due course the bolt of Harris tweed arrived and was ceremoniously presented to the Nawab, who was simply delighted with it. Some time later, Tacklow inquired when we were going to see him wearing a coat of it, and the old man chuckled and said that he did not think we would ever see *that*. Tacklow, surprised, wanted to know why ever not, and His Highness, rolling about with mirth, said that he had had the material made into two suits of pyjamas.

Well, I suppose they were beautifully warm in the cold weather. But just imagine how *scratchy* they must have been! Unless, of course, he had them lined with silk, in which case it would have been a lot like going to sleep in a Turkish bath.

Harris tweed was not the only thing of ours that he coveted. We had acquired a seven-seater Hudson that was large enough for the whole family (including Kadera and Mahdoo and an enormous amount of luggage) to travel in. One look at this impressive vehicle and His Highness lost his heart to it. He walked round and round it, patting it, opening and shutting the doors, stepping in and out of it and trying all the seats in turn, like Goldilocks trying the Three Bears' chairs and beds, and finally getting his driver to put the hood up and down (it was an open tourer, much in vogue in the twenties). I could see Mother getting distinctly nervous and I knew she was visualizing Tacklow making a present of it to the Nawab: she was fond of the Hudson, and knew that the seven-seater models were going out of fashion and were few and far between, so that her chances of getting a replacement were slim.

The old man tore himself away from it at last and only about an hour later, when he was about to take his leave, did he ask Mother if she would consider selling it to him. He was prepared, he said, to pay her twice the price she (or rather, Tacklow!) had paid for it — or three times, if twice was not sufficient compensation for its loss. He wouldn't even *consider* Mother's suggestion that we try ordering a brand-new seven-seater car from the makers on his behalf, which would do him much better, since our car had already clocked up a good deal of mileage* — not to mention wear and tear on the tyres and the chassis. No, a new one was not what he wanted. The one he wanted was *this* one, and no other. So did Mother; and since she was not to be persuaded, His Highness left sorrowfully, giving the Hudson a final pat as he passed.

'Oh dear — !' said Tacklow, 'I'm afraid you'll have to let him have it.'

'No, I *shan't*!' retorted Mother, adding bitterly that she knew Tacklow too well to think that he would dream of accepting the Nawab's terms. In which she was right of course, for the rules against officials of the Raj accepting gifts other than perishable ones such as fruit, sweetmeats and flowers were very strict, though they were broken only too often. But not by my darling papa, who having been born honest was stuck with it. He simply did not know how to be anything else.

He wouldn't think of selling anything to his friend the Nawab, who

---

* We had bought it second-hand.

was also his employer, at a profit. That would not only be taking advantage of the old man, but would be seen by the entire population of Tonk, and certainly all the members of His Highness's enormous family, as a slick piece of bribery. So since Mother refused to part with the Hudson there was no more to be said. His Highness continued to take breakfast with us every Sunday, and each time he would ask to see the Hudson and give its bonnet an affectionate pat, as though to remind it (and us) that he hadn't forgotten it.

The whole thing began to wear Mother down, but as she knew perfectly well that we couldn't afford to part with the Hudson at its market price, and that we needed a car of that size in order to be able, when occasion demanded, to transport the lot of us — four Kayes (five if and when Bill was with us), Kadera and Mahdoo, plus our combined luggage which included Pozlo's outsize cage — she remained firm and refused to part with the car. Even when it began to look as though the weekly breakfast parties, which had been such sociable occasions, were now more in the nature of an excuse for the Nawab to take a fond look at the far from attractive object that he had fallen in love with. However, in the end a solution was found — possibly by the young Nunni-Mir, who shared his grandfather's passion for cars . . .

If it was only a question of size, surely it would be better for Mother to have *two* cars at her disposal rather than one seven-seater? (After all, her three children could all drive, and two normal-sized cars would take eight people comfortably and ten with a slight squash.) H. H.'s garages were literally stuffed with cars, all of them kept in A1-plus condition by an army of chauffeurs and their assistants, and Mother was invited to come to the palace to have a conducted tour of the garages, pick out any two cars she liked from the collection, and to do a straight swap: the seven-seater Hudson in exchange for any two other cars. Even Tacklow could hardly find fault with that.

Mother duly inspected the incredible array of cars, and heroically resisting the only chance she was ever likely to have to own a gorgeous Rolls Royce and/or a Bentley, selected a second-hand Wolseley and a small Morris Oxford. She drove the Wolseley and either Bets or I, or Bill whenever he spent a leave with us, drove the Morris Oxford. The Nawab's head chauffeur drove the Hudson away to the palace, the Nawab sitting happily in state in the centre of the back seat, smiling like the Cheshire Cat. Everyone was happy.

✣ Bill and three of his Frontier Force friends, Phil Edwards, Campbell Harris and 'Wee Andrew' Skeen, son of General Sir Andrew and Lady Maggie, arrived to spend Christmas with us, and one of the ministers took them out very early one morning, long before it was light, to sit up for a leopard that had been preying on the goats and cattle of a small village out in the *mufussal* and terrorizing the villagers, who complained that it took their animals by daylight and in full sight of them, showing no fear of man or of firearms. They were afraid it was a demon, for though the headman and the local *shikari* had both made several attempts to shoot it, their bullets had had no effect upon it. The possibility that both the headman and the *shikari* might be rotten shots had apparently not occurred to them. What *had* was that it might turn on them and become a man-eater; and hearing that there were some young sahibs holidaying in Tonk they hoped that they would be good enough to get rid of this demon for them.

A goat would be staked out as bait at a spot where there were trees in which *machans* could be built, so that the sahibs could sit up there to await the arrival of the leopard which, being fearless, would arrive with the dawning. And perhaps the bullets of the *Angrezi-log* would have more effect than their own . . . Thus the headman, Bill and friends, the minister and his *shikari*, all duly sat up in the *machans* — rough and ready platforms up among the branches that can be easily reached by any leopard, since those beautiful spotted cats are expert tree climbers — a fact that Bill confessed later that he kept on thinking about, for this was his very first taste of *shikar*. However, all went well, for the leopard had obviously come to despise the villagers whose goats and cattle provided it with such plentiful meals. Drawn by the tethered and very vocal goat, it strolled up, well after first light, to inspect this possible breakfast, and Bill shot it.

The entire party, plus corpse of leopard, turned up at the house, very pleased with themselves; and Mother photographed Bill and the 'demon' on the *kunkar*-covered drive in front of the house. If I can find a copy of that snapshot, it will be included in this book. But please, no letters from irate and virtuous 'animal rights' protesters. Just think first. Count twenty, slowly and then stop and consider. In those days — and until the very end of the Raj — the tiger and the leopard, the elephant, the black-buck and the white rhino, and indeed every species of animal — even the great bow-head whale — were in no danger of extinction. There were any number of them, and far, far fewer humans. It is only of late that the appalling population explosion of one species, *ours*, has led to every peasant who can afford one reaching for his gun and axe and a box of matches, in order to kill everything that eats his crops or preys on his livestock, and to chop down or set on fire the jungle that was its natural habitat. Did I say something of the sort in the first volume of my autobiography? Oh well, it bears repeating.

The main thing I remember about Christmas Day was that a *fu-fu* band from the town (hired for our benefit by one of the ministers) appeared before the bungalow in the dawn, to serenade us on our festival day. A very kindly thought, and much appreciated — though personally, jerked out of sleep by the incredible din that any *fu-fu* band can produce without even trying, I was not as grateful as I should have been. The band was accompanied by a few *nautch*-girls, who danced for us in the little *bara-durri* — the audience hall (see snapshot) that was attached to the house. One of the girls — she could not have been more than fourteen or fifteen — was a *very* pretty thing indeed, but the others were elderly and fat, and not in the least like my romantic idea of an Indian dancing girl. There was also, as an added attraction, a dancing bear and its bear-leader, which successfully ruined the whole show for me.

I had seen dancing bears before (there have always been too many of them in India), but only as a child, and Punj-ayah had never allowed us to go too near them. This one was the first I had ever approached. It was a sad and ragged bear, whose fur was matted and thick with dust, and as I came close to it I saw with horror that the lead chain, one end of which was held in its owner's hand, hung from an iron ring that had been thrust through a hole pierced through its nose, and that the hole was raw and bleeding. The bear reared up at a signal, and tottered about on its hind legs in time to the beat of a drum, and when it tried to stop its owner jerked angrily on the chain and the poor thing screamed and put its forepaws over its sore nose. I shrieked at the bear-leader, using every bad word that I could think of, and tore off up the path to the house in floods of tears to fetch Tacklow and beg him to *do* something — buy the bear, or have its owner arrested, or fined, or, preferably, beaten until he screamed as the poor bear had screamed. But to do *something*.

The bewildered bear-leader found himself on the receiving end of a tongue-lashing from the sahib that he probably never forgot, and Tacklow (who really should have been a vet or an animal trainer) sent for warm water and swabs, a bottle of Dettol and a pot of some soothing ointment, and while the bear's owner stared in astonishment, set about bathing the poor creature's nose, patting it dry and smoothing on ointment, all of which the bear accepted in the spirit in which it was done, without attempting to snap or even wince away from this strange but kindly hand. It just stood there as though it had known Tacklow all its life, and knew that this human could be trusted — probably the only one it was ever to meet that could, poor creature. I remember that Tacklow talked to the bear the entire time, and that it actually appeared to be listening.

Turning his attention again upon the bear's astounded owner (plus, by this time, a large and interested audience), Tacklow demanded to know if he had never heard the tale of the cruel bear-owner, and launched into a lurid tale concerning a man who in the days when Raja Jaichand was King of Benares made his living by travelling the country with a monkey and a bear that he had captured in the forest and taught, by means of great cruelty, to dance and do tricks. Then one day, while the captive creatures moaned and wept because they had been given nothing to drink for many hours and were parched with thirst, their owner settled down to sleep away the hot hours of the day in the shade of a mango tope without noticing that on the far side of a tree to which he had chained his animals there was a small pile of stones and branches that was a shrine of the Jungle Mother, Banaspati Mâî. The goddess, too, was asleep, for it was the hottest time of the day, but the moans of the bear and the weeping of the monkey woke her, and when she heard their tale and learned that they had been given neither food nor drink since the previous day, she enlisted the help of Hanuman, the monkey god, who called upon his people to rescue and avenge their brother, while she herself did the same for the bear. The *bandar-log* (the monkey-people) stole the keys from the sleeping man and, having released the suffering creatures, took their erstwhile owner captive in their place, chaining him and dragging him away into the forest, where they and the bear-folk treated him as he had treated their brothers, making him dance and do tricks for their amusement and biting or clawing him when he stumbled or fell or did not instantly obey them. They denied him food and drink for days at a time until his tongue turned black and he could not speak or scream for the dryness in his throat, and became mad with thirst. And always the bears and the *bandar-log* sat around in their hundreds, watching him and ordering him to dance for them — not as men dance, but as the *bandar-log* dance, on all fours, just as he had made his monkeys and the bear dance on their hind legs, burning them with hot irons when they tired. And so for many years they kept him prisoner, and only when at last he became too old and feeble to dance for them did they turn him loose to die of hunger in the forest . . .

'So be warned by his fate,' said Tacklow severely, 'for who knows but that one day one of the gods may overhear the cries of these poor beasts of yours, and deal with you as Banaspati Mâî and Hanuman dealt with the cruel master? And even if they do not, you may be very certain that when your time comes to die, the gods will see to it that you are reborn as a bear who will be captured by someone who will treat you exactly as you have been treating this one. Now take the *dewai* (medicine) and use it as I have done until the *baloo*'s* nose is no longer sore. And if I hear that you have not done so, I will petition the Nawab-Sahib to have you thrown into jail.'

The bear's owner grovelled in the dust, promising faithfully to look after his *baloo* in future like the doting father and mother of an only child, and backed away down the drive, salaaming at every step and looking scared out of his wits. Tacklow, forestalling what he knew I was about to say, got in first and said, a shade testily, 'No, we *can't* buy his bear. What would we do with it? Do have some sense, Mouse!' And, of course, he was right: it wasn't feasible. But oh, the tragedy of those bears! There are more of them now than ever, and the last time I was in Agra and drove out to take yet another nostalgic look at Fatehpur-Sîkrî, there seemed to be one of the wretched creatures — taken from their cool Himalayan forests to spend the rest of their lives in the dust and the terrible, glaring heat of the Indian sun — every 200 yards of the way. It hurts one just to *think* of it.

I told Tacklow that I couldn't remember hearing that story of the cruel owner and the performing animals before, and he laughed and said that he was not surprised, since he had invented it on the spur of the moment, there being nothing like a parable for putting across a message, and he thought it might even stick in the mind of that bear's owner with more effect than any threat, and make him watch his step. I do pray that it did.

* *Baloo*: bear. Pronounced *Ba*-loo. Not, as by Disney, b' *Loo*.

Chapter 19

~❊❊❊❊~

There were several shooting parties that Christmas, consisting of the Heir the Sahibzada Saadat, and half a dozen of his friends, the Meades and ourselves, and Bill and his friends. We would drive out of an evening into the open country, stopping off at a spot selected by the local *shikari*, who would meet us there accompanied by the headman of the nearest village and several villagers, leave the cars and, having spread out into a thin line across the plain, walk forward in the warm evening light that drew long blue shadows on the stony ground from the thorn scrub and datura bushes and the tall, dry clumps of pampas grass, while above us the setting sun freckled the sky with bright gold or peach-pink shreds of cloud, and the partridges began to call from the cover of the scrub.

Those 'rough shoots' were among the pleasantest things about Tonk, for they reminded me of the shooting camps of my childhood years when Bets and I, one each side of Kashmera, would follow behind the guns as they walked up game-birds across the scrublands on the far side of the river at Okhla. Here, as there, the line would walk forward, the guns separated from each other by about fifty yards, while the rest of us — Mother, Mrs Meade, Bets and myself, the *shikari* and the villagers — walked either alongside one of them or somewhere in between. The line would put up partridge and quail, pigeons, pea-fowl and snipe and the occasional duck or guinea-fowl. Sometimes a hare, and once or twice a leopard — though these last were allowed to lope away unharmed, as was the occasional porcupine. At the end of the evening, when the sun had set and the first stars began to glimmer in the sky, we would walk back to the cars and distribute the bag between the guns, the *shikari* and the villagers.

Tacklow seldom took a gun out with him on these rough shoots, for as I have said elsewhere he was an indifferent shot; except, oddly enough, when it came to snipe, which are supposed to be among the most difficult of birds to shoot. But he would miss far more of the slower birds than he hit, and instead took the opportunity of walking alongside Bill, of whom he had seen very little of late. Bill, seizing the first chance he had had of having a private word with his father, confessed that he had become involved in what he described as 'rather a sticky situation' and was badly in need of help and advice.

Bill had arrived in Tonk in such an unusually subdued frame of mind that even the prospect of bagging a leopard had done little to cheer him, and when I inquired as to the reason for this gloom, he admitted that he had got himself into an 'awful jam', but that talking about it wasn't going to help, so would I just shut up. I remember leaping to the conclusion that he had got himself embroiled with some unsuitable cutie (1920s slang for 'bimbo') and was wondering how to get rid of her — Bill was always falling in love with some girl or other. He had been doing so ever since his preparatory school days, but they never lasted long. However, he said crossly that this was serious. It was, too.

I no longer remember the details of the drama. But it seems that a friend of Bill's, a fellow subaltern, who had been living beyond his means and got himself badly into debt, had taken to writing cheques that he knew would bounce. He had come to an arrangement with his bank (or, more likely, a money-lender) to lend him enough money to pay off his debts, with the proviso that the sum must be repaid, plus a fairly exorbitant interest, within a stated time, but since he appeared to be a bad risk he had to get some friend to stand surety for the loan and repay it if he himself failed to do so. He had asked Bill to stand surety, assuring him that there was not the *slightest* risk involved — all that he would have to do was sign a bit of paper to this effect, and long before the date on which it must be repaid came round he, the friend, would have paid it in full, for he had already cabled his father and followed it up with an express letter explaining the whole situation. So Bill need have no anxiety about the money not being repaid, and he would have saved his friend from getting into serious trouble with his regiment, who might well cashier him. Bill, of course, signed. 'I couldn't possibly have done anything else, could I?' protested Bill, defensively, telling me all. 'How *could* I have said "no", when poor old — Phil or Tim or Jim or whoever — was in such a hole? And how could I *possibly* have known that his old skinflint of a father would let him down by sending him a "let this be a lesson to you" lecture instead of the money?'

I remember inquiring priggishly if it had not crossed his tiny mind that it was not only stupid, but downright dishonest to put his signature to a solemn promise that he *must* have known he couldn't possibly keep, if he were called upon to do so. Whereupon Bill bit my head off, but had the grace to confess that it never occurred to him for a moment that it would come to that. Now that it had, the only thing he could think of was to tell the whole sad story to Tacklow — which was, he admitted, the main reason why he had suggested that he plus a couple of friends should spend their Christmas leave in Tonk — in the hope that Tacklow would be able to think of some solution to the problem; in other words lend him enough money to pay off the money-lender. But now he had begun to wonder what would happen to him if *his* father, too, should prove as flinty-hearted as his friend's had been, and had spent sleepless nights trying to summon up the courage to break the news. I assured him that Tacklow would never behave like that, and urged him to 'tell all' and get it over with, instead of trailing around with a face like the chief mourner at a funeral. But poor Bill hardly knew Tacklow, and since his confidence in fathers had been badly shaken by the behaviour of his friend's parent, it took him some little time to screw up his courage and come out with the whole sad story.

Poor Tacklow. He had so hoped to be able to save some of the money that the Government of India had paid him for his work on the Treaties, but the extra expense of bringing his family out to India with him, and paying for their keep and expenses in Delhi and Kashmir, and buying the Hudson, had absorbed every anna of it; and now the 'rainy day' money he hoped to put aside from his salary as President of the Council of State in Tonk, plus anything else he could raise, was going to have to go towards paying off this outrageous debt contracted by his son. For he paid it, of course. There was nothing else he could do, since Bill was of age and could not plead that he did not understand what he was letting himself in for. I don't remember, after all these years, what the actual sum was; it would, in any case, probably seem laughably modest these days. But at that time it seemed to me enormous. I couldn't see *how* he was going to raise it, and had visions of him getting caught in the same sort of trap that Bill was in. But Mother said that he had arranged for an overdraft, something he had previously always steered clear of, and that with the help of that and his savings, it would be managed. But we would all have to try to economize for some time to come.

An unnecessary warning, since I don't remember a time when we didn't!

The incident was never mentioned again, and now that he knew he was off the hook Bill's spirits rose as dramatically as though a tangible weight had been lifted off his shoulders, and the rest of that Christmas holiday was a great success.

I never heard if Bill's friend ever repaid the money or not; if he did, it would only have been in dribs and drabs and over a long interval, for a subaltern's pay was far from lavish, and since the young man in question was one of those breezy and ebullient types with a fondness for horses and gambling, and a tendency to 'play it off the cuff', it is my guess (without wishing to be uncharitable) that he quite genuinely forgot all about it after a few months, and left Tacklow holding the baby. Bill certainly never paid it.

✕ The Raj, as I have already mentioned, had formed a habit of holding 'Weeks' during the cold weather — 'Lahore Week', 'Calcutta Week', 'Lucknow Week' and so on. These 'Weeks' consisted of several days of non-stop socializing and festivity which included gymkhanas, racing, polo tournaments, a military tournament and any number of parties and dances attended by all the prettiest members of the Fishing Fleet — the 'Week Queens' who had a beau in every Cavalry Cantonment in India. The greatest of these 'Weeks' was the 'Horse Show Week' in Delhi, which, apart from the Horse Show itself, was crammed with entertainment that included a huge Viceregal garden party, dances, a ball at Viceroy House and another, always a lavish fancy-dress affair, at the IDG — the Imperial Delhi Gymkhana Club.

Tacklow had already arranged for Mother, Bets and me to spend three weeks in Delhi, which included the Horse Show, but following Bill's disclosure it seemed highly unlikely that we would be able to attend. However, after an anxious interval in which a great deal of calculation and much scribbling of sums on the back of envelopes went on, Tacklow took a deep breath, increased his overdraft to danger-point, and decided that we could just manage it. Mother had already written to 'Aunt Bee' Lewis — the combative spinster who had had charge of us during our years of exile in an English boarding-school, and now lived in Southampton — sending my measurements and asking her to buy me a really pretty dress for the Viceregal Ball. It would be the first 'ready-made' dress that

207

I had ever possessed, since all the previous ones had been run up by some 'little woman round the corner'.

This extravagant garment (I believe it cost all of £15 including the postage) would certainly have been countermanded if it had not already been bought and posted, and Mother fell back on the verandah *darzi* for the rest of our dresses, for the materials for which we went shopping in the cloth shops in Tonk's bazaar.

I remember I designed a ball dress for myself in a very cheap green satin and yards of mosquito netting that the proprietor of the shop had dyed exactly to match. Skirts were still short and waists still ignored, so it had a long bodice, with a full skirt that started about mid-hip and consisted of short 'handkerchief points'. But in order to conceal as much as possible of those piano legs, I had a wide hem of the green-dyed net edging the green satin points. It was a great success, and I cherished for years a newspaper cutting from the society gossip column of the *Civil and Military Gazette*, which reported both the Viceregal Ball and the Horse Show Ball that year, and included a reference to Miss M. Kaye: 'looking very pretty in a ravishing green satin and net confection, which was quite the prettiest dress at the ball'. *Did* I preen myself next morning! I kept that cutting until it literally fell to pieces. It was the high spot of the year for me.

I bought yards of shimmering pale blue Bokhara silk, shot with lavender, which the enthusiastic *darzi* made up into a Louis Quinze-style ballgown on the lines of the one that Madame de Pompadour wears in the pastel portrait of her by Maurice Quentin de la Tour, with the difference that in place of embroidery, I painted a design of garlands and flowers in oil paint. The material took it wonderfully, and the *darzi* contrived a magnificent Louis Quinze crinoline out of whippy slivers of bamboo and two-anna-a-yard muslin, which we dipped in rice-water starch. It made the most gorgeous, though ephemeral, fancy dress, and was as great a success at the IDG's big fancy-dress ball as that green satin and mosquito-net confection had been at the Viceregal Ball. The only disaster was Aunt Bee's expensive off-the-peg model. But that story comes later.

Fortified by our bazaar-bought and *darzi*-made finery, Mother, Bets and I, accompanied by Kadera, set off for Delhi; this time, in the interests of economy, in the Wolseley. Thereby saving ourselves the price of four train tickets and the cost of railing the car. Tacklow had been a bit doubtful about this, but Mother, having pored over a selection of road maps and asked the advice of any number of local citizens who professed to be familiar with every road, track and river crossing within a radius of a hundred miles, was quite sure that we could get ourselves and the car to Delhi. We started off bravely, weighed down to the gunwales with bedding rolls and baggage.

For the first hour or so we drove along something which could, at a pinch, have been called a road, but which, without any warning, suddenly petered out into a sandy track that meandered off into nowhere between walls of casuarina shrub. Mother followed it, *faute de mieux*, for about a mile, until it, too, vanished in a waste of sand, and we were not only lost but found ourselves in a spot where there did not appear to be a sign of habitation for miles around.

It is almost impossible to imagine finding oneself in a similar 'Empty Quarter' in the India of the present day, and from what I have seen of it and its exploding population I don't think that there can be any left. But even in those far-off days one could always be certain that if only you were patient and prepared to wait for a while, sooner or later, in even the loneliest and most desolate tract of land, a wandering goatherd and his flock, or some lone traveller on foot, would appear out of the sun-glare and the shimmering heat-haze that lay like a vast expanse of shallow water across the empty plain, reflecting rocks and thorn scrub, kikar-trees and pampas, so that they seemed to float like ships or islands on a glassy sea.

There was no point in turning back, or ploughing on into the sandy waste, without even a compass to show us which way to go. So Mother pulled up in the scant shade of a clump of casuarina, Kadera spread a travelling rug on the sand and brought out the picnic basket, and we all sat down and ate sandwiches and Mahdoo's superlative curry puffs, drank orange squash from Thermos flasks and waited for rescue. Which duly arrived in the form of an elderly gentleman, armed with a *lathi* and balancing a large bundle on his head, who had been attending a local fair and was returning to his village. The trackless plain held no mystery for him, and he was delighted to be offered a lift home in the car — he had never ridden in one before, he said. Bets and I crammed in together alongside Mother, Kadera and our rescuer and his bundle took over the back, and the expedition pushed on.

I use the word 'pushed' with intent, because that is what we did for most of the next mile or so; the sand got deeper and deeper, and Mother kept on stopping while Kadera, Bets and myself and our passenger got out to tear branches of casuarina and sheaves of pampas grass which we spread in front of the wheels before pushing the Wolseley out of a particularly intractable patch of sand. It was hot and exhausting work; and worse was to come, for our passenger informed us that we had to ford an unbridged river. At this point even Mother began to consider turning round and going back. But our passenger was made of sterner stuff, and he urged us to press on. His village, he said, was only a short distance away from the far bank of the river, and he would wade across and fetch help in the form of ropes and volunteers to push and/or shove. So on we went.

The river, when we reached it, was less of a hazard than we'd feared, for there had been no rain for at least two months and it had shrunk considerably. The main channel was not more than five yards wide and barely two feet deep at the ford. But, judging from the wide expanse of silver sand on either side of the water, it was a good deal wider and deeper when in flood, and it was this sand that was the trouble. It took what seemed like hours to get the car across it, and we should never have done it without the help provided by our passenger, who, as he had promised, waded across, and after disappearing over the higher ground that lay on the other side — leaving us sitting collapsed in the small patch of shade provided by the car — eventually reappeared accompanied by about ten or fifteen stalwart villagers armed with ropes and a horde of fascinated children, the majority of whom were barely knee-high to a beetle.

I fancy that they must have become used to rescuing stranded motorists, for they went smoothly into action. There was a good deal of noise, but no arguments as to how to tackle the problem; and after an endless interval of shouts and yells of encouragement, the Wolseley was pushed, tugged and half carried across the powdery sand and on to the firm wet sand at the river's edge. Mother, terrified of flooding the engine, drove with extreme caution across the ford, and encouraged by shouts of advice from her squad of helpers, and delighted squeals from the chorus of cherubim, took the shallows on the far side at speed; aided by those who manned the ropes, she managed to cover quite an appreciable distance on the dry sand on the opposite side before getting stuck again. However, we were across!

Once free of the sand we soon reached the village, where the women offered us cups of milk, fruit and freshly cooked chapattis, and — like most women in a country of small outlying villages — were friendly and forthcoming, once they had got over their shyness, asking a hundred questions, laughing themselves into stitches at Bets's and my stumbling attempts at Hindustani, and congratulating Mother on her fluency in their tongue. Bets and I taught the assembled cherubim 'Little Miss Muffet',* in the vernacular, which was very popular. All in all it was quite a party, and I remembered it when, much later on, I heard horror stories about travellers who had attempted to drive over country where there was no main road, and been practically held to ransom by 'simple villagers' who demanded enormous sums, paid in advance, before they would give any help. At no time did these people, most of whom had probably never seen a white face before, so much as *hint* that they would like to be paid for their help. They had given it out of pure good-heartedness — as they gave the food and drink. Mother hadn't got much money with her, but she gave our passenger — who had to be pressurized to take it — as much as she could spare, and asked him to distribute it to the helpers who had got us across the ford; and he insisted on coming with us to set us on our way and see that we did not miss a field track that would take us on to a passable road.

We parted with him with regret, and ploughed on across unmapped country, hoping for the best; and luck was with us, for towards sunset we actually managed to reach civilization in the form of a little Dâk-bungalow, where we put up for the night and ate the familiar Dâk-bungalow dinner of 'a couple of Chapattis and a *murgi* grill'. (There was once a topical song sung by the comic in a musical comedy put on by the Simla Amateur Dramatic Society at the Gaiety Theatre, in which every verse ended with that line. Tacklow used to sing it to us. But although I can remember the tune to this day, those are the only words that survive.)

Once again we would be sleeping under canvas in New Delhi, for the members' quarters at the IDG had been booked out for Horse Show Week, and the overflow were put up in tents. Our particular tents were not even in the Club grounds, but on the racecourse a short distance away. That was a lovely interval. A brief taste of fun and glamour after a

* *Muffety Mai bhaiter hai*
  Dood or roti karter . . .
  Burra s'muckra cupera puckera
  Bargia Muffety Mai!
      (Punj-ayah's version)

spell in the wilds of Rajputana and life as it must have been lived by members of the East India Company a century and more ago.

Our tents were spread out under the shade of a line of gold-mohur trees, and separated from the rails of the race track only by a gravel path and a strip of lawn. We would be awakened in the brilliant Indian dawn, clamorous with birdsong and glittering with dew, by horsy friends who started each day by riding on the racecourse and would draw rein when opposite our tents and shout to us to wake up. And every morning, as I scrambled out of bed and into a dressing-gown, and ran out to greet them, I used to congratulate myself smugly on the fact that however late I had gone to sleep on the previous night — or rather the small hours on that same day! — I always looked my best first thing in the morning: I could thank the Lord for a Grade A complexion that didn't need any make-up to improve it, and was probably given me in compensation for a regrettable figure.

I don't remember the names or faces of any of the young men I danced with during that glamorous Horse Show Week, so I presume that for once I wasn't in love. Yet I do remember having a perfectly lovely time. This, once again, was the Raj at play; and it was wonderful to be young and to be part of it, with all of life ahead of you. The whole of Delhi smelt of flowers. Sweet peas and carnations, delphiniums and roses, pinks, hibiscus, jasmine and orange-blossom grew and flourished in every garden, while bougainvillaea and trumpet-flower poured over rooftops and walls in a blaze of colour; and when darkness fell the air was heavy with the sweetness of night-scented stock, moon flowers and *Rhat-ki-Rani*; and always, somewhere within hearing, a dance band or a gramophone would be playing the sweet, sugary melodies of that era: 'You Were Meant for Me', 'You're the Cream in My Coffee', 'The Birth of the Blues', 'What'll I Do?', 'Always', and 'Fancy Our Meeting' . . . Odd how they still come back after so many long years.

Bob Targett was still around, and I danced with him and laughed with him, but realized that Tacklow had been right: I wasn't his type of woman at all, and I would never have been a success as his wife. Bets and I struck up a lasting friendship with the wife of Alan Riley, A. I. R. Riley, who ran the Delhi Flying Club. His wife, who was Dutch (her maiden name had been Van Oz), had been nicknamed 'Ooloo' long before she set foot in India, where *Ooloo* means 'owl', and is widely used as a term of abuse — 'You son of an owl!' However, 'Ooloo' stuck and a more inappropriate name for the witty, amusing, beautiful (she was like the young Lauren Bacall) and attractive wife of A. I. R. Riley you couldn't imagine. We both loved her dearly — as did almost everyone she knew, and we saw a lot of her, since she and Alan lived in one of the Club Quarters. Dear Ooloo! — how you used to make me laugh. You had a lot to do with making my stay in Delhi, and the Horse Show in particular, a memorable time in my life.

I have, as I have said before, never had any use for horses. I took a dislike to them from an early age, and since I am also no gambler, race meetings have never been my cup of tea. I have attended a good many, but only because I have been taken by some friend whose company I enjoy, and who seems to think he is doing me a good turn by taking me to see a sport that he is sure I must enjoy as much as he does. And because I have lacked the nerve to blot my social copybook by admitting that race meetings leave me cold — except (there is always an exception) when I happen to be personally acquainted with at least half of the amateur jockeys, and know the rest, together with most of my fellow race-goers, by sight. Only then does the whole jamboree become entertaining to me. Which is why I actually enjoyed the Delhi races.

To give an example of their unique entertainment value, there was the occasion when a friend of ours, one McCandlass (better known as 'Loopy Mac'), whose enthusiasm for riding was not matched by his skill, when competing in an owner-riders race sponsored by the business community, came tearing into view on the first lap and, to wild cheering from his supporters, a full two and a half lengths ahead of the field. Unfortunately there was a narrow side track ahead of him — possibly for the benefit of any rider who had lost a stirrup or otherwise come to grief and wished to retire from the race. But since his horse was in fact bolting, and not even faintly under control, it made straight for the side track and tore off down it — followed by the entire field, who either thought this was the correct way round, or whose horses had also got the bit between their teeth and intended to forge ahead or else . . . The whole lot, following Mac's lead, shot off the course and disappeared with the speed of diving ducks into a fairly dense patch of wooded land, which at that time bordered one side of the course. After lengthy but unknown adventures, they eventually emerged, looking exceedingly sheepish, wreathed in strands of creeper and assorted greenery and brushing twigs and bits of bark out of their hair.

There was also a more dramatic occasion when one of the amateur jockeys parted with his mount a mere yard or two from the winning post, and crashed to earth among a forest of hooves. At which point a girl rose like a rocketing pheasant from her seat in the stand, and, shrieking his name over and over again, fled down the aisle and across the grass, scrambled over the rails, and, still screaming, flung herself down on his recumbent form yelling, 'Speak to me, Johnny! *Speak to me!*' Whereupon his wife broke the deathly silence that had fallen upon the stands by tutting impatiently and remarking in a carrying voice: 'Silly bitch! He'll never forgive her for this.' I gather she had got used to her husband's frequent straying and come to terms with it.

You didn't get those sort of dramas included in the price of the tickets during Ascot week or Newmarket. The only tragicomedy of that exciting Horse Show Week was provided by the 'ballgown' that Aunt Bee had selected for me much earlier and posted weeks ago to mother, c/o the Imperial Delhi Gymkhana Club.

It had been waiting for us in the Secretary's office, and proved to be a dazzling confection in heavy white *crêpe de Chine*, lavishly embroidered with glimmering silver beads, each one shaped like a daisy and attached to the material by a small central bead. It really was the prettiest thing, and did credit to Aunt Bee's taste; for, frankly, I had been dreading the arrival of some flouncy thing in pale pink with a high neck, puffed sleeves and frills in all the wrong places, 'suitable for a young girl'. I regretted that it wasn't longer, for hems, after a decade of twenties knee-length-or-above fashions, were at long last beginning to edge downward, which was good news for girls like myself whose legs were far from shapely. I had rather hoped that the London shops would by now have taken the plunge and opted for long skirts, even though the Raj had not yet got around to them. I also regretted (not for the first time) that I wasn't a lot slimmer, for those shimmering daisy-heads (I have one or two of them to this day) did tend to make me look slightly like a stranded salmon. Still, it was not only an attractive garment, but one that was definitely not *darzi*-made, and I set off for the Viceregal Ball feeling definitely pleased with myself.

It was the custom for Delhi hostesses to give large dinner parties prior to the Viceregal Ball, and although I don't remember who my hostess was, I do remember that her house was in Old Delhi, not far from Maiden's Hotel and the Kudsia Bagh, that there were two unexpected guests who had arrived in Delhi only that day — I think relations — and since there were not enough dining-room chairs to go round, an extra two were hastily brought down from the bedrooms or wherever, and that I, as the most junior member of the party, was given one of them, a cane-bottomed chair of local manufacture.

I enjoyed that dinner party. My partner was a young man I knew, and the one on the other side was a cheerful and chatty type, and the conversation flowed like Tennyson's brook. It was only when the meal was over and our hostess rose, signalling that the ladies would now remove themselves to drink coffee in the drawing-room and queue up for the dressing-tables and the bathrooms on the upper floor, that disaster struck.

Turning from left to right and back again, to talk to one or other of the fellow guests I was seated between, I had not noticed (it had not occurred to me to even think of it), that those glittering little daisies had worked their way through the holes in the basketwork seat of my chair. It was only when I attempted to rise, and found that I couldn't, that I realized what had happened. And by that time it was too late, for one of those gallant young men had sprung forward and helpfully jerked my chair away. There was a rending noise, and I stood up. But with a large, blank, daisyless patch on my behind and between sixty or seventy glittering daisies strewn all over the carpet. One of life's darker moments.

Mother shrieked in horror and my hostess in sympathy, while *khitmatgars* and guests scrabbled around picking up the twinkling pieces of the fallen flowers. But it was no good; the dress was a total write-off and there was no way I could go on to the Viceregal Ball wearing that ruin, since apart from that daisyless patch on its seat, the *crêpe de Chine* had been ripped in several places, giving the assembled company a private view of my petticoat and camiknickers. There was nothing for it but to streak for home and change into another dress. One of my fellow guests nobly offered to run me back to my tent on the race course and I accepted the offer thankfully; once there, I changed hurriedly into the green-satin-and-dyed-mosquito-netting confection that had already received an Hon. Mensh. in the social columns — and which anyway, suited me a lot better than those daisies — and we arrived, late and panting, well after the remainder of our party, but otherwise in good shape.

That was my first look at the finished and furnished Viceroy House and I thought it an enormous improvement on the old Viceregal Lodge in Old Delhi. It was the most magnificent building; something out of a fairy-tale, with its sweeping stairway of white marble — open to the sky. Its huge corridors lined with uniformed men of the Viceroy's Bodyguard of tall splendid Sikhs, all of whom in their towering turbans looked to be at least seven or eight feet high. There were not only flowers in the Mogul gardens, but in every room and all the long corridors, reflecting themselves, together with the dancing guests, in the black marble walls of the great ballroom, which had been polished until they resembled sheets of black looking-glass. I could see myself in them waltzing to the strains of 'Always' or 'Alice Blue Gown' and laughing because life was such tremendous fun — in spite of the ruination of my first expensive evening dress, and having to arrive late at the ball. Tacklow used to be fond of quoting a verse from *The Ingoldsby Legends*, Barham's translation of Horace's '*Eheu fugaces, . . . Postume, Postume!*' 'Years glide away, and are lost to me, lost to me!' except that they are not lost to me. That ball in the new Viceroy's House is still, with much else, a glittering fragment that remains clear and bright in my memory.

It was in that same cold weather season that one of the many practical jokes, with which Sir Edwin Lutyens had booby-trapped his Viceroy's palace, went off with startling success on the occasion of the first New Delhi Viceregal garden party. Sir Edwin had decorated each corner of the roofs of the two wings of the house with enormous shallow bowls of red sandstone on short stems, each one standing in a marble, or possibly sandstone saucer. The bowls were in fact fountains which, when turned on, filled up with water which brimmed over and fell in a silver veil into the saucers below, from where it was recycled to fill the bowls again, or else rerouted to water the gardens. I had seen them tried out on a hot still day the year before, and thought how very pretty they looked, and what an original and brilliant idea they were.

Brilliant, my Aunt Fanny! I don't believe for a moment that the old boy didn't know exactly what would happen, and probably regretted not being there to laugh his head off when it did. For half-way through that particular garden party, a light breeze got up . . .

Well, I don't need to describe what happened, you can visualize it for yourself. All those pretty, frilly, diaphanous silks and muslin confections, those fabulous embroidered saris and the elegant wide-brimmed hats, the crisp, starched muslin turbans, the top-hats, and the gaudy uniforms of the ADCs on the stretch of garden nearest the house, scattering like leaves in an autumn gale, and stampeding for cover.

⚹ Mother, Bets and I spent a lovely three weeks in New Delhi. But back in Tonk, tragedy had struck darling Tacklow. He had put Pozlo back into his cage after his usual evening walk, but for once forgot to put the cover over it, which he normally did after sunset, since Pozlo preferred to sleep in the dark. Just at that moment one of the Nawab's relatives had dropped in to pay an informal call on him, and Tacklow merely closed the cage door and hurried out to greet his visitor. The caller did not stay very long, and having seen him into his car, and watched it leave, Tacklow came back into the drawing-room and was about to call for the lamps to be lit when he heard a sudden frantic squawk from Pozlo, and hurrying into the dining-room (where the doors, like all those in the bungalow, were set wide, for the weather was beginning to warm up) saw that there was a wild cat clawing at the cage and that Pozlo was lying on the floor of it. The cat streaked out of the room but Pozlo was dead ... He had gone to sleep as always, with his head tucked between his wings, on the perch nearest the top of his cage, and by a sad stroke of bad luck, too near the bars of his cage. The sun had gone down and dusk was gathering in the rooms, and he had not heard the cat, which had clawed at him with a taloned paw. It was sheer chance that one of those talons had pierced the back of Pozlo's fluffy little head, and killed him instantly — he had only had time for that one squawk as he died.

It is almost impossible not to grow fond of an animal or a bird that obviously dotes upon you, and Pozlo had made it plain from the start where his heart and devotion belonged. No one could have resisted such patent adoration, and Tacklow became devoted to that endearing little bunch of green feathers. When he had had to leave us in Kashmir and go down to Rajputana, he had insisted on taking Pozlo with him — 'to keep me company'. And Pozlo had done just that. And now he was gone.

Tacklow was devastated. I really think he could not have been as shocked and bereft if it had been one of his children who had been killed. At first he couldn't believe it, and tried to revive the little bird with brandy, and when he realized that there was nothing he could do, he fetched his gun, went out to look for the wild cat which had retreated to the rock-strewn waste land behind the kitchen quarters, and shot it. Even though he liked cats. He cried for Pozlo as, more than forty years later, I too was to cry bitterly over the death of an even smaller piece of fluff and feathers — a little budgerigar named Hamlet whom I had adopted practically from the egg, and who, after a few years of devoted companionship, I had to have put down, because he had acquired a cancerous growth that was killing him painfully. I remembered Tacklow that day, and I knew how he must have felt: except that it had been much worse for him, for he must have been so lonely and Pozlo had been such an adoring companion — spending most of the working day perched on his shoulder, snuggled up close to the curve of his neck, from which vantage point he would reach up occasionally to nibble lovingly at Tacklow's ear, or growl reprovingly and inquire, when anyone else came into the room, '*Now* what?' (a phrase I am afraid he had picked up in his early days from me, when I was busy and did not welcome interruption).

Chapter 20

~⚜~

In spite of being born and spending the first years of my life in India, I still had no idea what a hot weather in the plains can be like — let alone a hot weather in the plains of Rajputana. It was something that I was about to find out from personal experience; for though Tacklow's contract was exceedingly generous on the matter of leave (to all intents and purposes allowing him, as far as I could see, to take as much as he liked, whenever he felt like it), certain matters connected with the state *and* needing his attention had cropped up, and until they were sorted out and settled, it was impossible for him to leave Tonk. And as Mother would not go without him, and we could not go without her, we all stayed on well into the hot-weather months.

It was an experience that I would be called upon to endure many times in the future, and one that I never got used to. But this was not only the first time, but quite the worst, largely due to the fact that there was no electricity in Tonk. Therefore no fans, no fridge (they hadn't been invented yet), no ice. And in place of sixty-watt bulbs, there were only kerosene lamps and the occasional Petromax, both of which hissed and flared and generated enough heat to make the hot rooms a great deal hotter.

Outside, the sun blazed down out of a cloudless sky that was not blue, as it is during the months of the cold weather, but a curious washed-out steel-grey; and during most of the day, between an hour after the sun rose and an hour before it set, the land seemed completely deserted. No humans, no animals, no birds. The only thing that moved was the landscape, the earth itself, that danced and jigged and quivered in the heat-haze, and an occasional dust-devil that, snatched up by some wandering breath of air, whirled across the stony ground and died again. Even the nights were not black, but a thin, washed-out grey, and every now and again one would see the horizon begin to darken threateningly and know that another dust-storm was about to blot out the scorching land.

We sat the heat out for weeks in Tonk, and then the *Lou* began to blow, and life became bearable.

The *Lou* is a hot wind that blows across Rajputana in the months before the monsoon breaks and, but for the *kus-kus tatties*, it would merely add to the discomforts of hot weather. But Mother Nature has thoughtfully provided a weapon against it. The *kus-kus*, whose roots, woven into a curtain and hung in any open doorway where there is a through draught and kept soaked with water, cool the hot air with dangerous efficiency. Dangerous because unlike a modern air conditioner you cannot control its temperature; when the thermometer in your verandah is registering a hundred and fifteen degrees in the shade, the inside rooms can easily drop to a mere sixty or seventy — which can lead to a severe chill on the liver, if you don't watch it.

We fell into the hot-weather routine that entails spending every day in the dimness of a closed and shuttered house which, when the *Lou* is blowing, can be beautifully cool. Too cool in fact for the Residency doctor, whose HQ was, as far as I remember, Ajmer, but who visited us at intervals and insisted that we wear cummerbunds to protect us from getting chills on the liver. As soon as the sun neared the horizon and the shadows began to stretch out long and blue on the hot dust, we would emerge like troglodytes into the last of the daylight, to walk or drive and make the most of the cooler evening air. Every door and window in the house was then opened wide, and our beds were carried out to the *bara-durri*, where, under our mosquito-nets, we would spend the night in comparative coolness. But at the first blink of dawn we would wake and hurry indoors; and before the sun rose every door and window would be closed again and every split-cane *chik* (blind) on the verandah unrolled to its fullest extent, in an attempt to keep as much as we could of the night's coolness trapped indoors.

In the late spring of 1929, in order, I imagine, that Tacklow could make himself familiar with the affairs of Tonk, he returned to Simla, taking us with him. So Bets and I, who had been living for this day, saw again the small hill town in which we had both been born, and where we had spent so many happy summers of our childhood.

This time we did not, as in the old days, take the little train that puffs and chugs its way laboriously up the interminable twists and turns of the railway track that links Kalka, on the fringes of the burning plains, with the cool summer capital of the Raj, but drove up instead in the two cars, which we had arranged to leave in a couple of garages below the Cecil Hotel in Simla — the rule still held that no cars except those of the Viceroy and the Commander-in-Chief were allowed in the summer capital.

Every foot of that road was dear and familiar, and I drove up it with a lump in my throat and mentally singing Alleluias at the top of my voice. The road on which Emily Eden, Kipling, Henry and John Lawrence, and many a Governor-General of the East India Company (and, later, Viceroy of the Raj) and my own grandfather and father in their youth had travelled on, in *tongas* or palanquins, in the days before the railway was built, still, for the most part, ran parallel to the track, rising up slowly from the hot lands, along bare hillsides where nothing grew but sun-scorched grass and tall clumps of candelabra cactus. Kipling, who travelled on that road many times, has described it in a number of his stories and verses, and it has not changed much since his day; or mine.

✄ The air changed and became cooler and the hillsides greener and more leafy as we left the plains behind; and soon we were among the pines and the familiar sights and scents of my enchanted childhood: ferns and pine-needles and wafts of the delicious scent of the wild climbing roses that the garden centres call 'Himalayan Musk'. Presently we saw the signpost that marks the turn leading upwards to Kasauli and Sanawar, and the one that leads down to Dugshai — the little military cantonment to which Tacklow had been posted on his arrival in India as a raw young 'griffen' in 1889. From there he would cross the Kalka–Simla road, and climb the steep hillside above it to sit and study for his language exams in the peace and quiet of a small British cemetery that dated back to East India Company days, when Sir Henry Lawrence, of Mutiny fame, first established a school for the sons of army men in Sanawar.

The Dâk and PWD bungalows, which had been built a day's march apart for the convenience of travellers, and the bazaars of little hill villages that now boasted ramshackle but surprisingly efficient garages where petrol was sold by the can, were unchanged. And so too, when at last the road parted from the Jatogue tunnel and swept round the slope of the mountain, was Simla . . .

We stopped the cars at the edge of the road and sat there staring at it, finding it difficult to believe that we were seeing it again, and that after those nine long years of exile it had not changed. There it lay, sprawled along the top of a ridge of the foothills and bright in the evening sunlight, with its bazaars pouring down to the valley below in a cascade of flat tin rooftops, and the pine- and deodar-clad heights above it dotted with the houses, hotels and offices of *Sahib-log* and rich Indians. There was Christ Church, standing out ivory white against a backdrop of trees and buildings; and there, at the opposite end of the town, perched up on a hilltop, was that Victorian monstrosity, Viceregal Lodge, its windows, like many others from Summer Hill to Chota Simla, glittering like diamonds as they caught the late afternoon sunlight.

Tacklow had arranged for us to stay at the Grand Hotel in the 'Cottage', a wooden building separate from the rest of the hotel which was built out on a hilltop at one end of the central section of Simla. The public rooms, the entrance hall, sitting- and dining-room and so forth, were on a comparatively level plot of ground. But from there the rest rose up sharply, the guest-rooms, bisected by the steepest of drives, rising with it in tiers on either side. The most convenient rooms were those nearest the public rooms, and the best ones, though approached by a steep walk (up which the older, stouter and less agile guests preferred to let their rickshaw-coolies pull them), were the suites built on the flat of the hill, from where the views were superb. The cottage, however, lay some way below these, and could have been visible to them only as an area of red-painted corrugated-tin roofs; for the drive, having reached the crest of the hill, dived sharply downwards for a couple of hundred yards to end at the front door of the cottage, which had been built to fit neatly on to a flat-topped bit of rocky ground that jutted out of the hillside. The building, like most of those in Simla, was constructed out of the lightest possible materials, wood and tin, and this one had the usual corrugated-tin roof and was surrounded by a wide, glassed-in verandah, from the edge of which one looked straight down a terrifyingly long drop on to the tops of trees and the roofs of other houses built far below. We were, in fact, perched upon the top of a small hiccup of rock on an exceedingly steep hillside.

I had not been allergic to heights during the first fifteen or sixteen years of my life, and could not understand it when I suffered a bad attack of vertigo while climbing a smallish mountain in Switzerland called Mont Cray, whose name is graven into my memory when much else has left no mark. I had suddenly found, when nearing the top, that I couldn't move, hand or foot, and had to be escorted down, inch by inch, by two infuriated members of the party who had wanted to reach the summit. I have seldom felt so humiliated. But though looking down from the edge of our verandah brought back a horrid memory of Mont Cray, earlier memories of playing in the garden of Chillingham, and similar Simla gardens poised on the edge of precipices, helped me to get over it; and after the first day or two I ceased to worry. This, after all, was where I came in . . .

The 'cottage' consisted of a round, single-storey building with a large and somewhat dark centre room, out of which the bedrooms and bath-rooms led, and since the road that led down to it was a cul-de-sac, and we took all our meals except tea in the hotel's dining-room, you can see that in order to eat, shop, visit friends or go for walks, we were faced with a stiff climb to the top of our cul-de-sac, followed by an equally steep descent down to the dining-room or the town, and the same in reverse when we returned to our eyrie. The result was admirable. We all became beautifully svelte.

Immediately after breakfast on the morning after our arrival, Bets and I set out to explore and were enormously relieved to discover how little Simla had changed. Everything was just as we had left it, with two notable exceptions. As in old Delhi, too many of the shopkeepers on the Mall whom we had been on familiar terms with had retired or moved away or died, while their children with whom we had played had grown up and married; the girls to leave home and become mothers of large families, and their brothers to attend colleges or acquire wives and jobs in far-away metropolises such as Calcutta and Bombay. We had forgotten that nine years is a very long time in the East, where children are often betrothed while still in short socks, and are married and have children of their own at an age when a western child would still be struggling with homework.

None of the older generation, all of whom were now grandparents, even great-grandparents, recognized us, and only a handful remembered us — or pretended to do so. The only noticeable exception was one of the men who worked in the 'waxwork' shop, who, long ago, we would watch by the hour together as they patterned pieces of plain dark cloth intended as wall-hangings, cushion-covers or shawls, with lotus lilies and sprigs of blossom, and a gaudy assortment of birds, bees and butterflies. Even he did not immediately recognize us, but after we had reintroduced ourselves, and possibly because we had once been such dedicated admirers of his skill, he managed to recall us well enough to ask after Punj-ayah, our long-suffering but much loved ayah.

As for the kids we used to race down the one-in-one slope of the Lucker-Bazaar hill on our way to school at Auckland House, they were all grown men — fathers of families and heads of households, and totally unrecognizable. The only other way in which Simla had changed was its size. The place had shrunk. I had thought of it as a very large town. The distance between Scandal Point and the Cecil Hotel, for instance, or Harvington to the Bandstand on the Ridge — which I used to walk six days a week, there and back, when in the care of the dreaded Nurse Lizzie — had seemed an enormous distance to the short legs of a child. Yet now they were no distance at all. A fifteen-minute walk at most. The Town Hall, which I remembered as an imposing building, was nothing to write home about, while as for the Gaiety Theatre, on whose boards Bets and I had pranced and danced in so many children's shows, it was *tiny*. How *could* we have fitted the entire dancing class on to it for the rainbow ballet in *The Lost Colour*, one of the last children's plays that I had appeared in before being shipped 'home' to England and boarding-school?

I was to spend part of three separate 'Seasons' in Simla. But since I never kept a diary or any written record of my life, I cannot, at this date, be any too certain what year this or that happened in, or in what order. For which reason I shall steer clear of dates. What I *am* clear about are the events of that first return to the much-loved town in which I was born.

Sandy Napier, a schoolfriend of my brother Bill's, who spent much of his school holidays with us and had come to be regarded as a member of the family and a brother-by-adoption, was also in Simla that year, having been made an ADC to the Governor of the Punjab. So was Bob Targett, and a number of other friends from Delhi. And, of course, 'Buckie' — Sir Edward Buck, Head of Reuter's and still greatly loved by all the children of his friends, as he had been when Bets and I were small.

Buckie — or to be accurate, the Times Press in Bombay — had just published a revised and more up-to-date version of *Simla Past and Present*, a book he had written over twenty years before at the bidding of Lord Curzon, one of the earlier Viceroys of India, who had just discovered that the house he was living in had originally been lived in by that excellent author, artist and Queen of Snobs, the Lady Emily Eden — sister of the deplorable Governor-General, Lord Auckland, who back in the days of the East India Company had, almost single-handed, brought about the disastrous Afghan war of 1840–42. Lord Curzon, who had evidently read and enjoyed Emily's chatty and catty account of her time in India, wanted a book about the Simla of her day and his, and Buckie had duly come up with one, which he dedicated to Curzon. The reprint, much updated, was dedicated to another, and more recent Viceroy, Lord Reading . . .

To anyone interested in the history of a town — once made world-famous by the tales that were written about it by a young newspaper reporter by the name of Rudyard Kipling (see *Plain Tales from the Hills* and *Kim*), Buckie's *Simla Past and Present* is a must, and I was charmed to see the updated version prominently displayed in every bookshop one passed. Buckie himself had retreated to his beloved house, Dukani, perched on its hilltop some six miles outside Simla, above the little village of Mashobra. When at last Bets and I got around to paying him a visit, we left our rickshaws on the mule-track behind Oaklands, the house in which as children we had spent two happy summers, and instead of going on by road, we climbed up from there by the almost invisible goat-track which had been our favourite way of reaching Dukani in the old days.

Buckie was at home, and delighted to see us; as was his old head-*mali*, Kundun, and Kundun's *bibi* (wife), both of whom, apart from some grey hairs, were surprisingly unchanged. Dukani too had not changed — though like Simla, it had shrunk a bit in the course of time. I had remembered it as much larger. The bunches of violets that patterned the wallpaper in the guest-room in which Bets and I had always slept when we visited Buckie of old were a bit faded, and blotched here and there with the faint stains of damp. But otherwise we could have occupied it only yesterday. The lower verandah was still banked with the pots of cinerarias that had always been Kundun's pride, and Buckie's cluttered study was reassuringly familiar.

We spent a wonderful afternoon there, and when the time came to leave, Buckie said that we must sign his guest-book — a bulky volume that took up a lot of space on his overcrowded desk, and was full of the names of those he had entertained at Dukani during the years. Many of those names were famous, or have become famous. But what interested me most were certain topical verses by Tacklow that had appeared in the comments column of the guest-book to mark various weekend visits by my parents. I wish I'd had the sense to ask Buckie if I could copy them out, but I didn't think of it. It was pushed out of my mind by an intriguing coincidence that still fascinates me. Buckie had said: 'Let's look back and see when you two last visited me; it's bound to be here.'

It was. There were our names in handwriting that was still childish and unformed. But what made it startling was the date, which, except for a single numeral in the year, was the same as the one we had only just written after our names on the current page of the guest-book. We had returned to Dukani ten years to the day after our farewell visit in 1918. We stood and stared at it unbelievingly, and a little later, walking back down the narrow hill path to our old home, Oaklands, we both half expected to meet ourselves round every turn — two small girls in short brown dresses, brown strap-shoes and khaki *topis* (those large pith-helmets that all *ferengis* wore as a protection against heat-stroke) — scrambling up the familiar goat-track to play in Buckie's garden with Kundun's latest baby; as, somewhere back in time, we are certainly still occasionally doing.

✕ That we should join the Amateur Dramatic Club goes without saying. After all, both of us, and Mother before us, had appeared on the boards of the Gaiety Theatre a good many times already. And though compared to the vast expanse of stage that we remembered it seemed to have shrunk to the size of a pocket handkerchief, Simla would not have been Simla without it. So naturally we joined the players, and appeared in our first grown-up play in walk-on parts. Mine consisted of a few lines of the 'Madam is not at 'ome ziz morning' genre (I played a French maid) and we don't think Bets spoke at all. As far as we can remember she merely delivered a parcel from a dress-shop, and that was that. But we were jointly responsible for designing the costumes and the set, and we really went to town on that.

The play, entitled *Vanity*, was about a spoilt musical comedy star who gets her come-uppance (that's all I remember about the plot), and the action throughout took place in the drawing-room of her flat in Mayfair. This gave us a lovely chance to discard a rough sketch put forward as a suggestion by an old acquaintance of ours, Mr de la Rue Brown, the manager of the Gaiety. The 'de la Rue' had been suggested many years ago by some humorist commenting on the manager's habit of standing outside the door into the green-room, which gave on to the Mall, smoking a long cheroot for the larger part of the day. Brown had instantly adopted it. No one knew how old he was, but he had been the manager in Kipling's

KASHMIR

Right: The avenue of poplars was planted to hold up the raised road that runs the length of the valley from Baramullah to Srinagar. It was raised to help keep it above the water level in time of flood, though it is not always successful in this.

Left: Spring in Kashmir – 'It's magic!'

Below: Nanga Parbat, 'the naked mountain', seen from Khilanmarg on the opposite side of the valley.

Left: The Red House.

Below: Kadera, our bearer, prop and stay of our family for close on a quarter of a century. He is holding Angie, who thought as highly of him as we did.

Left: His Highness Hari Singh, Maharajah of Kashmir, opens an exhibition of Kashmiri arts and crafts. He is wearing a wonderful coat of gold Benarese brocade.

Left: Mahdoo, the 'Flench cook'. He had, when young, worked for a Frenchman who taught him to cook.

Above: Breakfast at Sonamarg. 'Smiler Muir', Mother and two guests, on trek.

Far left: Angelina Sugar Peas making loving noises at Mother, whom she adored. She was a lone orphan, picked up in the jungle by a *shikari* who gave her to Bets and me, but she attached herself to Mother at first sight.

Left: View from the Black Marble Pavilion, Shalimar Gardens.

Below: A picnic in the valley. Self and Bets picking wild irises. Angie does not mean to be left behind. That's her clinging to Bets's skirt. The whole valley smells of irises in the spring.

Left: Lotus lilies on the lakes.

Above: Tony Weldon (Hon. AB NBN), with Bets riding pillion.

Right: General Sir Andrew and Lady Maggie Skeen. Lady Maggie put an end to my first engagement.

Below: HB *Carlton* from Gupter Ghat, Dāl Lake. This is the boat we were in, anchored off Gagribul Point, when the unknown couple put on a parting show for us.

Below: A party on the roof of HB *Carlton*. *Left to right, front row*: Babs Babbington, Bets, lovely Rachel Maxwell and Bill, who was much smitten by her. *Back row*: Jimmy Godwin and 'Jug' Stewart, who married Norman Hartnell's sister, Topsy.

Above: Peggy Spence's wedding reception in the garden of the Kashmir residency. Bets and I did the flowers for it, despite considerable resistance from Mrs Hart's Kashmiri gardener.

Below: A *shikarra*, the 'taxi' of this eastern Venice bringing a guest to our boat.

Left: Me, Mother and Bets on the prow of HB *Carlton*.

Right: Scandal Point, Simla. The Ridge Road branches off to the left and the Mall goes on in the shadows, to the right. The hill in the back is Jacko, and the spire belongs to Christ Church, where both Bets and I were christened.

Below: Moll, Bets and Judy Birdwood, somewhere on the hill road below Simla. Probably to visit someone in Kassouli, because the only cars allowed in Simla are the Viceroy's, the Governor of the Punjab's and the Commander-in-Chief's – Judy's father.

Above: A picnic in the Simla hills. *Left to right*: Bets, Bill, Sandy, 'Sailor' Boyle and Mother.

Above: The line-up for the last night of *Vanity*, performed by the Simla Amateur Dramatic Society at their own Gaiety Theatre. The cast take a final curtain call, with Bets on the far right and me second from the left. (The leading lady is wearing the disputed 'cocktail outfit' – *trousers*! very daring in the twenties!) The photograph appeared in the *Statesman*.

Left: Me (believe it or not), taken by some European photographer in New Delhi in the winter of 1928–9. Can't recall the name of the photographer – he didn't last long. Having struck twenty, I have thankfully cut off my hair and taken to wearing flashy earrings with evening dress.

Below: Sandy (ADC, at Barnes' Court, to the Governor of the Punjab).

Above: The Black Heart Ball, Simla. I am wearing all Mother's opals, and carrying the ostrich-feather fan. The dress is copied from one my great-great-grandmother wore in Regency days; or that was the idea, but since the portrait of her stops just short of her waist, it's mostly guesswork!

TONK

Left: First view of Tonk.

Below: His Highness the Nawab of Tonk and Tacklow sitting overlooking a lake where they went duck shooting.

Above: Major Barton, the Nawab of Tonk and Tacklow, 'President of the Council of State'.

Right: Our house. The square open-sided bit on the left is the *bara-durri*, where one can receive guests, take tea, or during the hot weather have one's bed taken out at night.

Below: The Nawab comes to breakfast.

Above: The Nawab sends an elephant to take us sightseeing. Bets, Sandy and me.

Left: On our way back we are entertained by the headsman of a village that we are passing through.

Right: The Tikka-Sahib.

THE NAGEEM BAGH NAVY

Left: The drawing-room of our houseboat, the HB *Carlton*. Mother and me on the sofa, Bets behind the camera. Mother's watercolours are on the walls, together with some of her 'Chinoiserie'.

Right: The Nageem Bagh Navy – the fleet at anchor. HMS *Fairy Queen*, HMS *Carlton* (flagship) and HMS *Midget*.

Below: The Nageem Bagh Navy. *Left to right*: Captain (Andy), First Officer (Mike), Midshipmite (self), Bo'sun (Enid) and Cabin-boy (Bets).

Above: The Club's bathing-boat on Lake Nageem, which is said to be bottomless.

Left: On the bathing-boat. *Left to right*: self (having bathed), Mother, Bets and the Andersons, Andy and Enid, about to bathe.

day, and according to himself, for many years before that. He had always seemed to us to look as old as Rip Van Winkle, and he still did. He hadn't changed a whisker. What's more, he was still the old tyrant he had always been. Fortunately he had a soft spot for us, and did not raise too much fuss when we vetoed his suggestion for the standing set, and substituted one that, believe it or not, was considered positively daring.

Brown's idea of the décor of a theatrical star's Mayfair flat had been incredibly dowdy and pedestrian and, judging from photographs of previous drawing-room comedies put on by the Simla ADS, exactly like every one of its predecessors. Bets and I threw out the chintz-covered chairs and sofa and the matching curtains, and substituted draped satin, a couch piled with cushions, and 'pouffes' in place of chairs, added one of those then fashionable floppy Parisian pierrot dolls, and topped it off by muralling the walls with decorative blossom-trees and weeping willows à la Erté.

That set was a terrific success, and every night of its run earned a spontaneous round of applause when the curtain rose on an empty stage for Act I. Our dress designs were equally novel and gained us a good many approving paragraphs in the press; though they were the cause of a spectacular row between the leading lady, a Mrs Jane Franklin, and the number two lead, whose name has escaped me.

My part in the play happened to be as the curtain rose, and on the first night the applause for the set very nearly led to my missing my entrance, because this was something I was not prepared for. The scenario called for the curtain to rise on an untenanted room in which a telephone had just started ringing . . .

Brief pause (I had been instructed to count five slowly) and then: 'Enter briskly a French maid from centre door. She crosses stage to where the telephone stands concealed by the skirts of a crinolined doll' (a ghastly but very popular 1920s gimmick) 'and picks up phone: "*Allo? Allo?*"' — and so on. But that round of applause for the set had not been anticipated by anyone; and it drowned out the telephone. I dithered wildly on the far side of the door and was finally pushed on by our flustered producer, and very nearly earned a second ovation for my dress. I had designed myself a classic maid's outfit, complete with very saucy cap and distinctly frivolous apron but in lilac and lace instead of the traditional black and white. It was at least original and, combined with that particular set, very effective.

When it came to designing the Act I outfit for the leading lady, Bets and I decided that she ought to wear something really arresting that would establish her star-status on sight. We came up with lounging pyjamas, which at that date were still considered to be a very daring innovation. (*Trousers?* — very 'fast'!)

Slacks and pyjamas for women were still a fairly new idea in the world of modern fashion, and despite the fact that in Asia women had been wearing them for centuries, they had not yet been taken up by Anglo-India, so the pair we designed for Mrs Franklin created a mild sensation. Since the set and its furnishing was pastel-coloured, we had the lounge pyjamas made up in black satin, decorated with a modernistic design of flowers painted on to the material with ordinary oil paint, and both Mrs Franklin and the director were delighted with the effect. Not so the second lead . . .

The row blew up during a rehearsal in a building called the Chalet — a sort of annexe to the men-only United Services Club further up the hillside, where dances were held twice a week, and parties were occasionally thrown by members of the Club. I had brought along a coloured sketch of the trousered outfit, and while our leading lady and the cast applauded it, our number two lead was simply furious. This, it turned out, was because her part called for her to make a brief appearance in the third and last act, daringly clothed in nothing but (wait for it) a nightdress! Believe it or not, she had apparently been looking forward to creating a sensation by rushing on stage in such intimate garb. But now, she complained bitterly, if Mrs Franklin were to make her first appearance in Act I wearing a pyjama suit (which incidentally covered her up from top to toe in black satin and was about as unrevealing an outfit as you could wish for), it would completely ruin the impact of her own entrance in Act III, and she wasn't going to stand for that. Either Mrs Franklin turned down the pyjamas or she, Mrs Whozit, would leave the cast — So there!

Tacklow had warned us that amateur theatricals have a knack of leading to an incredible amount of animosity and in-fighting over the most trivial of questions, and had illustrated from a hilarious list of personal experiences, designed to encourage us to watch our step, and, like Brer Rabbit, 'lay low and say nuffin'. His stories had made us laugh a lot, but most of them seemed so absurd that I think we both took them with a large pinch of salt. But here we were, in our first grown-up show at the Gaiety, bang in the middle of a dust-up of fantastic proportions, complete with tears, fireworks, hysteria and threats of a walk-out. It was unbelievable, and forgetting Tacklow's stories of similar shenanigans and his advice as to lying low and saying nothing, I unwisely rushed in where St Michael himself might have feared to tread. I suggested that there was a gap of a good two-and-three-quarters of an act between the leading lady's first entrance and the brief appearance of the number two seed wearing a demure white nightdress. Surely no one in the audience would, by then, remember what the leading lady had been wearing, let alone make any connection between very mod black satin lounging pyjamas and a very ordinary nightgown!

This tactless olive-branch was not well received. It merely incensed both combatants even further, and they turned on me, as the designer. At which point the director, who had been horrified by the threats of resignation, entered the fray with disastrous results. He suggested that as the stage directions did not include lounging trousers, but *did* mention the nightgown, perhaps — er — perhaps Mrs Franklin might . . . ? But alas, Mrs F. fancied herself no end in those black satin piggies, and nothing was going to induce her to part with them. If Mrs Whateverhernamewas didn't like them, she knew what she could do about it. Her part was not all that important anyway, and there must be dozens of girls in Simla who would be able to take it on at a moment's notice.

At this point the director, panic-stricken, re-entered the fray like a rocket. Bets and I, finding ourselves temporarily ignored by all three combatants, beat a hasty retreat up the narrow staircase that led to the upper rooms of the Chalet, and half-way up collapsed on to the steps at a point from where we could listen unseen to the battle raging below, and were overcome by gales of helpless giggling. I hadn't laughed so much since my school days, and I can't think why the whole affair should have struck us both as being hilariously funny. Perhaps because we were both still young enough to think of our elders and betters as 'grown-ups', or because we hadn't quite believed Tacklow's stories about the temperamental fireworks that so frequently enlivened anything to do with amateur theatricals. Yet here we were, seeing a magnificent example of them on our very first show.

I don't remember how the fracas ended. But Mrs Franklin obviously won on points, because she wore the pyjama-suit in Act I during the entire run of the show (one week!) and added a very long ivory cigarette-holder for extra effect (and I don't remember any of the male members of the cast complaining that she had ruined their bit of business in Act II where they light up a cigarette). The nightdress in Act III got a round of applause all to its little self, possibly provided by Mrs Whozit's husband and her friends and supporters but more likely because, believe it or not, in those innocent days, to run on to a stage wearing nothing but a nightgown (even such a non-see-through as Mrs Whozit's) was considered pretty *risqué* and almost tantamount to streaking. The Simla audience loved it.

Since Sandy had become an ADC in attendance on the Governor of the Punjab, Bets and I got asked to all the more frivolous dances and parties at Barnes Court, the Governor's summer residence, while Mother, with a reluctant Tacklow in tow, had a lovely time going to all the sixteen-button-glove affairs — balls, white-tie dinner parties, lunch and garden parties. I had thought Delhi was a very social place. But it was nothing to Simla. There were dances and fancy-dress balls given by the Most Hospitable Order of the Black Hearts — founded in 1891 and consisting of a Grand Master, a Prelate and Knights, all bachelors or grass-widowers (married men whose wives had not been able to accompany them out to India were permitted to qualify as Knights Bachelor).

The Prince of Wales (the one better known as the Duke of Windsor) was made a temporary member during his ill-fated visit to India.

The object of the members was to repay collectively the hospitality they had received individually from Simla hostesses, and the parties they gave were certainly memorable. Their uniforms on these occasions consisted of black knee-breeches with evening dress, a red shoulder cape ornamented with the black heart of their order, and another black heart worn suspended from a red ribbon around their necks. The motto of the order, which appeared on all their invitations and official stationery was: 'He is not so — as he is painted', the missing word being only known to members. The story goes that the first Grand Master and his Knights, having chosen a motto, arranged for a painter in the Simla bazaar to paint it tidily on a large notice board that would be displayed on the occasion of any Black Heart festivity. The industrious fellow obeyed, but his English was very sketchy and he mixed up two of the words, transposing the fifth and the last; when this was pointed out, he blotted out the fifth, leaving a rather grubby blank (the paint underneath had not been dry), and the first of a long list of Grand Masters, instead of hitting the ceiling, shouted with laughter and told him to leave it like that, with a tidy black bar in place of the grubby grey blotch. The Order would keep the missing word a secret and let outsiders try guessing what it was.

My own bet — knowing India's fondness for muddling up sentences — is that the original motto was to have been 'He is not so black as he is painted'* and that the sign-painter from the bazaar was worried by the idea that any sahib should seriously wish to paint himself black. (Why black, for goodness sake? Why not, if he really wants to be a different colour, a nice shade of copper? Or better still blue, like the Lord Krishna?) But to become a *Kala ardmi*, a black man? No! There must be some mistake, and it was up to him to put it right. I bet it was that.

My first invitation from the Black Hearts in Simla (they had hosted at least two in Delhi) was to a fancy-dress ball, preceded by a dinner party at the United Services Club. Other parties for invitees were being held all over Simla, and as far as I remember the main shindig was timed to begin after the dinner parties were over and the guests given time to arrive at the Chalet, where on this occasion — and possibly on others as well — all the guests, from the Viceroy and his wife to the most unimportant teenager present (who might, that year, have been Bets) were, on arrival, marshalled into line and made to make their entrance into the ballroom one by one and feet first, through a pair of black curtains and down a chute, at the bottom of which two masked Knights of the Order waited to catch them and hoist them to their feet. The Black Heart parties were nothing if not informal.

I had been to the Bachelors' Ball in Delhi dressed as the young Queen Victoria, and I went to this one as my great-grandmother, the mother of the Sophia with whom Tacklow used to spend fishing holidays in Scotland when he was still only a schoolboy. (There is a portrait of her by Raeburn — now somewhere in America, I gather — in Regency dress and with her hair cut short and curled and held up on the top of her head by a *filet* in the fashion made famous by Madame Récamier in the days following the French Revolution, and first made popular in England by the notorious Lady Caroline Lamb, who, having publicly snubbed Lord Byron at a London ball, fell violently in love with him and created one of the greatest scandals of the Regency years.)

Since Tacklow was against cutting my hair off, I curled the ends and piled it up on the top of my head, and Mother lent me her opal tiara, necklace and earrings for the occasion, which made my evening.

Since time is running out for me, I shall not attempt to track events

* *'Devils are not so black as they are painted'* — (?) Thomas Lodge.

down by laborious research, but just tell them as things that happened to me in Simla — date unknown. There was the occasion, for instance, when Simla was hit by a smallpox epidemic, and we were all ordered to be vaccinated.

The majority complied, and I remember the shock Bets and I got, climbing up the hill from the lower road below the main bazaar and about to bypass the Cecil Hotel, when we remembered that a particular friend of ours, one Walter Harvey of the F and P, was staying there. We decided to look him up, and having been told by the man on the desk that Mr Harvey was in, we went along and banged on the door. Walter's voice demanded to know who was there, and having found out, invited us cordially to come in. When we did so we found that his sitting-room was empty, but that the door into his bedroom was ajar: 'Come on in,' urged Walter, 'if you don't mind seeing me in pyjamas. I'm in bed.' We pushed open his door and went in, to be greeted with enthusiasm, until, somewhat belatedly, he said: 'Hey — don't come too close! You'd better stay by the door. The doctor says I've got smallpox.'

He had too! It turned out that of all the people at Army Headquarters, plus their wives and families, Walter had been the only one who refused flatly to be inoculated. I forget what his reasons were, but they can't have been merely frivolous. After all, he was an intelligent chap. But he was the only European in Simla to disobey that order; and he was the only one to catch smallpox. He survived. And before one of the rabid anti-Raj lot starts yowling about 'racial discrimination' — yes, everyone in Simla, and throughout the bazaars, who did not refuse to be inoculated as Walter had done, was inoculated, and the epidemic was contained.

There must have been a fair number of casualties among the native population, as smallpox is endemic throughout India, and compulsory inoculation would not have been possible in a place like Simla Bazaar. But only one of the Europeans whom we all knew died of smallpox that year, and I am not sure if she was involved in any way with that particular epidemic. She was the pretty niece of Sir Ernest and Lady Burden, who had been invited to spend a season with them and, like Walter, had refused flatly to be inoculated. Her reason, we were told, was religious. I don't know if that was merely a rumour or the truth. What is true is that the only two *ferengis* who refused inoculation both caught smallpox. The rest of us went around with itching arms and got away with it. Maybe the Lord was underlining the point that He helps those who help themselves?

After all, one of His apostles was a physician, and surely He would not have included Luke among the chosen if He had disapproved of doctors? (No; I haven't forgotten that He also chose a traitor. Or that He provided us with brains and a mind of our own.)

Bob Targett was up in Simla for the hot season. I saw quite a lot of him and discovered, with relief, that there was no slightest stirring of that previous romance; or of embarrassment either. Only lots of liking still. Which was just as well for me, as it didn't take long to discover that Bob was already heavily involved in a rather tricky romance with a gay grass widow whose charms — and experiences! — I could not have hoped to rival. But what with Bob and Sandy and Walter and a few other bachelor acquaintances, we were never short of partners at any of the many dances and dinner parties, and though for once I was completely fancy-free, and had been, surprisingly, ever since the disappearance of Donald from the scene, I must have been in love with life instead of in love with love that season. Because one of my clearest memories is of walking — no, not walking, dancing — dancing, skipping, running, along the Mall from the Combermere Bridge to the Cecil Hotel on a misty afternoon. I've forgotten what errand I was on, or if I was just out for a walk. All I remember was the feel of light raindrops, (in Scotland they would call it a Scotch mist) fingering my face and running down my mackintosh, and a wonderful sense of lightness and happiness. I had come back to my starting point, and found that all was right with my world.

❊ 6 ❊

'Song of India'

Chapter 21

꧁ஜ꧂

I 'came of age' that year. A magic date which in those days was twenty-one, but has now been reduced to eighteen, and already looks like being reduced to sixteen. The occasion was celebrated with a dinner party and dance at the Cecil Hotel, and I remember, with regret, that when my parents asked me what I wanted for my twenty-first birthday present, I asked for an evening dress that I had seen in one of the European shops on the Mall, and, of all the silly things, a wildly expensive ostrich-feather fan to go with it. Tacklow did his best to persuade me to choose something that would last. But I had set my heart on that dress, and even more so on that fan, for huge ostrich-feather fans were all the rage that year, and the *Tatler* and the *Sketch* and all the glossy European magazines were full of lovely ladies carrying them.

I got my dress; and the fan. And have regretted it ever since, for it would have been nice to have had a memento of that auspicious landmark in my life, that I could have kept for the rest of my days. A piece of jewellery, or silver — which, incidentally, would by now have increased enormously in value and probably ended by becoming an heirloom. As it was, the dress, a frothy and exceedingly fragile affair consisting of layer upon layer of silk net that shaded from orange to lemon (and to be honest, did not particularly become me), became limp and tattered in no time at all, while that spectacular fan, which matched it in colour and created a mild sensation in the ballroom of the Cecil Hotel, fell victim to those rapacious little insects that we used to call 'woolly bears' who can (and do) eat anything that comes their way. Only the tortoiseshell sticks of that fan lasted for a few years, but in the end the woolly bears munched their way through those as well. And for some forgotten reason, no photograph seems to have been taken of me wearing that glamorous outfit.

The only thing — apart from the memory — that I have left to remind me of my long-ago coming-of-age is a very small pile of moonstones which are all that is left of a beautiful but incredibly fragile necklace Sandy gave me because, he said, they were the only stones except diamonds (which he couldn't afford) that could be worn with an orange and lemon dress; they picked up and reflected any colours near them like soap bubbles.

He was right about them reflecting other colours. They do. And they looked wonderful with the fan and the twenty-first birthday ball dress. But alas, that dream of a necklace was as fragile as if it had indeed been made of soap bubbles. The slim oval stones were held together with loops and bands of gold barely thicker than a spider's web, a necklace such as only an Indian craftsman could have made. It broke too easily, and each time it broke and was mended, a few moonstone drops were lost. In the end it got too small to go round my neck; I tried sewing the remains on to a dress and lost even more stones. By now only a tiny handful, enough to fill a thimble, is all I have to remind me of my coming-of-age party, and of Sandy and Simla, and the band of the Cecil Hotel playing 'Fancy Our Meeting', 'Tea for Two' and 'Always' . . .

My gunner brother, Bill, whose unit was stationed that year in one of the North West Frontier outposts — Razmak, I think — came up to Simla to stay with us for a few days of his leave. He and Phil someone, one of his gunner friends, had spent the main part of it in Kashmir, where they had hired a houseboat between them and evidently had what Bill described as 'a whale of a time'. In the course of which, it eventually transpired, he had become engaged to be married.

This bombshell having been dropped into the collective family lap prefaced by, 'Oh . . . er . . . um . . . and by the way — ' it was not at first taken very seriously. Dear Bill had been in love with one damsel or another from his prep school days, and we all remembered the carry-on there had been over a lovely creature he had become temporarily attracted to during his final days in England before he sailed to India (the one who would insist on calling him 'Billy-boy'), and the swiftness with which she had been superseded in his affections by a 'smashing' girl in the course of the voyage out. But at least he had never got as far as being engaged to any of them.

This time it was evidently serious. However, his chances of actually marrying for some years to come were almost non-existent, since the

Army still stuck firmly to its rule that no officer might marry without his Colonel's permission before he attained the rank of Major or the age of thirty, whichever came first. And few, if any, Colonels were going to allow one of their young subalterns, with no private means, to launch into matrimony and the raising of a family before he had learned his trade and proved himself. However, Bill's main reason for spending the final days of his leave in Simla was not to see his family or celebrate his twenty-third birthday (or even my twenty-first) but to break the news of his engagement, and buy the ring. The style of token that his betrothed had in mind, explained Bill, was unobtainable in such outposts of Empire as Razmak or Bannu or wherever.

The object of his affection turned out to be a girl we had already met in Delhi during Horse Show Week. Her father was a Lieutenant-Colonel in, I think, some Corps or other, or possibly in one of the many Punjab Regiments, and she had a brother who was also in one of the Indian Army Regiments. She and her mother had been spending the hot weather in Kashmir, in a houseboat on the Jhelum, and Bill had met her at a young people's party at the Residency and, in his usual fashion, instantly fallen in love. I have to admit that I can't think why. In general, the girls he fell for were outstandingly pretty and this one — let's call her Bertha — though by no means plain, was nothing to write home about. Just a nice-looking girl with a figure that showed to advantage in a bathing suit, a costume in which she appeared in most of the snapshots of her which Bill produced for our inspection. He seemed to have spent his holiday, in company with a gang of like-minded young friends, on the bathing boat at Nageem, and his nights dining, wining and dancing either at the Club or at Nedou's Hotel, finishing up by floating off in pairs in *shikarras* across the moonlit lake, to join up again in the pallid dawn when everyone returned to their separate houseboats — where they would sleep until one o'clock and meet again at Nedou's for a late luncheon before driving back to Nageem, and repeating the whole programme again.

Had it not been for the engagement, we would probably not have seen Bill for so much as a day of his leave. As it was, he decided that the occasion was important enough to make him tear himself away from his love in order to break the news to his family in person. And then of course there was that ring. Bertha apparently felt the same about rings as Lady Maggie had. An engagement did not count without a ring on the right finger, and that was that. Bill had taken Bertha to look at one or two in the shops of several Kashmiri jewellers on the Bund, but she had not thought much of them, and it had been decided that he would buy one in Simla. The only trouble was that he doubted he had got enough money in his account to cover the transaction, and should it come to more than expected would Tacklow please come up trumps and lend him enough to make up the difference?

Tacklow, looking a little worn, agreed to do so, though Bill had still not repaid that other debt. But he inquired how Bill thought he was going to afford the expense of feeding, clothing and housing a wife on a budget that did not even run to paying for a modest engagement ring. Weddings, he pointed out, were expensive items on their own, let alone honeymoons and all that came after them. 'Oh, not to worry,' said Bill buoyantly; he wouldn't be able to get married for at least seven years, unless of course, as he had explained to Bertha and her parents, he should become a Major before then, which he didn't think was very likely. However, Bertha had promised to wait for him, and by then he would have saved up enough money to cover the extra expenses, and his pay would have gone up considerably. Everything would be quite all right, we'd see!

Mother, who had received the news with every sign of dismay, visibly relaxed, as I suppose we all did. In Mother's youth, seven years wouldn't have seemed like an eternity, as it would today. Victorian brides had always gone in for long engagements, in particular those who followed their men out to the further parts of a widespread Empire. Sir Henry Lawrence's wife, Honaria, had waited for nine years, living on nothing but scraps of news from him (and in those days it took half a year to get a reply to a letter from India to England), until he was able to send for her to come out and marry him. And she was only one of many. Which I suppose was partly why the idea of a seven-year engagement didn't seem as weird to us then as it would today. Certainly Bill was taking it very calmly.

Bets and I, both incurably romantic, thought he was being truly heroic. To have found and fallen in love with the only girl in the world for you, the one you wanted to spend the rest of your life with and to find that she felt the same about you, and then discover that you couldn't marry her and live happily ever after for seven years — (by which time, of course, you'd both be old!) seemed too cruel, and our hearts went out to poor Bill.

We needn't have bothered. The very next day Bill asked me to accompany him to a jeweller's to buy the ring. He said he wanted my advice, and I remember feeling flattered. But in fact it was a confidante he needed, for there was something he wanted to get off his chest and, having pledged me to secrecy and extracted a solemn vow that I wouldn't breathe a word of it to anyone, especially not the family,* he blurted out the whole unhappy story as we walked along the Mall on our way to Hamilton's, the jeweller's.

It seemed that he and a friend, a Phil someone who was a fellow gunner, had hired a small houseboat between them, and they had met Bertha at a Residency dance on the first night of their leave. Bill had been very taken with her from the start; she was an excellent dancer, and they had partnered each other for most of the dances that evening, and from then on were regarded as 'a pair' at all the subsequent parties attended by their 'crowd'.

About half-way through that leave, several members of the crowd who were due to return to their units in the plains had thrown a farewell party which began with dinner at Nedou's Hotel, followed by dancing and drinking at the Srinagar Club and, when the band packed it in, a late-night picnic on Char-Chenar Island, a little island in the middle of the Dāl lake to which the members of the party had arrived in pairs in *shikarras*. Someone had brought a wind-up gramophone, and there had been the usual mounds of sandwiches, salads and cake, and most people had donated a bottle of something or other, ranging from wine, spirits and liqueurs, to beer and lemonade.

Bill said that he supposed it was the mixture of these that had been his undoing, for he had learned early on, first as a prefect at Repton and later as a 'snooker' at the Shop, that it was almost impossible for him to get drunk: because long before he reached that stage, he would be sick; a humiliating habit that he was never to outgrow but which had its useful side, since he never got rowdy, maudlin or belligerent; just vaguely happy — generally prior to being as sick as a cat.

He must have been slightly more than happy by the time the *shikarras* landed their passengers back at the Dāl Gate, from where they dispersed to their various hotels, guest-houses or houseboats, because he said he didn't remember anything about the homeward journey or how he had managed to get himself to bed. He woke some time towards mid-morning

* Since this was over half a century ago, I feel it is now 'time expired'.

in bright sunlight, and with a cracking headache, and received the first shock of the day from Phil, who he found fortifying himself with mugs of strong black coffee supplied by their solicitous and experienced *manji* (boatman). Phil had ordered more of the same for his fellow-sufferer, and lifting his mug in salute said: 'Here's to you both. I hear I have to congratulate you.' 'Whatever for?' inquired Bill morosely, gulping black coffee.

Phil looked surprised and, apologizing for speaking out of turn, said he hadn't realized that it was going to be kept a secret. To which Bill had inquired, what secret? What on earth was Phil blathering on about? And Phil had said: 'Your engagement of course. Bertha told me last night when we were all milling around saying goodbye to each other, that you and she had just got engaged to be married. She didn't tell me that you wanted to keep quiet about it for the time being, so I supposed . . .'

Now in those days there was an unwritten law in Kashmir concerning couples who took moonlit trips on the lakes, particularly when the lotus lilies were in bloom. It was believed (and frequently proved true) that no young man who took a girl out in a *shikarra* on those enchanted waters when the moon was full could resist proposing marriage to her. Or she accepting. For which reason any engagement entered into under those conditions would not be considered valid unless repeated on the following morning in full daylight, and preferably before witnesses.

Bill, pale green from shock and hangover, admitted that he hadn't the faintest idea what he had said or done from the time the picnic party had landed on the island. The whole thing from then on was a blur. Scrambling hastily into his clothes and without even bothering to shave, he fled from the boat, grabbed the first *tonga* he saw and, urging its driver to get as much speed out of his horse as possible, made for the bund where his girlfriend's parents had moored their houseboat; with the intention, he explained to me, of saying, 'Look, old girl, I don't remember what I said to you on the way back last night, but whatever it was, for God's sake take it with a tablespoon of salt!' Or words to that effect. He did not, however, get the chance . . .

Bertha had gone out shopping, and it was her Mama who received him. And instead of the frosty reception he expected from her, she advanced on him with a beaming smile and outstretched arms and, addressing him as her 'dear boy', embraced him fondly and said how pleased she would be to have such a nice son-in-law. And that, said Bill mournfully, tore it. He couldn't possibly, he insisted, explain to her (as he could have to Bertha) that he had been tight as a newt on the previous evening and hadn't a clue as to what he had or hadn't said or done during at least a third of the festivities. 'So I said the only thing I could think of,' confessed Bill. 'I said I couldn't get married for seven years. Which is true of course; her parents must know that. And she's sure to get tired of me long before that. It's not as if she hasn't got loads of boyfriends.'

I wanted to know what on earth he was going to do if his Bertha turned out to be truly in love with him, and the faithful type who was willing to wait for him for years on end. Was he prepared to marry her when the time was up? Bill merely looked uncomfortable and said it wouldn't ever come to that. It seemed that both she and her parents had agreed that in view of the length of the engagement, it would be better not to publish any notice of it in the newspapers — to avoid having to publish a cancellation at some later date, hazarded Bill, hopefully. I was less sanguine, because of the ring —

We chose one at Hamilton's that morning after long deliberation. The deliberation was over price rather than design. Bill's means, as ever, were strictly limited, and as he had no intention of getting deeper into debt if he could help it, he confided to an elderly assistant at Hamilton's the maximum figure he could run to, and urged that it be kept as far below that as possible. We ended up with a small sapphire between a couple of slightly smaller diamonds. As this offering was to be given to his fiancée by Bill in person when they met again in Kashmir, which would not be until his next leave, and since we too planned to spend the autumn in Kashmir, the ring was handed over to Tacklow for safe-keeping when Bill returned to the Frontier a few days later.

✣ Amateur dramatics and the Gaiety Theatre continued to play as large a part in my adult life in Simla as they had during my childhood, and to live up to their reputation for fun, feuds and drama. They also brought me a valued friend, one Judith Birdwood who would in the future, after becoming Judy Messel, turn professional and, under her maiden name, design any number of shows for the Cambridge Footlights and the Marlowe Society, for whom she was designer and wardrobe mistress for thirty-eight years. Her father, later Lord Birdwood, was at that time General Sir William Birdwood, Commander-in-Chief, India. Judy had been charmed by the set and costumes for *Vanity* and had come round the back when the curtain came down after the first night to congratulate

243

me. We sat together in the green-room talking for hours until old de la Rue Brown threw us out. Later on the two of us managed to get involved in other productions, notably an Edwardian musical comedy, *Miss Hook of Holland*, *A Persian Garden*, *The Constant Nymph* and *Faust*.

I was to have played the soubrette in *Miss Hook* and sung one of the hit songs in that show — 'A Little Pink Petti from Peter'. But alas, after rehearsing for weeks my eyes went bad on me, and the eye specialist at the Walker Hospital ordered a week in bed in a blacked-out room — no reading or writing. And, thereafter, spectacles of all dreary things. It was a blow, and when the show was performed I had to watch (through dark glasses and from the back of the stage box) my understudy bringing the house down with endless encores of 'Pink Petti from Peter'. But although I was out of the show, I had, in partnership with Judy, designed the costumes and sets, and contributed a personal touch that turned one number, the modern one, into a spectacular success.

All 'dated' musical comedies put on by the Simla Amateur Dramatic Club invariably included one 'modern' song, slotted in among the original earlier ones. The one we used for Miss Hook of Holland was 'Tip-Toe through the Tulips' — which in those days was new. Someone had worked out a dance that was meant to turn it into a spectacular number for the entire chorus, but it fell sadly flat until I had a sudden brainwave, which, I am delighted to say, worked a treat. We had a whole lot of paper tulips made in the bazaar, and attached each one to a dart, borrowed from the Darts Club. The dancers carried baskets full of these, and sowed them in lines all over the stage by the simple expedient of dropping each dart with a firm flick of the wrist that drove the point into the wooden floorboards of the stage, and made it possible for the chorus boys and girls to tiptoe through these rows of tulips. Practice made the chorus perfect, and as a final encore, they picked the tulips and stashed them back into their baskets — thus clearing the stage for the next bit of hi-di-ho.

I was exceedingly proud of that simple but most effective bit of stagecraft, and also of a few more that I dreamed up for a production of *Faust*.

I can't remember which year *Faust* came into. Probably 1930, when Judy invited me to spend six weeks at Snowdon, the C-in-C's house in Simla, to help her and her musical brother, Chris Birdwood, put on a production of Gounod's *Faust* at Davico's ballroom. Though it could have been in 1931 when I was staying with friends of Mother's, Mr and Mrs Bevan-Petman — parents of the artist Hal Bevan-Petman, who was to become, and remain, a dear and much admired friend of my family's until the end of his days. The dates of those two separate visits remain vague to my mind, though I remember that after leaving the Bevan-Petmans I spent a few days with the family of Cyril Drummond, Headmaster of the Stapleton Cotton School, and that while I was there his wife won the silver medal for the best watercolour in the Simla Fine Arts Society's annual show, with a painting called *Mist-swept Kuds*.* Why do some things stick while others escape one? I remember that while I was there I shared a bedroom with a friendly and charming young daughter of the house named Chloë.

My stay at Snowdon was memorable for several reasons, one of them being that a touring theatrical company, the first I had ever come across in India, arrived in Simla and played for at least two weeks at the Gaiety Theatre. Their repertoire included a musical comedy and that grim and great play, *Journey's End*. The company called themselves the Quaints — a name guaranteed, I would have said, to put off the most enthusiastic theatre-goer. But they turned out to be far from quaint, and Judy and I were bowled over by them. One of them, a young man who sang and danced in the musical offering and took the part of the hero-worshipping young officer who gets killed at the end of the last act of *Journey's End*, was to make a great name for himself on both stage and screen: he was the future Sir John Mills. I can't claim to have recognized his performance as particularly outstanding, because we thought they were all outstanding, and Judy and I, reeling under the impact of such excellence and profession-alism, were horrified by the fact that contrary to the time-honoured practice of all the amateur dramatic shows, no floral tributes were handed up to the actresses at the final curtain. This injustice would have to be put right.

We hurried back to Snowdon seething with indignation and, first thing next morning, sent for the head *mali* and gave detailed instructions as to baskets that were to be bought in the bazaar, and filled with the best flowers that the garden and the glasshouses could produce. These must be ready in time to be handed in at the stage door of the Gaiety Theatre at such and such an hour that evening, and a *chupprassi* was detailed to

* *Kuds*: hillsides.

take them in one of the Snowdon rickshaws. Our combined pocket-money did not run to the boxes of chocolates which often accompanied the leading lady's flowers but we could manage the baskets and the ribbon, and the *mali* and assistants surpassed themselves. The floral tributes were a great success.

The only other thing that I remember with great clearness about the Quaints' visits to Simla was that on one of the nights, returning from the theatre through a blanket of thick monsoon mist and drizzle down the winding, tree-lined drive that led to the side entrance of Snowdon, the two leading *jampanis* of the four who pulled my rickshaw suddenly stopped dead, and, dropping the shaft, retreated to join those at the back, leaving me looking out into a misty darkness illuminated only by the blurred yellow lights of a pair of rickshaw lamps.

In rainy weather the rickshaws were enclosed in waterproof hoods and coverings that left the occupant dry, but gave him or her only a narrow slice of rain-spattered glass to see through. The *jampanis* too were protected from the wet by long capes and hoods of mackintosh, and all rickshaws were fitted with a pair of oil-lamps that were lit after dark. Judy's rickshaw was ahead of mine and I could see, past my own lamps, two faint jogging blobs of yellow that were her rickshaw lamps vanish into the dripping misty darkness. I couldn't think why my own had stopped so abruptly until a movement just beyond the small circle of light caught my attention. Something that showed pale against the blackness of the dense forest of rhododendron, oak and deodar lining the edge of the steep bank on my right. Something yellow and spotted, and with two brilliant points of green light that, as they moved, caught and reflected the light of the rickshaw lamps . . .

It was a leopard, returning from foraging on the hillside above, which had been checked by the passing of Judy's rickshaw, and would probably have waited to let my own go by if the *jampanis* hadn't happened to spot it and dropped the shaft to take refuge behind me. That sudden stop had obviously alarmed the leopard more than the sight of it had alarmed the *jampanis*, for it hesitated for a full minute, its tail twitching angrily, obviously wondering whether to turn and go up the hillside. Then, abruptly making up its mind, it sprang down on to the road immediately in front of me, paused for a brief moment to turn its head and stare straight at me, unblinkingly, with those brilliant green eyes, before vanishing silently into the misty darkness below the far side of the drive.

My valiant *jampanis* gave it a moment or two to get clear before emerging discreetly — looking extremely sheepish — and we set off after Judy, who wanted to know what had held us up. I said that we had prudently waited to give right of way to a leopard, and Judy merely remarked that the woods were full of them. She was right, of course. In those days India was full of leopards and during my years there I saw a good many of them. But that one is forever bracketed in my memory with Simla, the Gaiety Theatre, and a touring theatrical company called the Quaints.

Chapter 22

Chris Birdwood's production of *Faust* was, as far as I remember, in the following summer. This, then, would have been the year in which Judy asked me to stay with her, so that we could work on the scenery and costumes, and I eventually stayed on in Simla with several other friends in order to do the same for two or three other amateur dramatic shows.

Judy and I were given a free hand with the dresses and sets, and everything else was up to Chris, who was at that time masquerading as an ADC to his father, the Commander-in-Chief. He did not appear to be doing a stroke of work in that line, and seemed to spend his days lying on a sofa in the drawing-room at Snowdon, reading sheet music. I suspect his appointment (which was pure nepotism) was due to prolonged nagging on the part of his doting mother, dear Lady Birdwood, and that Sir William must have given in after a hard struggle. But at least when it came to pulling strings, Chris was in an excellent position.

He managed to borrow the Viceroy's band, complete with bandmaster, to act as orchestra, and had no difficulty in rounding up all the best singers available. And a very talented lot they turned out to be. I wish I had had the sense to keep a programme, but I didn't so I don't remember the name of anyone who took part, except for the one who took the part of Marguerite, a Lady Crosthwaite, of whom more later. Nor do I remember why the opera was staged in Davico's ballroom and not in the Gaiety Theatre; probably because the Gaiety was fully booked for the season by the time Chris decided that he would like to have a stab at *Faust*. In fact, Davico's made an excellent and much more commodious theatre, for it boasted a large gallery at one end that doubled as a dress circle, and the stage at the other end was quite as large as, if not larger than the Gaiety's.

It had no facilities for painting scenery, but we were allowed to use the Gaiety's, and Judy and I spent the larger part of each day in overalls, sloshing paint on to canvas. We had decided on a very dark setting for

Act I, which was to be Faust's study — a Tudor-style chimneypiece off-centre (large enough for Mephistopheles to step through), the walls covered with tapestry, and only two pieces of furniture: a table and a chair.

The chimney had been easy enough, but our medieval tapestry looked too obtrusive and we didn't know how to tone it down, until I had a sudden brainwave. The studio at the Gaiety was properly equipped for scene painting, which, for the benefit of the uninitiated, consisted of two rooms, one above the other; the upper with the slit cut in the floor which allowed you to lower the entire backcloth through it, so that you didn't have to stand on a chair or a ladder to reach the bit you wanted to paint, but just lowered it (the canvas was fastened to a roll that could be turned by a handle, so that you could sit or stand to paint whatever part of it you wanted). We let down our far-too-gaudy tapestry, so that only a small part of the top remained visible, and then emptied along it the contents of the buckets of dirty paint water in which we had been washing our brushes. It could have been a disaster, but in fact worked a treat. The water poured down across our stylized over-bright trees, castles and huntsmen, fleeing deer and pursuing hounds, toning them down drastically, but leaving them still visible, so that the whole backcloth looked as though it was hung with a superb and very ancient and dusty tapestry.

The only other bit of scene painting that posed problems was the scene in the cathedral, where Marguerite prays to a statue of the Virgin, which keeps on turning into Mephistopheles. We got stuck over this for some time, but another rare brainwave solved it triumphantly. We cut an oblong slice out of a cathedral pillar, stretched coarse grey net across it, and fixed a wide tube of heavy black cloth to the back of the whole thing, plus red electric lights that could be operated manually when needed. Mephistopheles would be wearing a black velvet cloak lined with red satin, and the idea was that he would stand on a pedestal inside the black tube, with his cloak wrapped about him so that none of the scarlet showed. When the footlights were on (and the red lights inside the tube off), no one would see him, and when they were faded out and the red lights came on, he would drop the black cloak and be seen clearly through the net. Well, the red lights worked all right, but unfortunately the oblong in the pillar was still glaringly visible as an unexplained niche of black from the moment the curtains went up. No amount of grey paint on the net disguised it, and the general opinion was that we had better scrap the hole in the pillar, fill it in with canvas and settle for Mephistopheles stepping out from behind it whenever the score called for it. Fortunately — or perhaps unfortunately — my brain clicked into action and produced a beautiful solution. This too worked like a dream.

We cut the oblong into a pointed niche and painted the canvas to look as though it had a carved stone edging, and I chalked a coloured statuette of the Madonna on to the net with coloured pastels. It is always a thrill when a far-fetched gimmick actually works in practice, and I admit to being slightly stunned at the success of this one. The footlights caught the pastels, and the Madonna looked as solid as though she had been carved out of marble. But when the red lights behind the net were gradually brought up and the footlights faded out, it looked exactly as though the statue was turning into the devil. It was a wild success. The only snag was that I had to draw the whole thing all over again, and in frantic haste, before the curtain went up on that scene. It proved impossible to shift the scenery without shaking the net; and as soon as it was shaken the pastel came off the net in puffs of coloured chalk. I redrew the Madonna at least ten times in six evening performances, two matinées, the dress rehearsal and a couple of trial runs in order to co-ordinate the bringing up and fading out of the footlights with those inside the pillar. I got pretty good at it, I can tell you! There is, however, a snarky and well-known saying to the effect that 'pride goes before a fall' and mine was doomed to bite the dust.

The Viceroy had been holding a Governors' conference in Simla that week, and it had seemed a good idea to someone or other to suggest that His Excellency should bring all his gilded Governors to see the final performance, and advertise it as a special performance in aid of famine relief. His Excellency, probably only too willing to have this pack of VIPs taken off his hands for one evening, consented and, as soon as that news got around, there was a scramble for seats. Everyone who was anyone wanted to be there, and one could safely say that if the terrorist wing of the Quit India Movement had managed to toss a bomb into Davico's ballroom that night, the Raj would have come to a grinding halt there and then.

Just think of it! The Governors of every single province in the land, together with the Commander-in-Chief, India, and any number of Members of Council and other assorted bigwigs, headed by the Viceroy himself. It was equivalent to the entire royal family, the Prime Minister and his Cabinet, and the leaders of the armed forces and heads of police and intelligence, all gathered together under one roof, and you can imagine what a dither the cast was in. Not to mention the harassed chaps who were responsible for security.

Everyone's nerves were slightly on edge, but any tension Judy and I might have suffered was relieved by one of our amateur scene-shifters. These were all members of the Viceroy's band, and by this time they all knew the score backwards and could have taken over from the prompter without a qualm. This one was obviously word-perfect, for carrying a heavy roll of canvas across the stage, he tripped on a piece of carpet and came a terrific cropper. Sitting up dazedly and tenderly feeling his chin, he did not, as expected, come out with a few forceful words, but intoned instead in a mournful baritone: 'Never will I trust me powers again!' It was a quotation from something that Mephistopheles says to Faust: ('If she prefer your flowers to these gems, never will I trust my powers again!') and it sent Judy and me off into helpless giggles. Which was just as well, for the rest of the show was a nightmare.

The house began to fill up, the VIPs arrived, and so eventually did the Viceroy. But back-stage, panic was raging — the so-and-so who was playing Mephistopheles (I've no idea what his name was so I shall call him Mr M.) had not arrived. Frantic phone calls failed to trace him. There was no question of an understudy being sent on instead, for the drawback to ambitious amateurs in a small town putting on an opera is that there is not likely to be more than one really good tenor, baritone, bass or soprano to be found in a restricted community. In fact one is lucky to be able to produce one of each!

Poor Chris was nearly demented, and he was preparing to go out in front of the curtain and say that he was terribly sorry, but the show would have to be cancelled, when (most unfortunately) Mr M. turned up — tight as a newt. Totally, gloriously, absolutely plastered. I still don't know why the producer and the more senior members of the cast didn't give up at once and scrub the whole thing. But I imagine that their collective nerve failed them at the thought of having to go out and inform the distinguished (and by now impatient) gathering that the baritone was higher than a kite and in no condition to appear before them, so would they please all go home. Instead, they attempted to delay the proceedings by getting the band to play the overture twice, while some of them alternately pushed Mr M.'s head into a bucket of cold water and forced him to drink black coffee, while others did their best to get him into his costume, all of which he took with the greatest good humour.

✂ The house-lights went out and the band launched into the overture for the third time, and we were off!

Fortunately for everyone concerned, there were not that many people in the audience who were familiar with *Faust*, and no one seemed to have noticed that the overture was an exceptionally lengthy one and taken at a somewhat leisurely pace. Or that there was an over-long gap between its final chord and the parting of the curtains. Since this was the last night, I had no worries about the scenery and the costumes. I knew they were all right, because I had watched every performance, and had plenty of time to alter anything that hadn't worked in practice. Visually, the whole thing was a triumph, and Judy and I, feeling justly proud of ourselves, had been smugly anticipating an impressive spate of compliments from the last-night audience. But we had not been prepared for the mayhem that one intoxicated performer can create when well and truly flootered. Nor, alas, had the rest of the cast; having begun the evening feeling every bit as smug and certain of success as Judy and I were, they had been thrown into a dither by the failure of one of their stars to turn up and, by the time the curtain went up and they realized what they were in for, were all in a state of near panic.

Faust, who under the circumstances had the most reason for being anxious, was not in his usual good voice, but he did his best, and all went well until the entry of the villain of the piece. Judy and I had been particularly proud of the way we had worked the conjuring up of the devil, and on every previous performance it had gone like a breeze. Faust had to fling down one of those flash-fireworks (a jazzed-up version of the things we call *partarkas*) and Mr M., who was standing behind the black curtains at the back of the Tudor fireplace, peering through a narrow chink between them as he waited for his cue, had only to step forward, flinging wide his black, scarlet-lined cloak, as the flash went off and the audience automatically flinched back and shut their eyes against the glare . . . And there was the devil — conjured up out of darkness and thin air! It had always gone splendidly. But not tonight.

The flash, as ever, went off beautifully. But when the audience stopped blinking, nothing had changed. Faust was mouthing wildly at the prompter, as though hoping for some assistance from there, and a muffled and furious voice could be heard expostulating with someone in the wings. The next moment, Mephistopheles shot on to the stage head first, propelled with some violence by an infuriated hand on his back, and having regained his balance, strolled amiably on towards centre stage, nodded affably to the audience and waved merrily to the unfortunate conductor (I can't remember whether Chris was actually in the hot seat that night or whether it was the bandmaster) to indicate that he could start. Surprisingly, he was in tremendous, though slightly erratic, form. Alcohol imparted a distinctly fruity edge to his voice, and the audience gave him a tremendous hand. Only those who had seen the show before realized that his entrance had not been all it should.

We brushed through the next act pretty well, and once again, only those in the know realized that there was anything untoward. Allowances are, in any case, made for amateurs. I don't suppose many of the audience that night were familiar with the opera, and the rest do not seem to have noticed anything odd about the extremely exuberant behaviour of our Mephistopheles. After all, why shouldn't the devil be pleased with himself?

We sailed through the next couple of acts, with a terrific display of high spirits and not too many missed cues and musical gaffes on the part of Mephistopheles, and Judy and I had begun to breathe again when along came my *pièce-de-résistance* in the Cathedral. I re-drew my Madonna and besought the stage manager to try to persuade Mr M. to stand still — which he had always done before, though I had my doubts as to his ability to do so tonight. And how right I was. To begin with, he took a dislike to being incarcerated in the tube of black cloth at the back of the pillar, and in the end had to be put there forcibly. Annoyed by this, he flung back his black velvet cloak, displaying its brilliant satin lining, and when Marguerite, played by Lady Crosthwaite (who in addition to a well trained soprano voice, possessed a character on the lines of that formidable battle-axe, my Aunt Molly, and was known by one and all to be exceedingly quick on the draw), launched into her prayer to the Virgin, he behaved abominably. Discovering, as though for the first time, that the net in front of him was thick with coloured chalks, he began to flick it off in little puffs of powder; and when that palled (by which time there was little left of my statue) he stuck his head out of the side of the pillar and, having spotted various friends in the audience, yoo-hoo-ed cheerfully at them. I could have killed him. I really could. And so could Lady Crosthwaite, who, on her knees by the footlights, couldn't see what was happening above her head but realized that the audience was beginning to laugh.

The awful thing was that it *was* funny. I had so wanted the performance to go without a hitch on this special occasion, and this ghastly man had ruined it. But exasperated as we were, neither Judy nor I could stop laughing; we practically rolled in the aisles. The only person who could see nothing amusing in it was our poor leading lady, who was furious. She was to become even more so during the last act, which wasn't really the inebriated Mr M.'s fault so much as whoever was in charge of the scene-shifting. (Not us, thank heaven.)

In the last act Marguerite is discovered in prison, about to be hanged for the murder of her illegitimate child. This was Lady Crosthwaite's big scene and she looked terrific, togged up in a long white robe and with her splendid blonde wig (hitherto done up in plaits) loose and flowing all down her back. The prison cell called for no special scenic effects, and Judy and I, still weak from giggling, were congratulating ourselves that at least there was nothing here that the inebriated Mr M. could ruin. We wronged him. Our scene-shifters, understandably flustered by the weird goings-on, had failed to notice that the backdrop had not been lowered to its full extent, and that there was a gap of at least six inches between the bottom of the dungeon wall and its floor (an error that must be fairly easy to make, because years later I saw exactly the same thing happen at a London theatre, on a very star-studded occasion indeed! — the opening night of Sir James Barrie's last play, *The Boy David*, starring Elisabeth Bergner in the title role).

Since the last act of *Faust* takes place in the cell of a medieval prison, and the backdrop in question was painted to represent dark stonework, the scene was pretty gloomy and that six-inch slit showed up as a brilliant strip of light. Well, that wouldn't have mattered too much, because sooner or later someone back-stage would have spotted it and had it eliminated. But unfortunately, the interval till someone in the front of the house hurried round to get the backdrop lowered was a good deal longer than one would suppose, because it hadn't occurred to anyone that it wouldn't be corrected in double-quick time. Glaringly obvious to the audience, it was, on account of the darkness on the other side, barely visible to those back-stage. By the time we had woken up to the fact that the back-stage lot hadn't spotted it, and managed to get around to the stage door and sounded the alarm, the harm had been done. For on the far side of the canvas our Mephistopheles, still as merry as a mayfly, had decided to dance a jig in time to the music, and the sight of a pair of long-toed scarlet slippers, attached to two or three inches of scarlet legs, performing an Irish jig, proved too much for the audience. They began to laugh, and found they couldn't stop. Gales of laughter spread through the house and once again the wretched Marguerite found herself trying to sing to an audience that was literally rolling about in its seats if not actually in the aisles. And once again, although I could willingly have strangled that infuriating man, I found myself laughing as helplessly as any of the convulsed audience.

Fortunately, this state of affairs didn't last very long. As soon as the back-stage lot found out what was going on, the backcloth was hastily lowered and the scene returned to the gloom of the dungeon. The audience mopped its eyes and pulled itself together, a shaken and furious Marguerite and a rapidly disintegrating Faust got on with the final act, and when at last the curtain came down, it fell to thunderous applause, presumably because the audience was feeling slightly ashamed of itself and was trying to reward the other members of the cast for gallantry in the face of overwhelming odds. As for Judy and me, who could have wept for the ruin that had been made of the scenery and effects we had been so proud of and had taken so much trouble over, we had to admit that in spite of our rage and disappointment we had laughed ourselves into stitches, and that it had been one of the most entertaining nights of our lives.

✼ We were fated to have at least one more of the same in Simla, this time at the Gaiety Theatre, when Lady Crosthwaite (late Marguerite) put on, for a single night, a performance entitled *In a Persian Garden*. It was in aid of some charity or other, I think for Lady Dufferin's Fund for Medical Aid to the Women of India. And I don't know how Judy and I came to be mixed up in it, because I can't remember doing any scene painting or costume designing for it. Yet we were obviously in on it from the beginning because we attended every rehearsal, and were always on call, for some reason or another.

The show consisted of a series of *tableaux vivants* taken, vaguely, from someone's illustrations to the *Rubaiyat of Omar Khayyam*, and each tableau was accompanied by a singer who sang the matching quatrains, standing in front of the curtains which parted, when the singer had finished, on the appropriate tableau. I imagine that Lady Crosthwaite must have been one of the singers along with some of the cast of *Faust*. Lady C. was the mainspring of the whole show, and she cracked the whip with enthusiasm over anyone who had anything whatever to do with it, beginning with old de la Rue Brown, who, having managed the theatre from way back in the 1880s, considered that he owned it and did not take kindly to being chivvied about. Neither did the Viceroy's bandmaster, whose men were again acting as orchestra, and had taken to referring bitterly to the proceedings as: 'This 'ere Perishing Garden!'

Lady C., besides being a notable battle-axe, had considerable social pull, which she had used to co-opt a number of young Indian royals to appear in two of the tableaux. These privileged infants would turn up for rehearsals guarded by phalanxes of retainers, and decked with the most amazing jewels, which had an alarming habit of coming detached from their settings or simply falling off as the result of inadequate fastenings, to the fury of Mr Brown, who was forced to turn sweeper and personally brush out the premises after every rehearsal, or risk having the resident sweeper and cleaners accused of pocketing some missing trinket worth a small fortune. Not, I feel sure, that the royals or their attendants would have noticed the loss, or troubled to make a fuss about it if they had. Probably the jewels were only their second-best, and hardly worth bothering about. Or that was the impression I got one evening when I trod on an emerald and diamond earring, fringed with seed pearls, and handed it over to the senior lady-in-waiting in charge of its four-year-old owner. She didn't actually say, 'What — that old thing?' but I got the impression if she'd been the one to tread on it, she would have dropped it into the nearest waste-paper basket. It was the sort of incident that made me realize how incredibly, fantastically rich most of the ruling princes were.

The dress rehearsal of the 'perishing garden', which had an invited audience, many of them relatives of the cast, turned out to be even more hilarious than the last night of *Faust*, and if it is true that 'a bad dress rehearsal makes a good play', then the play ought to have been one of the best ever, for nothing seemed to go right. Lady Crosthwaite (never the most tactful of women) lost her cool and bit everyone within sight, which had the unfortunate result of inciting several insulted males to retaliate in kind, while reducing the rest to nervous jellies.

There was a short sharp encounter early on with Mr Brown over the lighting of one of the tableaux, 'Myself when Young' — the part of 'myself' being taken by the obedient but bewildered heir to one of Rajputana's greatest kingdoms, while the accompanying quatrain was slightly unsuitably sung by a sahib in full evening dress, white tie and tails, the lot. The audience enjoyed the encounter to the hilt.

For some reason Lady C. took a dislike to the lighting of this tableau. Too yellow, I think. She rose from her seat in the stalls like some over-clothed Venus rising from the waves, and, ignoring the invited audience, called a halt to the proceedings and shouted authoritatively for Mr Brown. When that wizened character eventually sidled out from the wings she demanded that he should scrub the yellow lights and try the amber. This was eventually done, only to be greeted by a howl of horror: 'No, no, *no!* Mr Brown. That's terrible! No we can't have that, try the pink.' The pink was duly tried, with even less success, as was the green, and Lady C. eventually called for blue. Nothing happened. 'Blue, Mr Brown,' repeated Lady C. fortissimo. The lights remained stubbornly green. 'Mister Brown!' trumpeted our directrice, 'I said I wanted to try the blue lights. Blue! Mr Brown! *Blue lights.*'

Old Mr Brown's head protruded from the wings looking exactly like an elderly tortoise in spectacles: 'Ain't no bloody blue lights!' snarled Mr Brown, and stumped away to go to ground again in his office. The audience was entranced.

The incident of the blue lights, however, was not the only unrehearsed side-show that evening for, owing to a deplorable lack of rapport between the curtain-raiser and the scene-changers, the curtains on two separate occasions parted prematurely, disclosing work still in progress. On the first occasion, the lovers who were supposed to be sitting underneath a bough and sharing a flask of wine, a book of verse and thou, prior to singing in the wilderness, had dutifully taken up their positions. But far from being alone together, they were accompanied by a couple of beefy stage-hands in their shirt-sleeves who, oblivious of all else, were engaged in hammering nails into the bough in order to keep it securely in place. Their horror at being suddenly put on display to a considerable audience was greeted with a howl of mirth, which rose to a crescendo when both men made a simultaneous dive for the wings in the manner of a rugby tackle. That really did bring the house down. It was greeted with yells of 'Goal' and 'Off-side' and similar tribal noises.

I don't know why this sort of thing should be so funny, but it is; and Judy and I were not the only two who, from our privileged seat in one of the boxes, fell about laughing, and once we had started, could not stop. From then on, to the embarrassment of the cast, every scene — and every song too! — was greeted with gales of mirth and uproarious applause, and I can only suppose that this demoralized everyone backstage. The same style of incident that had ruined the earlier tableau was repeated, to even greater enthusiasm on the part of the house, by the most elaborate of the tableaux: the one that was supposed to show the 'Courts where Jamshyd gloried and drank deep' and which happened to involve the greatest number of juvenile royals.

This time a different assortment of back-stage helpers, also in shirt-sleeves and wearing the most deplorable trousers, were disclosed moving busily to and fro, backs to the audience and bottoms in the air, placing gorgeous cushions and bolsters in position, and oblivious of the fact that several of the 'court ladies' were clearly hissing between clenched teeth and rigidly smiling mouths: 'Get off the stage! — the curtain's up! *Get off the stage!*' Well, they got off in due course, and by much the same rugby-tackle fashion as the others had used — a frantic dive into the wings and shouts of 'Goal!' from, I suspect, several members of the Viceroy's band. The show itself, when it came on, was a great success and raised a nice, solid sum in aid of the charity it had been put on for. But the paying customers, who greeted every song and its accompanying tableau with polite applause, didn't get half the fun for their money as the invited audience that had laughed themselves into hiccups over the dress rehearsal.

Among the many other things that I remember about my return to Simla as a grown-up are two people and a story. One of the people was a young man who was to become known to half the world as 'Jai', His Highness the Yuveraj of Jaipur — I don't think he was the Maharajah yet — an incredibly handsome young man and every bit as charming as a Prince in a fairy-tale. The other was a blond and good-looking young Scandinavian by the name of Aage Thaarup, who had taken rooms at the Grand Hotel and set up in a modest way as a hatter. (He eventually became hatter to the Queen and half the fashionable ladies in London.) I was fascinated by those hats, and even more so by the fact that the young designer had a habit of trying them on himself. Greatly daring — and having saved up for several months — I 'bespoke' one in my price-range, a very small black felt hat rather in the style of a pancake. I remember him telling me severely, 'Now remember, in zis hat you have only ze one eye!' He then jammed it on his own head, well over his left eye, to illustrate, looking, I have to admit, far more attractive in it than I did, for he, like Jai, was a most beautiful young man and a pleasure to look at.

The story was one that was told me by old Mr Bevan-Petman, when I was staying with him and his wife in the summer of — I think — 1929. They were old friends of my parents and lived during the summer in one of the oldest of the Simla houses, a big three-storeyed wooden house with wide, glassed-in verandahs and large dark inner rooms, built on and partly into the steep hillside above Davico's ballroom and the road that led to the Lucker bazaar and Snowdon. From those glassed-in verandahs one looked out on to a most wonderful view, fold after fold of foothills and valleys stretching away on to the high mountains and the long line of snow-peaks that lay along the horizon. The house was surrounded by a small flower garden and a well-stocked vegetable one, that like all Simla gardens appeared to be pegged to the steep hillside by a few tall deodars. Above these lay the thickly wooded acres of Jacko Hill.

All Simla gardens, in particular those on the slopes of Jacko, were apt to be raided at frequent intervals by bands of the monkey-folk — the brown, thievish, noisy *bandar-log* who haunt the forests and chase each other across the tin-roofed houses. But I had been a guest of the Bevan-Petmans' for at least a week before it occurred to me that during that time I had not seen a single monkey on their premises. And this at a time when the cherries were ripe, not to mention the peas and french beans.

Normally Simla is as full of the *bandar-log* as a London garden is of sparrows, since Jacko, the hill that many of the houses are built on, has on its highest point a temple, complete with a resident priest, dedicated to the monkey god, Hanuman, who holds a prominent place in Hindu mythology. The top-storey windows of all our houses, and many of the lower ones too, were screened by wire-netting to keep the *bandar-log* from stealing anything that happened to catch their fancy and was small enough to carry away — items such as spoons and forks, articles of clothing, and anything edible. Groups and troops of them were an integral part of Simla's scenery, and the clatter and clash of half-a-dozen monkeys chasing each other across the red, corrugated-tin roofs of our houses became as familiar a sound to us as the shrill whistling of the kite-hawks that wheeled above the bazaar, or the sough of the wind through pine-needles.

I began to look out for the creatures, but though the rest of Simla was still as infested by monkeys as ever, I never saw a single one on the roofs or in the gardens or the orchard of the Bevan-Petmans' house, and one day, having commented on this to my host, he told me the reason.

It seems that until a few years earlier the house and grounds had been plagued by hordes of monkeys who would descend like locusts upon the kitchen garden and the orchard, as soon as the produce of either was nearing the point where it would be ripe enough to pick, and strip it bare. They seldom ate the flowers, but they enjoyed tearing the heads off them and would rampage through the garden like a gang of nasty little boys, snatching off the heads of the roses and carnations or whatever was in flower, and pelting each other with them. And despite all the careful netting of vegetables and fruit, the erecting of scarecrows, the yard-strings that when touched activated rattles, plus a dozen other tricks of the trade, very little survived their depredations. Nor did wire-screens succeed in keeping the house completely secure from their pilfering fingers.

I don't remember for certain what it was that pushed the harassed household to the breaking point, but at a guess it was probably an incident that old Mrs Bevan-Petman described to me with considerable bitterness, and which after a lapse of several years still rankled: the sight of a large dog-monkey sitting on the bough of a pine tree crooning to itself as it carefully pulled to pieces a satin and lace petticoat that she had bought only an hour before at a sale of embroidery by the pupils of a Mission School in Kalimpong, and had left for not more than five minutes on one of the verandah tables, still wrapped. I bet that was the final straw, and I can just see Mrs B.-P. running screaming to her husband demanding vengeance. She was not a patient lady. Anyway, whatever the cause, it was sufficient to send her husband reaching for his gun . . .

Bevan-Petman senior was known to be one of the best shots in India. But until now, however severe the provocation, he had never even considered shooting one of the *bandar-log*, for the simple reason that a great many Hindu citizens of India regarded them as sacred — or at least semi-sacred — by reason of being under the special protection of Hanuman. But by this time, he had had it. If the opposition wanted war they should have it, and from then on he shot monkeys. With, I may say, the approval of his servants; particularly his Muslim head *mali*, who, given any encouragement, would have started shooting them long ago.

The *bandar-log* took a little time to realize that they were up against serious opposition, but as their casualties mounted the message finally got across, and their raids on the Bevan-Petman estate got fewer and farther between until, at long last (I believe it took a full year) they ceased altogether, and there came a time when for several months at a stretch not a single member of the tribe was either seen or heard on the premises. The B.-P.s congratulated themselves on their victory and were a trifle scornful towards fellow-sufferers who flinched from copying their tactics. But they congratulated themselves too soon.

One day, and without any warning, an army of monkeys descended *en masse* from the forested hillside that lay beyond the Bevan-Petmans' domain, and attacked the house. It was, insisted my host, a carefully thought-out exercise, for they had obviously encircled the place before launching their attack. 'They came at me from every direction, screaming, grunting and shrieking defiance. It was terrifying,' he said, and the humans took to their heels and rushed for the house, though not in time to prevent a number of monkeys getting in through doors and french windows that had been left open. Mrs B.-P., the bearer and the head *mali* could all handle a shotgun, and they and Mr B. -P. ran from window to window, firing, while the rest of the household snatched any weapon they could and laid about them with polo-sticks, squash racquets, walking sticks and anything else that came to hand. Mr B.-P. described it as being exactly like a Tom Mix cowboy film, in which the Indians attack some lonely farmhouse, and that it should have been uproariously funny — if it hadn't been so frightening.

He said the creatures kept it up for what seemed like ages, but was probably not more than the inside of an hour, and then they called it off as suddenly as they had started it. One minute they were still fighting to get in at the windows, shrieking, biting and clawing, and the next they had vanished into the forest. Their casualties had been heavy, and later that day the victors buried the vanquished in a mass grave in the orchard. And from that day on, no monkey had been known to come within several hundred yards of the Bevan-Petmans' grounds. Personally, I think the whole story is a very scary one. There is something very frightening about animals having the same kind of brains as humans — and using them in the same way. I wasn't sorry to leave that house.

Anyone who wants to know more about Simla's *bandar-log*, and their temple on the crest of Jacko, can find it in a book by Raja Bhasin, entitled *Simla, the Summer Capital of British India*, which contains dozens of stories about that once fabled little town.

Chapter 23

꙰ᘓᕽᏂᕽᘎ꙰

We left Simla a few days after my twenty-first birthday, to drive to Kashmir; Mother at the wheel of the big car, with Tacklow and most of the luggage aboard, and Bets and I taking turns to drive the small one, with Kadera to keep an eye on us. I don't remember much about that journey, except that the monsoon rains had been heavy that year, particularly in the north, and the floods were out in the Kashmir valley, though not too badly to hold us up.

That journey was to become so familiar and, much as it often scared me, so dear, that sometimes still, on nights when I cannot sleep, I drive along that road in my imagination, having first decided which one I will take, for there are three ways into the delectable valley. The one by Abbottabad, which I have already described; the one via Murree, and the last via Sialkot and Jammu and the Banihal Pass, which I still think is the best one to approach it by. Because, after you have zig-zagged up that treeless mountainside, with its interminable hairpin bends — and its frequent horrific reminders, in the way of wreckage strewn across the barren slopes far below you, of what can happen if you take them too fast, or if your brakes fail — and when you have negotiated the long dark, dripping tunnel at the top, you suddenly come out on to a wonderful panoramic view of the valley spread out at your feet, far, far below you, green and blossoming and beautiful, ringed with snow-peaks and looking, after the bleakness on the far side of the tunnel, like a skylark's view of Eden.

I don't remember which route we took that year, but I'm pretty certain that it can't have been via the Banihal, because driving up that fearsome road would have scared me stiff and I couldn't possibly *not* have remembered it! But I remember that old Ahamdoo Siraj had not failed us, and the houseboat he had hired for us was ready and waiting, half-way between Gagribal Point and the Dāl Gate, which is the place where the

Jhelum river flows into the Dāl through a water gate that can be opened or closed according to need. The houseboat he had rented for us was the H. B. *Carlton*, which was, at that time, one of the larger boats on the lakes. It seemed enormous to me, and I couldn't see how on earth it was going to negotiate the narrow waterways and canals that led out to Chota Nageem, where Ahamdoo had arranged a more permanent mooring for us.

Bill had managed to get a few days' leave in which to come up and meet us, and we found him waiting at the Dāl Gate, where we all piled into *shikarras* and were rowed across to the H. B. *Carlton*.

We had been afraid that Bill would have brought his fiancée along to meet us, for the fuss and bother of arrival after a long tiring day was hardly the setting that any prospective in-law would have chosen for a first meeting. Fortunately, however, he had not been able to see her himself, for she had been out when he arrived unexpectedly early — several hours earlier than we had — and called briefly at her parents' boat. He had left a message saying that he would be along later in the evening to take her out to dine and dance, and now he bathed and changed into his dinner-jacket, and having asked the *manji* to call up a *shikarra* and arrange for a *tonga*, apologized to Mother for having to go out on our first evening together, and was rowed away to the Dāl Gate.

The next few minutes remain fixed in my memory because it taught me a sharp lesson about making judgements. Bill had looked far from cheerful, and I wondered if Mother, who was never very quick on the uptake, had noticed it. She was leaning out of the window watching him go, looking as all those thousands of women must have looked, back in the dark days of the 1914—18 war, as they watched the troop-trains that were carrying their men away to the battlefields of France and Flanders pull out of a railway station. She had seen so little of him as a child or a schoolboy or a cadet; and even less of him as a soldier. Now she was going to lose him to an unknown girl. It cannot have been a happy moment for her. But all she said as she watched him leave was 'I do hope she'll like us.' Not 'I hope we'll like her,' you notice.

Mother and I had never got on very well. Bill, her adored firstborn and her only son, was her pride and joy, while Bets, as the baby of the family, was her darling and her pet. I came somewhere in the middle and as far as she was concerned didn't count for very much — which had never worried me because I came first with Tacklow, first of his children

I mean. Mother came first with him. I must have been about sixteen or seventeen when it first dawned on me that my mother, instead of being a fount of wisdom (as, in the manner of most children, I had imagined her to be) was in fact a rather silly woman. For example, she confessed one day that she had not wanted another baby while Bill was still so small, and that she had done everything she could think of to get rid of me — 'The sort of things all your married girlfriends seem to know about and advise you to do,' said Mother blithely; adding with a distinct tinge of irritation that she had done everything they advised, but none of it had worked.

What a thing to tell me of all people! Yet she would have been horrified if anyone had accused her of being tactless or unkind in telling that tale to the least-loved of her brood, when all she thought she was doing was having a grown-up talk with a daughter who was now old enough to realize babies were not discovered under gooseberry bushes or brought by storks. There was no malice in Mother. She just didn't think — or not very often. Yet seeing her face as she watched Bill leaving us, and hearing her express the hope that his girl would like us, I was proud of her; for I know that if I'd been in her shoes I wouldn't have been able to say that! It also made me realize that that sort of thinking cancelled out any amount of silliness, as well as explaining why Tacklow was still so much in love with her after all these years.

But in the event she didn't have to worry for long, for in considerably less than half an hour a *shikarra* bumped alongside and Bill catapulted in through the dining-room windows, beaming from ear-to-ear in the manner of the Cheshire Cat, and bursting with good news. It seemed that he had arrived at his fiancée's houseboat, clutching the small velvet box that contained the engagement ring, only to be fended off before he had had a chance to present it. For Bertha had fallen in love with somebody else and no longer wished to marry Bill. She had been incoherent with apologies, and Bill, torn between relief and embarrassment, had apparently managed to blurt out something about hoping that she would be happy and that they could remain friends, before hastily removing himself.

Tacklow was asked to take charge of the ring again until such time as Bill could flog it, which he subsequently did, at a loss, as no one who has ever been in the same position will be surprised to learn. Mother shed a few relieved tears and Bill celebrated by going solo to the Nedou's Hotel dance where, inevitably, he met yet another, 'absolutely smashing girl'.

'The trouble with me,' confessed Bill at breakfast next morning, 'is that I fall in love with every girl I meet, and I don't know what to do about it!' 'Keep off the drink,' advised Tacklow drily. But except on that one inexplicable occasion, drink was not, and never would be, a problem with Bill, for the simple reason that he could not hold it. A blessing in disguise if ever there was one.

The matter of his nuptials having been settled to everyone's satisfaction, Bill returned in good spirits to his battery, and the H. B. *Carlton*, which was to be our temporary home for the next few weeks, was poled out to the *ghat* that Ahamdoo had hired for us a mile or so away, not far from the Nageem Bagh lake.

One of the great charms of living on a houseboat in Kashmir used to be that you could move your home, plus your entire family and its belongings, from place to place as the whim took you — always provided that you had made sure that there would be a *ghat* available for you to tie up to at your journey's end. No one can really appreciate the charm of Srinagar and its chain of lakes until they have sat at ease on the flat roof of their boat and watched the world go by as a team of stout Kashmiris (or if their boat is small enough, their *manji* and one or two of his relations) pole them through green willow-bordered waterways, spangled with lily-pads and the brilliant, flashing jewel colours of kingfishers, to emerge into bright sunlight and find themselves moving grandly through the main street of one of the outlying suburbs, for here, as in Venice, many of the streets are replaced by canals. I had passed this way often in a *shikarra* but never before from the vantage-point of a houseboat roof, and it was like watching a play from a seat in the front of a dress circle.

Every houseboat has a 'cookboat' in which the *manji* (who usually doubles as the cook) lives with his family, and has his own 'working' *shikarra* in which the staff can go shopping and generally fetch or carry. This last is a strictly utility craft and does not boast padded seats or a canopy, as the 'taxi' *shikarras* do, and when a houseboat is on the move, it is trailed behind the cookboat which follows behind the houseboat. So we made a stately procession as we moved to the rhythmic chant of the men who were poling us. These poles are enormously long and must be exceedingly heavy, but they handle them with the ease of long practice, dropping them into the water at the front of the houseboat, and walking back along the duckboards pushing them, until by the time they reach the end of the boat there is only a scant yard of wood left above the water for them to push with their shoulders, before hauling the great, dripping poles out and walking forward, trailing them, to repeat the process.

Our floating home glided us past an ancient mosque, shaded by chenar trees and fronted by a wide flight of stone steps that ended in the water; past a little Hindu temple whose tall, pointed roof glittered blindingly in the bright sunlight, because it had recently been retiled with plates of tin taken from the sides of kerosene tins, which may sound unromantic, but in fact looked wonderful. An excellent lunch was served as usual, in the middle of all this, but Mother, who had been making pencil sketches all morning, became aware that there was some slight hitch in the proceedings and a certain amount of whispering in the pantry between courses. She asked if anything was wrong. No, no, said the *manji* — it was nothing. A slight inconvenience only. His wife was in labour, that was all. They had not expected it for another week, it was a pity that it happened today, but there was nothing for the Lady-Sahib to worry about.

Mother was appalled. The very idea of that unfortunate girl having a baby in the overcrowded cookboat, with no privacy at all, and while it was being poled by hired coolies, and her husband and his brother were cooking a three-course meal for us, and various members of her family were falling over each other helping to wash dishes — ! The boat must be pulled into the bank and moored at once and the coolies sent home and no more cooking must be done until the baby arrived and it was certain that all was well with its mother. We could easily stay here until then, and send for coolies at a later date.

It was the *manji*'s turn to be horrified. He wouldn't dream of stopping the boat for such a trivial reason. It would be *shuram ki bhat** and his wife would be terribly upset to think that she was the cause of it. What would people say? He was plainly shocked to the core, and Mother had to give in, though she spent an anxious day and night. We arrived safely at our moorings, having been served tea *en route* at the normal time, and dinner (four courses) on the dot. There was no further word from the cookboat but Mother did not sleep well, wondering if she should send for the nearest woman doctor. She need not have worried. The morning dawned cloudless and bright, and the first thing we saw when we looked

_____
* Shameful talk.

anxiously at the cookboat was an enchanting baby boy, roughly the size of a small cottage loaf, sitting propped up on the prow of the cookboat, wrapped in a gaily coloured blanket, wearing a red and gold cap on his head and looking as chipper as a cricket.

Our *ghat* turned out to be on a spur of land that was almost an island, on which the rich Indian who owned it had started to build a two-storey house where he and his family could spend the summer months. But when it was almost finished, something must have happened to make him change his mind, for he abandoned it, and rented out the land as a *ghat* instead. The unfinished house acquired the reputation of being haunted, though no one knew why. The only reason why we never entered it was because the sun, rain and snow of many years had played havoc with it and made it too dangerous a place to go wandering around in. Willows, poplars, weeds and wild roses had grown up around it, and there were several large chenar trees and an ancient wild cherry that must have been there long before the house was built.

The mooring itself was on a quiet backwater known as Chota Nageem (small Nageem), separated from the larger lake of that name only by the Nageem Bagh Bridge and the main road that leaves Srinagar to circle the Dāl and touch, in doing so, no fewer than four of the gardens with which the Great Moguls gilded the lily that is — that was — Kashmir. And since the entire island was included in the fee that was paid for our *ghat*, we found ourselves in possession of enough space to accommodate at least three more houseboats. Which was our good fortune, because the only drawback to having one's houseboat moored at Nageem itself was that even at that date it had become much too popular, and by now was getting grossly overcrowded. There were places where cookboats were moored parallel to and far too near their houseboats, which led to a certain amount of friction between the holidaying occupiers. One of them, goaded into action, sent a crisply worded letter of complaint to his next-door neighbour, pointing out that her *masalchi* had taken to flinging the dirty water in which he had been washing her dishes straight into his drawing-room windows, and that this practice must now cease. Since he signed his letter 'Russell of Liverpool', the lady on the receiving end leapt to the conclusion that he was being frivolous and, unaware that he was in fact Lord Russell of Liverpool, signed her apology 'Mary Magdalen of Jerusalem'. He was not amused.

Nageem was a deservedly popular spot, for though it is quite a small lake and cannot compare in size with the Dāl, Nasim or Gagribal, it is the deepest of all the lakes (local opinion insists that it is bottomless) and, being fed by underground springs, is also the cleanest and clearest, which made it an excellent place for swimmers. It also boasted a large bathing boat (only one, at that date!), which was moored well out on the lake opposite the Club, and furnished with changing rooms, a bar, and diving boards from which, for a small sum, one could bathe, dive, or just sit around talking and sipping gimlets, a popular local drink with the Raj, consisting of gin, Rose's lime juice and ice. But the overcrowding that was due to its popularity was not the only drawback to acquiring a *ghat* on Nageem. A worse one was the almost total lack of privacy.

No conversation was private, and a disgusted young American friend of ours, globe-trotting through India, complained that he had been told that the immoral goings-on of the holidaying British in Kashmir were beyond belief, but that in his opinion anyone who had the 'noive' to be immoral on a houseboat deserved a gold medal for Courage Beyond Call of Duty. He had a point there, for it is impossible to move in a houseboat without rocking it gently, and creakingly, at every step. In addition to which, no word spoken in a normal voice went unheard.

The same went for the wooden-built huts, hotels and guest-houses of Gulmarg, which had given rise to endless stories. The best known of these concerns a middle-aged Major on leave who, arriving at a late hour of night at Nedou's Hotel in Gulmarg, was given a notoriously draughty single room, untenanted for the past week and the last-but-one of a row. His journey up from the plains having been a particularly exhausting one, he went straight to bed — and to sleep. Only to be rudely awakened (the phrase can be taken literally) by the arrival of an amorous couple in the end room who, it soon became clear, had no idea that the next-door room was no longer unoccupied.

The unfortunate Major found himself forced to listen to a good deal of scampering and scuffling, punctuated by maidenly squeaks or guffaws of manly laughter and occasional protests that suggested that the pair were attempting to take each other's clothes off. Presently the unwilling listener was regaled with the sound of a crisp slap and a male voice inquiring roguishly, 'Whose little bottom is this?' followed by a flurry of squeaks and giggles, the sound of a second slap and a breathless soprano voice demanding, 'And whose little bottom is *this*?'

At this point the Major's patience snapped, and he sat up in bed and said loudly, 'Oh, for Pete's sake make up your minds whose it is, and let me get some sleep!' A frozen silence descended on the next-door room and was not broken again. By the time the Major surfaced and came out to have his breakfast next morning, the couple in the end room had not waited to be identified, but had 'folded their tents like the Arab, and silently stolen away'.

There are several versions of this story, which leads me to suppose that a similar occurrence happened fairly frequently, probably every time that a casual visitor, unacquainted with the acoustic hazards of the wooden walls of Gulmarg's rooms, arrived in that enchanting resort unexpectedly. The last time that Bets and I visited this much-loved haunt of our youth — it was more than sixteen years after the British too had packed their belongings and silently stolen away — we had booked rooms at Nedou's Hotel and were charmed to discover that the single-plank pine wall that separated our bathrooms was not only thin enough to allow us to chat to each other while we were in our baths, but there was actually a knot hole in it large enough for me to hand my cake of soap through it to Bets when she discovered that she had not been supplied with one of her own.

But on looking back across the years, I think the best description of the flimsiness of the partitions that divided visitor from visitor in the pine-built huts of Gulmarg and the houseboats of Srinagar was voiced by a precious young man, newly arrived from England and experiencing the drawbacks of life in Kashmir for the first time: 'But my dears, I *assure* you! I can hear the people in the next room changing their *minds*!'

One learned to live with it. It certainly made life more interesting and was quite possibly the main reason why, ever since the families of the *Sahib-log* first took to escaping to the hills to avoid the hot weathers, the hill-stations they favoured acquired a reputation for being hot-beds of scandal. Kipling certainly played a large part in this legend with the publication of his *Plain Tales from the Hills*, a widely read collection of short stories based on Simla scandals and dedicated to 'the wittiest woman in India' — a title eagerly claimed by at least a dozen would-be Mrs Hauksbees, though it was almost certainly meant as a compliment to his mother, the pretty, witty Alice Kipling, who before her marriage had been one of the beautiful MacDonald sisters.

The view of Raj society as a suburban forerunner of the scandalous goings-on that made the blue-blooded denizens of Kenya's Happy Valley set so notorious is still, after all these years, a widely held one — particularly among writers who were not even born when the British quit India. Personally, I don't believe it was nearly as bad as they make out; in contrast with what is considered to be normal behaviour in the present day it was, of course, laughably fusty and sedate. But even at its worst it had one redeeming feature: its scandals nearly always turned out to have a comic side to them, at least from the onlooker's viewpoint, though I don't suppose that those directly involved found them so wildly funny.

We once missed being eye-witnesses to a famous piece of drama by a matter of yards — four or five hundred at most, the distance that separated our secluded mooring from the scene of the action on Nageem. But we heard all about it at first hand from friends at Nageem who, metaphorically speaking, had seats in the front row of the stalls; and also second-hand from any number of others who were nowhere near Nageem but had passed on the story in convulsions of laughter . . .

It concerned an attractive and light-minded lady whose houseboat was moored at Nageem and whose husband was spending ten days of his leave fishing on the Bringi, a trout stream some ten or twenty miles from Srinagar. Finding all that time at her disposal, his wife rashly resumed a romance that had had to be put on the shelf when her husband arrived up on a month's leave. She should have known better, since not even a water-beetle, let alone an illicit lover, could stir among the close-packed ranks of houseboats around Nageem without someone noticing, and commenting on it. Word of the resumed relations with her Don Juan seeped out to other fishermen on the Bringi and, inevitably, since men are worse gossips than women, reached the ears of her husband, who returned with all speed to Srinagar two days before he was expected.

According to the cognoscenti, who are always with us (and endorsed on this occasion by the enthralled occupants of at least half the other boats on Nageem), the lady and her admirer had been celebrating their last-but-one evening together by dining *à deux* on her boat before going on to dance at the Club, when her husband suddenly appeared on the scene. Ignoring both of them, he marched straight across the dining-room and, without speaking a word, disappeared briefly into the bedroom section of the houseboat, to reappear with his service revolver in his hand.

Fortunately for everyone concerned, the sliding windows on the lake side were wide open, for it was a warm evening; and the Don 'stood not upon the order of his going'. Though unsuitably attired for aquatics, he did not hesitate. He dived straight out of the window into the lake and swam off into the sunset, encouraged by a revolver shot which missed him by inches but brought at least half of the houseboat population of Nageem rushing to the windows or up to the roofs of their boats. They must have had an excellent view of the ensuing drama, for the irate husband, hitherto invisible to the majority of his audience, ran up to the roof of his own boat from where, only slightly impeded by his hysterical wife, who was clutching his arm and shrieking '*No! No! No!*' at the top of her voice, he proceeded to scare the daylights out of his onlookers, as well as the lover and the lady, by driving the former to swim under water and, every time the poor chump's breath gave out and his head showed, carefully placing a shot just near enough to force him to dive again.

History does not relate the end of their story. It just stops there, like so many Raj stories. To follow it up would have been considered bad taste and an infringement of privacy, mere vulgar curiosity, in fact. As far as the Raj was concerned scandals, particularly of the domestic variety, were more likely to draw shrieks of laughter than raised eyebrows, while the more notorious of its erring ladies acquired colourful nicknames such as the 'Charpoy Cobra', 'Bed-and-Breakfast', the 'Passionate Haystack' and the 'Subaltern's Guide to Knowledge', by which they were known from one end of the subcontinent to the other. All very reprehensible, I suppose, yet it had one redeeming feature. There was seldom any real spite or viciousness in the gossip and scandal-mongering; something I discovered to be one of the great differences to which I had to adjust when the Raj ended and I was back once more in my native land. Here there was no trace of humour in the whispers of the tale-bearers whom I was to encounter; only plenty of envy and malice, and a lot of real cattiness. Perhaps it was the loss of Empire that had soured the once tolerant and easy-going islanders so thoroughly. Or perhaps they had used up all their reserves of good temper in surviving those long, agonizing years of war, with its terrible toll of death and destruction. I don't know.

❋ 7 ❋

'Life is just a bowl of cherries'

Chapter 24

~❊~

We had been delighted with the size of our island and the privacy it gave us. But we were not to remain in sole possession of it for more than a few days, for shortly after our arrival we met and offered mooring space to the Andersons, a honeymoon couple who became lifelong friends. Andy — Ronald Anderson (I believe his old friends used to call him 'Ronnie' but he was always Andy to us) — was a Sapper Captain, based in Peshawar, and since neither he nor his bride had taken kindly to the lack of privacy on Nageem, we took pity on them and invited them to share our nearby but more spacious *ghat* in Chota Nageem. A day or two later, while collecting our mail at the Post Office on the Bund in Srinagar, we were hailed by an old friend, Colonel Henslow, whom we had last met when he was bear-leading the young Duke of Northumberland a year or so before. Now here he was again, and once more acting as guide, mentor and family friend to another, though far less exalted member of the peerage, a Michael Something.

I don't think any of us caught the name, which had been distinctly mumbled. (It sounded like 'Gazi' and turned out to be Guernsey.) The Colonel explained that he and Mike were staying at Nedou's Hotel for a few days, and pressed us to return there and have luncheon with them. Which in the end we did.

Mike Something turned out to be a charmer, and from the start we all got on tremendously well together — as we had with Andy and Enid. So it was no surprise when he and Colonel Henslow turned up at Chota Nageem the next day announcing that they couldn't wait to exchange their rooms at Nedou's for a houseboat, and asking for advice. Mike was fascinated by the H. B. *Carlton*, which he compared most favourably to the boredom of living in hotel rooms. But while he prowled enthusiastically through the houseboat, and fraternized with the Andersons and their sealyham (the little dog had greeted him as an old friend, for Mike, like

Tacklow, was good with animals), the Colonel took the opportunity of having a private talk with my parents, on the excuse of wanting to be taken on a tour of the island.

He felt he had to explain, before letting things go any further, why he and Mike happened to be putting up at Nedou's Hotel instead of — as might have been expected — at the Residency, or in one of the state guest-houses or houseboats which were normally put at the disposal of any visiting VIPs, from Members of Parliament or the peerage to film stars on holiday.

The fact of the matter was that Mike was, officially, in dire disgrace and in consequence travelling more or less incognito. (Hence the name by which he had been introduced, which was a secondary title and the one by which he had been known until he succeeded to the earldom, for he was in fact the Earl of Aylesford.) He was also, to all intents and purposes, 'out on parole' in the custody of the Colonel, with orders to keep a low profile and do nothing to attract the attentions of the press — or anyone else! — until such a time as his family, and the Army, were prepared to pretend that his misdeeds had been forgotten, and that it would be safe for him to return home.

Poor Mike! He told me the whole story in detail later on, and I laughed myself into hiccups over it though I could clearly see why the Establishment and his family must have wanted to wring his neck. But then I could also see Mike's point of view because my darling Tacklow, that most unmilitary of men, had also been ordered into the Army against his will. There had been some excuse for this in Tacklow's day, when Victoria was still firmly on the throne and the children of Victorian parents did what they were told and that was that! But I found it hard to believe that the same sort of thing was possible in my own day and age.

Mike's family, however — not to mention his relations and godparents — had taken it for granted that he would follow his late father's footsteps and serve in the same regiment. He had, he assured me, put in a plaintive protest, because he didn't think he was suited to a military career and had been considering becoming an explorer. But this had been brushed aside, and he ended up as a subaltern in whatever regiment his father had served in. Once there, he discovered that he had been dead right in thinking that the army was not for him. He was the squarest of square pegs in a round hole and it was not long before he lined up in front of his CO and asked for permission to send in his papers and leave the Army.

He swore that he had not expected any serious opposition. But his family and relatives appear to have thrown a collective fit, and followed it up by a series of harrowing scenes that began with 'Don't talk rubbish, boy', and advanced to an incredulous 'Have you taken leave of your senses?' before descending rapidly to anger, arguments and a general shouting match and ending, inevitably, in tears and pleas of 'Think of me', 'Think of *us*', 'Think of your poor *father*'. (Mike's poor father had been killed in the First World War, so he didn't remember him all that well!)

Mike said he had found it all very wearing, but had stuck his toes in and refused to budge until, finding that they could do nothing with him, they appealed to the most important of his godfathers to talk him out of it. Which, in Mike's opinion (and mine too), was a really dirty trick, since the godfather in question had not only been a personal friend of his father's but happened to be King George V.

Well, as Mike said, what *can* you say when your monarch himself has you up on the mat and asks you as a personal favour to please reconsider? . . . 'He was so *nice* about it,' explained Mike in extenuation. 'If he hadn't been so nice I might have been able to stick to my guns. But as it was, I couldn't just stand there and say "No", could I? — could *anyone*?'

He had given in, of course; and it had proved a fatal mistake. Because once having returned to duty it hadn't been long before he realized that he really could not cope with army life and the sooner he made this quite clear to one and all, the better. This decision received strong support from a like-minded friend who had only been waiting to see how Mike had fared before following his example and sending in his own papers. I don't remember the friend's name, or anything more about him, but apparently the two of them discussed the matter at some length before coming to the conclusion that the only course left open to Mike was to go AWOL for an extended period, thereby forcing the authorities to lose patience with him and throw him out.

The friend decided not to waste time arguing his case, as Mike had done, but to abscond with him, and the two packed a suitcase apiece, pocketed their passports and as much money as they could scrape together, left brief messages to be delivered to their families and their commanding officers and took off for France.

Considering that Mike had already made one determined effort to get out of the Army, you would have thought that his regiment would have been pleased to see the last of him. (His friend's, on the other hand, evidently took the departure of their escapee with admirable calm.) It was not so, however, with Mike's lot, who seem to have gone straight up into the stratosphere. For no sooner did they learn that he had made a break for liberty, and was now on the loose in foreign parts, than they dispatched the Military Police — or whoever deals with absconding soldiery — in pursuit. And I suspect, though this is only a guess, that his family too must have hired someone to chase after him and bring him back, for according to Mike's account of his subsequent adventures, there would seem to have been a plethora of human bloodhounds baying on the trail.

His version of those adventures was probably embroidered a good bit here and there, but they certainly made hilarious listening. The two of them appear to have had a number of hair-breadth escapes from capture, including one from a modest commercial hotel in a small and unimportant town, miles away from the tourist trail or any place of interest. No one, they decided, would dream of looking for them in such a dull, out-of-the-way dump as this. But within a day or two of their arrival a young and excitable member of the staff, with whom they were on friendly terms — Mike had a talent for attracting friends and allies wherever he went — scratched on their door to warn them in a dramatic whisper that there were a couple of sinister characters below, possibly plain-clothes *flics*, who were asking to see the hotel's register and inquiring about two young Englishmen who, judging from the description they were giving the receptionist on the desk . . .

It was dark, and to make matters worse it was raining; and Mike's account of their flight by way of an exceedingly ancient and very slippery apology for a fire escape, and their subsequent, and successful, efforts to muddy their trail, was hysterically funny. From his family's and the Army's point of view, however, the whole, rousing, round-and-round the mulberry bush business must have been exasperating, and I still cannot understand why they let it go on so long. Eventually, however, they did what they ought to have done from the first — called off their respective bloodhounds and left the two fugitives to their own devices, in the sure knowledge that sooner or later they would run out of money, and get bored to bits with supporting themselves by part-time jobs on farms, or washing dishes in city cafés, and come home. Which of course they did.

You may have noticed — I have only just done so myself — that in all these Keystone Kops chases there never seems to have been any trouble over passports; nowadays no one could possibly go swanning around the Continent without having their passport demanded of them with depressing frequency.

Anyway, once it became clear that no one was prepared to waste any more time or money on playing silly games of hide-and-seek, the whole escapade became a bore, and they returned sheepishly to the fold. Mike's friend seems to have got off fairly lightly, being allowed to send in his papers and leave. But Mike was dismissed from the service, and officially disgraced, 'His Majesty the King having no further use for his services' — or whatever the formula is. Colonel Henslow was roped in to take him out of the country and keep him out, until such a time as the scandal he had created had died down and been forgotten. But over a decade later His Majesty the King (not the same one, for he was dead, but his successor, George VI) was to find a use for Mike's service after all. For when the Second World War broke out, Mike managed to get himself commissioned into — I think — the Artists' Rifles; and returning across the Channel with them to fight for King and Country, he was killed somewhere on the Continent in the black year of Dunkirk and the fall of France.

But all that was still far ahead of us. By the time Colonel Henslow and my parents returned from their stroll around the island the Andersons and Mike were on the best of terms, so when Colonel Henslow asked for permission to share our mooring (provided he and Mike could find and rent a suitable boat and our *manjis* were agreeable) the ayes had it. Ahamdoo Siraj, who had found us the H. B. *Carlton*, found a small, two-bedroom boat for them and they duly moved in.

Parked one behind the other, our houseboats with their cookboats made an imposing fleet. I don't remember what happened to the Colonel, except that he left us at this point. I presume he realized that Mike would be all right with us, so he could safely go off to visit old friends on the Frontier. Anyway, he vanished from the scene, to rejoin us some time later, and he was never a member of the Nageem Bagh Navy.

✗ It was Andy who founded the Nageem Bagh Navy, and dubbed the H. B. *Carlton* the Flagship. The whole thing was invented one night when he and Enid and Mike were having dinner with us on our houseboat. The party had been a hilarious one, and Andy had declaimed a nonsense poem about a ship called the 'Walloping Window-blind', and another, from the *Bab Ballads*, that numbered among its crew and a 'Bo'sun Tight and a Midshipmite and the crew of the Captain's gig'.

By the time the party broke up that night we were all life members of the NBN. Andy was the Captain and Mike was the First Officer, 'Number One'. I was the Midshipmite and Enid the Bo'sun Tight (Bets and I never called her anything but 'Bo'sun' to the end of her days — which, as I write, was only the other day. *Kiwa Grabrata*, dear Bo'sun! Be seeing you), Bets was the Cabin Boy, Mother the Quartermaster and Tacklow the Paymaster-General, while the Andersons' sealyham was, of course, the Dog-watch. We designed and made a flag to fly on the flagship (I have it still) and a motto, which was also a password: '*Kiwa Gabrata*'* — which loosely translated means: 'This Puzzle's the Beetle.' But please don't ask me why. It had a reason once, but I've forgotten that too. Oh woe!

℀ I find it hard to describe in words, let alone pin down on paper, the sheer *fun* we had with our Navy that autumn. I only know that looking back on those days through the long, leafy avenue of the years, they stand out as one of the happiest times of my life — a time in which we never seemed to have stopped laughing. And just to add an extra touch of champagne fizz and sparkle to those light-hearted, laughter-filled days, Mike and I fell in love.

That we should have done so was more or less inevitable, for Kashmir, as it was in those far-off times, might have been made for lovers. To begin with, as I have already said, it was purely a holiday resort and all those young men, who had left the stifling heat and toil and discipline of offices and cantonments behind them and come up there on leave, threw off the restraints that work had imposed on them and got down to enjoying themselves. They went fishing, camping or trekking, went riding through the woods around Gulmarg or lazed on houseboats and bathed in the lakes. And every evening except Sundays most of them went dancing.

Those who hadn't already got a girl collected one, and night after night, when the dancing was done, they saw her home in a *shikarra* by moonlight or starlight, or, more often than not by the pale yellow light of dawn, serenading her the while with the strains of some sentimental record played on a wind-up gramophone. If they owned a car, they drove her

---

* Our crest was a water-beetle.

back, frequently by the way of the lake road, branching off on to the one that winds up the hillside to Chasma-Shahi, the 'Imperial Spring', which is the smallest and, with one exception,* probably the most attractive of the many gardens with which the Mogul Emperors adorned the Kashmir Valley.

This particular garden had been designed and built to the order of that most loving of husbands, Shah Jehan — he who raised the Taj Mahal to the memory of his adored wife who had died giving birth to their thirteenth child. From here you could look down and see all Srinagar city and miles of the valley laid out below you: the Takht-i-Suliman and the fort of Hari Parbat; the winding silver ribbon of the Jhelum river, and the narrow waterways that link the many lakes — Gagribal and the Dāl, Nageem and Naseem, Nishat and Harwan, and very far away, the shimmer of Manasbal and the Wular lake.

Chasma Shai was a favourite spot for moonlight picnics, and I have been to so many parties that have ended up here in the small hours among its fountains and flowerbeds, that to this day I never see a full moon without thinking that only a few short hours ago it would have been shining down on that dear familiar garden.

It was looking at its best that September; there were still lotus lilies in bloom on the lake, though not in the numbers there would have been in high summer, and all around the lakes the poplars and willows were beginning to turn gold, while here and there a chenar tree would show a hint of apricot or orange that would in time deepen into flaming scarlet, but at present was only a warning that once again the year was moving towards winter. Many of the holiday-makers, their leave over, had already left, and others were making preparations to leave. But since their places were taken by people moving down from Gulmarg, where the nights were getting chillier, Srinagar seemed almost as full as ever. The Nageem Bagh Navy continued to flourish, and we made plans for autumn-winter manoeuvres.

We had already decided to stick to the original crew as the only 'life members', and anybody else who joined would do so only as Able Seamen

---

* The exception being Nasim Bagh — the Garden of the Breezes — one of the most imaginative gardens ever made, which was destroyed by the Indian Army, who replaced it with a barracks and a few tatty flowerbeds and gravel paths encircling a small, tin-roofed bandstand. *Ugh!*

— 'the crew of the *Nancy* brig'. The first three of these were Tony Weldon, that long-time friend from the days of the Red House, followed by John Sykes and Sammy Woods. I can't remember the names of any of the others, but I don't think there were more than half-a-dozen at most, for our standards were strict, and consisted, among other things, of a thoroughly silly story that was tried out, without their suspecting, on each candidate. If he or she did not laugh themselves silly over it, they were out. The joke was a simple one and squeaky clean . . .

An absent-minded professor attending a 'white-tie' dinner was handed a dish of mashed potatoes by a waiter, and to the consternation of the elderly lady sitting next to him, he ignored the spoon and, dipping his finger-tips into it instead, he rubbed them into his hair. 'Professor Bleep!' gasped the horrified lady, 'that is *mashed potatoes*!' The professor gave it a startled glance, and said: 'Dear me, so it is! I do apologize — I thought it was spinach!'

The members of the NBN thought this pre-Monty Python joke simply hilarious. But I am sadly aware that nowadays it would probably have fallen flat, and that any similar test set up in these enlightened times would be either crudely vulgar or cringingly blasphemous (preferably both) in order to get a laugh. But to return to the NBN, one or two otherwise excellent 'possibles' fell at that spinach fence without knowing they had done so, which for some reason caused more amusement among us than if they had passed with honours. It was, by itself, a cause of endless amusement and gales of laughter.

The Navy, mostly *en masse*, picnicked in turn on two small islands, the Char-Chenar on the Dāl and Sonalanka on Gagribal lake; danced six nights a week either at Srinagar Club or Nedou's ballroom — finishing up on a lawn at Chasma-Shai, playing gramophone records and watching for the dawn. We paid several visits to Gulmarg, driving as far as Tanmarg, where we left the cars and rode up on *tats* on the unmetalled pony track that winds up through the forests, to have drinks at the Club and lunch in the garden of the new café that Nedou's had just opened, attached to the Gulmarg branch of the hotel. Once we rode on up through the forest to picnic on Apharwat — at Khilanmarg, the Meadow of Goats, where the tree-line stops as though drawn by a ruler, and the snow-line begins; and once we spent an entire day fishing for snow-trout in the Ferozpore Nullah, which lies a mile or so above, below the pony track.

Whenever the Navy was not manoeuvring *en masse*, Mike and I would go off alone to drift about the lakes in a *shikarra* that he had hired for his personal use. He used to play a series of records in rotation. A favourite one, kept for moonlight picnics, was 'You Were Meant for Me', and whenever he played it he would sing the words to me.

Mike was not yet twenty-one, and it was a measure of how seriously he had offended his family and relations that they should have sent him so far from England when he was just about to come of age. Twenty-one: would you believe it? A milestone that would, had he toed the line and behaved himself, have been commemorated with a ball at Packington and/ or Aylesford, plus various other celebratory gestures of congratulation and rejoicing such as wining and dining the indoor and outdoor staffs, lighting bonfires, and similar forms of hey, nonny, nonny! As it was, he had to make do with a dinner and dance at the Peshawar Club, laid on by the NBN.

With that occasion in mind, I took out all my savings and bought a dazzling two-piece evening outfit in a sale at a dress shop on the Bund, owned and run by a Mrs Viva Fraser. It consisted of a short, shimmering, pale-pink dress sewn all over with thousands of tiny crystal beads and decorated at the neck and hem with darker pink roses and pale emerald leaves in small china beads, worn under a matching coat of the same length: the two together weighed a ton! The costume had been imported from France, and I thought it was the most beautiful outfit I had ever seen, even lovelier than Mother's opal-beaded evening dress. I could not understand why it had not been snapped up by someone else the moment it had gone on display. Well, that was obvious, if only I had used my head.

Skirts were on their way down yet again, and most evening dresses now swept the floor. And apart from being a bit *démodée*, a two-piece affair needed to be worn by someone with good legs and a slim figure — the slimmer the better. Short skirts and several million beads do not look their best on size sixteen girls with piano legs. Besides which, it had initially been too expensive for the average memsahib until, having been tried on and reluctantly discarded by women with more money and far more sense than myself, it ended up in the end-of-season sale, where, against all advice, and begobbered by the charm of those shimmering, glimmering beads and the exquisitely embroidered roses, I bought it. And wore it only twice. Once at Mike's coming-of-age party and a year later at some first night — or perhaps last night — at the Gaiety Theatre in

Simla, where, having gone back-stage to congratulate some performer, I was pounced upon by a frantic producer and begged to run like the wind to the chemist's, about two or three hundred yards further up the Mall, to get some special form of restorative that was desperately needed by one of the cast who was feeling faint and threatening to walk out.

Cotten and Morris, the chemist in question, ran an all-night emergency service, and clutching the required prescription and a few rupees, I fled from the green-room, tore down the Mall by the light of the road lamps, collected the prescription, and panted back — a bit slower this time — and was about three-quarters of the way back when I realized that I was running alongside a thin, glittery line of light — not much thicker than a dew-hung cobweb — that seemed to stretch right down the length of the Mall. I put my hand out without stopping and caught it. It was a thin length of cotton, strung with little crystal beads and, checking to look behind me, I saw that there was a second line, running back to the chemist's . . . I had caught a loose thread of the beaded coat on something inside the green-room (it turned out to be a basket of flowers that was waiting to be presented to the leading lady) and I had unravelled a good half of my coat and heaven knows how many crystal beads out in the Mall.

I never wore that outfit again. It did *not* suit me. But I cut off and kept the swags of roses as a souvenir of the NBN days, and because I thought I ought to be able to sew them on to something else. I never did, and I still have one of those fragile swags, tucked away in a sewing basket somewhere in the attic.

✂ Oh, well — all good things must come to an end at last, for 'Golden lads and girls all must, as chimney-sweepers, come to dust'. The Captain, the Bo'sun and the Dog-watch were the first to go. The lone chenar tree high up on the side of the Takht-i-Suliman, which was always a signal that autumn was about to take over the valley, had already turned scarlet, and Andy's honeymoon leave was over.

Colonel Henslow returned to collect his charge and fulfil various tentative arrangements that he had made for the two of them, and to hear — and hopefully approve — a number of plans for the near future that had been made in his absence by the NBN in Council. As for us Kayes, we too would be leaving Kashmir soon, *en route* for Abbottabad where Bill, now stationed there, had made arrangements for us to stay for a week or two on our way to the plains. The Fleet therefore left its anchorage at Chota Nageem and sailed *en masse* for another, temporary one, off Gagribal Point. This was the usual practice for those who had spent their holiday at Nageem and suchlike places, since departing buses and cars left for the plains from a point near the First Bridge. And that meant leaving any distant mooring a good hour earlier, if one intended to drive as far as Murree or Abbottabad, let alone Rawalpindi, before dark. An early start was essential, and the houseboats queued up to be as near as possible to Gagribal Point or the Dāl Gate.

We arrived a day early so as give the Bo'sun a chance to do some last-minute shopping, and just after we returned, laden with parcels, Kashmir laid on a special matinée performance by way of farewell . . .

The boats of departing holiday-makers were packed fairly close together, and all the founding members of the Nageem Bagh Navy were about to have lunch on the roof of the flagship when the midday calm was shattered by an unseen female — English and possessing an admirable pair of lungs and an astonishing command of bad language — who was yelling abuse at the top of her voice. The yells were accompanied by loud splashes, and the uproar brought the occupants of every boat within hearing range rushing to the windows or roof of their boats, prepared to leap into the lake and rescue someone from drowning. It was not necessary.

Looking across a short stretch of water, the enthralled audience, now numbering hundreds, had an excellent view through the open windows of a nearby houseboat, and of its temporary tenant sitting at his dining-room table with his head in his hands. I don't think anyone ever saw his face, for he never said a word. He just sat there with his shoulders slumped and his head down, flinching occasionally when struck by a piece of houseboat crockery, or some other form of missile that was being hurled at him by a young virago who was raging round the room, picking up and throwing in the general direction of the open window, anything that she could lay her hands on.

Most of it, luckily for him, made it through the window, to splash into the lake, while we all watched riveted by the drama and the sheer variety of ammunition that whizzed past the victims' head to splash or plop into the lake. Plates, cups, saucers and glasses of every shape and size, gramophone records, bottles of assorted drink, jugs and sugar basins, a large china serving dish and at least two teapots, and finally — like some sort of grand *bonne bouche* — a wind-up gramophone that sailed majestically out into the sunlight and descending, hit the water with a colossal splash.

The effort it must have taken to heave this last item out through the window must have been too much for the shot-putter, or else she had finally run out of breath and adrenalin, as well as ammunition, for she turned on her heel and vanished into the bedroom end of the houseboat, followed by the wailing *manji* who had been standing well clear of the action, wringing his hands and calling upon Allah and a variety of saints as he watched his property being destroyed. Another member of the houseboat's entourage entered cautiously and, becoming aware of the interested audience outside, hurried to the windows and closed the wire-gauze fly-screens. And that was that, as far as we were concerned. We never discovered what it had all been about, though everyone had a different theory to fit the evidence. But you see what I mean about the majority of scandals in the days of the Raj tending to verge on the farcical.

This had an even more ridiculous postscript, for an hour or so later (by which time the ex-tenants had left by a back way) the *manji* could be seen directing salvage operations from the roof of his houseboat, bustling to and fro and leaning out at dangerous angles to point and shout down instructions to his team to indicate where it might be worthwhile to dive for fish-plates or a teapot, and urging them not to tread on any unbroken bit of glass or crockery and to be careful about bringing up the gramophone. It was, for some reason, a lot funnier than the original crockery throwing — though it did not amuse the *manji*.

Andy, the Bo'sun and the Dog-watch, with Andy's bearer, left their houseboat at dawn on the following day, and the rest of us set our alarm clocks, and got up early enough to see them off with a ceremonial salute fired by Mike from his shotgun. There was a distinct nip in the air, and Mike had had to put on his army greatcoat because he was cold. And, as the sun came up behind the long range of mountains that wall the eastern side of the valley, we could see that the snows had already began to creep down towards the tree-line.

It should not have been a sad occasion, since we would all be meeting again in a few weeks' time in Peshawar for Mike's coming-of-age party; and after that Colonel Henslow and Mike were hoping to persuade Tacklow to help them lay on a trip down the Ganges — something that Mike had set his heart on. There were also various other plans afoot, including one for Christmas. But in spite of all this, it was certainly not a very cheerful occasion; I suppose because in our heart of hearts we all knew that a very special time, an almost perfect time, had ended; and that however much fun we had in the future, it could never be quite the same as this time . . . Because 'Once Upon a Time' never comes again.

🞷 Our stay in Abbottabad was, not unnaturally, something of a come-down after the heady, holiday days in Kashmir, and I don't remember much about it except that we played a lot of golf, and much to my surprise I became quite good at it. Then at last we were *en route* for Peshawar, leaving the mountains behind us and heading for the plains once more. We stopped briefly at Akbar's fort at Attock, to pay a call on the commander of the fort who was a friend of Tacklow's, and then, crossing the bridge that spans the Indus and brings you back into the North West Frontier Province, found ourselves greeted on the far side by the NBN in full fig: naval caps with *Kiwa Gabrata* cap badges all correct, the Dog-watch barking an ecstatic welcome, and the orange, brown and green NBN flag flying at the fore. It was a gorgeous surprise, and the beginning of another week of non-stop laughing and sheer, light-hearted fun.

I don't remember where Mike and Colonel Henslow stayed — probably in Deane's Hotel or else in a chummery with Sammy Woods and John Sykes. But we were put up by the Captain and the Bo'sun in their palatial bungalow, and the code-name of the operation was given out as 'Let Battle Commence!' Andy steered us up the Khyber, where our first stop was, very suitably, at something that from a distance looks surprisingly like a battleship that has come to rest on a hilltop. This is in fact Shaghai fort, which stands guard at the mouth of the pass. Its garrison stood us cold drinks and showed us all over it, pointing out the 'Anderson Loop-hole', which was the invention of our Captain, who was called upon to explain how it worked.

From there we drove up the long winding road of the historic pass, ending up at its far end at Landi Kotel, where we were stood lunch by the Khyber Rifles who were on garrison duty there. We signed our names in the guest-book in order of NBN rank, adding our rank under each name, and including a verse of the Walloping Window-blind; and I drew the crest of the NBN, that puzzled beetle, at the head of the column. And thirty-four years later — long after the North West Frontier Province had become part of a new country called Pakistan — Bets and I were invited to go up the Khyber again, and to have lunch in the mess, which happened to be garrisoned again by a detachment of the Khyber Rifles.

And there, looking back in the guest-book, were the names of the NBN of joyous memory. Though, sadly, when I went there again almost two decades later, the book had gone, and every officer in the mess, including the CO, had not even been born when our light-hearted Navy wrote nonsense in the mess-book at the top of the Khyber on a day half a century earlier.

The rest of our stay in Peshawar was as much fun as the first Nageem Bagh Navy days had been. We all lunched together whenever we could, sometimes at the Club, sometimes at Deane's Hotel or at one of the chummeries, and sometimes at Andy and Enid's, and we spent several hilarious hours deciding on the tunes the dance band would play at Mike's party. I still have a grubby sheet of Peshawar Club paper on which a list was scribbled down in various different hands; it includes 'The Music Goes Round and Around', 'Life is Just a Bowl of Cherries', 'You Were Meant for Me' and 'I'm Looking Over a Four-leafed Clover'. Anyone remember any of these? Alas, I doubt it!

Mike struck twenty-one on the last day of October, and his party to celebrate the occasion was a wild success, though I went close to ruining it for myself by *insisting* on wearing that pink beaded shift and coat. Apart from weighing a ton and being much too hot, it must have made me look exactly like Miss Piggy in one of her flashier outfits, something that I only realized when I caught sight of myself in one of the long looking-glasses in the ladies' cloakroom of the Peshawar Club. I had entered the room among a group of girls, and was not aware of the glass until, turning suddenly, I caught a glimpse of myself and thought, 'Golly! That woman looks exactly like a raw sausage that's been rolled in the Christmas tree glitter!' And then suddenly realized that it was *me*! That was one of life's darker moments. But even that salutary shock did not spoil my evening for me. For I had been the guest of honour at the dinner party before the ball, and Mike, who by that time had drunk a good deal of champagne, danced more dances with me than he should have done. We sat out several of them, and it was while we were sitting arm-in-arm in a secluded corner of that shadowy, lantern-lit garden that he suddenly asked me if I would consider marrying him. He had, he said, hinted at this on several occasions, but hadn't had a positive reaction from me, and he hadn't spoken out because he was still only a minor who could be ordered about and told what he could or couldn't do. But tonight he was his own man, and he could do exactly what he wanted to. No one could dictate to him any longer: 'So how about it, darling — could you bear having me around for the rest of your life?'

Well, that was the rub. I was very fond of Mike and of course those hints he had made had not been unnoticed. On the contrary, I had thought about them, and him, a great deal, and though I did not want to admit it, even to myself, I could not make up my mind if I would have cared for him as much as I did if he'd been plain Mike Smith or Green or Brown. Because I had to admit that the idea of becoming a countess, and the châtelaine of two great houses, was enormously alluring. Far too alluring, for it got in the way of deciding whether the answer to his question was 'yes' or 'no'. And then there was always that famous Gerald du Maurier reply: 'I'll be ready in five minutes — no, make it three!'

Did I feel that I could say that, without hesitation, to darling Mike? No, I couldn't. Because I would *love* to be a countess! — not because I would love to be his wife. And then there was still the matter of age: I was *older* than he was. I don't know why that pressed so hard on my conscience, because after all, it was only a matter of weeks. But a girl of twenty-one feels well and truly adult, while a boy of the same age is still only a boy ... I would be regarded not only as a gold-digger, but as a cradle-snatcher. It was all very difficult, because if he had been the 'Mr Right' — that legendary knight-on-a-white-horse whom too many girls in my generation had been brought up to believe in, *surely* I would recognize him as the only man in the world for me, instead of dithering like this?

Half of me — no, let's be honest, three-quarters of me wanted to shout: '*Yippee!* I've pulled it off! The glass slipper fits me, and I'm going to be a countess — a countess — a countess ... *Wow!*' But the remaining quarter of me was the daughter of that painfully honest man Tacklow — who I don't believe ever told a lie in his life — and a granddaughter of the Dadski who, happily launched on a successful career as an Edinburgh architect, had given it all up and gone off to become an impecunious missionary in China, because he believed that God had spoken to him ordering him to do so.

Lastly, but it counted for a lot, I knew very well that Mike had had too much to drink, and I was not going to land him in the sort of mess that Bill had only just escaped from. So, adding it all up, I fell back on the reply that seems to have been popular with Victorian misses who weren't sure of their own minds: the 'Oh, but Mr Lambswool, this is so sudden!'

gambit. I asked for a bit more time to think it over, because 'such an idea had never entered my mind' — which was a black lie if there ever was one! Whereupon Mike suggested that I start thinking about it at once, and we exchanged a fervent embrace, which left a sprinkling of beads on the breast of his dinner-jacket and did no good at all to my lipstick, and went back arm-in-arm into the ballroom singing 'Life is Just a Bowl of Cherries' at the tops of our voices.

Chapter 25

~꧁꧂~

The party ended with bacon and eggs and black coffee around four
o'clock, and a day or two after that we left Peshawar in the dawn, bound
for Sialkot, where we all had breakfast in the Sialkot Dâk-bungalow and,
after an affecting farewell and a lot of uproarious NBN-ing, parted with
the Andersons and a couple of Able Seamen, who had accompanied us
as far as Sialkot in order to give us a really good send-off. That done, we
drove on to Lahore taking Mike and Colonel Henslow with us. These
two were unexpected eleventh-hour additions to our party, for they had
meant to stay on in Peshawar until the end of the month. But as Mike
said, 'We've had a lovely run for our money, but we'll only spoil it if we
try and keep it up too long. Besides, Andy and the rest of them up here
have got to stop playing and get back to work, and Sir Cecil and you lot
have to leave for Delhi. The Colonel and I are the only ones who haven't
got to go to any given part of the country, and I'd like to see Delhi. Would
you mind very much if we came with you?'

Put like that, Tacklow could hardly refuse, but there was one snag. We
had been invited by a long-time friend of my father's, Sir Geoffrey de
Montmorency, then Governor of the Punjab, to break our journey from
Peshawar to Delhi by spending a few days with him at Government
House. The idea of having to drop off Mike and the Colonel in some
hotel in Lahore while we swanned off to spend the next few days in gilded
comfort at Government House seemed a bit unfriendly, and when that
sudden request to go south with us was made on our last-but-one day in
Peshawar, Andy had suggested that we ring up G-H Lahore and ask if
we could bring a couple of guests with us.

After all, argued Andy, those gilded caravanserais were large enough
to put up an army, and more than half their job consisted of putting up
VIPs by the dozen, at short notice. So why not offer them these two?
So we did. We rang up Government House and asked for the ADCs'

room, where the phone was answered by that long-time friend of our family's, Sandy Napier. Sandy replied with the greatest cordiality that of *course* we could bring Lord Aylesford and Colonel Henslow with us. Plus the entire House of Lords as well if we so wished; the more the merrier, and he would fix it. What did we think that ADCs did for a living? — Or words to that effect.

So thanks to Andy we set off gaily for the capital city of the Punjab, where we received a rapturous welcome from Sandy and Jimmy Maynard, the other ADC. Later on, when he was free to greet us (since despite all the flippancy from Andy and the ADCs, Governors of Provinces worked hard and long), there was a distinctly less enthusiastic one from Sir Geoffrey when he realized that the elderly man whose hand he was shaking was not the unknown VIP he had automatically agreed to put up, but the youth beside him, who looked young enough to be this Colonel fellow's grandson! For we had entirely forgotten, in that exchange of light-hearted badinage on the telephone, to give Sandy any idea of the age of the prospective VIP, and either he, or Jimmy Maynard, had picked up an ancient and long out-of-date copy of *Burke's Peerage* when checking on Mike's name, and decided in consequence that Mike would be an elderly greybeard with at least one bedsock in the grave.

Well, you wouldn't have thought that mattered very much, would you? Neither would I. Though I was to learn better; because it seemed to have offended against that Great Panjandrum, St Protocol, who in the days of the Raj was a very Big Pot indeed. Even Indian princes who ruled over vast tracts of country and possessed riches beyond the dreams of western avarice bowed to it; scheming and plotting to get a greater number of 'guns' to add to the total of those fired in their honour when they went visiting the Viceroy or some Governor of a Province, or on various state occasions. An extra gun, which was in the gift of the Government, could be used as a bribe or a reward, and its power was enormous, while deadly feuds between memsahibs who considered they ought to have been placed higher at a dinner table than some other memsahib whose husband's rank was lower than her own were all too common. Even elderly women were not above jostling each other in order to pass through a door first — or merely go ahead of someone else. It was unbelievable. Yet it happened. This was the first time I had seen it in action. But not, unfortunately, the last.

Since Government House never used handwritten or typed lists of guests, the order in which diners would be seated, and the daily bulletins that chronicled the arrival and departure of guests, were always printed; and as there happened to be a fairly large dinner party on the night of our arrival, and it was now too late to alter the guest list, the name of the Earl of Aylesford, who outranked every other guest apart from H. E. the Governor (who represented the Viceroy, who represented the King — I hope you are still with me?) had been partnered at the table by Her Excellency the Lady Governess, with the next most senior lady — a stout and bespectacled dame who had the misfortune to be slightly deaf — on his other side.

I don't know which of the two was the more surprised to find themselves seated next to a stripling who could not possibly have been less than half a century younger than either of them. Mike, however, took the situation in his stride, behaving as though he were a favourite nephew talking to a couple of elderly aunts with whom he was on the best of terms. I remember thinking that he must have learned how to chat up old ladies from having to cope with a difficult grandmother (he had!). But it did not occur to me until some time later that his old dragon of a grandmother must, in her prime, have been the notoriously flighty Lady Aylesford, who had caught the roving eye and, for a time, the heart of that portly, naughty old rip, King Edward the Seventh of rollicking memory. No wonder Mike was good at chatting up old ladies!

Our host, on the other hand, was deeply disapproving. Though I don't see why, because, after all, the sacred rules of Protocol had not been broken. But for some reason Sir Geoffrey thought that he ought to have been informed earlier that this VIP whom he had been landed with was a young thing only just turned twenty-one. He was extremely starched and stuffy about it, and Sandy and James were hauled up before him next morning and told off in the crispest terms.

I don't remember anything much more about that particular stay at Government House, except the sight of Lady de M. sweeping into breakfast on what appeared to be a tidal wave of dogs. It seems that Her Excellency had a passion for small dogs, not shared, I gather, with her husband or the staff, and regarded with horror by her unwary guests, who having sprung to their feet on the arrival of the Lady and her pack, frequently found themselves treading on small bits of hair and fur that barked shrilly and nipped at their defenceless ankles. We were also privileged to snatch a glimpse of Her Ex. and the pack driving through the Mall one morning in what looked like a very elderly Daimler, with its hood down. Her Ex. was seated regally on the back seat, literally surrounded by her canine friends: dogs to the left of her, dogs to the right of her, plus an overflow of dogs on the folded roof of the car; all of them yapping in chorus. A dignified Indian equerry sat in front beside the driver, both in the household uniform, and there was also an ayah somewhere; which means that the Daimler must have had a couple of extra flap seats, as in London taxis.

Her Excellency, recognizing us, waved her parasol in an affable salute, and in doing so managed to dislodge one of the pack — a Peke, if memory serves — which fell into the road, landed, fortunately, on its feet, and chased after the car, shrieking at the top of its yap. Apprised of its fall by the helpful yells of sundry pedestrians, Her Ex. ordered the car to stop, and the beautifully uniformed equerry, still managing to look dignified, ran back and collected the creature. Her Ex. waved a gracious hand at the crowd (which in India can be counted upon to collect on the instant to stare at the slightest deviation from the normal) and, the Peke having been restored to its fellows, the car moved on in a cloud of dust and a shrill chorus of yapping. Mike subsided abruptly on the edge of the pavement, put his head in his hands and laughed himself silly, explaining, between hiccups, that now he had seen everything!

Back in Delhi we settled into Number eighty-over-one, The Mall, a small, white, flat-roofed house which had been built as a more permanent shelter than the sea of tents set up on the plain outside Old Delhi for the guests attending the Great Durbar of 1903. Tacklow, who had work to do in Delhi on behalf of Tonk, had hired 80/1 for a few weeks. Then, to the inexpressible joy of Bets and myself, we would be setting off on a trip down the Ganges by river-boat from Gurrmuktasa, to that dearly loved haunt of our childhood, Narora, at the head of the Ganges Canal.

It was Mike who had been responsible for this. He had been leafing one day through one of Mother's enormous collection of photograph albums (she was a compulsive album keeper) and had come across one that contained photographs of one of the Ganges trips that she and Tacklow and some of their friends used to take every year — camping each night at a different spot, and shooting for the pot. The photographs had fascinated Mike, and after seeing them he had badgered Colonel Henslow to persuade Tacklow into arranging a similar trip, and taking them with him. The Colonel had done his best, but Tacklow had been evasive, and I don't think he would have agreed if I hadn't gone to him with my problems the day after Mike's coming-of-age party and asked for his advice.

He listened to me thoughtfully, and when I had finished he looked at me over the top of his spectacles with what I used to think of as his 'Mr Bennet' look and said, 'You seem to have thought it all out fairly clearly for yourself, darling. So what do you want me to say? Socially and financially, young Mike would be what my generation would have called a "catch", and your mother would probably be the envy of all her friends who have marriageable daughters. He is also a very nice child and he has charming manners. I like him. But he's a Peter Pan. He hasn't really grown up yet, and I'd say that he's still too young to be thinking seriously of marrying and settling down — because one can't even make a guess yet at what sort of person he will become when he does grow up. I'm not going to make up your mind for you, because that is something you've got to do for yourself. But give it time, darling. And until you have made up your mind, one way or the other, my advice to you is to say nothing of all this to anyone else: not to your sister, or any of your girlfriends. Not even to your mother — in fact specially not to your mother, because she's going to be so disappointed if nothing comes of this, and I won't have her upset. Remember your *Uncle Remus*'* — 'Tar-baby ain't sayin' nuthin' and Br'er Fox he lay low'. You do both, my Mouse!'

That last was good advice, and I took it to heart. I also saw exactly what he meant by saying Mike was still Peter Pan. But then that was one of the things that made him so lovable, and the less sensible half of me decided obstinately that until he chose to grow out of it, I would be Wendy to his Peter — and to heck with being too old for the role! All the same, I still wavered, and the next time he brought up the subject of marriage — and I have to admit that he did not exactly ply me with proposals (merely mentioning the subject now and again and not appearing unduly disappointed when I continued to prevaricate) — I told him that since arrangements for the Ganges trip had now been fixed up, and we would be seeing each other daily and hourly for over ten days on end, I could safely promise that he would have an answer on the last day of the

---

* *Uncle Remus, Legends of the Old Plantation* by Joel Chandler Harris.

trip. To which he replied lightly, 'Oh, good! I shall keep you to it . . .' and went on to talk cheerfully about something else.

I remember thinking that he seemed very sure of the answer, that perhaps he knew, though he had never shown the smallest sign of it, that he was a 'catch', and that therefore the very idea of being turned down had never even crossed his mind. The thought was a disturbing one and I am sure quite untrue. But it worried me a bit at the time, because that stay in Delhi, during which Mike and I saw as much of each other as we had in Kashmir, had also shown me a couple of disturbing things about my lovable Peter Pan that had never once shown up, even faintly, in all the Nageem Bagh Navy days or during the festivities in Peshawar. He drank too much and he could not hold his drink. Nor did he know how to choose friends: anyone who flattered him and laughed at his jokes was 'a terribly good bod! — we must enlist him as an Able Seaman!'

He collected a crowd of hangers-on from the bars at Maiden's Hotel, the Cecil, the Old Delhi Club and New Delhi's IDG, and they sponged on him mercilessly. A typical example was a night on which Bets and I were dining with him at Maiden's. There were only four of us to begin with, Mike and a friend of ours, one John Gardner of the Central India Horse, whom we had introduced to Mike, and whom he had invited to make a fourth. Unfortunately we had started the evening with a few drinks in the bar, and someone — probably the barman, or a waiter (Mike was staying at the hotel) — had addressed him as 'M' Lord'.

There were not all that many peers of the realm skating about India in those days, and one or two young men, who were already a bit tipsy, caught the name and turned to stare, as did several grizzled topers with very fruity-looking noses. I saw one of the latter lean over and speak to one of the barmen in an undertone, and presently he came across to Mike with an outstretched hand and said, 'You're Aylesford, aren't you? Thought I recognized you. My old man used to be a friend of your father's. I rather think we met shootin' somewhere. Don't suppose you'd remember. Name's Bloggs (or whatever). Jimmy Bloggs — ' Mike gazed at him a bit woozily. It was obvious that neither the name nor the face meant anything to him. But then he was always a friendly creature who attracted people as fly-paper attracts flies, so he smiled vaguely and shook the outstretched hand, and within five minutes he was being introduced to a whole clutch of total strangers, and was standing them drinks.

They did not leave us when a waiter touched Mike's arm and said that the dinner he had ordered was ready, they merely followed us to our table and suggested in hearty tones that we and they put our tables together and make a party of it. They were all pretty merry by now, and Mike could see no objection to this: he liked parties. And when dinner was over and one of them suggested that we all go off to dance at the IDG in New Delhi, Mike was all for it. But I noticed that when the bills for the dinner were discreetly produced not one of the freeloaders who had gatecrashed our party stayed to pick one up. They all with one accord faded rapidly away in the direction of the men's cloakroom on the excuse of 'spending a penny' or collecting their coats and hats, leaving Mike to sign for the lot of them. Nor did any of them suggest paying for themselves when they returned. The bills were forgotten as we all piled into cars and set off for the Imperial Delhi Gymkhana Club, which in those days lay on the far side of New Delhi, near the racecourse and the lovely little tomb of Saftar Jung. Nowadays, worse luck — so fast and so swiftly has the city grown — there is no open country beyond Saftar Jung's Tomb, only an ocean of new suburbs, wave after wave of them as far as the eye can see.

We arrived at the IDG and swept into the hall in a mob. There must have been at least fifteen of us, all told; and here, once again, the pattern was repeated. While Bets and I retired to the ladies' room to primp and preen, Mike's new-found friends vanished into the Gentlemen, and from there into the ballroom, leaving Mike and John Gardner landed with signing for the entire party. John, who was later to become a good friend of Mike's, had no feelings of *noblesse oblige* towards that crowd of parasites and thought Mike was an ass to allow himself to be sponged on in this manner; nor, as a subaltern, could he afford to pay for half of them. He signed for himself, which as the invited guest he need not have done, and since none of the hangers-on returned to the hall, Mike signed for the rest. 'I like this friend of yours; he's a good chap,' approved John, telling me what had happened, 'but he doesn't seem to have cut his milk teeth yet. He oughtn't to let himself be conned into footing the bill for that lot of freeloaders, and you should tell him so. What that boy needs is a keeper!'

He did of course. And his charm was such that when he really needed one, there always seemed to be one there to step into the breach and give him a helping hand. John was to become one of these, but though I tried to be one, I made a botch of it; I suppose because I was still too callow and inexperienced to cope. And trying to cope with Mike on the loose in Delhi, no longer as a minor but officially and legally grown-up and master of his fate, was a little like having to control that proverbial cannon that has broken loose on board ship during a storm at sea. The example I have just given, of how we began an evening in Old Delhi as a decorous foursome dining at Maiden's Hotel, and ended up in a riotous party in the Gymkhana Club in New Delhi, was merely one of many similar evenings. On one occasion the night's entertainment ended in my helping one of the hotel bearers put Mike to bed in the small hours. I thought he was dead — or anyway, dying — and, being scared to death, I insisted on waking up a doctor (presumably the hotel's resident medic), who was not pleased. Nor was Mike when he heard about it. He wanted to know how I could have made such a silly fuss about it, when I should have helped hush it up!

The trouble was that almost every evening, when the day's work was over and shops and offices shut, the British gathered on the lawns of their Clubs to 'eat the air' as the delightful Indian phrase puts it, listen to a band, and drink gimlets and whisky sours, gin slings, pink gins and a variety of other short drinks with fearsome names. Later on (probably driven in by mosquitoes) they would gather in hotel bars and places where they could drink, by this time suitably dressed in dinner-jackets for dining or dancing, or whatever entertainment they had planned for the evening. (Yes, they *did* always 'dress for dinner', even when dining alone in their own bungalow, and even when camping in the jungle! That at least is truth and not legend.) And in these places they might occasionally be accompanied by one of the lawful owners of the land. Not very often, because caste Hindus, although not totally forbidden all forms of alcohol, as Muslims are, prefer to do their drinking in decent privacy behind closed doors.

This 'sundowner' drinking was a long-established habit among the Empire Builders, and Mike took to it like a duck to water. He had never once been drunk during our unsophisticated Nageem Bagh Navy days, only, at most (and then only very occasionally), getting what in those days we would probably have called 'tightly slight' or 'slightly sozzled'. Which to my mind proves that drink was something he could take or leave. He didn't need it in the euphoric days of the NBN when we were all riding high on clouds of laughter and silliness and sheer high spirits. There wasn't all that much drinking in the NBN because none of us could afford it. Not even Mike, while Colonel Henslow held the purse-strings. But the partying in Delhi was on a different level from the youthful fun-and-games in Kashmir. There was a lot more drinking, for one thing, and far too many parties finished with Mike getting well and truly plastered.

I couldn't handle it. And for a rather silly reason: when he was sober he was in love with me, and he could be so very sweet. But when he was drunk, I ceased to be special and became someone of no importance at all — a faceless stranger who merely happened to be a member of the party he was in that night. Well, there is that old saying: *in vino veritas*, isn't there — 'In wine is truth'. I was reminded of that too often in those Delhi days. Particularly on those occasions when I realized that it was high time that Bets and I went home and, saying goodnight to him, realized that he had not the faintest idea who I was.

I had tried, on the first occasion that I realized he had too much to drink, to persuade him that he had had enough. But that had been a hopeless failure — as anyone who has ever tried that will know! All I got was a degrading row, beginning with Mike drawing himself up to his full height and staring at me like some pompous Peter the Great who has been insulted by one of his *moujiks*, and demanding, in a voice that could be heard from one end of the room to another, if I was '*daring* to shuggess that he had had too mush to drink. Because if sho . . .' Anyone who has ever been silly enough to argue with someone who is well and truly plastered can take it on from there. I don't suppose the scenario varies very much.

I retired in tears, and Mike, waking next morning with a terrible hangover (serve him right!), couldn't remember the details. Only that he had been drunk and exchanged a good few wingèd words with someone — he wasn't even sure with whom, but as soon as he could see straight, he swallowed a couple of Maiden's Hotel's special blend of prairie oysters* and, I imagine, a lot of black coffee, and came rushing round to 80/1 The Mall. When finally admitted, he went down on his knees and apologized in dust and ashes, promising faithfully that if only I would forgive him, 'just this once', such a thing would never happen again — never, never, *never*. After a tearful scene in which I seem to remember we both wept buckets,

* The standard Raj remedy for a hangover: a raw egg in a mixture of Worcestershire sauce and other unexpected items.

peace was restored and for a day or two, everything came up roses. Then *bingo* — we went back to the same routine.

I never again made the mistake of trying to stop him drinking once he had 'drink taken'. I merely left the party the minute I realized that I had ceased to be me and become just-one-of-those-present. And every time that happened Mike would arrive at 80/1 next morning and go through the same hoops again: grovelling, apologizing, coaxing, swearing that if only I would forgive him that he'd never, ever . . . Oh dear! The truth was, of course, that he felt, at last, that he was his own man, and no one could make him do anything he didn't want to do, ever again. There used to be an old music-hall song in Tacklow's day that sums it up beautifully: 'I'm twenty-one today! Twenty-one today! I've got the key of the door, never been twenty-one before! Father says' (in Mike's case, Mother) 'I can do what I like, so shout "Hip-hip hooray" I'm a jolly good fellow, twenty-one today!' Yes, he was twenty-one and he was throwing his hat into the air and getting his teeth into freedom — and enjoying every single minute of it! Plenty of time ahead in which to sober down and start toeing the line.

The only thing that I find strange, having lived in a world that was still enormously influenced by Victorian values and morals, is the fact that in all my early love affairs, sex never even got a look in. Girls like myself just *didn't*. And that was that. Had I been asked to give an opinion based solely on my own experience, I would have gone on believing that this was the norm, and that only around one in fifty of my contemporaries had ever fallen by the wayside. However, I have since learned, with genuine surprise from popular novels, that the wholesale slaughter of young men during the 1914–18 war, and the harsh fact that when a girl saw her particular young man off to war she knew that her chances of ever seeing him again were small, had broken down the sex-barrier in Europe fairly sharply; and that from then on it became pretty shaky.

Well, maybe; but the Raj was still in many ways a backwater, left reasonably undisturbed by the winds and tides of change, and by and large the majority of its Fishing Fleet did *not* sleep around, and the ones who did were few and far between. But it was interesting to note that as soon as one of these dashing creatures lost her virginity, she couldn't *wait* to try to persuade her girlfriends to follow her example. A fact that suggests that the 'fallen' longed to be back in a huddle with the cosy majority instead of knowing that they were still very much out on a limb and considered to be 'fast', the worst label you could slap on a young unmarried woman. I can remember one of these modern and emancipated young women, who had been prodding me about my love-life, saying in superior tones, 'Do you mean to tell me that you haven't been put through your paces yet? For heaven's *sake*! — how *Victorian*!' And in restrospect I am inclined to sympathize with her. But I also feel enormously grateful for the fact that only one of the young men with whom I enjoyed a romantic flirtation let his feelings get out of hand and became a nuisance. Otherwise, it really was a case of 'No sex please. We're British.' And only the other day, reminiscing about old times with someone who had in his rollicking youth been a handsome and dashing young heart-breaker, he said: 'It was pretty difficult for young men like myself, you know. All of us bouncing with *joie de vivre* and raring to go, because where single girls were concerned, sex was definitely out. You lot just wouldn't play, and we knew it and didn't try it on. But grass widows were considered fair game, and there were always plenty of those around. Married women who had been sent up to the hills to escape the hot weather, and were left husbandless for weeks on end, had a field day. They used to mow us down in droves! Remember the one who was nicknamed "The Subaltern's Guide to Knowledge"? Yes, I bet you do! Well, that's how we coped with the situation; I don't know how you "nice" single girls managed.'

Nor do I, really; it certainly wasn't because we were frigid, so I can only suppose that fear of the possible consequences of sleeping around had been so deeply and successfully embedded in our subconscious that it had become more than strong enough to keep even something as powerful as the sex-urge in check. As for all that 'Keeping myself pure for the "Right Man"; one alone to be my own, one alone to share my caresses' stuff, it was so much eyewash: icing-sugar on the cake. For you have to remember that in those days birth control was still pretty much in its infancy, and abortions were performed by sleazy back-street practitioners whose addresses were not easy to come by; nor, thank heaven, did young men setting out on a romantic date carry condoms in their pockets. The very idea would have been enough to take all the romance out of an evening. And oh, how romantic we were!

We sipped imitation champagne and held hands under the tablecloth while somewhere on the far side of the room some would-be Bing Crosby — or possibly the great man himself on a record — moaned tunefully about moonlight and roses bringing memories of you, or some other top-of-the-pops. And when we danced to the sweet melodies of George and Ira Gershwin, Buddy de Silva, or a new young composer called Noël Coward, it was cheek-to-cheek, and we really did feel, as we clung together and swung around together on those crowded ballroom floors, that the *words* of the songs we danced to were true — 'Heaven, I'm in heaven'*. . . We didn't really *need* all that panting, sweating and struggling together among the sheets which nowadays, according to our cinema and TV screens, is regarded as the inevitable — and boringly familiar — ending to every good party; preceded, I gather, by the baldly unromantic question 'Your place or mine?' *Ugh!*

✻ That Delhi interlude was not a very happy one for me. But it ended at last. To be followed by a halcyon period, another of the wonderful slices of my life that, like the NBN, is marked with a white stone.

---

* Yes, I know that tune belongs to the 1940s. But it also belonged to my generation.

Chapter 26

~⊱⊰~

It was no surprise to me that after Mike had seen Mother's photographs of the Ganges trips, and heard her stories, and Tacklow's, of the trips they had made in the past, he had set his heart on doing the same. For I too had been fascinated by those snapshots, and had always resented the fact that there was a strict rule, originally formed and thereafter firmly enforced by Sir Charles Cleveland, that under no circumstances whatever were any children permitted to join the party. I would have given anything to be included in one. And now I was going to be.

Sir Charles had been dead for some years now. He had died of cancer and was, I believe, one of the first humans to have a cancer treated by that comparatively new discovery of Madame Curie's, which she called 'X-rays'. As far as I remember, a fragment of radium had been enclosed in a small metal container and implanted in Sir Charles's body, in the hope that it would burn away the cancer. It didn't. It merely killed him in what must have been an agonizing manner. Tacklow said that it had only been an experiment, and that Sir Charles, who had never been afraid of anything, had volunteered to play guinea-pig, knowing what he was in for if it didn't work. Which sounds so like him. Dear Sir Charles! He was a great man in every sense of the word. Kashmera, his *shikari*, was, however, still very much alive, as were several of the men who had been recruited for those previous Ganges trips; and these, together with Mahdoo and Kadera and the English-speaking down-country bearer who was shared by Mike and Colonel Henslow, made up our crew.

I can't remember whether we drove or went by train to Gujrowla. By train, I imagine; because we would not be coming back that way. But I do remember how heart-warming it was to see again the old iron railway bridge that spanned the great river at Gujrowla looking exactly the same as it did in the days when we used to transfer there into small river craft, to cross to the far bank where carts would be waiting for us to take us

303

inland to whatever shooting-camp had been laid on for the Christmas holidays.

Kashmera had made all the arrangements for this trip, as he used to do for Sir Charles and Buckie, Tacklow and Mother; and the two big wooden boats lay waiting for us under the shadow of the bridge. These boats were typical of the kind that had carried the river traffic for centuries before steam and trains were even dreamt of, let alone invented, and their design had not altered for hundreds of years. They were clumsy, flat-bottomed craft, fashioned entirely from wood in a manner that would surely have been familiar to Noah.

The larger one, which took the crew and the tents in which we would camp, plus all the necessary provisions, was sketchily enclosed at one end by a wooden deck under which gear could be stored and, I presume, members of the crew could shelter from the sun. That is, if they had no objection to being packed like sardines, for I see from a snapshot in Mother's photograph album that on this occasion we carried no fewer than *thirteen* in the 'staff' boat. This inflated number was because the boats were carried down-river by the current and needed very little in the way of steering, beyond the occasional hand on the clumsy wooden rudder, or a touch from one of the even clumsier oars that all such boats carried. But on reaching its journey's end — in our case Narora — the boats must return to base against the current; and the only way was by manpower. A team of coolies hauled the boats up-river by means of heavy hemp ropes, singing as they plodded forward, in the manner made famous by the Volga boatmen. Two men could easily have brought one of the boats down-river, but it needed a team of at least eight to drag them back to the point from which they had started.

The drill was that our boat, which was not so heavily loaded, went on ahead, to be followed at a more leisurely pace by the boat carrying the crew and the tents and all the rest of the clobber. Only Kashmera and one of his friends, and Kadera if he should feel like doing so, came on the first boat. Our object (or rather, Mike's and Colonel Henslow's) was to shoot mugger — the man-eating crocodile of the Indian rivers. I suppose a day will soon come when even these horrid murderers will become an 'endangered species' and people like the long-vanished *Sahib-log* will be accused of 'wantonly killing this poor, harmless animal to the point of extinction'. Bet you! But in the twenties the rivers swarmed with muggers, whose annual toll of villagers, men, women and children, snatched as they filled their water-pots, bathed, washed their garments, watered their cattle or just paddled and played on the wet sands at the river's edge, was horrific. Every ford had its resident murderer, and so did every village; and those who lived and made their livelihood on the banks of the Ganges, boatmen and fishermen, paid the heaviest price.

I never felt any sympathy for the mugger. (Or for a snake or a spider either, though that is only because they give me the creeps, and not for any sensible reason!) But I wouldn't be sorry to hear that muggers were no more, and I shall never forget the excitement of floating silently down that enormous, winding river and wondering what one would see round the next bend. If, as happened fairly often, there was a basking mugger or *garial* — the long-snouted, fish-eating crocodile that is hated by all Ganges fishermen, who blame it for poor catches — lying out in the hot sand near the water's edge, Kashmera would let our boat drift gently into shallow water until it grounded, and study the creature through binoculars to see if it was a large enough specimen to shoot. Or if it was a mugger at all. For a basking mugger, even a large one, is never very easy to spot, since not only are they almost invisible once the silt that coats them has dried to the exact shade of the sandbanks around them, but they take good care to lie at the precise angle at which a water-borne log or similar piece of flotsam, drifting down on the current, would lie when it was stranded. Many a careless calf or goat, coming down to drink, has been deceived by this ruse!

A baby mugger or *garial* was, except on one occasion, left to get on with it. But if Kashmera approved, either Mike or Colonel Henslow, depending on which of them had shot the last one or particularly wanted this one, would jump ashore and, with Kashmera in attendance, stalk the creature by whichever route or direction Kashmera advised. This usually necessitated a long, hot, inch-by-inch crawl over acres of the fine silver sand that lies on either side of India's rivers and affords very little cover beyond the occasional tuft of coarse grass or ragged clumps of casuarina.

Only when Kashmera confirmed that the Sahib under his charge had reached a position where he had the best chances of hitting his target, would he whisper, '*Maro, Sahib*' and the hot, silent stillness of the day would be broken to bits by the reverberating crash of a rifle shot and a sudden, violent ripple of movement all along the river, as the quarry, together with scores of mud turtles who had been basking in the sand along the river's edge — almost invisible, as was the mugger, by reason of the silt that coated them — simultaneously flipped up and plopped into the water with the speed of light, while an astonishing number of birds — most of them hitherto unnoticed — abruptly took to the air: the white egrets that we used to call 'Dobi birds', which had been dozing above their reflections in the shallows, and are an integral part of any Indian river, and a variety of small brown birds such as sandpipers which had been resting in the scant shade of casuarina scrub.

The mugger too, unless hit in a really vulnerable spot, can more often than not get away — and live. For it only needs one swipe of that powerful armour-plated tail to land the creature back in his own element, and muggers, like cats, would appear to have nine lives. If the stalk *was* successful, the corpse was marked with a small flag fastened to a stick driven into the sand, and left for the second boat to collect on its way down-river in our wake. We would stop and go ashore to have a delicious picnic lunch prepared by Mahdoo, and drift on in the afternoon until we found a really attractive place in which to camp, where we would stop and wait for the cookboat to catch up with us. Kashmera and one or two of his assistants would skin the muggers and/or *garials* that had been shot that day and rub salt into the skins, which were then pegged out to dry so that they could be in a fair condition for the Cawnpore tanneries to turn into suitcases, handbags, attaché cases, shoes or whatever.

On the first night of that trip both boats set off together, ours leading, and we stopped as soon as we were far enough from Gujrowla to avoid being pestered by pi-dogs and small boys, set up camp and ate the dinner that Mahdoo had prepared for us. But for the remainder of the trip, both luncheon and our evening meal depended on what the men had managed to shoot for the pot. For no sooner had we selected a campsite than Tacklow, Colonel Henslow and Mike, accompanied by Kashmera, and with Bets and me as onlookers, set out in search of food. Game in those days was easy to come by. The open country on either side of the river swarmed with partridge and quail, sand grouse, snipe, wild duck, teal, hares and any number of black-buck. Tacklow was a poor shot, but Mike and Colonel Henslow were excellent, and since Kashmera was as good as either of them, we — and the thirteen members of our entourage — fed royally.

It was an unforgettable trip, and one that no one will ever again be able to emulate. Since then the population of India has doubled and then tripled and now quadrupled, and where, in my time, there was nothing but open and empty land between the little villages and the occasional town, I am told that these days village touches village. And once, many years later and long after India had become independent, when I was talking over the old days with an old, old boatman, whom I had known as a young man in the days when I was a child, he sketched a wide gesture with his outstretched palms, and said sadly, 'Once there were many, many *kala-hirren* (black-buck). But now there are none left in all this great land!' Well, he was wrong there, for there are a few, though I think they won't last much longer, because there isn't going to be any room for them!

But back in the autumn of the last year of the Roaring Twenties the lovely, empty land was alive with *kala-hirren* and any number of game birds. And night after night we went to sleep to the flicker of firelight and the voice of the river as it whispered and chuckled and rippled its way between the moored boats.

I have said somewhere before that though I was born among mountains and will always think of the Kashmir-that-was as the most beautiful country in the world, the plains of India, and the great rivers that flow across them, have a particular and inexplicable hold on my heart and imagination. I have never really been able to explain why this is so. But every inch and every hour of that trip down the Ganges was pure joy. It was something to do with the size and the flatness of the land. The sense of enormous space. The mile-wide river and the vastness of the empty land which, despite its size, was dwarfed by an even more enormous sky that reduced everything below it to pygmy proportions. The huge circle of the horizon that, whichever way one turned, was always there, so that one stood, a tiny creature no bigger than an ivory chess pawn, in the middle of such a gigantic circle that it was difficult to understand why it did not curve — as nowadays one can see the land or sea curve away below one from the window of an aeroplane. I could never decide at which time of day I liked it best; at dawn, or midday, sunset or night. At dawning, in that clear, pale light that casts no shadow and seems to make the earth shrink down and become as flat as a threadbare Persian carpet, stretching away around you, with the river a smooth expanse of glass and the world so quiet that you could hear the smallest fish jump in the shallows under the far bank, or the fall of a dead leaf on to the sand.

It is in the early dawn that wild duck and geese and teal that have been feeding during the night on the croplands that surround every small village return to the hidden backwaters of the river, where head-under-wing they drowse away the hot days until the sun nears the horizon and it is time for them to wake again for the evening flying.

The skies of early dawn are usually empty and cloudless, and beginning to turn the same dusty shade of duck-egg green that the Georgian architect, designer and decorator Robert Adam used so often in the magnificent houses that he built. But sometimes the night will have left behind it a thin scatter of clouds, wisps and shreds of vapour that will catch the sun while it is still a long way from the horizon, and blaze gold against the green. And presently the cool duck-egg green will turn to yellow, until at last the whole sky is that colour. It is then that the birds awake and sing in chorus; and suddenly there are shadows where no shadows have been before, and a million million dew-diamonds flash and glitter from every twig or stone or blade of grass, as the sun lips the horizon and, as Kipling wrote, '. . . the Day, the staring Eastern Day, is born'.

I loved every minute of those spectacular Indian mornings, and would often set a small alarm clock under my pillow so that I could wake up in time to watch the darkness fade and the sky turn from grey-blue to Adam green and primrose-yellow and from there to the silver and the brilliance and the gold. It was a spectacle that grabbed my heart as a child and has never let go, even though I know that by now most of the empty spaces and the silence will have gone.

The day was almost as alluring. The incredible blue of the sky and the distances. The glitter of the slow-flowing river. The lines of white egrets pricking along the shallows and the flocks of emerald and turquoise parakeets that whirled, shrieking, out of nowhere, to settle briefly and drink, before rising in a chattering mob and whisking themselves away again. The miles and miles of silver sand, blindingly white in the blazing sunlight, and patched here and there with sparse outcrops of grass and casuarina and a green shrub that was always bright with vivid yellow flowers, and whose name I have forgotten — if I ever knew it. The way that heat danced on the sandbanks, so that the horizon and the entire landscape leapt and quivered as it presented you with a series of enthralling mirages — castles and camels and silver lakes, and sudden glimpses of green woods and waterfalls. And except for the gurgling of the water under the prow of our cumbersome craft, no sound but our own voices to break the hot, sun-bleached stillness.

The evenings were always spectacular, since heat and dust are wonderful materials for light to work with. And once again, as the sun sank towards the horizon, the sky would turn back from blue to apple green, streaked and splashed with every colour on an artist's palette. There were never very many clouds, but those there were lit up the sky, evening after evening, until it blazed with wisps and scarves and explosions of molten gold, bright apricot and rose-pink. Whichever member of the Heavenly Host is responsible for Indian sunsets not only makes a spectacular job of it, but does not have to stoop to repeating a performance, since the repertoire seems to be endless. Every evening I would think, 'This is the best *ever*! — it's gorgeous, it's wonderful, it's out of this world. If only I could paint it.' But I couldn't: the splendid transformation scene was always over too quickly. But when it had gone, there was still the night.

Oh, those nights on the Mother of Rivers! The moonlit ones were wonderful, but the starlit ones were better. I had watched many night skies since the night when Tacklow took me up to the Ridge at Simla and gave me my first lesson in astronomy. I can't have been much more than five years old at the time, but he hooked me on astronomy for life. Yet when I look at the night skies now, or read about them or watch TV programmes about them, it is the night skies as I saw them on that Ganges trip that I remember best. I'd never seen the stars quite so clearly before. Perhaps there had been a rainstorm somewhere not too far away — a foretaste of the winter rains that, long after the monsoon has ended, can spoil a camp, or a trek, in northern India. We certainly did not have a drop of rain or even an overcast day during that trip. But if there had been rain somewhere just beyond our vision, it would have helped to clear the dust and made the stars brighter. And then, of course, the month was November, and the monsoon, which had ended in early September, had been heavy enough to have cleared the air and laid the dust in a fairly drastic manner. Also it was now eleven years since the Great War had ended. Time enough in which to dissipate all the corruption that bombs and high explosives, gas attacks, petrol fumes, disease and death had created. The terrible epidemic that had swept round the world in the wake of that war — killing as it did so, many more men, women and children than all the bombs and ammunition had been able to do — had passed, and the bodies of those dead had long ago been burned or buried, or carried away in their thousands by India's rivers, and the land (by now a far emptier one) had had plenty of time in which to cleanse itself of the man-made foulness that war had bred.

The fact that the death-toll of 1917 had been so high — higher in India I believe than almost anywhere else — was already being made good. But the land was still relatively empty, for whole villages had been wiped out, and that meant far fewer cooking-fires and cleaner air.

I don't remember on which night of our trip there was a full moon, or whether the 'dark ones' came at the end or the beginning. I only remember standing out under a starlit sky and suddenly seeing it as I had never seen it before. 'The stars in their courses', each one keeping its own station as it spun through space, some so near that it seemed as though I could reach up and touch them, and some so far away that it was easy to believe that I was watching something that had blinked that blink long before the pyramids were built — before Babylon was built or Troy fell, or Alexander the Great crossed the Indus to invade India. Or perhaps even further back still, when dinosaurs roamed the world and the star I was watching had already blown itself to pieces so long ago that I was only watching something that had not been in existence for uncounted centuries.

It was as if I was seeing the night sky in what we would now call 3-D, and though I have never seen it quite so clearly again, that is the way I still think of it: when I first saw it in an unpolluted sky and remembered the words of David — if he really was the author of the Psalms — and I can paraphrase slightly: 'When I consider the heavens, and the wondrous works of Thy hands, what is Man that Thou art mindful of him?' What indeed? When you look at some of the things that mankind has been doing on this planet, I can't imagine!

But then there is no reason to suppose that we are the only world He created. There may be thousands of others; and any day now we may easily discover that we have succeeded in making this one expendable. If so, serve us right! No one can say that we haven't asked for it!

✳ With freedom to choose a new campsite each evening, we stopped for preference where there were trees under which we could pitch our tents, and if possible, shrubs and pampas grass, and low, sandy cliffs at our back. The sites that we chose were sometimes on the right bank of the river and sometimes on the left as the lie of the land dictated, but always near trees or tall grass; with the result that, after the silence and solitude of the sun-baked hours, the brief and beautiful period of twilight and dusk — in Eastern lands so quickly over that it seems to be little more than a breath drawn between day and darkness — was by contrast as clamorous with sound as though the invisible conductor of an orchestra had let his baton fall and released a torrent of music.

Flights of homing birds, chattering, quarrelling and gossiping, would appear out of nowhere until the trees seemed alive with them. Each evening there were peacocks crying from the cane-brakes and partridges calling from every clump of grass, while out on the river the wild-duck would wake and take off for the evening flight in line after talkative line. This uproar lasted only a short time, but as the last of the sunset faded and the first stars began to shimmer in the darkening sky, the day-time birds fell silent and the owls and the nightjars took over; and from somewhere far out on the plains beyond the river, a jackal-pack would raise its hunting cry, beginning with a single mournful long-drawn-out howl that was repeated several times, until the whole pack took up the cry and howled together in a yelping, wailing chorus.

On white nights the pi-dogs of the nearest village would provide a back-up to the eerie howling by baying at the moon, and sometimes one would hear the maniacal laughter of a hyena — a sound I could have done without. But I never minded the jackal-packs in full cry, perhaps because that sound had been a familiar part of my childhood for the first ten years of my life. As familiar was the peacock's harsh, mournful cry, which I loved and still remember with deep affection, because that cry woke me up each day at dawn, and was one of the last calls to be heard in the dusk.

We would always stop, if Kashmera could manage it, within walking distance of a village, because the old *shikari* and his boatmen enjoyed company and liked to have a bazaar, however small, within reasonable reach; as did Mahdoo, who preferred to shop daily for items that did not keep well in the heat, such as milk and butter and fresh eggs, vegetables and fruit. So there was generally a good deal of coming and going between the camp and the nearest village after dark when the campfires were lit. There were always *tulakdars* and grey-headed village elders who remembered Tacklow and Mother from those yearly trips down the Ganges during the war years and the early twenties, and who asked for news of people like Sir Charles and Buckie and the others who used to pass that way in the old days. They were sad to learn that Sir Charles was dead and sent their respects and messages to Buck-Sahib and 'Soppy'-Sahib and Bunting-Sahib and their congratulations to those younger sahibs who had now become the fathers of sons who, undoubtedly, would one day in the future come drifting down-river to talk to the sons and grandsons of the men who had known their fathers.

Sometimes they would bring gifts with them: a handful of walnuts, or a stick or two of sugar-cane or a slab of *halwa* made from buffalo's milk sweetened with *gur*, which is raw sugar, and boiled and boiled until only the solids remain, when a few chopped pistachio nuts and a drop or two of attar of roses are added before the sweetmeat is flattened and shaped into bars, and — on very special occasions — wrapped in skin-thin pieces of pure, beaten silver. Sometimes a *tulakdar* would proffer a *nuzzer* consisting of a few rupees in a small handkerchief, and this Tacklow would touch and return, as is — or was — the immemorial custom of the land. I have heard that nowadays too many ex-rulers of princely states have taken to accepting the money instead of merely touching it. In which case I imagine the custom will not last much longer!

These old gentlemen, the village elders, would squat down on their heels (an art that Bets and I had once been able to emulate without thinking, but by now, alas, had lost) and chat in the firelight with Tacklow, filling him in with the news and gossip of their village, and asking for information about the doings of the wide world beyond. For this was well before the coming of radio and the TV which now blaze the news into every hamlet, however small and obscure. It was rare for a newspaper to reach these small groups of farming folk, and rarer still for one of their number to be able to read and explain it to their neighbours.

They would also as a matter of course lay their problems before Tacklow, and ask him to adjudicate on such vexed questions as the rightful ownership of crops grown on a disputed field, or what damages should be paid by a villager whose cow had broken into someone else's vegetable patch and eaten or otherwise destroyed at least half of the crop with which it had been planted. And once we were visited by the wailing and distraught family of a small girl who had been taken by their long-time enemy, the local mugger, while she had been filling her *lotah* (brass water-pot) at the water's edge, only the previous evening. Tacklow promised that we would do our best, and handed the problem over to Kashmera, who was taken off to be shown the exact spot where the tragedy had occurred, and regaled with endless stories of this particular mugger's victims and the failure of all the attempts by the local *shikaris* to put an end to its depredations.

It seemed that that particular murderer had been around for a good many years and, though wounded on several occasions, had always managed to get back into deep water and recuperate. Traps had been laid for it in the form of pieces of rotten meat loaded with poison, and though the bait had been taken and there had been no sign of the mugger for the next week or so (as was its habit when wounded by a rifle bullet), no sooner had the village decided that it *must* be dead and that it was safe to relax their guard, than some unwary human, or his cow or goat, was snatched as they waded into the river to fill a water-pot, or to drink.

Kashmera studied the marks on the wet sand where the child had been taken and learned all he could of the creature's habits, and announced that the camp ought to stay where it was for a day or two. I don't mind telling you that all of us took the greatest possible pains to watch our step whenever we went too near the water. It wasn't all that comfortable knowing that there was one of those revolting, scaly horrors somewhere near at hand, watching us to see if there was a chance of making a sudden rush, or just a single sweep of that powerful tail that could hit us into the river where we could be snatched and dragged down into the deceptively peaceful Ganges.

Kashmera knew a lot about muggers; he had studied them and their behaviour for years. He also knew a great deal about this particular stretch of the Ganges, its quirks and its currents, from having accompanied Sir Charles and his friends on countless shooting trips on the river since the days when Charles and Buckie were young men and he himself was only a boy learning his trade from an older and more experienced *shikari*. He had taught Bets and me, when we were still in short socks, how to tell the size of a mugger by the marks it left upon the wet sands as it crawled out of the river and turned to face the water at the angle of a stranded log, and — when it slithered back into the water again — to tell whether it had been startled into leaving, or merely decided that it was time to go home. Best of all he taught us the best places in which to lie up and watch for one to leave the water, and how to reach that vantage point by crawling to it across open sand — a trick we found useful when attempting to catch sun-bathing river-turtles.

It was fascinating now to see him studying the sands at the water's edge for a good mile up-stream and down, and (using Tacklow as interpreter) telling Mike that the creature would not be likely to show himself near the spot where he had taken the child for at least a week, and probably longer. 'For the mugger knows well,' said Kashmera, 'that always, after a killing, the folk of his village throw rocks and unpleasant things into that spot and are careful to avoid that part of the bank, both for their own safety and for their animals. Or, if they use it, they only do so with great caution, and carrying arms. Therefore he will not show himself near the place until they forget and become careless again. So tomorrow we will look for him either on the far side of the river, or well up- or down-stream.'

We had done so, and Kashmera had thought right: the mugger showed himself towards noon on the following day, about a mile up-stream of our camp and on the same side of the river, at a spot where it was almost impossible for anyone to take a shot at him, for here the banks were high and overhung by thickets of lantana and elephant-grass, and the current ran fast and deep, undercutting the land and scouring out the earth from around the roots of kikar-trees and casuarinas. Besides, the creature was so beautifully camouflaged that left to myself I would never have spotted it. Not even with the help of binoculars, for it lay along a narrow mud ledge barely wide enough to accommodate its armour-plated body, and only just clear of the water, a foot at most.

Lying there, parallel with the clay bank, the sludge at the bottom of the Ganges already baked on it to a patchy silver-grey by the sun, it blended so perfectly with the tangle of roots and the stripy shadows of the overhanging vegetation that it was very nearly invisible. It certainly would have been to me if Kashmera hadn't whispered to me and directed my binoculars to the exact spot. And even then it looked more like part of the bank than a living creature.

Mike had suggested risking a shot at it, but Kashmera advised against it, on the grounds that unless one can hit a mugger in one of only two of his vital spots — neither of which at this date, I can be sure of, though I *think* one is in the neck, just behind the eyes and the other in the spine (Kashmera's ghost, if it is still around, must be disgusted with me) — the creature's reflex action when it is hit is a violent, jack-knife jerk that flips it back into deep water in the space of a split-second, where, however badly it may be wounded, it is likely to recover in due course.

Lying out in the sun on a narrow ledge at the foot of that long, high stretch of bank, its blunt nose towards us, it presented the smallest possible target; there was no hope of being able to get a shot at it from the opposite side of the river, for that distant shore had already withdrawn from view behind the dancing, shimmering curtain of heat-haze. In the end, after a lot more argument between Mike and Kashmera (inadequately translated by me) and the fact that there *was* no other way of approaching that scaly old murderer on the ledge, I was firmly told to stay where I was, while Kashmera and Mike set off to see how close they could get to the creature before risking a shot. Fortunately there were several trees among the scrub on the bank which enabled them to fix the spot they were aiming for, and they set off to make a wide detour that was planned to end a short, hopefully silent, stalk that would bring them out about 100 yards up-stream of the mugger.

It didn't work, of course, though in the circumstances I suppose it was worth trying. I lay and watched the mugger through Tacklow's binoculars, in the intervals of keeping a lookout for any sign of movement among the scrub and the tall grasses which would tell me where the stalkers were. I didn't see any, but there are always lookouts who warn the wild creatures of the approach of man. In this case, I gather, a king-crow that had been snoozing in the shade of a peepul tree had woken up and given the alarm. I was too far away to hear it, but I happened to be looking at the mugger and I saw it slide noiselessly off its ledge into the water. And that was that. Some time later, Mike and Kashmera appeared pushing their way through the vegetation at the edge of their overlying bank, and waved to me to stay where I was, while they scrambled down to the water's edge and walked back to examine the marks that the enemy had made, before clawing up the bank and rejoining me.

Kashmera confirmed that it had been the village mugger, and that they would have to hope that it would come out again in some more easily accessible spot. It did so in the late afternoon, a good two miles downstream of where we had seen it that morning, on the far side of the village. A panting villager arrived at the double to bring us the news, but by the time Mike and Kashmera got there, a horde of small children, vengeful friends and playmates of the little girl who had fallen victim to the mugger, had driven it off by throwing stones at it. And the next day it was back again on that inaccessible ledge at the foot of that long stretch of high bank. This time Mike and Kashmera and a couple of the boatmen took one of the boats across the river and, having hauled it up-stream and out of sight, let it float down again on the current. For it seemed that the wildlife on the river was as familiar with boats floating silently down it as they were with those being noisily towed up it, since this was something that had been happening for 1,000 years or more.

Kashmera was of the opinion that if Mike were to try by land again, a bird or monkey would be certain to cry the alarm, for the thickets were full of both. But if we came down silently on the water, not a bird would squeak. It was our best bet — though he owned that it was not easy to fire from the deck of a moving boat and he did not know if the young Sahib had ever attempted such a shot before. Mike said of course he had; when he was shooting a duck or goose from a punt, and that anyway, if we kept the boat as near as we could to the right bank it ought to be a gift.

Chapter 27
~~✕✖✕~~

As far as the boat was concerned, the whole exercise went as planned. Mike seems to have knelt on the floorboards and, resting the rifle barrel on the edge, fired at a range of, at a guess, no more than fifty or sixty yards as the boat came level with the mugger.

The crash of the shot appeared to coincide exactly with a violent jack-knife leap on the part of the sleeping mugger, which whipped round and in the same flash of a second disappeared into the river. '*Damn!*' lamented Mike. 'Oh, damn, damn, *damn!* I missed it! How *could* I have missed it?' But he hadn't; for when we stopped the boat at the campsite, and he and Kashmera walked back along the top of the bank and climbed down at the point where it had been lying, there was a gout of blood on the ledge and Kashmera, examining it, said that he had certainly not missed it, though he had not hit it at either of the vital spots that would have paralysed it and prevented that automatic jerk that had catapulted it into the river in one leap. 'But I think the Sahib may well have killed it,' said the old *shikari*. I asked him why he thought so when there was such a very little blood, but he said that it was the *kind* of blood that mattered, not the amount.

We spent one more day at that campsite, and though there was no sign of the mugger, the village *shikari* told Kashmera that there was a large *garial* whose favourite basking spot was on the sandbank on the far side of the river, and that the village would be greatly obliged if one of the sahibs would shoot it, for its depredations had led to a marked shortage of fish on that particular stretch of river. Indian villages hate the *garial* even more than they dislike the mugger, for the mugger only kills an occasional human — who will soon be replaced, if female — and a few goats or a calf, whereas a big *garial* needs many *seers* weight in fish to fill its stomach, and deprives the fishermen of their livelihood and the public of a valuable source of protein. Colonel Henslow was ferried across the river in a boat belonging to one of the fishermen in the village and, after a prolonged stalk, bagged a large *garial*. We all went across to photograph it, and I *think* it was the same day that Mike caught a baby *garial* in an unorthodox manner, though I can't be sure . . .

Its mother can't have told it everything, because it had crawled much too far away from the water, and since Mike had left his rifle in the boat he snatched a fish-spear from one of the boatmen, ran after it as it scuttled away towards the water, and speared it in the shallows. He had been looking out for baby muggers or, preferably, *garials* (whose skins are much finer) because he wanted to have the skins made into an attaché case or possibly a pair of shoes, and the grown mugger or *garial* has too coarse a skin for fine work — the divisions between its plates are too deep and after being cured and tanned may crack.

On the following day, after a careful recce by Kashmera and the village *shikari* on both sides of the river, both up-stream and down, had showed no trace of the mugger, we struck camp and moved down-stream. But we can't have gone much further than a mile when a panting, wildly waving figure appeared on the river-bank beside us, trotting along in our wake and pausing occasionally to make a megaphone of his hands to shout unintelligible words. 'It is the mugger,' translated Kashmera. 'They have seen the mugger,' and he steered our boat into the bank.

Well, they hadn't actually. And if it had just been a case of spotting it lying out on the bank as before, we would not, I think, have gone back for it. But that was not the case, as the panting messenger explained when he finally caught up with us. One of the villagers who had seen us off that morning had walked back up-stream in pursuit of a cow that had strayed from the herd, and having turned back had sat down to rest at the edge of the bank and become aware of an odd noise that was, he explained, like someone groaning, and seemed to come from below ground.

Leaning over to see what it could be, he had become aware that directly below him, and almost at water-level, there was a cave in the bank, or rather the entrance to a cave, and though scared out of his wits by the peculiar subterranean sound, curiosity got the better of him and he climbed cautiously down to discover what was making it. The entrance to the cave was partially under water, but it sloped back and up into the earth, and the strong stench of musk and decayed carrion told him that he had found something that I believe is rarely discovered: the home-cave of a mugger.

Keeping well to one side of it, and greatly daring, he had peered inside. But all he could see was the darkness and the glint of the water — and the unmistakable gleam of the creature's eyes. It was enough; and scrambling hastily back up the steep side of the bank, he tore back to the village, shouting the news, and returned with a small crowd of people at his back, including the village *shikari* who said this was a sahib's work, and sent off a runner in pursuit. The boats pulled into the shore and Mike and I and Kashmera, plus the excited messenger, walked back up the sands to our most recent camping ground, and a further mile up-stream to the cave, now surrounded by villagers armed with sticks and *lathis*, prepared to prevent the mugger from emerging, though this was something I don't think anyone could possibly have prevented if the creature had had the strength to do so, because the entrance was obviously somewhere well below the water-level and this was merely the top end, in which he could breathe, and keep his larder until it was sufficiently rotten to suit his taste.

He was breathing now, but with appalling difficulty and in great pain. Though I never thought I could possibly feel sorry for a mugger, I was sorry for this one as it lay in the dark, emitting agonizing groans with every breath it was struggling to draw.

Mike had brought a small pocket torch with him which we strapped on to the barrel of his rifle with that sticky elasticated bandage material from Mother's first aid box. Watching him climb down to the lowest edge of that overhanging bank, I was scared stiff that the mugger would rush forward to attack him and that if he stepped back he would go straight down into deep water with the creature on top of him, for he had little or no room in which to take avoiding action, and only two options. He could either leap to one side — providing he didn't slip in doing so — or go straight back into the river. I didn't like the idea of either.

Nor did the other spectators, Kashmera least of all. He kept on exhorting me to tell the Sahib that he must be careful. 'Tell him that a mugger is always very dangerous until it's dead, and this one is not dead yet! Tell him that he must be ready to move sideways very quickly. *Not* back.' Mike moved cautiously to face the cave mouth and, bending down to peer inside, flicked on the torch for a brief moment and stepped aside hastily. It was a whopper, and right back in the cave, and he would have to shoot him there and could only hope to goodness that the bullet didn't ricochet off a rock or something solid in the back of the cave, and get him — Mike — on its way out. An observation that did nothing towards soothing my nerves! But there was nothing else for it and, crouching down again, he got his rifle up to his shoulder, switched on the little torch again, fired, and almost in the same second, jumped sideways to the left of the cave mouth.

The crash of the shot in that confined space was incredibly loud, and though the bullet hit it between the eyes, the creature's reflexes were still enough to make it rush forward and collapse just inside the mouth of the cave, where Mike gave one more shot just to be on the safe side. It was as well that it lurched forward, for otherwise I don't believe we should ever have got it out of that noisome cave. Certainly none of the villagers would have faced crawling inside in order to drag out the corpse. But as it was, it was easy enough to put a rope round its neck and haul it out and along that stretch of high bank until we reached a shelving beach once more.

The creature was not as large as it had looked when alive, but it was a fair size all the same, and sure enough, when its stomach was cut open that evening (after the skin had been removed and rubbed with salt, and rolled up in a piece of sacking ready to be dispatched to the Cawnpore tanneries) it was found to contain the forearm of its last victim, together with several small and unbroken glass bracelets. These and the bone, we learned later, were, together with a good many other grisly relics, collected and burned as the ritual demands, so that the ashes of the deceased could be consigned to the river.

Kashmera found the whole episode enthralling. He said that in all his years as a *shikari*, and the many times he had accompanied Cleveland-Sahib on his shooting trips down the Ganges, he had only once before come across a mugger's cave. And that had only been because a particularly heavy monsoon had brought down great chunks of bank and exposed it. And never before had he heard of anyone shooting a mugger in its lair. I imagine he lived on that story for the rest of his life.

I can't remember whether it was after this or before it that we camped for two days in a grove of silk-cotton trees near a little village called Puth, in the hope, which proved a vain one, of seeing butterflies. This was because just once in all their Ganges trips, my parents and their party had tied up there and found that a particular creeper that grew there was in full bloom. Tacklow said he was not aware of having seen it before (he was no botanist!) but that it had a small and rather undistinguished white flower with a strong and very sweet scent, and that it climbed all over the surrounding bushes, almost smothering them, and was smothered in turn by hundreds of thousands of butterflies. Not just Monarchs, which have a habit of swarming in that manner, but butterflies of every size, kind and description, drawn by the heavy scent and gorging themselves on the honey. He knew a lot about butterflies and had once collected them. But this was the only time he had ever seen them in such numbers, and so hypnotized by the scent and drugged by honey that they made no attempt to avoid the humans who stared at them and put out a finger to touch them, or the birds which gorged on them.

The villagers had told him that this always happened once every year, during the flowering time of the creeper, but that one never knew when it would be. And Tacklow told me that ever afterwards they had tried to arrange to visit Puth at the time the creeper would be in flower, but had never managed to get it right again. Either they were far too early, or just too late! And since the men all had pressing work awaiting them in their respective offices when the all-too-short holidays were over, and could not loaf down the Ganges like we were doing, there had never been any question of staying on for a few days in the hope of seeing a creeper come into flower. Yet every year after the 'butterfly year', Tacklow had hoped against hope to hit the right date again, until a dire year when they found that some of the villagers had ploughed up an acre or so of the ground where the creeper had grown and sown it with Indian corn.

Mother had taken a snapshot of the butterflies, but nothing had come out but a blur that might have been anything — or nothing. Many years later, hundreds of miles to the north-west of the great subcontinent, when Bets and I saw the same sort of sight — thousands of Monarch butterflies (we used to call them 'potato butterflies' because they could always be found fluttering about the potato creeper in our garden in Simla) smothering the lantana bushes on the banks of the Chenab river, within sight of the Kashmir snows, and I took at least half-a-dozen colour transparencies of that fantastic sight, the result was the same. A blur of colour that could have been anything. For even though by then I had a far more sophisticated camera with a much better lens, it had not been quick enough to freeze or make sense of the vast cloud of fluttery, shimmery butterfly wings.

If Tacklow hadn't promised to be back in Tonk by a certain date I think he might have stayed another day or two hoping for the creepers to flower. But he could not wait any longer, and nor could he identify that particular creeper among the many that grew along the river-bank and in the open country behind it — or on the rough ground that had once been a cornfield.

The only large town that we passed on that trip was Benares. It is one of the most sacred towns in all India and, seen from the river, one of the oldest and most beautiful. I don't know where the name 'Benares' came from, probably from some fifteenth- or sixteenth-century British adventurer's mispronunciation of 'Varenese' which was its old name, and is again now. Holy men of all persuasions flock there, as do men and women who wish to obtain merit or petition the Gods for a particular favour — a male child, or a cure for sickness. And very many — those who can afford it — come there to die, for the most flourishing industry of the town is death. Ceaselessly, by day and night, the smoke from the funeral pyres rises like incense in some medieval cathedral as the bodies of the dead who have come there or been brought there to die are burned among the *chattris* (umbrellas) near the river's edge, so that when the fires die down the ashes will be consigned to Mother Gunga who will carry them to the sea.

The air can never be free of smoke, which draws a thin, gauzy veil over the high, cliff-like wall of ancient domes and towers and temples, peepul trees and palaces, that rises above it; and the long flights of stone steps that lead down to the burning-*ghats* at the water's edge are, from sunrise to sunset, as crowded as Jacob's Ladder with pilgrims or mourners ascending or descending.

I am told that the time to see Benares is in very early morning, when the pyres of the previous day have burned out and the next ones have yet to be built and lit, and the wide sweep of those ancient stone stairs can be seen, uncluttered by the bee-swarms of humanity. Well, we couldn't break camp in time to reach it by sunrise, and it was nearly midday by the time the current took us slowly down past that beautiful frieze of domes and temple-tops and the lovely white marble palace of His Highness the Maharajah of Benares. By that time humanity had taken over with a vengeance, and not only the steps but the river for at least thirty feet out from the shore was black with people bathing, and uncomfortably full of boats of every size and shape, of which ours was only one among many.

Right: Some officers and crew of the Nageem Bagh Navy. *Left to right*: Enid the Bo'sun, Bets the Cabin-boy, self the Midshipmite, Andy the Captain, and Mike the First Officer. The Quartermaster, Paymaster, Dog Watch and sundry Able Seamen were absent on 'shore leave'!

Below: Mike on his twenty-first birthday. Pencil sketch by M. M. Kaye.

Above: Cap'n Andy and Chief Petty Officer John Sykes.

Left: The NBN on lifeboat drill, Peshawar.

'Row for the shore sailor,
Row for the shore!
Heed not the rolling billows
Or the breakers' roar!'

DOWN THE GANGES
A Shooting Trip: Garhmuktesa to Narora

Top left: Bets, Mike, self, Colonel Henslow at one of our camps.

Above: Mike's catch, the man-eating mugger.

Top right: Mike spears a small *gharial* (a fish-eating crocodile).

Right: Mike watching the man-eater he shot loaded on to the second boat.

CHRISTMAS CAMP
– tiger-shoot at Pirwa

Above: The camp on Christmas Day, Pirwa. *Clockwise:* Tacklow, Campbell Harris (he at least is enjoying himself!), Bill, self, Mother, Bets.

Above right: Tacklow, beaters and Saadat, the heir apparent, the tigress and her cub.

Right: The tigress and the elephant that bolted.

NUNNI'S WEDDING TO A BRIDE FROM BHOPAL

Left: The twelve-year-old bridegroom looks out of his carriage on the special train.

Below: The palace, Bhopal.

Below: Guests arrive for the wedding at Bhopal.

Above: The Nunni-Mirza, waiting for his 'Wedding Special' to arrive.

Above: Guests from Tonk arriving in Bhopal in some of the Nawab's collection of cars.

Right: Saadat (no comment).

Right: The Citroën expedition led by Georges-Marie Haardt takes a brief halt in Kashmir. Geoffrey Wright, Mike, Bets, self and the artist Alexandre Jacovleff – his paintings were wonderful.

Below: Colonel Waddington and Georges-Marie Haardt, the leader of the 'Yellow Journey'.

Above: Mother sketching.

Below: A birthday party. Guests were required to arrive as 'tourists' and to act the part in a short film written and cast by the owner of a small hand-held film camera. *Left to right:* self, Bill, Babs Babbington, Sylvia 'Snip' Coleridge (who later made quite a name for herself on the stage and screen), her sister, 'Tiny' Coleridge, and Bets.

Above: The wedding of Molly Baines and 'Bolshie' Tatham. Bolshie ran the polo at Cowdray Park for many years, after leaving the Indian Cavalry.

Above: The Garden of the Breezes, Nasim Bagh, now cut down and replaced by barracks.

Left: Country boats on the Jhelum river, Srinagar.

Below: Party in Gulmarg. I don't remember who the people sitting next to me are. The nearest to the camera is Edna Bakewell and the man standing by Bets is Edna's husband, Bruce, the Forest Officer, both of them dear friends of ours.

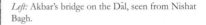

Left: Akbar's bridge on the Dāl, seen from Nishat Bagh.

Right: The entrance gate to Chasma Shai, 'the royal spring'. This was only a very little garden but much loved. This is the lower level, which is all flowerbeds. The higher level, where the only pavilion stands, is mostly lawns. We used to picnic on these. When the band packed up, many of the dancers, provided there was enough moonlight, ended by driving out to this little garden, to wait for the sunrise. So this is not a bad place to say goodbye to Kashmir.

Left: The Dāl Lake. The Shalimar Gardens are behind the fish-spearer's right hand, among the trees on the far side of the lake. In those days the lakes were crystal clear and almost weed-free. You could watch the fish swimming between the stems of the lotus and the water-lily pads.

Below: Mother with the *manji* of the houseboat and family, on Char-Chenar Island on the Dāl Lake.

Below: Reflections in the water in Shalimar. Geoffrey Wright, self and Mother. The highest peak in the background is Mahadeo.

Right: Mother sketching the Black Marble Pavilion, Shalimar Gardens.

Left: Tacklow, Yda, Geoff Dimsey and self (I'm not sure who is sitting next to me!) on the bathing-boat.

Right: Bets as a butterfly. Dinner and cabaret in aid of – I think – Zenana Hospitals. We made those wings ourselves. What's more, they opened and shut!

Below: Me appearing in a cabaret show in Srinagar. We didn't have much in the way of theatres in the Raj, so we provided our own, and amateur theatricals of every sort flourished.

Above: Bets's Chinese dance – 'Little Lacquer Lady'.

Below: One of the Sunday afternoon picnics, off the Meerut Road.

Right: Self off to a Viceregal garden party (not the one that was blacked out), wearing my second-hand finery.

Below: The 'sextet' in the porch of the Underhill Road Chummery in Old Delhi. *Left to right:* W. H. P., Bets, self, Bill, Pam (Cosgrave), Neil.

Below: Bets and W. H. P., their engagement snapshot. (He refused to be called 'Henry', and since Mother already had a 'Bill' in the family and he didn't care to be called 'William', he settled for his initials and was from henceforth W. H. P.)

Above: Neil and W.H.P. outside the Underhill Road Chummery in Old Delhi.

The left bank, opposite the town is — or was in those days — surprisingly empty. Apart from a scattering of reed-built huts and a few more solid buildings that looked as if they had been started but left unfinished, it seemed to have been ignored by the housing trade. The sandy shallows on that side, and much of the surface of the river, were full of strings of faded marigold flowers which are by tradition used to adorn the dead as well as to garland honoured guests and holy men, and other VIPs. Odd, when they have been used for so many centuries as funeral flowers.

I remember regretting yet again that I hadn't had the sense to take a paintbox with me. But my admiration for the spectacular town was ruined by the horrid discovery that what I had taken to be just another, though more venturesome swimmer, dog-paddling down on the current, was in fact a partially burned corpse. And that the lifelike movements that had given it an illusion of keeping itself afloat were caused by scavenging fish and river-turtles tugging at it as it was carried down-stream.

It was not that I hadn't known about such things, because I had since my early years of childhood. The holy books of Hinduism direct that bodies should be burned and their ashes consigned to the nearest river, preferably the Ganges. But wood is expensive, and since very many of the poor cannot possibly afford the expense of priests and a pyre, it is considered permissible — particularly in times of war, plague or famine, when there are many corpses to be disposed of — to place a live coal in the mouth of the deceased before consigning it to the river. This one had probably been slipped into the water on the quiet from somewhere a longish way up-stream, and left to the mercy of the current. It should not have horrified me, but it did. And though it had never occurred to me that I might one day attempt to write a book, the seeds of a novelist, to whom all is grist to the mill, must have been there. Because years later, when I was at work on my first India novel, *Shadow of the Moon*, I remembered that corpse and described it going down-river, tugged this way and that by scavenging fish and turtles, so that it looked alive.

✳ Throughout that lovely journey Mike had behaved like an angel. He was enjoying every minute, and it showed. Tacklow had been asked by the old Nawab if he would please shoot a tiger that had been taking too heavy a toll of the herds of the villagers of Pirawa, a small hamlet near the border of his state. He had also suggested that we should use the occasion to lay on a camp for the Christmas holiday and ask anyone we wished to join it. His heir and some of his relations had expressed a wish to be present, and he himself would give the orders to lay on a camp for the occasion, and see to all the details of the shoot. Tacklow had accepted with pleasure, and we had already asked my brother Bill and one of his friends, Campbell Harris. And now Mike, having heard of it, badgered my parents to let him come too, on the grounds that he had never been on a tiger shoot before — and might never get such an opportunity again, since tiger shoots were not in everyone's gift, and were apt to be reserved for the senior ranks of the 'Heaven-born' or visiting bigwigs and brass-hats.

I don't think Tacklow thought much of the idea, since Mike and I had been living in each other's pockets for a good many weeks on end now; what with the Nageem Bagh Navy, the NBN reunion and Mike's twenty-first birthday celebration in Peshawar, our stay at Lahore and then in Delhi, followed by this Ganges trip, Tacklow thought it was high time we took a break from each other's company. However, it became impossible to refuse, and after all, it only meant another ten days at most. Mike was wildly excited at the prospect, and could talk of nothing else during our final days on the river. The whole trip had been an enormous success — and then, on the day that we were due to reach Narora, where our trip ended, Mike sprained his ankle.

I don't remember how he managed to do it. Presumably by putting his foot into some old rat-hole that had been enlarged by a snake or a mongoose for a temporary home. All I do remember is that while the tents were being set up at our last-but-one campsite, Tacklow, Colonel Henslow and Mike had gone off to shoot partridge, or anything else that was suitable for the pot, and Bets, Mother and I had not accompanied them. We had stayed on the campsite to watch the birds coming home to roost in the trees overhead, and to admire what looked like being a really spectacular sunset; and saw Mike, looking pale grey under his tan, hopping painfully to the camp with one arm round Tacklow and the other round Colonel Henslow.

Mother, who had attended first aid classes throughout the Great War years and never travelled anywhere without a first aid box, soaked a roll of bandages in cold water and bandaged up the swollen ankle as well as she knew how, but could not commit herself as to whether it was only sprained and not broken. Mike was obviously in great pain and the sooner we got him to a doctor the better. That, however, was easier said than done. As far as we knew there was not a qualified doctor within miles. But Kashmera assured us that there was a skilful *dai* (nurse) at Narora, and if we left immediately after breakfast next morning, we could reach Narora by mid-morning. If she proved to be useless — which he refused to believe — we could get the Sahib to the railway station and on to the first train to Delhi, as the next best thing. He would send a runner immediately to Narora to enlist the *dai*'s services.

Mike had a nasty night but managed to drown the pain in a good deal of brandy, with the result that he had a hangover next morning to provide a counter-irritant to the ankle. We left Mahdoo and Kadera and the rest of the second boat's crew to strike camp and follow us, and left for Narora as early as we could, taking only Kashmera and two crew men.

This hasty voyage on the final day of our journey was a sad anticlimax. We had meant to take it slowly, savouring every last precious minute of it, because all of us knew that this was something that we were never likely to do again. Not 'us Kayes', anyway. I suppose Mike could, if he had really felt like it, have repeated the trip; though not with people like my parents and Kashmera, who knew and loved every last curve and bend of that fabled river, its shoals and shifts and sandbanks, the high bluffs and the lantana and pampas grass and the occasional groups of trees, mango and silk-cotton, neem and Dâk trees, and the grey-greens of casuarina and the tall broomstick palms.

As it was, we took it as fast as we could, keeping to the main current and not bothering, when we rounded an outflung arm of land, to look out for the grey shape of a mugger or a *garial* basking in the sun near the water's edge. In places where the current slowed, Kashmera and two boatmen would man the two huge, clumsy wooden oars, and hurry us along. And when we reached Narora, the *dai* was waiting, and so were four coolies from the canal-works with a stretcher who under the *dai*'s orders, carried Mike up to the nearest Canal-bungalow — the one that we used to stay in when Bets and I were children and paid our annual visit to Narora.

The *dai* turned out to be an ancient, witch-like old village woman, grey-haired and wizened, with bony, wrinkled hands, and wearing a not over-clean sari which she kept on twitching into place in order to hide her face, whenever it fell away — which it did every other minute. Mike took a dislike to her on sight and began by saying he wasn't going to let the old hag touch him, and that she probably had at least six diseases which he could catch if she did. There followed an exhausting argument, which in the end I won, though not until I had become so exasperated with him that I would have enjoyed slapping him. He gave in eventually, and sulkily allowed the old creature to have him transferred from the hut to a mattress that was laid on the ground. Having got him there, she squatted down beside him, very carefully removed the bandages and felt his ankle with the tips of her long, bony fingers, announcing after a moment or two that the Sahib had only sprained his ankle and the bone was not broken, and she could put that right at once. Which, believe it or not, she did. Mike was fascinated. He hadn't come across the ancient Indian skill of massage before, but he swore the old lady had drawn out the pain with her fingers and got all the wrenched muscles straightened out again.

She told him he must rest it as much as possible for a week or two, but otherwise he was OK, and she advised against going off to catch a train to Delhi for the next couple of days. So Mike stayed in the Canal-bungalow, while the rest of us camped as usual in tents set up in a grove of trees above the canal-works on the banks of the river, where it widens out and slows because it is held back by a weir, and by the great sluice-gates controlling the water that flows into the Ganges Canal.

It was lovely to be back in Narora again, even though our friends the Perrins were no longer there. But it had been a mistake to let Mike sleep alone in the Canal-bungalow, with only his bearer and a *chowkidar* who was employed by the Canal Company to keep an eye on him. He was cheerful enough while we were all there with him, and after a comparatively long spell of sleeping under canvas on camp-beds, I think we all rather envied him in his more spacious and civilized bedroom in the Canal-bungalow. But once we had said our goodnights and left him, he found that even with his own bedding the regulation *narwar* bed provided by the Company was not all that comfortable and that he could not sleep — not even after counting flocks of sheep. Finally he gave up the attempt and stood himself another slug or two of brandy, which proved far more effective than the sheep. So much so that he ended up by finishing the bottle and sending his bearer down to his tent to fetch another.

I knew very well that Mike wasn't an alcoholic, or even on the way to becoming one, for he hadn't drunk more than two regulation 'sundowners' every evening, and one, or at the most two, *chota-pegs* — small whiskies and soda — between dinner and going to bed, during the entire trip. I think it was a combination of a lot of petty things — sheer fury at being confined to bed with a still swollen ankle, finding, when he could not sleep, that he had no one to talk to, and general frustration because a *narwar* is uncomfortable to sleep on unless you are used to it, aggravated by being made to stay still, or told that he couldn't do what he wanted to do when he wanted to do it; plus the disappointment that a trip that had been so much fun, and such an enormous success, should be spoiled like this at the very last moment, and that he might even have to spend another day — even two — supine on this wretched *narwar* while the rest of the party carried out the prearranged programme for the final day in Narora: fishing for *chilwa* on the weir, and for *maseer*, the great fighting fish that are the salmon of India's rivers, in the mile-wide waters above the Canal head.

There was also the fact that he was in pain, and that Mother's first aid box contained neither painkillers nor sleeping-pills, and that all we carried in the way of drugs was brandy and a few aspirin. Whatever the cause, Mike consoled himself by getting beautifully tight and waking up in a filthy temper and with the hangover of a lifetime. What he needed was loads of sympathy and a couple of prairie oysters and I was in no condition to offer either. Because the one thing I had no idea how to deal with, and felt that I could not and would not cope with, was a drunk. And I, too, was feeling on edge and far from calm and controlled, for after all, this was to have been the day on which I decided my future, and presumably Mike's. Well, I suppose you could say that at least I did that, because we ended up having one hell of a row.

It was a thoroughly undignified one, in the course of which I remember getting tied up with a truly ghastly sequence of yes's and no's, when Mike yelled at me that he supposed that my answer was 'no' and I yelled back, 'Yes — I mean *no!* — I mean yes, it's no! . . .' Oh, dear; youth, youth! What chumps we can make of ourselves.

In the end Mike shouted at me that in that case he was returning to Delhi that very day, and what's more he was going to marry the first nice-looking girl he met — *so there!* And having got that off his chest, and forgetting in the heat of the moment that he had a sprained ankle, he stormed out of the bungalow — ruining his exit by a howl of pain as whichever foot it was hit the floor, and thereafter limping furiously away in search of Colonel Henslow, while I shouted after him with equal fury, '*Good!* I'm *delighted* to hear it! I hope she turns out to be an alcoholic shrew, which is what you deserve!' — or words to that effect.

I have to admit that I really didn't believe for a moment that he meant what he said. I thought it was just Mike in a rage, and that like all those other times in Delhi when he had drunk too much and been rude and insufferable, he would be around first thing in the morning, apologizing in dust and ashes and promising never, never, never to behave like that again. And when he and Colonel Henslow actually did leave an hour or two later — I forget what excuse he and the baffled and embarrassed Colonel cooked up to explain their abrupt departure (the necessity of getting to a hospital, I imagine) — I was truly relieved, because I felt that this was a point of no return, and that what I had to decide now was not so much 'yes' or 'no', but just how many more times (if I made it 'yes') I was going to accept the apologies and the promises never, never to offend in this manner again. I had already begun to feel that I had done so far too often. I needed a few Mike-free weeks to straighten things out, and we would do that together when he arrived in Tonk for the Christmas camp and the tiger shoot.

But Mike had meant exactly what he said, and within a week of arriving back in Delhi — where, as far as I can remember, he parted with the Colonel, who had other commitments — and on his own for the first time, he seems to have collected the old gang of scroungemongers again. Once his ankle was out of plaster, they swept him off to another dance at the IDG, where someone introduced him to a prominent member of that year's Fishing Fleet, one Amber Orr-Wilson, an ex-model — the job had not the star-status that it acquired in the years after the Second World War, but was still considered fairly 'dashing'. She was not merely 'the first nice-looking girl' that Mike met on his return to Delhi, but a spectacular creature with the figure which one would have expected from a model, and she had already caused more than a few ripples in Peshawar.

There had been, for instance, the occasion when, at a dance at the Peshawar Club, she and her partner had been dancing the tango so superlatively that the other dancers had stood back to watch, and let them have the floor. Undeterred, they continued to dance until it dawned on the spectators that either a button or a bit of elastic, or both, had given way and a vital part of Amber's underwear was gradually descending. Amber herself did not become aware of this until she suddenly discovered that her ankles were caught up in a loop of lace and satin. Stopping, she looked down to see what it was, and then gracefully stepping out of her 'smalls', she freed herself from her partner, stooped down, picked them up and, carrying them at arm's length, sailed across the ballroom floor and handed them, with the maximum publicity, to the scarlet-faced youth who was presumably her host, saying in bell-like tones, 'George — park my knickers, will you?' At which there was a roar of laughter and a good many people clapped.

Women's underwear, in those days, was still considered to be 'unmentionable' (heavens! how far we have come!), and most women, myself among them, would have been speechless with embarrassment if caught in the same predicament. I remember being inordinately impressed by that masterly exhibition of *savoir-faire*. For you have to be a member of my generation — and of the Raj too, which still preserved a code of morals and behaviour that, if no longer Victorian, still hovered on the fringe of Edwardian — to realize what a quantum leap that gesture of Amber's was in the direction of the distant future. Those of my parents' generation — Victorians all — were profoundly shocked, while my own laughed our heads off, and rethought a good many of our attitudes.

I imagine that I lost Mike from the moment that Amber first met him and decided that this was the one she wanted. I simply wasn't in her class; and even without that silly quarrel and the screaming-match that ended it, if she wanted him, I feel sure she would have annexed him without any trouble at all.

I didn't realize that I could stop dithering as to whether I wanted to marry him or not, and that I could now, to quote a future pop-song, 'colour him gone', until Tacklow and Mother both received charming letters from him. He thanked Tacklow for laying on the Ganges trip for him, and told both of them what fun it had been and how much he'd enjoyed it, didn't even mention me in either letter, but ended both by saying that he was afraid he would not be able to come to Tonk for the Christmas camp after all, because he had had a telegram from his mother to say that she would be coming out to Delhi for Christmas, and would be staying with friends who hoped he too would stay with them. He was *so* sorry . . . etc., etc., but it couldn't be helped, and he wished them both a very merry Christmas and New Year. And that was that.

I didn't see him or hear from him again for several years, though I did hear about him from certain kind friends who took care to keep me *au fait* with all the gossip about him and Amber. It seems that they swanned around India together, and on a return visit to Peshawar — where he did not look up the Captain and the Bo'sun or any ex-member of the NBN — he managed to break all the rules by smuggling Amber, dressed as a man, up to Razmak, a men-only frontier post which in those days was strictly off limits to all British or European women.

This, when discovered, raised a terrible furore, and the story goes that when the officer in command of the garrison at Razmak was telephoned by some irate brass-hat in Peshawar and asked if it was true that an Englishwoman had actually been smuggled past the sentries into tribal territory and was present in Razmak, he admitted it, and asked, on behalf of the entire Mess, if they could please keep her for a day or two before sending her back. She was a dazzler, was Amber.

Mike very nearly married her. But on the eve of the wedding,* assisted apparently by a collection of his bachelor friends who were giving him an eve-of-wedding party, he got gloriously tight, and treated Amber as he used to treat me when under the influence — as though she was some unattractive stranger who had gatecrashed his party and could therefore be spoken to as rudely as possible. That attractive creature, Amber, was not used to this sort of thing, and the result was a terrific row, in the course of which the lady tore off her engagement ring and threw it in his face, announcing that as far as she was concerned the wedding was off — for good! And stormed out. She (like me!) expected him to turn up the next morning full of apologies and penitence, and when he didn't she telephoned his flat and got no answer. His mother and his best man and a selection of his friends all insisted that they hadn't an idea where he was, which could possibly have been true, because Mike, with a good deal of assistance from his resourceful mother, Lady Guernsey, had phoned ex-Able Seaman Tony Weldon NBN,† whom the two of them had prevailed upon to accompany the escapee on an expedition to Canada's Hudson Bay, all expenses paid and starting at *once*. They would be responsible for booking all the tickets and for ship and hotel accommodation.

Tony said he jumped at it: 'Well, who wouldn't?' And the two of them disappeared for the next couple of months into Hudson Bay and the

* In London.
† Who happened to be in London at the time.

enormous, trackless forests of Northern Canada. The wedding was called off, and, naturally, the reception; and by the time the fugitives returned to civilization, if there were any bits of broken hearts lying around, they had all been thrown away with the bathwater. In the event Amber married an Italian Marchese, thus becoming a Marchesa and châtelaine of one of those fairy-tale villas on the shores of one of the Italian lakes. But she must have been one of 'those whom the gods love', for she died, still young and beautiful, from cancer.

As for me, I continued to think that I still had a choice in the matter of Mike's hand and heart until I received a long and chatty letter from one of the Delhi debs (who had never been a particular friend of mine) telling me in great detail all I didn't want to know about Mike's new girlfriend. She said she 'thought I ought to know'. (Oh yeah?) Well, I suppose she was right, at that. But I remember glooming around the camp that Christmas, feeling lower than an earthworm and unable to enter into the Christmas spirit.

Chapter 28

~⁂~

The camp was one of those lavish ones that the princes of Rajputana went in for in a big way. Wooden floors covered with *durries* — druggets — and strewn with Persian rugs. Proper beds ornamented with brass knobs and curlicues, dressing-tables fitted with cheval-glasses; tin baths; sitting-rooms complete with cretonne-covered sofas and chairs, and elegant writing tables provided with writing paper embossed with the state's crest in gold. In those days princes liked to do things properly.

On Christmas morning there was a long line of camp servants standing ready to present my parents with the customary festival '*dollies*', flat, rush platters piled with fruit and all kinds of *metai* — sweetmeats. After Tacklow had distributed largesse, the guns — Tacklow and Bill, Campbell Harris, and the heir, Saadat, together with three or four of his friends and several courtiers — went off to walk up partridge or shoot snipe on a nearby *jheel*. I didn't go with them, and spent the afternoon sulking in the company of the lone elephant which had been brought along to act as a stop for the beat that was scheduled for Boxing Day.

The elephant was as bored as I was, and I began to have a fellow-feeling for her as she rocked restlessly to and fro in her pickets, shifting her weight from one foot to the other and inventing various ways of passing the time. I've always liked elephants, and I owe this one a debt of gratitude, because I ended up watching her silly games and being amused by them instead of brooding about the end of my love affair with Mike. One of the many ploys that got her — and me — through the long, hot, drowsy hours of that last Christmas Day of the restless twenties was a very simple one, but fascinating to watch. She would pick up a handful of dust from the sandy soil to one side of her and, having placed it carefully on a small pile on the top of her head, swing her trunk down to the opposite side and blow it off, repeating the operation with neatness and elegance, and never once failing to blow off the little pile that she had placed on her head. She had a whole repertoire of these silly games, and when she got bored with one, she would turn and look at me, before producing the next, to make sure that I was paying proper attention to her.

Thanks to that silly young elephant and to the tiger-hunt, I forgot to brood on my personal affairs, and I can't even remember now on what day the beat was held, only that we had to wait until we received proof that the tiger was in that area. Bait, in the form of some hapless (and very vocal) goat or young buffalo calf, had been staked out at various points in the landscape to which it was hoped to lure the tiger, and only when the local *shikari* arrived hot-foot with news that the tiger had killed one of these unfortunate creatures on the previous night, was the beat laid on. By which time it was far too late for Bill to take part in it, since he had to leave in time to be present for the New Year's Day parade in Kohat. The beat consisted of as many men as could be raised in the nearby villages, reinforced by some of the Nawab's token army, and every man who cared to arm himself with a *lathi* or ancient shotgun, firecrackers, drums and anything that could make a noise. The country around the camp was true 'tiger-country' — which meant that it in no way resembled the jungle as depicted by Hollywood in films such as *The Jungle Book* and *Kim*. Here the land was largely open plain, liberally scattered with low, scrub-and-tree-covered hills. And almost everything that grew there was the colour of gold or sun-bleached grass. A tawny country where the thin lines and criss-cross black shadows might have been specially designed as cover for tigers.

Tacklow and the others had been taken on the previous day to see the *machans* we would occupy for the shoot — half a dozen small wood and string platforms about the size of a child's bed, fixed high up in the tallest of the sheshum trees, and each capable of holding at least two to three people. Tacklow, for whom the shoot had been laid on, and the head *shikari* were to occupy the one in the most favoured position, on the level ground of a narrow valley between two steep little hills, with the longer of the two hills at his back. Mother and I, who were 'onlookers only', were given the next *machan* in line. And at the foot of the same hill, at intervals of roughly 100 to 200 yards, were Saadat's and the best shot among his equerries; then the one that should have been Bill's, and was now occupied instead by Bets and Campbell Harris, and finally one containing two more of Saadat's suite.

As soon as news was received that the tiger had killed, a runner went out with the news to the waiting beaters, who had presumably been camping out on the plain well beyond that hilly tract where the *machans* had been built, while extra beaters and the elephant were hurried out to the spot. We left as soon as we had finished breakfast, and followed in cars (the Land Rover had not been invented in those days), bumping over the open plain and raising clouds of dust in the process, stopping when we came up with the advance guard. This was as far as we could go by car, explained the head *shikari*, for where the little hills began there was too much thorn-scrub and tall grass, and too many trees to allow for the passage of cars.

Saadat had been anxious that one of us should make use of the Tonk elephant as a sort of moving *machan*, and urged me to ride on it. But I had not spent a couple of afternoons in that creature's company without coming to the conclusion that she was still too young, and far too imaginative, to be trusted with a tiger beat. I therefore refused the offer as politely as I could, to the obvious relief of the *mahout* (its handler), who showed no enthusiasm for taking his ponderous charge into the fray, and withdrew her, thankfully, behind the cars and the small group of drivers, onlookers and gawpers who seem to materialize out of thin air anywhere one stops in India, even in the middle of what had seemed to be an unpopulated desert.

We started off on foot and in single file along a narrow beaten track that had been made by those who had built the *machans* only a day or two earlier, while the head *shikari* talked in an undertone, explaining where the beaters were and the signal that would tell them that the guns had taken up position and they could begin to move forward. The tiger, he said, was a particularly splendid specimen, and a good many of the minor princes whose states touched the borders of Tonk had tried and failed to shoot it. It was also possible, he added carelessly, that its mate might be in that area, since there had been reports of a tigress which had been preying on the herds of the villagers not far from Pirawa, some months ago. Tacklow inquired where the tiger had taken the kill, and the *shikari*, like the young Mark Twain, was happy to be able to answer promptly: he said he didn't know. Well, we were all to know within a minute.

The direction in which we were going took us in a half circle about a clump of pampas grass, and turning to the right, we came in sight of the tall sheshum tree in which the first of the *machans* had been built. Tacklow and the *shikari* came to a sudden halt, and so did I, a mere pace behind them. For of all places to choose, the tiger had carried his kill to the patch of open ground that had been thoughtfully beaten flat for him by the feet of the men who had built those elaborate *machans*. What's more, he had brought his entire family with him, so that they could share the weekend joint.

Fortunately, they had finished eating. Which was lucky for us, because if we had arrived in the middle of their lunch things might not have turned out so well. As it was, the entire family was taking its ease after stuffing itself with food. They were all there, father, mother and two three-parts grown cubs, lounging in the thin shadows of the sheshum tree and lazily licking the blood from their paws. They had seen us in the same moment that we saw them. But only the father of the family moved. He stood up and stared at us over the top of a low thorn-bush, and I saw for myself, for the first and thank heaven the last time, a tiger make use of those two whiter-than-white patches above his eyes. He dropped his head, so that the two patches, topped by a jet-black bar, looked exactly like a second pair of eyes: enormous eyes that glared at you with far more effect than the staring yellow ones below. Mother, behind me, said in a whisper, 'What's the matter? What are you stopping for?' and the *shikari* hissed, '*Chup*' (be quiet!) and gestured forcibly with his left hand, urging us to go back — slowly — slowly! We obeyed, for by that time even those who could not see what we were retreating from realized why we must move as carefully as though we were playing a deadly game of Grandmother's Steps. Both the *shikari* and Tacklow brought their rifles up, inch by inch, into the firing position, and when they eased off the safety catches the double click sounded terrifyingly loud in that petrified silence and drew an ominous growl from the tiger. And then at last we were round a spur of the hillside, and out of sight, and the *shikari* said, '*Bargo!*' — (run). And *did* we *bargo*!

The whole terrifying incident couldn't have taken more than two or three minutes. But it felt like hours. No. Not hours: it felt as though everything had stopped and that a clock that had always been ticking away somewhere wasn't ticking any more. I can't describe it better than that. Nor can I at this distance make an accurate guess at how near or how far we were to the tigers, because my long sight has always been much better than my short sight — which for many years now has been almost useless. But if I *had* to make a statement, and stick to it, I would say the distance between the tigers — the tiger, rather, because once I looked at him I never looked away — and myself, was not more than ten paces. I could even have counted his whiskers! He was *that* close! And I have often wondered if a maddening recurring nightmare that centred upon a tiger, and which afflicted me for close on twelve years after my father's death, could be traced back to those few minutes of total terror in which I had time to notice every single detail of the Pirawa tiger's face, including the way in which his lips twitched back from his teeth in something that was not so much a snarl as irritation at being interrupted at an inconvenient moment.

Once safely out of sight and range, the *shikaris* held a hasty conference, as a result of which another four excessively makeshift *machans* were hurriedly constructed and strung up in the trees on the far side of the hill from the original ones. There were fewer trees on this side, and Mother and I were finally helped to scramble up into a rickety arrangement of rope and branches of dead wood that strongly resembled a crow's nest, and was not all that far off the ground. But then, as the *shikari* explained (not very comfortably), since neither of us would be carrying a gun, we could use our hands to hold on to the main trunk of our spindly young dâk tree.

We couldn't see Tacklow, for although there were many more trees on this side of the hill few of them were of any great size, and their foliage, which had seemed so scanty below, was at its thickest at eye level. As for the other guns, they too were out of sight; and when the sounds of their departure could no longer be heard, the heat and silence of midday descended upon the jungle, and we had nothing to do but wait for the signal that would tell the beaters that everyone was in place. It seemed to go on for ever, and Mother and I, getting bored and more and more uncomfortable, began to talk in whispers. I for one was quite sure that if the tigers had any sense at all, they would have walked out at one end or the other of the line of *machans* long ago and vanished into the open country. I couldn't believe that the creatures would hang around after being disturbed at their lunch. But Mother said that all tigers must be so used to seeing the odd villager or two walking through their territory, that the sight of us wouldn't have bothered them in the least, especially as we had turned tail and retreated as soon as we saw them. Only if the cubs had been a lot younger would we have been in trouble, for then the tigress would probably have charged us on sight.

We had begun to wonder if my first guess had been right, and the tigers had cleared off and the beat been cancelled, when someone not so far away fired a shot. It was evidently a signal, for immediately, from somewhere very far away — so far that if it had not been for the windless silence of that torpid afternoon we would never have heard it — came a faint noise that in these days could have been the throb of an aeroplane's engines or a tractor reaping and cutting in a distant hayfield, but at that time and place could only mean that the beat had begun and that a mile or more away a long line of men and boys had begun walking towards us, shouting and hallooing as they beat the grass and the scrub with their *lathis*, banged enthusiastically on drums and tin cans, blew on cow-horns and occasionally fired off some antiquated fowling-piece lent for the occasion by a village headman or *shikari*.

At first that distant hullabaloo was hardly more than a throb of blood in one's eardrums, but it gradually increased until at long last it became disturbing enough to upset the siesta-ing wildlife, and presently the shadowy thickets of thorn-scrub, lantana and dried grass began to give up a variety of jungle creatures which would appear suddenly and, despite the carpet of fallen leaves, for the most part silently. Gorgeous peacocks, their splendid tails folded and held high, and accompanied by their harems of demure and dowdy wives, were the first to appear, picking their way across the forest floor at a pace that showed that they were not seriously alarmed, and passing directly below us to disappear into the forest behind us. A mongoose — there were several of these — and a thoroughly irritated porcupine, rattling its quills crossly as it hurried past, was followed by a jackal; and there were also a family of pigs and a grey wolf — one of the kind who made up the wolf pack in *The Jungle Book*. That was a terrific thrill, because I had never seen one before, and I was only to see one other* in all my life. It looked exactly like the drawings of Akela in the Mowgli stories, and it too made hardly a sound as it trotted past us over that layer of fallen leaves.

As the noise of the beat got louder and nearer, the animals that ran before it did so at greater and greater speed. Flustered jungle-cocks and a large variety of birds, a few black-buck, at least a dozen *chital* (the small spotted forest deer of central India) and several more pigs. And then at last, with the beaters already pouring down the hillside in front of us, the sound of a rifle-shot from Tacklow's *machan*, followed less than a minute

* Correction: three others. But only one more in the wild.

337

or two later by the arrival of the beaters, swarming around the foot of the tree in which Mother and I had our *machan*. I began to scramble down so that I could find out whether Tacklow had shot the tiger, and Mother yelled at me to get back for heaven's sake and not to take risks. But I couldn't see how there could possibly be any risk; not with a mob of beaters surging around between the tree-trunks. I had actually got one foot on the open ground when the tigress stood up and roared.

There followed one of the funniest sights that anyone could hope to see — if they were looking at it from a safe place: the inside of a tank or armoured car for preference. At the time it wasn't in the least funny to anyone who was there. For my part, I was up that tree so quickly that, like a famous character of the immortal P. G. Wodehouse, I 'almost met myself coming down'. I have never been so scared or moved so quickly. As for the beaters, every one of them flung away whatever weapon they had been beating with, and made a frantic attempt to climb the nearest tree.

Unfortunately, there were not nearly enough trees to go round, for apart from the ones that, for lack of anything larger, had been lumbered with our *machans*, the remainder of those within reach were either saplings or the occasional spindly kikar-tree. The result was like one of Gustave Doré's illustrations to *The Flood*, which depicts swarms of terrified and scantily clad humans clinging like bees to the tops of trees and anything that floats, as the rising water gets down to drowning the world. I only wish I had thought to photograph it, but at the time I was every bit as scared as they were.

What had happened was that, towards the end of the beat, one of the cubs had lost its nerve and, instead of sticking with its more experienced parents, had streaked up the hill by itself, and was running down the opposite side, in between the scrub and the saplings. The *shikari*, glimpsing it and deciding that it was the tigress, clutched at Tacklow's arm and said, urgently, '*Maro! Sahib — maro!*' (kill). It was a difficult shot, because all Tacklow could see was something orange and stripy bounding towards him between grass and lantana bushes, and as he was the first to admit, he was not a good shot with a rifle. However, he was that day. The shot killed the cub, and its body catapulted down the hill and fetched up behind a clump of bushes, where even with the help of his binoculars he could not tell which tiger he had shot, for all that he or the *shikari* could see was a small glimpse of orange-coloured fur.

Since there is a hard and fast rule that states that once a beat begins no one moves until it is completed and the beaters have reached and passed the *machans*, there was no way of verifying which tiger had been shot until every member of the beat was accounted for. But what no one knew was that the tigress had taken the same route as that cub and, looking down from higher up on the hillside, had presumably spotted Tacklow's *machan* and its two occupants and lain down to watch them in a shallow cavity under an outcrop of rocks. Lying there unseen, she had allowed the beat to go past her — some of them actually across the very rock under which she was lying — and the *shikari*'s theory was that it must have been the smell of her cub's blood that had made her stand up among the rocks and roar.

Tacklow, quite as startled as everyone else, pulled off another brilliant shot that brought her body sliding down across the rocks and the steep side of the hill below, to come to rest almost at the foot of his *machan*. No one saw what happened to the other cub. But quite a few of the beaters got an excellent view of the tiger. They said it obviously knew all about beats and how to deal with them, because it hadn't even been hurrying. Apparently it had merely strolled off in a leisurely manner, parallel to the line of beaters, who halted abruptly the minute they saw it (for tigers have been known to charge a line of beaters with fatal effect), merely intensifying their yells and drum-banging and waiting prudently until it disappeared from view.

Tacklow did not discover that he had shot one of the cubs until the *shikari* spoke to the shaken beaters and learned that there was no danger of the tiger suddenly appearing among us, as the tigress had done. Only when the *shikari* announced that we could all come down did Tacklow verify that his first shot had killed a cub, a discovery that ruined his day, for one did not shoot tiger cubs: it was one of those things that was 'not done', and I have seldom seen him more upset.

The *shikari*, however, took a different view. He simply could not understand why the Sahib was so downcast when even he, the *shikari*, had thought what he saw was the tigress, and had urged the Sahib to shoot — which he had very sensibly done, and with the greatest skill considering that he was aiming at a moving target of which they could get only brief glimpses between the lantana bushes and the tall grass. In the opinion of the *shikari* the Sahib should be congratulating himself for pulling off a magnificent double. And anyway, it was clear that the cubs were already weaned (it was surprising that their father had not already turned on them and attacked them!) and in a few months' time both would have been preying on young calves themselves. These *Sahib-log* who sentimentally refused to kill tiger cubs and pregnant tigresses did not know — or care! — what it was to be a poor villager whose livelihood frequently depended upon the yield from a single cow and its milk and droppings, and, hopefully, its calves — and who would be left destitute if their cow was taken by a tiger.

I have to admit that I saw the *shikari*'s point, though I too was sorry that one of those cubs had been killed, and glad that the tiger had escaped. Though not for long, poor creature, because only a few months later it finally fell to the gun of one of the neighbouring princes, who was not only a superb shot but had already accounted for the deaths of a long list of tigers and made several previous abortive attempts at shooting this one, since it was rumoured to be of record size for that part of Rajputana. And was, too.

It was late afternoon by the time we trudged back to where the cars and an increasingly large number of interested villagers awaited us. Tacklow may have been annoyed with himself, but he was clearly regarded as a hero by the assembled crowd. Garlands of marigolds, jasmine buds and tinsel appeared out of nowhere and were hung around his neck to the accompaniment of cheers and congratulations, and there tottered out of the crowd an old, old man, wearing nothing but a *dhoti* and a large, untidy turban, and supporting himself on an iron-tipped *lathi*, who clutched at Tacklow's arm and inquired in a quavering voice if it were true that he had shot a tigress, and when Tacklow admitted it, asked if there had been a scar on its forehead.

Tacklow said he was afraid he hadn't noticed, and inquired why the question had been asked. The ancient replied that he only wanted to know because the year before, while he was tending the cattle, a tigress had sprung out of the bushes and attacked a cow. And since it happened to be his cow, he had rushed at the tigress, whanged her over the head with his *lathi*, and driven her off. She had yelped and run away, bleeding profusely, which made him believe that if the tigress the Sahib had shot was the one that had attacked his cow, she would still bear the scar. And she did! I couldn't believe it. But when at last a couple of beaters appeared carrying the tigress between them, hanging head down by her paws, which were tied together and slung over a stout length of bamboo, we all rushed to look. And there it was. A year-old scar on her forehead that had only just missed her eye. There it is still, because her worn and battered skin lies on the floor of my son-in-law's study; and looking at it I find it difficult to account for the incredible bravery of that lone old man, armed only with an iron-tipped bamboo stave, going for a tigress almost twice his size and certainly weighing over three times what he did, and actually driving her off. Had it been me, I would have abandoned the herd and run like a rabbit.

We had a problem over the corpse of that tigress, for although it was no great distance by car back to camp, it was a long trudge on foot for two men carrying the dead weight between them. Since there was not enough room in the cars for the bodies of the tigress and her cub as well as the original passengers, it was decided to let the elephant carry them back to camp. An obvious solution, had the elephant agreed to it, which she did not. The moment she realized that these dangerous creatures were about to be put on her back, she swung her ears forward and, starting back in the manner of an elderly spinster who has found a burglar under her bed, gave a loud screech and took off for the wide blue yonder, her *mahout* (who had unfortunately dismounted and was standing beside her chatting to some friends) in frantic pursuit, shrieking alternate orders and imprecations as he ran. But it is a well-established fact that elephants, when they choose, can move at an astonishing speed — Kipling says of them, if an elephant wished to catch an express train, it would not hurry itself, but it would catch that train.

Watching this one practically vanish over the curvature of the earth's surface, I congratulated myself on having had the sense to turn down that ride, for if it reacted like this at the sight of a dead tiger, heaven only knew what it would have done had it caught sight of a live one — probably been half-way back to Tonk city by now! We didn't see the rest of the drama, because at that point we were loaded into the cars and driven away to the camp, leaving the head *shikari* and his friends to sort it all out. The elephant was back in her old place next morning, looking, I thought, rather subdued. Though that could have been imagination, for I had been feeling a bit sorry for myself of late.

Chapter 29

~※⚭Ҳ⚭※~

Three days later we were back in Tonk, and it was some time during that cold weather that Tacklow received an invitation for all of us to attend some celebration or other connected with the College of Princes at Ajmer, where the heirs and younger sons of India's 'royals' were — and still are — educated. This glittering shindig would last for several days and be graced by the presence of the Viceroy and Lady Reading, and include such gilded functions as a prizegiving and cricket match, a garden party and a state dinner. Mother, who adored any form of party and festivity, was delighted at the idea, but Tacklow was not in favour — largely, I suspect, on account of the expense, because I overheard him one evening explaining patiently to Mother that the exchequer was in very low water; even such seemingly 'free' holidays as the Christmas camp were anything but free, for in addition to the enormous number of people who expected to be, and must be, adequately tipped, there were always extras. And when those were added up, the total was always more than one expected — or had hoped. Besides, he had of late been granted a more than generous amount of leave, and it was high time that he settled down to steady work again. So no more junketing. We couldn't afford it.

The Nawab, however, had other ideas. He had not been too well of late and he said that he did not feel up to attending the festivities at Ajmer. His heir, Saadat, with Nunni-mia and their respective entourages, would of course be going; but he would like Tacklow to represent him, and he had already made arrangements for him and the Lady-Sahib and her daughters to stay at Tonk House in Ajmer. Most of Rajputana's royals kept a house in Ajmer, complete with a skeleton staff, for just such an occasion as this. I don't think that the old Nawab had used his for years. Nor do I remember if Saadat and Nunni and their personal staffs used part of it during the few days we stayed there. But I don't think they can have done so, because Nunni was rather a friend of Bets's and mine, and surely I would have remembered if he had been living in the same house — it wasn't a very big one! However, I don't remember much about the whole visit and had it not been for the disaster that it led to, I probably wouldn't have remembered anything at all.

What I do remember is that my darling Tacklow, whose idea of purgatory would, if admitted to, be a perpetual round of garden parties, receptions, state balls, banquets and similar functions, did his best to wriggle out of this; on the grounds that if anyone should act as stand-in for His Highness, it should be Saadat. But it did no good. His Highness wanted to be represented by Tacklow, and he wouldn't budge from that, even when the Assistant to the AGG Rajputana unexpectedly came out strongly on Tacklow's side — not, as I would have expected, because he too thought that the Heir Apparent was the proper person to represent his father, but for a more altruistic reason . . .

He wanted to save Mother, Bets and me from boredom and disappointment and, worse, from feeling snubbed. Even though we had all three been invited to the celebrations, we would find that this did not mean we would be able to attend the more glittering and exclusive functions. For instance, the only functions that Bets and I were likely to be asked to were the garden party and the cricket match (or was it polo? I can't remember). We would certainly not be asked to the state banquet. And it was more than likely that Mother would not be either. It was, you see, all a matter of precedence. Now that Tacklow had retired and was no longer in the service of the Government of India, but had 'gone private', his place, according to the Raj's rule-book of precedence, was a lowly one and would debar him and his family (particularly his daughters!) from attending the more glittering and exclusive functions, and leave only those that were designed for the *hoi polloi*.

Mother had pointed out a shade tartly that although Tacklow no longer had a right to a seat at the top table, he would on this occasion be representing His Highness the Nawab of Tonk, who had. But the Major shot that one down by observing regretfully that Tonk was only a minor state and 'outgunned' by so many of the senior and more powerful ones that a mere representative, who happened to be employed by its ruler, would cut very little ice. As to Tonk House, the Major was afraid that we could find we had let ourselves in for a most uncomfortable three or four days, since it was seldom used and had been allowed to fall into a shocking state of disrepair. While as for the staff . . . !

All in all he painted such a gloomy picture that, visualizing a repeat performance on a larger scale of my first disastrous dance at the Srinagar Residence and having no desire to be relegated to the ranks of a wallflower for three days on end, I sided with the opposition and could only hope that Tacklow would stick to his guns and refuse the invitation. Which he certainly would have done had it not been for Mother.

Mother had never cared a toot for precedence. In fact I very much doubt if she even noticed who sat where at *Burra Khaners* (big dinners) let alone who went in on whose arm or ahead of whom. She never gave a *Burra Khaner* herself (apart from anything else, I don't think Tacklow could have afforded it!). She only invited people she liked and who made her laugh, and if anyone took offence over her seating plans, she either never learned about it, or, if she did, refused to believe it on the grounds that no one could *possibly* be so petty. But, as I have said before, she dearly loved a party, and of late she had spent a lot of time living under canvas and wearing the gear that went with that — khaki shorts, knickerbockers and putties, sensible walking shoes and a khaki topi. Not that she hadn't enjoyed every minute of our trip down the Ganges and the Christmas camp. But she couldn't wait to put on her prettiest evening dress and go off partying, and didn't disguise her disappointment when Tacklow, after listening to the Major's discouraging talk, said that in that case he thought we had better give up the idea of attending the Ajmer festivities.

The Major said that he was sure that Tacklow had made the right decision. After which he changed the subject and we chatted a bit about this and that and he left.

Well, it was three to two against. But since the two were Mother and the old Nawab, they won easily. For when had Tacklow ever been able to refuse his darling Daisy anything that it was in his power, or his purse, to give her? While, as the Major had pointed out, the Nawab was his employer. So, of course, we went to Ajmer. And contrary to the Major's dire predictions, had a wonderful time there. This was largely because the new Viceroy, Lord Willingdon, and his wife, knew my parents, as did every ruling prince whose forebears had made a treaty with the Raj, which I presume meant all of them. Bets and I had met a good many of them and got to know their wives and daughters and it was nice to see them and their schoolboy sons and applaud their boys' skill on the cricket field, or at the prizegiving.

The focal point of the garden party, which I presume must have taken place in the college grounds, was a marble pavilion (or platform) reached by a long flight of steps and furnished with carpets, chairs and sofas and a scattering of small tables. Here the Willingdons were seated, together with a number of the more important rulers and their wives (the few who were not in purdah — most of them were in those days, as were all unmarried daughters who had reached marriageable age*) and a selection of the more senior British officials and their ladies. The rest of us circled around on the spacious lawns, or beside the long tables laden with sandwiches and cakes, while scores of liveried servants handed round cups of tea, and a band played.

The Indian guests outnumbered the British ones by at least ten to one, as was normal in Rajputana, since this was Rajasthan — 'the Country of the Kings'. Almost every 'King' was present, and there was a constant coming and going of people up and down the long flight of red-carpeted steps that led to the marble pavilion. It looked, I thought, a bit like Jacob's Ladder, and watching it, I noticed the Viceroy's ADCs were having to work hard, some of them leading guests up from the lawns while others escorted down those who had spoken to one or other of the Willingdons for what was presumably an allotted time, their place taken by a newcomer. Lady Willingdon, watching the lawns below from the vantage point of the pavilion, had spotted Mother just as tea was being served to her and those on the surrounding sofas, and, beckoning to an ADC, she sent him off to fetch my parents. I saw Mother being removed from a dense cluster of friends and acquaintances — she was always at her best at a party, for she possessed the invaluable knack of making everyone near her feel that they too were enjoying themselves. Led up Jacob's Ladder, she was plonked down next to Lady Willingdon and plied with tea and cake, and later Tacklow, too, was fetched up to the pavilion, where they both stayed until the tea interval was over and the Willingdons went down to do what was later to become known as 'a walkabout', meeting as many of the guests as possible — something that 'Mauve Marie'† was exceptionally good at.

---

* See the fatuous garden party in David Lean's film of *A Passage to India*!

† Marie Willingdon's favourite colour — and she made sure everyone knew it — was mauve. She liked to scold Mother for always putting an expensive mauve picture in her exhibitions, 'Because you know very well I won't be able to resist buying it!'

Bets and I, true to the Major's prediction, were not invited to the state banquet, but my parents were, and though the senior lady present went into dinner with the Viceroy, Mother found herself seated on his other side. It seems he had attended far too many state dinners of late, and been landed with making conversation to too many elderly '*burra mems*', so he had gone on strike and demanded to have at least one woman next to him who could be relied upon to entertain him and make him laugh. Tacklow's position at the table was probably a fairly lowly one — I know that it was a long way away from Mother and nowhere near Lady Willingdon, and also that he would never have noticed, or cared, where he was placed.

Bets and I were asked to a dinner party and 'gramophone hop' thrown by some of our age group, so we too had an enjoyable evening. In fact the entire visit was a great success, and the old Nawab — who considered that he and his state had acquired much *izzat* (honour) from the favour shown to his President of the Council of State by the Viceroy and Vicereine — was delighted. We hoped that Major Barlow, who as Assistant to the AGG Rajputana ranked only one step below his chief in the Province, and had of course been present, was equally pleased at the way things had turned out. But since Tonk was only one among many states that he had to visit, and (as he had pointed out to us) not one of the really powerful ones, we were not to see him again for many months. By which time so many other and far more interesting things had happened that we had almost forgotten about it. Unfortunately, the Major had not. But we were not to discover that until later.

The most interesting happening of the next year was Nunni-mia's wedding. Nunni was only twelve years old, but he had been betrothed to the ten-year-old daughter of a Bhopal nobleman, and their marriage was one of those token affairs in which the girl bride would spend the first three days of her married life in the care of her new mother-in-law and under the eagle eyes of the ladies of the *zenana* so that she could get to know something about her young husband before being returned to her own family until she was old enough for the marriage to be consummated. As his father's favourite son, and heir-designate after Saadat, Nunni was a very eligible bridegroom, and the *shadi* was celebrated with all the usual colour, pomp and ceremony of an Indian wedding. No expense was spared, and Tacklow became a little worried as to whether the state's exchequer could stand it. But our old Nawab doted on Nunni and nothing was too good for him.

A special train was laid on to take the wedding party to Bhopal from the railhead nearest to Tonk, and that alone must have set the old boy back quite a packet. Not to mention the fleet of cars and lorries needed to take us all there, which included the Meades and ourselves, as well as all the young bridegroom's kith and kin, every nobleman in Tonk and anyone in any position of authority, plus a host of Nunni's friends and any number of courtiers, servants and assorted retainers.

It soon became obvious that the train was going to be shockingly overcrowded, and Tacklow — who would be attending the wedding in his official capacity while his wife and daughters were going as invited guests — suggested that it would help towards easing the congestion if he and his family, their luggage and our two servants, were to travel to Bhopal by car. This would not only put our four-berth carriage and adjoining servants' carriage at the disposal of the wedding party, but allow him to be waiting on the platform to receive His Highness when the Nawab arrived at Bhopal, since the distance by road was a good deal shorter. The offer was accepted with undisguised relief, to the disappointment of Bets and me, who had been looking forward to the long, leisurely train journey which would have allowed us to gossip with the ladies in the purdah carriages.

However, the trip by road, though hot, bumpy and dusty, was not without interest and, since the Nawab had insisted on putting two of his best cars at our disposal, as well as picnic baskets full of delicious food and fruit and iced drinks in Thermos flasks, we were chauffeured like millionaires across the lovely, empty spaces and through the narrow valleys and low, stony hills of King's Country, and arrived, as Tacklow had said, well ahead of the wedding party from Tonk.

His Highness the Nawab of Bhopal was away, but he had left orders that we were to be put up in the New Palace — a disappointment, since I had hoped that it might be the Old Palace, the new one being one of those modern ones. I envied the Tonk party, who were housed in older and far more attractive buildings in the city.

The wedding party was greeted with garlands and a *fu-fu* band and much banging of tom-toms, and that night there was a men-only party, given by the bride's family. Everything looked set for a thoroughly pleasant occasion. But it was not to be. The very next morning a spanner was tossed in the works by the bride's father, who suddenly announced that the bride-price — the sum paid by the groom's family to the bride's father for the privilege of marrying his daughter — was insufficient, and that his *vakils* (lawyers) advised that it must be doubled. This, not unnaturally, led to considerable *gurr-burrh* or Indian uproar. For a time everything came to a grinding halt and it began to look as though we would all have to turn round and go home again. However, after endless argument and acrimony, my darling Tacklow, in whose lap this nonsense-work had landed, managed to sort it out and settle it to everyone's satisfaction.

That evening I saw the prettiest sight I have ever seen at any Indian festivity. Nor did I ever see anything like it again. Bets and I must have been to some party, probably dinner in the *zenana* quarter with the begums. Whatever it was, we ended up at a comparatively late hour of the night, sitting on top of a high wall in the dark, waiting to see a procession pass. The wall was one of a pair that ran on either side of a narrow street, somewhere in the old city, and presumably near the *zenana* quarters of some nobleman's palace, for several of the begums, shrouded in *bourkas*, were perched on the wall beside us.

It was a little like sitting up in a *machan* at a tiger beat, listening for the beaters to approach and wondering what would come out of the jungle opposite you. We could hear the noises of an Indian city all around us. But there was nothing and no one in the dark slot of the lane below us, until at last we heard drums and flutes and all the joyous din of a *fu-fu* band approaching from somewhere on our right, together with the bright flame of torches.

The torchlight and the noise came steadily nearer and suddenly the lane below us was full of men, some bearing torches, and the rest marching four or five abreast, carrying wands of leaves and flowers made from tinsel and glittering sheets of foil. I had seen these tinsel and paper flowers before, since they could be bought in almost any fair-sized bazaar throughout India. But I had never previously seen them put to such good effect, and it taught me an excellent lesson on the wonderful effect of a single colour used *en masse* as opposed to a dozen different ones . . .

The latter were merely gaudy, while the former could be magical — as here. The white flowers were small and silver, and barely noticeable among the mass of large pointed leaves, roughly the size and shape of mango or avocado leaves, and cut from green foil that glittered in the torchlight and turned to every possible shade of that colour as they rustled past us. The men who carried them wore dark coats and green muslin turbans, which made them completely invisible and created the illusion that Birnam Wood was on the move again, marching on Bhopal instead of Dunsinane.

I must have been told where they were going, and with what purpose. But if so I have no recollection of it. Only the picture remains; to become like one of those jewelled fragments in the rag-bag of offcuts thrown out daily by the costume department from the lovely costumes that Raymond Hughes designed for the film of my novel *The Far Pavilions*.

Considering that this was my first experience of a royal wedding in India, my recollections are remarkably few. Among them was a morning visit that Mother and I paid to the Senior Begum and her ladies. We arrived just as the Senior Begum was about to choose the jewels that she would wear for the wedding ceremony.

I don't think that we of the West have any *idea* of the riches that India used to take for granted. Not even Elizabeth II — or Elizabeth Taylor! — could match the state jewels of the richer princely states. Tonk was, as we had recently been reminded, a comparatively minor state; yet the selection of jewels that the Senior Begum's women had thought fit to bring with them staggered me. You've no idea what a picture it made. The old lady, who can't have been all that old (but then I was at the age when anyone over twenty-five was middle-aged) was sitting on a pile of brightly coloured cushions on a low platform under a roof that was all arches, supported by slender pillars. The room gave on to a balcony from which one could look out across the city through elaborately carved marble screens, for this was part of the *zenana* quarters, from where the occupants could look out unseen, but no one could look in.

The Begum was wearing a warm colour — probably orange or red — and her women passed by her in procession, each one showing her a piece of jewellery, displayed in a conventional velvet case that was presumably made by some modern jeweller, since most of the jewellery predated the boxes by at least a century. The contents of those boxes left me gasping, and I remember being deeply impressed by the casualness with which the old lady treated them. They all seemed to be fabulous, and I could not understand how she could dismiss so many with a careless flick of her hand after barely glancing at them.

Now and again she would lift a finger, lean forward, and look more carefully at some particularly gorgeous trinket before waving it away. She must have looked at and discarded at least twenty or thirty items before making her choice. I can't remember what it was, or even what colour she finally decided upon — only that it wasn't the one I would have chosen! I put in a strong plea for that one, and though she wavered for a bit, she eventually decided against it on the grounds that its beauty and superlative workmanship could only be appreciated at close range. Besides, the jewels did not glitter and so would have little or no impact when half shrouded in the gauze sari she intended to wear, which anyway, was the wrong colour.

I saw her point. If you had not been standing close to her you could well have believed that my choice was the real thing, and not jewellery at all. Because the set consisted of a necklace and bracelets that had been fashioned by some master craftsman to look as though they were garlands of jasmine blossom. The leaves had been carved from emeralds and the flowers were pearls — every one of them pear shaped and most beautifully matched — and except for the buds, at the centre of each flower was a yellow diamond. The things were a work of art, and I have never seen anything remotely like them again. Nor can I make a guess at what they must be worth now. But I could see why the Begum did not choose them, and she was right of course. In a country that uses garlands of fresh flowers not only every day, but every hour and minute of every day as a gesture of greeting or farewell, adorns the bride and groom and their many relations and friends with wreaths of roses and jasmine for the heads of its women, and drapes the biers of the dead with strings of marigold flowers, a necklace and bracelets of jewels made to imitate the real thing would, except at close range, be taken as just that.

On the day of the wedding two or three members of the bride's family took Mother, Bets and me to see the bride being dressed for the great occasion. Their house, like the one that the ladies from Tonk were staying in, was one of the old buildings in the city, and the only thing I remember about it is that it had no electricity and appeared to consist of a rabbit-warren of small, ill-lit rooms and long dark corridors, and that it smelt faintly of sandalwood and faded flowers, and strongly of damp and the slow centuries. The room in which we ended up, by contrast with all the others we had passed, was enormous, but I can give no description of it, because despite its size and its high ceiling it was lit by a solitary oil-lamp and the light from a single narrow window.

The room was also crowded with chattering women, some of whom we had already met, though it was difficult to recognize anyone in that gloomy dungeon. What with the inadequate lighting, the excited, giggling mob of girls and crones, all in their wedding finery and clashing with jewels, it was impossible to see if there was any furniture in the room or not.

As for the bride, all we saw of her was a bundle of red and gold gauze, crouched on its knees, head in hands and bent almost double, surrounded by a ring of waiting-women who were engaged in brushing and combing her hair, prior to smoothing it with scented oil and braiding it with jewels and jasmine buds. At present it fell to the floor in a silky black curtain that prevented us from getting so much as a glimpse of her face, even if she hadn't hidden it in her hands. I suspected that she was not only shy but was trying to hide the fact that she was crying, and I was grateful when Mother hissed in my ear that it was high time we left, adding indignantly that it was a shame to expect the poor child to meet strange foreigners at a time like this — she was after all, only *ten*.

We made our excuses and withdrew, and later in the day we saw the bride again, at the marriage ceremony; still a bowed, shrinking figure, draped in a splendid gold-embroidered sari and decked with necklaces, rings, bracelets and brooches of rubies and table-cut diamonds. We still couldn't see her face, or that of her bridegroom either, for the features of both were veiled behind a deep fringe made from strings of jasmine buds or pearls — I can't remember which of them wore what, but I *think* Nunni wore the pearls. I do remember thinking that his brocaded coat was far too tight and that he needed to lose weight, and also that if it wasn't for his outsize turban with its magnificent jewelled aigrette, and the drooping posture of his bride, he would have looked the shorter of the two.

I can still see them quite clearly, sitting side by side on a raised platform and under a fringed canopy in a courtyard of the bride's home, facing a crowd of wedding guests, most of whom were comfortably sitting cross-legged on the ground, while Tacklow and his family, and about a dozen more *Sahib-log*, were perched uncomfortably on small gilt chairs. And that's it. I don't even remember when all the uproar that followed began, whether it started while we were all still in Bhopal, or only after the Tonk contingent, accompanied now by the bride and a selection of her ladies and serving-women, got back to base. The latter, almost certainly, for Nunni would have seen little of his bride during the journey, since purdah rules are always more strictly kept when travelling. Anyway, whenever it broke, it was quite a bombshell.

The child-bride that twelve-year-old Nunni thought he had married turned out to be one of her aunts instead. A twenty-six-year-old one, at that!

Well, you can imagine the uproar and the coming and going between Nunni's family and the Bhopal girl's people. The latter were totally unrepentant. Their defence was that the Tonk lot must have known that no daughter of the house, not yet in her teens, could possibly be married while an older and close relative of the family remained unwed . . .

'Yes, of course we *said* we would give you our youngest daughter,' they admitted. 'For if we had not, your son might have refused to accept a wife more than twice his age, and created much difficulty for us all. But knowing that you would discover that there was still an older relative whose *shadi* had not yet been made, we were sure that you would recognize our predicament and know that it must be the aunt and not her young niece who would be the bride.'

That was the Bhopal family's case. But it did not wash. They had been careful to conceal the existence of the aunt, and all the agreements between the two families had made it quite clear that it was the ten-year-old who was to be the bride. As for Nunni, he had taken an instant and violent dislike to the unfortunate woman. He said she was exactly like a bossy nurse he had once hated, and also that she chewed onions, and if there was one thing he couldn't bear it was people who chewed onions! In short, he couldn't stand her at any price.

She returned to her family, and everyone was cross. For though the bride-price was eventually repaid and the gifts returned, the whole business had been an expensive waste of money and both sides were out of pocket and feeling very sour about it. All those parties! All that food and drink! All the new clothes and present-giving, the distribution of money and sweets, and the hiring of that special train — all wasted! No wonder the phoney bride had kept her face hidden and made herself look as small as possible — and no wonder her family had kept the room in which we had first seen her as near dark as makes no matter.

We had all been made fools of, and I was still young enough to be horrified by the discovery that grown-ups could lie and cheat and scheme and do each other down. But when our old friend from the early Simla days, the Diwan-Sahib, came down to stay with us for a few days, and I poured out the whole shocking story to him, he roared with laughter. It was plain, he said, that I still had plenty to learn about his country. And he assured me that any 'upper-class' Indian wedding (especially the ones involving royalty) that did not include a basinful of lies, trickery and nonsense-work would be unique. They *all* tried it on. 'Let me tell you,' he said, 'a story that my grandfather told me when I was a boy . . .' And he told me the tale of a little prince and his two half-sisters who, escorted by a solitary Englishman and accompanied by a vast cavalcade of servants and soldiery, horses, carts and guns, and scores of elephants, were taken to their respective weddings on a journey of many weeks, and of the chicanery and double-dealing that they met with by the way and on their arrival.

His story certainly made the recent goings-on in Bhopal seem mild by contrast, and I ended, as he had, by laughing and thought no more about it. But over a quarter of a century later, at a regimental dance in Ireland, a fellow guest, another army wife, told me that she had just heard that I had been born in India and had written a book about it (my first historical novel, *Shadow of the Moon*, had only recently been published) and she wondered if I would be interested in reading a diary that had been written well back in the last century by a member of her family who had served as an officer in the East India Company's Bengal Army. The diary, she explained, was not the original, but only a copy; one of the several that had been made for different members of her family. So if I'd like to read hers, she would be charmed to lend it to me. I said I'd love to, and the diary duly arrived at my army quarters. And believe it or not, the man who wrote it was the 'solitary Englishman' who had been charged with escorting that cumbersome wedding party that the Diwan-Sahib had told me about all those years ago, sitting in the *barra-durri* in front of our house in Tonk — !

Chapter 30

❦❦❦

Back in Tonk, Bets and I acquired a new pet, a baby brown monkey presented to us by one of the local *shikaris*, who told us that he had found it clinging to its dead mother in a nearby patch of scrub and jungle in which he had been shooting. (I suspect that he had shot the mother by mistake.) The tiny creature could not have been more than two or three days old, but already every hair on her skinny little body was covered with the eggs of fleas or lice, and our first task was to shave her — which we did with a razor borrowed from Tacklow. After which we gave her a bath in warm water to which we had added a spoonful of disinfectant, fed her with the aid of a rag dipped in milk, which she sucked with enthusiasm, and attempted to put her to bed in a wooden box which Kadera had supplied, complete with bars and a door. The baby, which we had named Angelina, and instantly shortened to 'Angie', would have none of it. Nature had taught her to cling like a limpet to her mother, and we were the next best thing. It was like trying to rid yourself of a particularly adhesive bit of flypaper, and when Mother tried to help us out by removing her, she ended up with Angie's skinny little arms and legs clasped tightly round her neck.

It was the beginning of a wonderful friendship. For the first time in our family history, we had acquired a pet who didn't instantly attach itself to Tacklow. Despite the fact that either I or Bets carried her around with us all day, fed her and allowed her to cling to one of our fingers through the bars of her box until she fell asleep (and woe betide us if we tried to free ourselves before she did), she made up her mind that Mother belonged to her, and that she belonged to Mother. Bets and I were merely 'staff', as were the rest of the servants, though she had her favourites, and Kadera definitely came top.

She was all eyes when she first came to us, eyes and hands (four of those) with a scrap of furry skin and bone to hold them together, and as

354

soon as she outgrew the habit of spending her days clinging to one of us and began to explore, we discovered that we had to find some method of controlling her destructive instincts. It was Kadera who solved the problem. He fastened Angie's box to a wooden platform nailed on to the top of a tall pole which he set up in the shade of one of the trees in the compound. A light metal ring of a circumference that allowed it to move easily up and down the pole was joined by a fine steel chain, roughly four or five yards long, to a small leather belt (originally a watch-strap!) fastened around Angie's small body. This enabled her to skiddle up and down the pole, taking the light ring and the lighter chain with her, and gave her a large circle of territory on the ground, and liberty to lie at the base of the pole, lie out on the platform or take shelter in the box, or, if she felt like it, sit on some of the lower branches of the tree.

Angie learned to use her harness in no time at all. She was as bright as a button, and the most endearing and loving of pets. I wouldn't, though, recommend anyone to acquire a monkey unless they are prepared to keep a close eye on it when it gets loose in the house, for the damage that an inquisitive creature with four hands can do in the space of two minutes has to be seen to be believed.

I don't remember which month Ramadan fell in that year, but at a guess it must have been in or around April, for the hot weather was just beginning to hint at the burning days to come when it ended, and the senior Begum invited Mother, Bets and me to the feast that celebrates its end. We accepted with pleasure, and as a gesture of thanks for the invitation, Bets and I decided to keep the last day of the fast ourselves.

Traditionally, the fast begins before daybreak and cannot be broken until darkness falls, thus allowing the faithful to eat or drink in moderation during the night hours. But while it is light they must not let a morsel of food or a drop of water pass their lips, which comes hard on those who keep it when Ramadan falls in the hot weather.

That day, in the dark hour before dawn, Kadera, himself a devout Muslim, woke Bets and me with a breakfast of tea, boiled eggs, chapattis and fruit, and when we had finished and he had taken the trays away, we tiptoed out on to the verandah, careful not to wake our sleeping parents, and up the flight of stone steps that led to the flat roof, to watch the stars fade as the dawn crept up in the east and the sky turned from indigo to green, to silver-grey, to primrose yellow, when the birds awoke and launched into their familiar dawn chorus. The weather was not yet hot enough to drive us indoors the minute the sun rose, or to make us shut every door and window in an attempt to trap the cool night air for as long as possible. But it was still hot enough, with the dry baking heat of Rajputana, to make us begin to hanker for a drink long before the morning was half over, and though hunger proved to be no problem, the lack of the normal set meals made the day seem intolerably long.

The party was to be held in the No. 1 Guest House, a white flat-topped building very like our own and looking down on us from the top of a little pointed hill just behind our house. We climbed up to it as the sun was setting and found ourselves engulfed in a scented swirl of women in ravishing saris and jingling, glittering jewellery, all of them talking at once. The Guest House, like our own, consisted of a single large high-ceilinged reception room, with bedrooms and bathrooms leading off it on either side and a dining-room on the third side. The whole was surrounded by a pillared verandah that could be enclosed by *chiks* which, when unrolled, made it suitable for purdah parties such as this. Since, in Eastern lands, the interval between the moment that the last rim of the sun disappears and that when darkness falls is a very short one, by the time we arrived, our hostess's serving-women were already rolling up *chiks*, for the sun had vanished and in the gathering dusk the faces of those in purdah could no longer be spied on by prying eyes.

The Begums were anxious, for dust and heat-haze had formed a cloud that lay like a veil of brown gauze above the line of the horizon, which might hide the moon for several hours; in the past it had been no unusual thing for a pall of clouds to hide it from sight for several days. But, fortunately, science had found a way of coping with that. All over Southern India, priests still leant from the minarets of their mosques to scan the skies for the first glimpse of the new moon, and nowadays, the moment it was sighted, the news would not only be cried to crowds immediately gathered below, but flashed by means of telegraph wires to all parts of the country. Even if the skies were overcast, the remotest hamlets could receive the news by means of primitive signals such as rockets, bonfires or gunfire, passed on over many miles.

In case the new moon was not sighted that night, it had been arranged that one of the ancient Tonk cannons should be fired as soon as the news reached the city. But in the event, no signal was needed, for as the dusk deepened that dusty gossamer veil began to shred away, leaving a clear lake of duck-egg green sky in which there floated a thin silver crescent.

It was barely more than a thread of silver, but at least half of the guests spotted it in the same instant, and the peacock scream of excited feminine voices drowned out the now unnecessary boom of the cannon and a clamour of gongs and conches from the house-tops and mosques of Tonk. Half a minute later the verandah of the Guest House had emptied like magic, as the Begums and their guests and their ladies turned and ran for the central reception room, which tonight had been cleared of furniture and contained instead a splendid buffet laid out on a long banquet table, every inch of which was invisible under a load of silver dishes piled full of delicious Indian food of every description.

The way those gorgeously clad women fell upon it remains one of my pleasantest memories of Tonk. One would have thought, seeing them, that they had all been starved for the entire month instead of only the light hours of each day, as they ran through the line of french windows, laughing, pushing, jostling, and grabbing at the food as though they were a crowd of unruly kids. Bets and I, catching the fever, ran with the best of them, though it was the drinks that we made for, for we both had uncomfortably dry mouths, and I remember draining at least two tall glasses of some fruit juice or other before I turned my attention to the food. It was a lovely party, and when we had all finished stuffing ourselves, and licked our fingers clean, we returned to the verandah again and watched a display of fireworks going up into the sky from somewhere in the unseen city, and listened to a pretty girl singing songs to the accompaniment of sitar and tabla, played by two older companions.

The nights remained cool for a little longer, making it unnecessary for us to move our beds out of doors. But every day saw the quicksilver in the thermometers in Tacklow's office and out on the verandah creep up a little higher, until one afternoon the first of the dust-storms arrived to warn us that the hot weather was well on its way.

At first it was just a slight darkening of the sky and, not being used to such visitations, I don't think we would have taken much notice of it. But the servants knew better. When they began to close the doors and windows Mother inquired why, and had her attention drawn to the curious brownish stain that was reaching upwards into the blue of the sky along the horizon. 'It is only the dust-wind,' said the Tonk men carelessly explaining that since it could at times come very quickly, depending on the wind, it was as well to be prepared. They stuffed newspaper under the gaps below the french windows and the doors, and Kadera put an indignant Angie into her bedtime box and brought her into the house.

The storm took some time to reach us, but when it did, it came with an awesome rush. The brown stain in the sky grew darker and darker until we had to send for lamps, and presently the first of the wind reached us and began to whine through the cracks and crevices under the doors and round the windows. By the time the storm reached us it was a whirling, seething wall of darkness that one moment was a hundred yards away and the next second had hit us so that we were in the centre of a whirlpool of dust and sand and flying debris. In spite of the paper that the servants had wedged under the doors the air was so full of gritty dust that we tied handkerchiefs over our noses. By the time it passed — which seemed an age but was probably not nearly as long as I think — it had left a thin layer of dust over everything, a grey, gritty coating that covered every inch of every single thing in the entire house, giving the interior the look of something that has lain on the sea-floor for long enough to collect a layer of sediment. It took days to get rid of it.

✵ That year we put off leaving for the hills for as long as possible, because Tacklow could not come with us. We had to make a guess at the probable day of the monsoon's arrival, and leave a good ten days before that, because the roads between Tonk and Delhi in places were mere cart-tracks that wound between patches of cactus, thorn-bushes and palms, and came out on to wide stretches of sand leading to the banks of unbridged rivers that could only be crossed by fords. The fords, used daily by cattle and casual wayfarers, were easy enough to cross in the dry season when the rivers were seldom more than two or three feet deep at their deepest. But when the monsoon broke, these same innocent-seeming streams, fed as they were by numerous little sidestreams, could become brown, roaring torrents in a matter of minutes.

We could not risk that, though we left it as late as possible and would probably have kept putting it off if Tacklow had not been required to go to Delhi for a few days on state business. Since he would only be staying there for two or three nights, it was decided that we too would break our journey at Delhi, and a telegram was sent off booking rooms for the four of us at the IDG Club. I can't say that I wasn't delighted to know that I was seeing the back of Tonk for the rest of the summer, even though it meant not seeing darling Tacklow again until some time in October. I had been lying awake for the best part of the cruelly hot nights of late, longing and longing to be cool again, and picturing the Dāl lake with its lotus lilies, and the Outer Circular Road at Gulmarg, with its view of the snow-peaks, its forests of deodars and pines, and the scent of pine-needles and waterfalls. It was difficult to believe at times that two such places as Kashmir and Tonk could exist in the same country.

We left as early in the morning as we could manage, having said our goodbyes on the previous day, Mother driving the big car with Tacklow sitting beside her, and Kadera and Mahdoo plus assorted luggage in the back. Bets and I, who were taking turns driving, followed in the baby Austin, with the rest of the luggage. And Angie accompanied the procession, sitting proudly on Mother's lap and pretending to drive, her skinny little hands on the wheel, and copying all the motions. Whenever we passed other monkeys — either brown monkeys or the grey, black-faced langurs, both species of which can be seen in large numbers all over India — she would drop her chauffeur-airs-and-graces, to look out of the open windows and hurl boasts or insults at them. Only when tired of pretending to drive the car would she leave Mother's lap and climb into the back seat to take a nap on Kadera's knee.

The IDG seemed very quiet and deserted now that most of its members and nearly all their womenfolk had left for the hills, as the Government of India made its annual migration to Simla in order to escape the rigours of the hot weather and the discomfort of the monsoon. As far as I can remember, only one memsahib had not joined the rush, her husband's job being one that tied him to Delhi. And, much to our delight, it was our dear friend 'Ooloo' Riley who had flatly refused to be shunted off to the hills, insisting that if Alan could stick it out in the plains then so could she.

Ooloo was, as ever, in terrific form, and Bets and I fell on her neck with shouts of joy. Her rooms were next to ours, which were in a double line of Club quarters facing each other across narrow grass lawns planted with gold-mohur trees, and a wide gravelled drive that led to the Club's dining-room. The trees were in flower and formed an avenue of shade and brilliant colour, and since our rooms were on the shady side of the drive they were degrees cooler than the ones at Tonk. And how marvellous it was to see electric ceiling-fans again — one in every room! I felt as though I had almost forgotten that there *was* such a thing as electricity, and was discovering its blessing for the first time.

We didn't see much of Tacklow, who I imagine spent most of his time arguing with *vakils* in stuffy offices in Connaught Place, and after only a night or two in Delhi he went back to Tonk by train — or, to be accurate, as far as Sawai Madhopur by train, where a car from Tonk met him. I have no recollection at all as to where Mother went, or why. I only know that it was something arranged at the eleventh hour between Tacklow and her and Ooloo Riley, who promised to keep an eye on us while she was away, and that Kadera remained with us to see that we were OK.

Left on our own — except for that couple of baby-sitters, Ooloo and Kadera — Bets celebrated the occasion by falling ill on the very first day of our independence. At first it seemed as though she had merely caught a slight chill — probably as a result of our last day in Tonk, during which the thermometers in the verandah and the *barra-durri* had been registering some horrific figure, while the main room of the house, in which Bets and I had insisted on doing her packing, was downright chilly from the icy stream of air that the *Lou* was blowing through the *kus-kus tatties*.

She had not been feeling too bright for the last day or two, but had not complained. It was only after Mother and Tacklow had both gone that she began to feel really ill. Luckily one of the resident club members, whom we knew well, was a doctor, and took a look at Bets and gave her a quick going-over. He told her to drink a lot of soft drinks and stay in bed for a day or two: 'No need to bother your Mother.' So we didn't, even though Bets had begun to look very pallid and sallow. But by the next day her skin was no longer sallow, but yellow — and a good bright yellow at that! Even the whites of her eyes were yellow. I had never seen anything like it before, and I was horrified. Ooloo and the doctor, however, took it fairly lightly. Bets had merely acquired a bad go of jaundice which, they told me, was a very common illness in India, and I was probably right about the *kus-kus tatties*.

Ooloo and I went shopping to Connaught Circus that evening, and bought a couple of pale blue muslin nightdresses and a yard or two of blue ribbon with which to 'tie up her bonny brown hair', because Bets's nightdresses were all pale pink and Ooloo said that pale blue was the only possible colour to wear with a yellow skin. And how right she was: all the others made Bets look yellower than ever, and pink was the worst of the lot. I don't remember how long she was on the sick-list, or how long Mother was away. Only that it seemed a very long time, and that just before it ended the monsoon broke, which was a marvellous relief after the grinding heat of the previous weeks. Suddenly everything seemed green again, and Bets revived in the coolness with surprising speed.

The only snag about the monsoon was that it flooded out the holes and burrows that for months past had been home to a large variety of creepy-crawlies, ranging from snakes to ants and including a particularly alarming specimen known as a 'jerrymunderlum', which *must* be an invented name, though I never heard it called anything else. It was a bright red creepy-crawly, about the size of a scorpion, and like scorpions it varied in size from quite small to large. It strongly suggested a cross between a scorpion and a miniature lobster, with a touch of spider thrown in. A real horror, and one that I don't remember coming across in my childhood. It flourished in Rajputana, and the first one I ever saw was in Jaipur. They must be hot-weather creatures, for I can't remember seeing them anywhere in the north, or in places where the winters are cold, and I had not expected to come across the beastly creatures in Delhi. But then I had never been to Delhi in the hot weather before.

I have always been terrified of spiders, and I was almost as terrified by these little horrors. There had been plenty of them in Tonk once the hot weather arrived, and whenever I saw one I would leap on to a chair and scream for Kadera, who would arrive looking resigned and more than a little scornful and deal with the enemy by picking it up in his duster and flicking it out of the nearest door — where, nine times out of ten, it would instantly be snapped up by some hungry bird. After which he would lecture me severely for making such a silly fuss over a harmless creature that neither bit nor stung, and tell me that I ought to be ashamed of myself. Well, I was of course. But that didn't stop me from leaping on to the nearest chair and yelling for help whenever I spotted a jerrymunderlum scuttling across the floor.

A day or two after the monsoon broke, while I was reading a book from the Club's library in the sitting-room of our quarters, the great-grandfather of all jerrymunderlums climbed up the back of the book and looked at me over the top of the page. I don't know how it got there without my knowing it, but there it was, peering at me and twitching its lobster-style whiskers, and I hurled the book from me with a piercing shriek that must have rivalled the Last Trump and brought Bets tottering out of the bedroom and Kadera at a run from the far end of the verandah.

The jerrymunderlum had gone to ground somewhere under the sofa, and Kadera, apprised of the reason for the uproar, stood and roared with laughter for at least a minute before launching into the now familiar lecture on the harmlessness of the poor creature and the *shurram* (shame) that I brought upon myself by behaving in this childish manner . . . etc., etc. Bets, who disliked jerrymunderlums almost as much as I did (but not to the point of being scared silly by them), retreated prudently to the comparative safety of her bed, while I continued to stand cravenly on my chair and Kadera hunted the creature under the sofa, muttering scornfully all the while about *garib kiras* and *bey-whakoof Missybabas.*

When at last the humble insect emerged from its hiding-place and scuttled out into the open, Kadera as usual dropped his duster neatly over it and, having picked up both, was on his way to the door to throw his 'harmless' captive out when he gave a loud yelp of pain and dropped it as though it had stung him. Well, it hadn't actually done that. But it had bitten him right through the folds of cloth, hard enough to draw blood, and I regret to say that at this point it was the turn of the foolish Missybaba to laugh her head off.

It proved to be quite a hearty nip, especially given the thickness of that cotton *jharan* (duster) which Kadera always carried slung over one shoulder. I dabbed it with disinfectant and put a plaster on it, just to be on the safe side, and after that Kadera treated those 'harmless' creatures with the respect that he accorded to scorpions, and stamped on them on sight. Fortunately their territory did not seem to range any further north than Delhi, and the one that bit Kadera was the only one that I remember seeing as far north as that.

Mother returned from wherever she had been staying and received a rapturous welcome from Angie (who had been moping around in her pitch behind the bungalow making sad hooting little noises to herself), and as Bets had stopped being a striking shade of gamboge, with the doctor's permission we set off for Kashmir.

The arrival of the monsoon made our journey to Kashmir a mixture of lashing rain, varied by brilliant intervals when the black ceiling of rain-clouds drew back to disclose a clear sky and a glittering, clean-washed world in which a myriad ponds and pools and puddles flashed like heliographs in the sunlight. We reached Rawalpindi, where we had booked for a night at Flashman's Hotel, in one of the bright intervals, and were disconcerted to find several messages from friends, including an urgent telegram from Ken Hadow, awaiting us at the hotel's reception desk, all of them urging us not to attempt to take the Murree road to Srinagar, because of the danger of landslides.

There were two other routes into the valley: one via Abbottabad and the other via Sialkot and the Banihal Pass. But since the Abbottabad one merged with the main Murree–Srinagar road at Domel and became one and the same for the remaining 109 miles of the journey, the chances were that there would be as many landslides on the last stretch as there were on the first. As for the Banihal route, well, for a start that entailed turning round, going back to Jhelum, and recrossing the bridge there. Which was something that Mother was not prepared to face a second time. She had arrived in Jhelum as a bride, and had crossed that bridge scores of times, pushing her baby son in his perambulator for an evening walk. But she had never before seen the Jhelum in flood, and it was a daunting sight. We had none of us liked the look of it.

The bridge, at that time probably one of the longest in India, since the river here is fully a mile wide, stands, in normal times, high above its surface, the tall stone piers splitting the smooth current far below the level of the road that carries all the two-way traffic of the Grand Trunk. During the dry season when the rivers run low, a full third of the bridge looks down on silver sandbanks or shallow water. But that day there were no sandbanks and no piers, and the iron girders of the bridge seemed to float on the surface of a brown, furious torrent that at first sight appeared to have no banks, and was in the process of turning into an inland sea. The racing, foam-streaked current was full of the debris of ruined villages whose mud-walled, thatched-roofed houses had been swept away by the flood and, together with the drowned bodies of cattle, whole trees and clumps of pampas grass torn from the bank, had piled up against the iron gridwork of the bridge, the road-surface of which would seem to be under water.

Mother had braked sharply at the sight of it. But the bridge guard had assured her that it was still safe to cross, though not for much longer, since the water was still rising. It only needed another tree-trunk the size of the last to add itself to the log-jam of flotsam and jetsam that had already piled up against it, and the pressure might become too great and a span of the bridge give way. He urged the Lady-Sahib to go while the going was good, and Mother took a deep breath and went.

It was a horrific crossing, made all the more alarming by the roar of the river as it fought its way through the impressive barrier of assorted litter which it was busy building against itself on the up-stream side of the bridge. Well, we made it. But you can understand why, having done so, Mother was not anxious to drive back to Jhelum and cross that bridge again — always supposing it was still standing — in order to brave the Banihal Pass.

In the end we decided to wait an extra night in Rawalpindi to see if things improved; a decision reinforced by meeting a fellow driver, recently arrived from Srinagar, who gave us a hair-raising description of having to reverse for nearly a mile along a stretch of road that was a mere ledge on the side of a cliff, some forty or fifty feet above the raging torrent of the Jhelum, until he found a place safe enough to allow a Kashmir-bound car to pass him — all traffic coming up from the plains having the right-of-way over those coming down, and both sections of road being equally perilous.

The following day, however, remained fine and sunny, and though clouds still hid the top of the mountain ranges and the news was still of bad conditions on the road, several intrepid drivers who, like ourselves, had been held up by the weather, decided to risk it and set off for the hills. Mother, consoling herself with the thought that the man who claimed to have driven backwards along a mile of edgeless road had at least succeeded in getting safely back to 'Pindi — and daunted, I suspect, by the size of our hotel bill — decided to follow their example.

We left 'Pindi basking in bright sunlight that stayed with us until just below Sunny Bank, two miles below the hill-station of Murree, where we plunged abruptly into a dense wall of mist and drizzle that reduced visibility to a matter of a few feet and forced Mother to switch on the car's headlights and slow down to a crawl. Murree is built on a hilltop, and once clear of its outlying fringes and driving down the winding road that dips down into the valley far below it, we were clear of the mist and the blanket of cotton-wool clouds that had blotted out everything around us and were in a rain-washed, sunless world under a lowering sky the colour of grey granite.

I don't remember if we met or passed any other traffic on our way up to Murree or down on the road between Murree and Kohala — which is on the frontier of Kashmir, where one pays a toll to cross the Jhelum river by a suspension bridge which spanned, that day, a turgid brown torrent that was almost as frightening as the one we had crossed earlier. But I do remember that the drivers of a number of cars and buses that were waiting on the weather, at both the British-India and the Kashmir sides of the river, were unanimous in warning us that the road ahead was in a terrible state, and that if the Dâk-bungalow had not turned out to be so full of stranded travellers (the *khansama* had informed us that by now the *Sahib-log* were sleeping two to a bed and in rows on the floor of the dining-room and the verandah, and that he could not provide shelter for anyone else — 'not even a mouse!'), Mother would undoubtedly have stayed there for at least that night.

However, she could not only see for herself that the *khansama* spoke the truth, but also see that the cars which had left 'Pindi less than an hour or two before us were not among the many that were parked here. Unless their drivers had lost their nerve and decided to stop at Murree, they had pressed on and were still ahead of us on the road. Inquiries at the toll gate supported the latter supposition, so Mother chanced it and drove on.

The road was in a reasonably good state, and we had no trouble until we arrived at Domel, where two rivers, the Jhelum and the Kishanganga, meet, and visitors to Kashmir pay another toll and have their baggage inspected. Here we ran into trouble, though not on account of our luggage. Angie, who up to now had behaved impeccably and been charming to one and all, took a sudden dislike to one of the customs men who came over to warn Mother about the perilous state of the road ahead and got a sharp nip for his pains.

Even at the best of times the roads into Kashmir can be terrifying. They had frightened me stiff on previous visits: in too many places they were cut out of the rocky sides of deep gorges, at the bottom of which, even in dry seasons, the penned-up waters of the Jhelum swirled and foamed as they raced down to the plains carrying with them the logs from the lumber camps far away in the forests.

The sheer drop between the edge of the road and the angry river varied from twenty to 300 feet, and the road wound and jack-knifed, so that driving up it (and worse still, down!) often gave the impression that one was about to drive straight into thin air. I love Kashmir dearly. It was and is one of my favourite places. Yet in that sad day — still mercifully a good many years in the future — when I was leaving it because the Raj had ended and India had achieved her independence, I could still think,

'Well, thank goodness I shall never have to drive along this petrifying road again!' It seemed to me the only good thing in all that sorrowful time.

But this was the first time I had driven along it in a high flood year, and all those pessimists at Kohala and Domel, who had advised us to turn back, or at least stay put, had been right; we should have paid attention to them. It was 'one-way only' for most of the way, belatedly enforced in order to stop anyone else having to reverse along that nightmare of a road with its hairpin bends and overhanging rocks. This held us up at frequent intervals, and gave the more fainthearted a chance to turn round and make for the nearest Dâk-bungalow — as several of those who had left 'Pindi ahead of us that morning had chosen to do. But Mother was nothing if not obstinate, and she refused to be beaten. As soon as she was given the signal to go, she went.

The road gangs were out, doing their best to clear a way for cars, and with their help we got over the first two or three bad patches fairly easily and began to think that this was not going to be as bad as we had feared. Until suddenly, turning a corner, the road vanished and we were faced with a vast, steep smear of mud and rocks and uprooted trees. The landslip had sliced off the entire mountainside in one enormous swoop, road and all, and deposited it in the river far below us. What's more, it was still falling. A slow-moving stream of liquid mud, full of stones and uprooted trees, was oozing steadily down the sheer mountainside, to slide over what had once been the road and drop straight down to form a dam at the foot of the gorge below; a dam that the swollen river was making short work of.

The landslip had swept away the outer half of the road, and with it the containing wall at its edge, and gangs of coolies were cutting back the fallen earth to try to clear a narrow track from what remained. Mother stopped the car, got out, and went forward to study the ground. Myself, I would have said it was impossible. Or at best, not worth the risk, for apart from the fact that liquid mud was still pouring steadily across that alarmingly narrow track, it was barely wide enough to take the car, and if it should skid even slightly, it would fall down that hideous drop below and into the river. But Mother thought she could do it. And she did. She made us all get out, Angie included, and went over alone, in bottom gear, with Kadera and several of the coolies holding on to any outstanding bits at the back of the car, in the faint hope of preventing it skidding off the road. Since there couldn't have been more than three inches to spare between the wheels and the edge of that drop, I don't know what good this could have done.

Only when she had got safely across, and we could breathe again, did it occur to any of us that there was a price to pay for pulling off this scarifying achievement: we couldn't go back. However bad the condition of the road ahead, we would *have* to go on, for apart from the near impossibility of turning round, it would mean having to repeat that bit of tightrope-walking in reverse! 'And if I'd thought of that before,' said Mother, 'I would never have done it — not for all the tea in China!' Yet, having pulled it off, there was nothing for it but to press on, which entailed repeating the same feat several more times. That was by no means the only or the worst bit, merely the first *really* bad bit.

The next worst was when Mother was again taking the car at a snail-slow crawl across another 100-yard wide smear of fallen mountainside (though this time, thankfully, not with a fifty-foot drop on one side of it) when a look-out far up the hillside above us yelled a warning of falling rock, and the coolies scattered like rabbits in every direction as a rock the size of a minibus came bounding down the mountain, hitting the ground at intervals as it came. Fortunately it didn't hit anyone, and missed the car by a large margin, which was just as well since Mother hadn't heard the yells — she could never have got out in time anyway.

There is no doubt at all that we should have listened those well-meaning people who had warned us to stay put until the situation improved a bit, and we paid for it by scaring ourselves silly. Still, we actually made it as far as Chinari, where the Dâk-bungalow managed to fit us in even though it was already full of travellers *en route* for the plains, who had also been held up by landslides and were not particularly cheered by Mother's description of the hazards awaiting them. I didn't envy them!

The road gangs had done wonders with the landslides beyond Chinari, and the next day, despite a few hold-ups, we were free by midday of those terrifying gorges and the unceasing thunder of the river, and driving once more on a flat, straight road through the long avenue of Lombardy poplars that leads to Srinagar. Peace — it was wonderful! Yet even here every ditch had become a pond and every pond a lake, while the Jhelum in spate was no longer the smooth and gently flowing stream that Mother had painted so often, but running fast and frighteningly high, streaked and dimpled with whirlpools that spoke of the hidden currents below, and dark from the earth and vegetation that it had torn from its once high banks as it swirled past on its way to Rampur and the gorges.

�֍ That year friends of my parents, the Moons, who had a house on the outskirts of Srinagar, roughly half a mile up-stream of the club and on the banks of the Jhelum, had allowed us to moor our houseboat alongside the bund at the end of their garden. We couldn't have been more grateful for it not only meant that we were within walking distance of the Church and the shops, the Post Office and Club and Nedou's Hotel, and most of the other places we were likely to visit, but it was an ideal spot for Angie. At the foot of the bund, and just above the grassy strip of land that bordered the river, stood a large tree whose branches overhung the *ghat* and shaded the front of our houseboat, underneath which we were going to set up Angie's house.

Well, we eventually did so. But not that day, for the river had risen so high that it couldn't have been more than a foot or two below the top of the bund on which, at first sight, our houseboat appeared to be sitting, embowered among the branches of a tree that should by rights have cleared it by any number of yards. In the circumstances, I suppose this was something that we should have foreseen. After all, we were only too well aware that the monsoon had been throwing its weight around this year, and that the Jhelum was in spate — and still capable of rising. But somehow we hadn't; and the sight of the currents swirling through the boughs of that tree, and of our two boats, houseboat and cookboat, about to be swept on to and over the bund and dumped upside down into the Moons' garden (because that was what it looked like) was no ordinary shock. For two pins I believe we would have sat down where we stood and collapsed into tears. It had been a nerve-racking day.

Our retinue, however, were made of sterner stuff: while Mother, Bets and I were staring in horror at our floating home, the *manji* and his friend were busy greeting Kadera and Mahdoo with the maximum of noise and enthusiasm, and before we knew where we were we were hustled on board where tea, hot toast and *pakoras*, plus a banana for Angie, appeared like magic. Mother, with visions of the boat breaking loose and being swept away down-stream during the night, would have bolted for Nedou's Hotel and holed up there until the river returned to normal. But she was shouted down by Kadera and the *manji*. The *manji* insisted that the worst was past, for the Weather Office had already reported a dramatic fall in the flood level, while Kadera remarked severely that if the *manji* and his family were prepared to spend another night on the river, the Lady-Sahib could be certain that it was perfectly safe to do so, and there was no need for her to start panicking. Needless to say, we stayed; and on waking next morning found our boat and the river a good deal lower than it had been the previous evening. Within a day or two you wouldn't have known that there had ever been anything wrong. Floods? — What floods?

As though in apology for its hostile shenanigans, Kashmir gave us another wonderful season. The sun shone, the lakes were strewn with lotuses and water-lilies, the Dāl had never looked more beautiful and, judging from the snapshots that survive, the Misses Kaye appear to have spent a good deal of time showing off — dancing, singing and acting in cabarets in aid of flood relief charities. (Bets did most of the dancing, while I did a bit of the rest.) In between rehearsing for these fund-raising entertainments we spent several wonderful weekends with Bruce and Edna Bakewell in their bungalow in the Lolab Valley.

We painted a lot — all three of us. Mother sketched, while Bets and I painted 'pictures'. Mine to illustrate verses or bits of prose that interested me: Rapunzel, for instance, Wynken, Blynken and Nod in their wooden shoe fishing for stars in the Milky Way, the Forsaken Merman, and Laurence Hope's Kashmiri Love Songs — 'Song of the Bride', 'Kingfisher Blue', 'Pale Hands I Loved Beside the Shalimar', and all those. Believe it or not, they sold very well. So well, in fact, that of all of the scores of illustrations I did in those days and entered for local art exhibitions, only two remain in my possession. And that was only because the *Illustrated Times of India Weekly* paid for the reproduction rights, after which they returned the originals to me and I kept three of them. One because I liked it, another, 'Ashoo at her Lattice', because I didn't (it was *not* a good bit of work and I tore it up), and the third because, like the first, my model for Ashoo had been the wife of the *manji* of our first houseboat. She was the most beautiful creature — like a Greek goddess.

Bets started by painting dancers and moved on to pencil portraits; she was very good at getting a likeness in pencil but not so good in colour. Eventually, since I could get the colour but not the likeness, we combined: Bets would draw the sitter, and I would colour the drawing. It worked rather well, and was a great help to our finances. Mother's sketches continued to outsell the two of us, though. Later, Bets too took to sketching, and became very good at it; and later still, after a few lessons from Hal Bevan-Pitman, she took to doing pastel portraits. These were — and still are — an enormous success, and they still keep her busy. She must have done hundreds of them by now, and is always meeting elderly people who say, 'You did my Mother/Father's portrait back in the thirties — mine too, when I was about five — I've still got them.'

We both took a hand in designing the costumes for the cabaret shows, and one in particular was a triumph. Bets was to do a solo dance as a butterfly, and we designed, painted and constructed a pair of wings from mosquito-netting and wire, fastened to her back so that she could open and close them. We also made a large mushroom — a most lifelike one too, though I say it myself — large enough for her to lie on, so that when the curtain went up she was discovered lying asleep on it, with closed wings. That dance was the hit number of the show.

I occasionally appeared in a chorus item, but left the solo dancing strictly to people like Bets, who were really good at it. But I did quite a bit of singing, generally as a twosome with some personable tenor or baritone, or supported by a chorus. The item I remember best was one in which, partnered by a dashing young cavalry officer, one 'Bingle' Ingle, we appeared on a darkened stage, sitting on a park bench in a pool of light thrown by a street lamp, and sang a song by de Silva, Brown and Henderson, entitled 'A Bench in the Park'. It went down well, and was to be encored in strange circumstances many years later, when, having unexpectedly hit the jackpot with a best-seller, I found myself one bright and sunny morning signing copies of *The Far Pavilions* in the book department of one of the largest stores in San Francisco. This junket must have been well advertised by my publishers, since every section of the available space appeared to be packed with book-lovers queuing up to part with what seemed to me an astonishingly large number of dollars in exchange for a book that weighed about the same as an overnight bag and which they didn't know if they would like. Among those trusting buyers, who should suddenly pop up out of the past but Bingle!

It seems that he had read a bit of the advance publicity in the local papers and, putting two and two together, realized that this M. M. Kaye must be the Mollie Kaye of his earliest appearances behind the footlights (the War being over, he had married and settled in America, where he had become a professional actor and singer). We greeted each other with considerable enthusiasm and, carried away on a wave of nostalgia, sang a reminiscent bar or two of 'A Bench in the Park', which went down well with the public. In fact the staff in charge of the book section assured me afterwards that it helped to increase the sales of the *Pavilions* considerably. However, to return to India and the long-ago thirties . . .

Chapter 31

Ever since I started writing down the story of my life, I have been uneasily aware that one day I would have to come to this part. It has, so to speak, been lurking in the wings: an ominous patch of shadow cast by something just out of range of the corner of one's eye, felt rather than seen. I also have an uneasy suspicion that I have written too much about the years up to date, merely in order to put off the evil day when I must write about the happenings of this particular time.

If I could ignore the whole episode and leave it out of this book, I would. But it explains so much of what came later, and without it, my darling Tacklow's subsequent behaviour would seem inexplicable. I am also happy to say that now I have come to it, I can't dwell on it at any length even if I wanted to, because at the time I didn't know what was going on. Tacklow never discussed it with me, and though I hate to admit it, I was far too busy enjoying life to realize that something was worrying him. Mother knew, but she too was having fun, and didn't really give him as much support as he needed, I'm afraid. In fact we both let him down.

It was, of course, that fatal visit to Ajmer.

Tacklow's immediate boss was Major Barton, the Assistant AGG Rajputana, who took his orders from the AGG,* a Colonel Someone, whose name I can't even remember. We had all rather liked the Major. He and his wife had stayed with us in Tonk on several occasions, and we had stayed with them at their headquarters at Deoli. We were, or so we thought, friends. But apparently the Major had objected strongly to having a subordinate who was not only his senior in army rank, but had been knighted. He seems to have cherished a suspicion that in the Neutral Territory of Ajmer, Tacklow (though his junior in the hierarchy of the 'F

---

* The AGG Rajputana (otherwise the Assistant to the Governor General) was a Colonel: *his* assistant, a Major, was Assistant to the AGG Rajputana.

and P' and the princely states of Rajputana) might be seen to outrank him. Which is why he had done his best to put us all off attending the Viceregal festivities at Ajmer. Unfortunately, that had failed and he had found his worst fears realized.

If only he'd told Tacklow the *real* reason why he did not want Sir Cecil and Lady Kaye to go to Ajmer, Tacklow would have seen the point at once. And the sense, too! But the Major was not a big enough man to do that and, alas, my father was far too unworldly a one to think of it himself. He didn't care a fig where he sat at table — above or below the salt! — and nor did his friends. Or Mother either. My parents were both of them genuinely untainted by the tediously snobbish rules of precedence, and couldn't have cared less who went in to dinner with whom. (Tacklow, no party man, would in any case have been wishing to goodness that he was elsewhere, either poring over his beloved stamps* or comfortably in bed with the *Times* crossword puzzle.) As for Mother, as I have already said, she adored parties — any party was fun to her, and she never failed to enjoy one. Neither of them would ever have suspected that precedence was the Major's Achilles heel, or that the fact that he and his wife had been publicly 'outranked' by someone technically subordinate to him, was gall and wormwood.

We were slightly surprised that he never came near us during the following months, even though we heard that he had actually passed through Tonk and had spoken to Saadat and one or two members of Council. We had merely supposed that he was in too much of a hurry. I can't remember who it was who first told me that Barton-Sahib had his knife into Tacklow, and why. At a guess, it was the Tikka-Sahib — a cheerful young man who delighted in gossip, always knew everything, and was a frequent visitor to Tonk. It could even have been one of the Begums, because this being India, almost everyone in Tonk apparently knew about it; and thought it was funny! Everyone, that is, except my parents, who until the balloon went up remained in happy ignorance.

Unfortunately, I can't give a detailed account of the various events that led up to what Mother called the 'Tonk Affair', although about a year after Tacklow's death she gave me a bulky sealed package that contained,

* He had been interesting himself for years in trying to catalogue Ferrarie's world-famous collection of stamps, which had been auctioned after the owner's death.

so she said, all the relevant documents concerning it that Tacklow had kept. These included his own account of everything that had been said or done as well as the letters he had written to her at that time — which alone accounted for almost a quarter of the whole, since throughout their married life, whenever they were apart Tacklow would write to her every day. There were also copies of a couple of letters that Mother had written (most ill-advisedly) to Saadat. *Everything* was there down to the last detail, insisted Mother in floods of tears, and she was giving it to me so that one day I could write it all down, 'so that everyone would know the truth'.

Well, perhaps she *did* possess a touch of the second sight after all, for at the time that she thrust that bursting file into my reluctant hands, I had no more intention of becoming a writer than I had of swimming the Atlantic. I was going to be an illustrator of children's books, another Arthur Rackham or Edmund Dulac. Never, *never* a writer! I took that file because I couldn't possibly have refused it, not with Mother dripping tears all over it, and behaving as though she was landing me with some kind of sacred trust. But as just then life was being pretty sticky for me without this as well, I locked it away in a suitcase and forgot all about it for the best part of another year. And when I did get round to it, it made me so *bloody** angry (it still does!) that if I'd been in India at that time instead of a bed-sit in London I really think I would have hitch-hiked to Tonk to tell Saadat and Co. exactly what I thought of them, and gone on from there to Deoli to try my best to strangle the Major with my own hands; confident that no jury would convict and that the verdict would be 'Justified homicide'.

I wept buckets over that file, just as Mother had done. My poor, darling Tacklow. I couldn't bear to think of what he had been through.

When I felt less murderous, I began to wonder what I could do with the file, and after spending hours and days of thought on it, I realized that there was literally *nothing* I could do. It had all happened several years before, and Tacklow himself was dead. It was finished. *Kutam hogia!* And I was a nobody; a penniless art student living in a sleazy 'bedsitter' off London's King's Road and managing to live on an income of one pound five shillings a week, which was the pension of an unmarried daughter of an Indian Army Officer (and lucky to get it, for if Tacklow had been

* Sorry. That's not a word I usually use, but it's the only one that fits here!

in the British Army I wouldn't have got anything!). I had no 'pull', and if Tacklow's friends had been unable to help him, of what use would I be?

In the end, I burnt the file. I couldn't bear to read it again and realized that I could do nothing about it. The past was the past, and the sooner I burnt it the better. Tacklow was where he would no longer care, and I couldn't spend the rest of my life lugging that bulging file of past misery and malice around with me like that tedious albatross. Anyway, I was going to be an illustrator, and I'd better get on with that . . .

Well, time catches up with one. I failed to make a living from my art, and ended up writing. And now, after all these years, I could almost wish (only *almost*) that I had kept that file. Because when it comes to details — names, dates, scraps of information, and so on — there is so much that I have forgotten; and what is left can so easily be dismissed as 'what the soldier said'. For instance, I can't even remember what the Begum's name was, because, as the senior lady in the state, she was *the* Begum: the others were merely 'so-and-so Begum'. I can only give you a rough outline of the 'Tonk Affair', which is probably just as well, as from what I recollect of the size of that bulky dossier, a detailed account of its contents would have taken up far too many pages and been insufferably boring.

The trouble started when Saadat, running true to the tradition of too many Mogul royals, suddenly turned against his young brother Nunni-mia — who until then had been regarded as the heir apparent — and with him, his mother the Begum. I can't remember what the quarrel was about, or who started it. But from what I know of the intrigues that seem to be an integral part of *zenana* life, I would say, at a guess, that some rival pretty lady had managed to steal the heir's affections, and was scheming to get a son of hers installed as heir apparent. Whatever the reason, Nunni and his mother fell from favour and the Begum suddenly found herself virtually a prisoner in Tonk, unable to leave the state.

None of this would have happened if the old Nawab had been hale and hearty, for Nunni was his favourite son and he doted on the boy. But the old man, whose health had been failing for some months, was now seriously ill, and a gang of courtiers, counsellors, palace favourites, servants and hangers-on had suddenly begun to reassess their positions and change their loyalties in light of the fact that there would soon be a new ruler in Tonk. As a result, any number of old alliances were broken and new ones formed; spies and tale-bearers proliferated, helping to stir up trouble, and 'Nunni's' Begum turned to Tacklow for help.

As the heir apparent, Nunni had been expected to finish his education at the College of Princes in Ajmer, but in order for him to do so, his name must be put down in advance as a prospective pupil, and a sum of money paid over to the school — presumably to cover a certain amount of the fees in advance. This sum Saadat had suddenly refused to pay, saying he had not yet decided who should be his heir! And since without it Nunni could not be entered as a pupil, 'Nunni's' Begum was anxious to pay it herself. But because she herself was not allowed to leave the state — and probably because the poor woman no longer knew whom she could trust — she wanted Tacklow to sell some of her jewellery for her, and see that it was paid over to the school.

This was something that Tacklow was not keen to do: he was well aware of how involved and dangerous intrigues in palace circles could be, and he had no desire to find himself being accused of persuading the Begum to part with her jewels, and pocketing the proceeds himself. And in the middle of all this, the poor old Nawab lay dying.

At first Tacklow would call at the palace once or twice a day, to sit beside the Nawab's bed holding his hand and talking to him; they had always been good friends, and the old man said that his visits made him feel better. Tacklow himself was sure that if only he would call a European doctor to treat him, there was a good chance that he would recover. But the Tonk *hakims* (doctors) bristled with rage at the very idea, and when Tacklow pleaded with Saadat and some of the senior councillors to allow an English doctor just to see the invalid and give an opinion, he found his own visits to the palace sharply curtailed. In the end, the old man himself asked to see an English doctor, and Tacklow sent for the nearest one: I don't remember where that would be, or what the doctor's name was. He was probably stationed in some outpost of Empire like Deoli. But when he arrived, Saadat said that his father had changed his mind and was 'too ill to see him'. Or Tacklow, either.

The doctor stayed in Tonk for a day or two, waiting on the chance of being called to see the Nawab, and in the end was allowed to. But he said the case was hopeless, although he too thought if the old man could be taken into an English hospital and be treated with European drugs, and allowed some peace and quiet — and fresh air — there was a chance of him recovering. But his room was crammed with relations, courtiers and servants, not a breath of fresh air was allowed into it, and his *hakims* were dosing him with water (in which strips of paper bearing charms or verses from the Koran written in cheap ink had been boiled), gold leaf, and even more expensive decoctions which contained emeralds and other precious stones that had been pounded to powder, or pearls dissolved in vinegar, 'medicines' that only a King could afford to take, and which, because of their value, must do the patient some good. Tacklow, who was fond of the old Nawab, tried to make the doctor stay a bit longer. Just in case . . . But the doctor said he had wasted too much time in Tonk already, and had too many other patients who were in need of care.

Despite all the peculiar nostrums, the old man hung on to life and raised enough energy to insist on seeing Tacklow, whom he begged, for the sake of their friendship, to look after Nunni and see that he was entered for the College in Ajmer. Apparently he had managed to see the Begum — or, more likely, she had managed to force her way in to see him — for he seemed to know all about the plots that were being woven to push Nunni aside. He also begged Tacklow to do his best for Saadat, who, he suspected, was also in danger of being pushed aside and superseded by another member of the family: 'Stay with him until he is safely seated on the *gudee* and cannot be deposed,' pleaded the old man, 'and promise me that you will not let Nunni or his mother be cheated out of their rights.'

Tacklow promised. What else could he do? But having regarded Saadat as the sole trouble-maker, he was somewhat shaken by the suggestion that there might be another candidate lurking among that swarm of brothers, step-brothers and sisters, and busy plotting a *coup d'état* that would oust both Saadat and Nunni from the succession. Tacklow was inclined to take that piece of tale-bearing with a large pinch of salt. But just in case there was something in it, he took the precaution of removing the keys to the Treasury and locking them up in his office safe, to ensure that when Saadat became Nawab of Tonk he would not find that a large proportion of its contents had mysteriously disappeared. Which but for Tacklow, very nearly happened, since within the next few days not only one group of anti-Saadat relations and their supporters demanded the keys to the Treasury, but two. And both were livid when they discovered that they had been impounded by Kaye-Sahib.

At this point Saadat, faced with the imminent prospect of power or a possible *coup d'état*, came to see Tacklow and begged him to stay on as President of the Council of State and, metaphorically speaking, hold his hand until such a time as he was firmly settled on the throne and had learned how to deal with the problems of rule and an unruly family.

Tacklow's contract with the old Nawab had still some months to run and he had been looking forward to the end of it. He had not enjoyed living in such a remote part of Rajputana. The heat and the dust-storms, the lack of electricity and made roads, the loneliness — most of all, of late, the loneliness. This last would not have worried him in the days when he was a carefree bachelor. On the contrary, as anyone who has read *The Sun in the Morning* will know, he enjoyed it. But Mother had changed all that. He was that rare creature, a one-woman man, and having found his one woman and fallen in love with her on sight, he remained in love with her for the rest of his life. He quite literally adored her, and every letter he ever wrote her was a love letter. There cannot be many women whose husbands still write to them, after a quarter of a century of marriage, as 'My own dear, darling Love . . .'

He had accepted the job in Tonk because he had two unmarried daughters on his hands, and a wife who loved the fun and gaiety, and the freedom from household chores, which life in India offered in the time of the Raj. But oh, how he missed us — Mother most of all. I used to think that I meant as much to him as he did to me. But that was before I read (some five or six years after Mother's death) the letters that he wrote to her during the Tonk period, when they had been separated so often, and I realized that her happiness was the most important thing in the world to him, and that I came a very poor second.

Tacklow had often written of a much-cherished plan of his for the two of them to return to China to spend a summer together in Pei-tai-ho, where they had spent a blissful honeymoon all those years ago. They would, of course, have to take the girls with them, unless those two decided to settle for one young man instead of several, and got married. But even if they didn't, there were plenty of young men in North China. And plenty of aunts and uncles with whom they could all stay until he could find a suitable house to rent and to live in.

Judging from some of the letters Mother kept, this had been a long-standing dream of his; and had the old Nawab not offered him that job in Tonk, the chances are that he would probably have moved on to China when his work on the Treaties was finished. But with his children having a whale of a time in India, and his darling Daisy urging him to accept the Tonk offer so that she could stay in India for a few years longer, I think he felt that he would be letting us all down if he refused.

Now, once again, with retirement and the prospect of a second honeymoon beckoning him, he wrote to Mother to tell her of the promise he had given the old Nawab, that he would do his best for Saadat — and for Nunni and the Begum (which might not be so easy since, if rumour were true, their interests could well conflict). Also that Saadat was pressing him to stay on for a further term as President of the Council of State when his term of office ended. This would mean at least two more years in Tonk. Probably three, and it was not a prospect he looked forward to. What did Mother think?

Mother was delighted. So much so that she even dashed off a hasty note to Saadat, with whom she had always been on the friendliest terms, thanking him for the offer and saying how pleased she was at the prospect of a further spell in Tonk, etc. It was a personal letter between friends, and one that should never have been treated as an 'official document' and filed as 'evidence'. She hadn't stopped to think before she wrote it, and plainly did not consider it to be of enough importance to mention to Tacklow: but Saadat showed it to one Abdul Karim,* a nasty piece of work, who passed it on to the Major. Nor apparently had she paid any attention to that remark of Tacklow's about 'not looking forward to the prospect of more years in Tonk'. She probably didn't even notice it, for the surviving letters written during this period make harrowing reading — if one reads between the lines. He never actually *asks* her to come to Tonk; but the fact that he is worried and lonely, harried by rumours of plots and counter-plots and the discovery that he can trust no one — that there is not one single person with whom he can discuss the situation in confidence, certain that whatever he says will not be distorted, and that someone will not soon be spreading a twisted and unrecognizable version of it throughout the city — is clear in every line.

He needed Mother at this time more than he had ever needed her, or anyone else, before. And he says as much, by implication, in every letter, even going so far as to say things like, 'If by chance you find that you could get away, you could always get the night-train from Delhi, and I could meet you at Sawai-Muderpore, or Sirohi, and we can drive back to

* No connection with our old bearer.

Tonk from there. But I quite see that you are tied by the girls, who can't be abandoned on their own . . .'

Why not, for heaven's sake? I was twenty-one! — coming up twenty-two. We had plenty of friends in Srinagar who would have kept an eye on us, and with Kadera and Mahdoo as well, we could have been left on that houseboat in perfect safety. I've never been able to forgive Mother for not going to him when he needed her so badly.

To cut a long story short, the old Nawab died, and Major Barton turned up in Tonk to represent the AGG Rajputana at the various ceremonies and festivities that accompanied the enthronement of the new Nawab of Tonk, His Highness Said-ud-Daulah Wazir-ul-Mulk Nawab Hafiz Sir Mohammed Saadat Ali Khan Bahadur Sowlat-i-Jung, GCIE. In other words, our old friend Saadat. And when that was completed, the Major, who on this occasion had elected to put up in the No. 1 Guest House, sent for Tacklow and told him that His Highness the Nawab-Sahib had informed him that he, Sir Cecil, had been 'putting pressure' on him, Saadat, to extend his term of employment in the state for a further three or four years. But since His Highness had no desire to do any such thing, he had asked Major Barton to speak for him, and to see that Sir Cecil vacated his house and left the state as soon as possible.

Tacklow, staggered by being given the sack in this abrupt and ungracious manner, could only suppose that some palace underling had been creating mischief on purpose, and hastened to tell the Major that he had got hold of the wrong end of the stick. He had had no intention of staying on in the job for longer than originally requested by the old Nawab. It was the old man who had asked him to stay until Saadat had learned the ropes, and Saadat himself who had implored him to stay on for at least a second term. There had been a mistake.

When, to his horror, the Major insisted that the only mistake had been his, Tacklow's, in thinking that he could 'twist Saadat round his little finger', Tacklow lost his temper and insisted that the allegations should be repeated in the presence of the new Nawab. This was something the Major had obviously expected — he'd have been stupid if he hadn't. Saadat was waiting in a nearby room, and was produced almost immediately. Tacklow said that, furious and insulted as he was, he couldn't help feeling sorry for the wretched man. He seemed miserably embarrassed, and he wouldn't look at Tacklow. Barton asked the questions and the Nawab said 'Yes' or 'No' to all of them until there was one totally insufferable one relating to the keys of the Treasury, made at the suggestion of Abdul Karim, the original snake-in-the-grass, that money and jewels were 'understood' to be missing from it. Saadat, presumably remembering how Tacklow had saved it for him, and knowing full well that but for Tacklow he would almost certainly have inherited a bankrupt Treasury, replied surlily that since he had no detailed knowledge of what was in it, he could not possibly be expected to know if anything was missing.

That question was hastily dropped. But he had endorsed the others, and when he had finished, Tacklow said to him, 'Nawab-Sahib, you know that this is not true. You cannot have forgotten so soon what you have said to me. Tell the Sahib the truth. For the sake of your honour!'

Well, he hadn't got any of course — not when it came to having to choose between beginning his reign by getting on the wrong side of the Assistant to the AGG Rajputana, and sacrificing Tacklow. For in the hierarchy of the princely states of India and the pecking-order of the Foreign and Political Department, an ex-Indian-Army Officer — even an ex-Head of Intelligence — once he has retired, cuts no ice compared with a working Assistant to the AGG Rajputana. It was perfectly obvious, of course, that the Major had been infuriated by the news that the newly enthroned Nawab had asked Tacklow to stay on in the same job. And equally obvious that he had not only shown it, but having scared the living daylights out of the poor man, shown him a way of escape by suggesting that it must have been Tacklow's fault, since he, the Major, was unwilling to believe that such an idea would ever have *occurred* to the Nawab; unless, of course, Sir Cecil had put it there, and bullied him into accepting it . . . ?

It could only have been something on those lines, and I imagine the unfortunate Saadat must have jumped at it. The only person who was stunned by all this and literally *couldn't* believe his ears was my poor Tacklow. For, having no conception of the offence that had been caused during that wretched stay in Ajmer, it never once occurred to him that the Major had avoided us ever since because he hated our collective guts, and he was totally unprepared for the sheer hatred that showed plainly along with the accusations. When Saadat wouldn't answer him, he turned on the Major and said: 'Since one of us must be lying, will you please tell us which one you believe?'

'I believe the Nawab,' said the Major.

Tacklow, even less willing to believe his ears, said, 'You are calling me a liar, in fact?'

'I am telling you that I prefer to believe the Nawab,' repeated the Major, and walked out of the room, followed by Saadat, who turned his head at the last moment and, looking at Tacklow for the first and the last time, gave him an imploring look accompanied by a faint shrug of the shoulders and a slight spreading of the hands that Tacklow said was an obvious apology and a plea that Tacklow would please understand why he couldn't help doing this. After which he scuttled away in the wake of the Number Two Seed Rajputana, followed by the Snake, who probably slithered.

✄ Well, that was all. A minor affair, you may think. But it shattered my darling Tacklow, who had always considered that anyone who took it upon themselves to govern a country and a people not their own *must* make it a matter of the highest importance to be just and truthful in all their dealings. That was Rule Number One with him; and to be told to his face, in the presence of the Nawab and one of his underlings, that he was a liar was as shocking as though a bucketful of pig-swill had been publicly flung in his face.

What he ought to have done, of course, was to leave immediately for Simla — or at least for Ajmer — and laid his case in person before the Top Brass. Instead of which, being Tacklow, he sat down and wrote to various senior officials who could have dealt with it. This meant that Major Barton got in with his own carefully doctored version well before Tacklow's letters were delivered. After that he hadn't a hope. Every single one of the men to whom he wrote wrote back to say, in effect, that he didn't have to worry, since no one who knew him would ever believe for an instant that he had bullied the Nawab into retaining his services, or lied to Barton. The very idea was so absurd that not one of his friends or acquaintances would take 'that fellow's' word against his — *But* . . . why on earth hadn't he gone at once to Simla or to Ajmer with his story, instead of letting 'that fellow' get in first? Didn't he *realize* that the F and P was practically a mafia when it came to backing their own members, and that they would stick together like glue?

Of course they were right. Barton got in first with a basinful of lies and soft soap (he may even have told the truth, and relied on his boss, as a 'member of the Club', to back him!). Tacklow kept all those letters. They were in the file labelled the 'Tonk Affair', and when I burned it I kept back one of them: because it was from a great friend of Tacklow's, and because I liked him. His name was the Hon. Sir Alexander Muddiman and he had, I think, been a member of the Viceroy's Council. I still have it.

In the end, when it was much too late, Tacklow went to Ajmer to see the AGG, who sent for Barton to ask him, in Tacklow's presence, why he had accused Sir Cecil of being a liar. And as if it was not bad enough to accuse Tacklow in front of Saadat of being a liar — and repeat it! — he insisted that he had never said any such thing. At *no* time had he ever accused Sir Cecil of lying. Pretty, wasn't it? He covered up his first two lies by lying a third time. And got away with it, of course. No wonder India got tired of the British and threw us out.

Mother didn't make things better by writing to ask Saadat to keep Tacklow on. It was one of the silliest things she ever did, because Saadat showed both her letters to Abdul Karim, who, having got hold of them, sent them to the Major, who pretended to believe that Tacklow not only knew about them but had put her up to writing them. In fact, he had never laid eyes on either of them, or known anything about them, and Mother had thought she was pouring oil on troubled waters and cleverly saving Tacklow's job for him. The first he knew of them was when he was shown them in the AGG's office. Poor Tacklow; he *did* have a rough time of it. And Tonk hadn't finished with him yet. There was still a final little bowl of swill to toss in his face before he left . . .

All his friends had told him off for not having the sense to leave Tonk at once and make tracks for Simla and the seats of the Mighty, to lay his case before them. But it hadn't occurred to them to ask him *why* he hadn't done so. He hadn't left because his contract with the old Nawab had still a few weeks to run, and he thought it was his duty to stay, because of the promise he had made to the old Nawab that he would do his best to protect the interests of Nunni and his mother. There wasn't much he could do for the Begum, for by now she was a virtual prisoner in Tonk. But he journeyed to the Begum's home state (I don't know that I ever knew what that was) and from there to Delhi, where he saw and spoke to everyone who might be able to help her, and pulled every string he could on her behalf, and on Nunni's. He managed at last to get the money paid on Nunni's behalf, and extracted a promise that she and the boy should be allowed to leave for the hills during the worst of the hot weather.

He had not received his own last quarter's pay, and was told, while in Delhi, that this would be paid to him by an emissary of the state who would be along any day now. Tacklow, having completed whatever business he had to do in Delhi, stayed on there, waiting for this man from Tonk, and eventually received a letter to say that Sirdar Bahadur someone-or-other would be arriving in Delhi the next day. The next day brought not the Sirdar, but another letter to say that the money had been deposited to his credit in one of the Delhi banks. It hadn't been, of course; nor had the bank ever heard of Sirdar Bahadur Whoziz and, after making inquiries of several other Delhi banks, they reported back to Tacklow that there seemed to have been no such person. And no money either. Tacklow gave up and left for Kashmir.

No wonder he wanted to get the hell out of India with all possible speed, and make for the country where he had met the girl of his dreams and been so happy that he still saw it through a golden haze of romance. And that is really why we ended up in China.

Chapter 32

~❦~

We didn't manage to get there at once. There were all sorts of arrangements to make. A house to be rented at Pei-tai-ho for one thing, and passages to be booked on a ship that would land us in China at the best time of year instead of the middle of winter, when North China is so cold that the sea has been known to freeze for three miles out from Ching-wang-tao, and most rivers are impassable.

Letters flew to and fro between Mother's family in Hong Kong, Shanghai, Tientsin and other Chinese cities, and the Post Office on the Bund at Srinagar (from where we collected our mail), as the details of our flit were thrashed out. In the end it took another year to make all the arrangements and get our passages booked for the right time of year. Meanwhile, Bets and I continued to have the time of our lives while the going was good.

That year, when the Srinagar season ended and one by one the house-boats, hotels and guest-houses emptied as the summertime visitors, tourists and holiday-makers packed up and left for the plains, we did not leave with them. Old Mr Nedou rented us the little cottage that stood in the grounds of the hotel. And here we settled in to spend what we imagined would be a very dull winter. It wasn't.

While the season was in full swing, and noisy with holiday-makers and dance-nights, I hadn't bothered to notice how many elderly people had retired in Kashmir, renting houses from local Kashmiris or the state and settling down with their cats, dogs and parrots to end their days in this beautiful, peaceful valley. There were any number of them, the majority being widows, since the Almighty has rather unfairly decided that women should, for the most part, outlive their men. Which is our bad luck.

These elderly dames were known in Srinagar as 'Yaks', because of their habit of wearing somewhat shaggy fur coats of local manufacture, which they habitually donned when taking their daily walks along the Bund to collect their letters from the Post Office, medicines from Lambert's the Chemists, or to cash their modest cheques at the bank. Bets and I got to know quite a lot of the Yaks, and we promised ourselves that if neither of us married, or if we did, and lost our husbands, we would come back to Kashmir and end our lives together as a couple of old Srinagar Yaks. And we might well have done so, if only the Kashmir we knew and loved had not become yet another blood-soaked battleground, torn to pieces because people who yelp of the sacred cause of 'Freedom' and the iniquity of 'Colonialism' think nothing of turning on their neighbour with tanks and bombs and hatred, and annexing his vineyard just as soon as they have got back their own.

My parents were not the only 'Brits' in Srinagar to have members of a younger generation staying with them that winter. Many of those who had retired to Kashmir, and several whose work kept them there, had young visitors staying with them — cousins, nieces, or Aunt so-and-so — and the winter months were enlivened by gramophone dances and a cabaret show in aid of the Ski-Club of India, functions which were held at the Srinagar Club, since both the ballroom and stage at Nedou's Hotel were closed for the winter.

Bets and I were inevitably roped in to perform in the cabarets, together with a chorus-line of girls and the invaluable Bingle — though I have no idea what he could have been doing in Srinagar at that time of year; I must ask him one of these days. He was probably ADC to the Resident or — being a young man of infinite resource and sagacity — had wangled some military appointment for himself so that he could keep in touch with an extremely pretty girl with whom he was temporarily enamoured. I remember he danced a minuet with her, wearing powdered hair, a satin coat and buckled shoes (costumes designed by the sisters Kaye, of course), and supported by an exclusively female chorus in panniers and white wigs.

The same chorus in different dresses (yellow net, if I remember rightly) supported Bingle and myself in another song and dance item. The song was one that still, after all these years, turns up again and again on TV or radio — 'The Sunny Side of the Street'.

The valley under snow was a most beautiful sight, and the only one of us who failed to appreciate it was Angelina Sugar-Peas (she had acquired the surname because the wooden box that was her home had once contained tins of that commodity, and advertised the fact by having the words printed right across one side of it). Angie, whose forebears came from Rajputana and were strangers to extreme cold, had never seen snow before and she took a dim view of it. We brought her in from the garden and established her on a little covered verandah at the back of the cottage, and Mother and Bets knitted her a series of woolly jumpers, the first two of which gave her hours of fun as she painstakingly worked out how to unravel them.

Having done so, she lost no time reducing them to a pile of wool, an operation that clearly fascinated her. I think she thought, from the way it ran out, that it was alive. Having reduced it to a fluffy mass and discovered that it was inedible — and also that without it around her she was uncomfortably cold — she tried draping it about her skinny little shoulders and, when it wouldn't stay there, carried it all into her hutch and hunkered down in the middle of it in the manner of a dormouse in its nest.

After that, Mother got the *darzi* to make her a couple of padded red flannel coats which proved a great success. She never even tried to remove them, so she had obviously worked out what they were for. Yet surprisingly, she never worked out a much simpler problem . . .

Bets and I used to bring her into our workroom — an upper room above the dining-room that was set aside for our exclusive use, but where Tacklow and Mother would usually join us (by invitation) of an evening, because it was the warmest room in the house. There was electricity in Kashmir, but it was erratic, to say the least. On an 'off-day' (or night) a sixty-watt bulb often produced less light than a Christmas tree candle. So electricity was seldom used for heating, and most houses (and all houseboats) relied on wood-burning stoves that stood in the centre of the room, circular tin affairs with a hole on top through which logs were fed, and another from which a chimney, in the form of a tin tube, led up, and out, through a hole in one of the window panes. Why Srinagar, with its wooden houses, was never destroyed by fire I can't imagine. But fires were rare, and these flimsy, makeshift heaters were remarkably effective. Once started and fed with logs, their tin sides would glow red with heat, and the very first time we brought Angie into the room, riding on Mother's shoulder, she gave a squeak of excitement at the sight of this glowing object and, before any of us could stop her, she had leapt down on to the floor and patted the side of the red hot stove.

Yelling with pain, she rushed to Mother to be comforted, and was petted and made much of. Well, you would have thought that once was enough. But believe it or not, every single evening she would prance into the room and circle the stove cautiously, obviously wondering if this hostile object would or wouldn't bite her again if she touched it. Would it? . . . or wouldn't it? We would shout at her to warn her (she knew perfectly well what 'No' meant). But the curiosity of her kind was too strong for her — she *had* to find out. She would stretch out a paw towards it, and then snatch it back again and again, but always in the end she couldn't resist giving it a quick touch. And burning her paw for the umpteenth time.

Oh well, it's a depressing thought, but we all do it, don't we? My revered kinsman Sir John Kaye wrote a contemporary account of the Afghan War which should be required reading in every Military Establishment. (He didn't call it 'the First Afghan War', because he didn't realize that there were going to be another four or five in fairly rapid succession — all of them ending in a British defeat.) Anyone who'd read his book would, you would have thought, have avoided getting embroiled in a second one. But did they? Not on your life. And when the curtain came down on the British Empire, and Russia decided that she could do better, did any of her generals or colonels or staff officers bother to glance at the accounts of the various British–Afghan brawls and the way they ended? Of course not. They barged bald-headed into the same old traps, and the Afghans routed them in the old familiar way. No one *ever* seems to learn by experience; their own or anyone else's. As Kipling wrote in 'The Gods of the Copybook Headings', 'And the burnt fool's bandaged finger goes wobbling back to the fire'. Poor Angelina Sugar-Peas!

We had expected to spend Christmas in Kashmir, but a telegram arrived from Bill asking us down to Kohat for Christmas week — accommodation fixed. Mother wired our acceptance, and the usual female wail of 'I haven't a thing to wear' was raised. Fortunately, Mother was one of those people who never throw anything away, and we had with us one of the trunks she had brought out from England. It was full of her old clothes — coats and skirts, evening dresses, bits of bead embroidery and fur.

Our verandah *darzi*, who had been having rather an idle time of it since the last cabaret costumes and Angie's winter wardrobe were finished, was set to work on producing new outfits from old for Bets and me to wear during Christmas week. It was the first time I realized that hoarding old clothes is not always a waste of space, for Bets and I set out for Kohat with what appeared to be completely new wardrobes, but were in fact what Tacklow called a 'cook-up' of attractive bits and pieces, some of which dated back to Mother's trousseau. We left Kashmir by the Abbottabad road and were lucky to get through as easily as we did, for the forests and hillsides were deep in snow, and most of the road was 'one-way-only', which made for slow going. But it looked unbelievably beautiful, for we had struck a good patch of weather and the sky behind the towering white peaks and the glittering Christmas trees was a cloudless cerulean, while every shadow on the snow was an impossible Reckitt's blue.

Bill's quarters in Kohat were half of a bungalow, and since the occupants of the other half had been invited to spend Christmas with friends somewhere at the opposite end of Punjab, they had given Bill the use of it for a week. The bungalow had a gruesome history, for it had been the scene of a spectacular incident that made headlines all round the world some time in the early twenties: the murder by a handful of tribesmen of a Major and Mrs Ellis, and the kidnapping of their seventeen-year-old daughter, Mollie. Mollie Ellis had eventually been retrieved by a Mrs Starr, an English nurse, who, braving the tribesmen, followed them up into tribal territory and, after a lengthy and hair-raising interval, managed to persuade them to return the girl.

The only other thing I remember in detail is that at one of the dances at the Kohat Club a prize was given to the regiment, unit or corps that put on the best amateur cabaret turn. I thought all the turns were excellent — competition was fierce! — but was delighted when it was won for the Sappers by a friend of Bill's, 'Jug' Stewart, who happened to be a member of our party on that occasion. Most of the turns were song and dance ones, but Jug went solo on behalf of his corps, and on the final vote won easily by rubbishing a dramatic and well-known Edwardian 'party-piece', 'The Green Eye of the Little Yellow God'. He recited this with actions to suit the lines, and though the earnest and patriotic Victorian who wrote it must have been spinning round in his grave with fury, Jug had his entire audience literally rolling in the aisles. We laughed so much that he had to keep on stopping until the house was quiet enough to hear the next few words, and his surprised and pained expression on these occasions was almost funnier than his action-packed rendering of such lines as: 'But for all his foolish pranks, he was *worshipped* in the ranks . . . and the Colonel's daughter *smiled* on him as well.'

That performance still remains a bright spot in my life, as does his wife, who had been Topsy Hartnell before she married Jug. Topsy later invited me to stay with her in Peshawar while Jug was away on one of the army's interminable 'exercises', and I spent a week with her, most of it, if memory serves, laughing. Her account of the hilarious happenings that had marked her brother, Norman Hartnell's, rise to fame and fortune as one of Europe's best-known *couturiers* really should have been taken down by a tape-recorder for posterity — except that tape-recorders hadn't been invented then. In later years her brother's name became synonymous with 'glamour'; famous for the lovely glittery embroidery that was a feature of his dresses. He became the Royal Family's favourite designer and wowed all Paris with the shimmering crinoline-style evening dresses that Queen Elizabeth (the present Queen Mother) wore on a state visit to France. He also designed the then Princess Elizabeth's wedding dress and the dresses of her bridesmaids, and, later still, the dresses that she and her maids-of-honour wore at her Coronation.

Topsy did her best to teach me how to wear clothes with the same flair that she possessed. But it was no use. I just hadn't the figure, and even the simplest 'little black dress' made by Hartnell looked as though it had been made by a verandah *darzi* when worn by me. But then high fashion was wasted on the India of the Raj, because one met the same people over and over again at the merry-go-round of dances, parties, balls and races.

I learned one important lesson early on. One of the Fishing Fleet had decided that when *she* came out to India she was going to knock the eye out of the Delhi men and missahibs by wearing really stunning models. She saved up her pocket-money for months and then spent it all, plus overdrawing her allowance for at least two years ahead, on two ravishing evening dresses and an equally striking garden-party and races outfit. And set sail for India, confident of teaching us all a little about high fashion.

Her first appearance was every bit as sensational as she had hoped. She looked marvellous in the sort of dress that every woman dreams of possessing — and most of us have the sense to know we couldn't wear successfully if we did. It had the lowering effect of making every other woman's dress in the Imperial Delhi Gymkhana Club look as though its wearer had run it up on an elderly sewing-machine that same afternoon. We were all green with envy.

The second dress was equally successful. But you tend to remember perfection, so the next time the first model reappeared, people said, 'Oh, you're wearing that heavenly dress again!' The third time it was worn, no one commented, and someone was overheard to say, 'She's wearing her old yellow (or whatever) number again.' And the same went, of course, for the second dress. The trouble was that in a station like Delhi — and there were dozens of them, Bombay, Calcutta, Simla, Lahore . . . you name it — there were too many dances attended by the same people, and what one needed was not two beautifully cut model dresses, but twelve to fifteen different little numbers, each one made in a different material, obtainable, astonishingly cheaply, from a cloth shop in the bazaar, and run up by that old genius, the verandah *darzi*. Better still, the entire lot could cost you far less than one 'exclusive model'.

This had its disadvantages, of course. I well remember seeing, among the new selection of materials at Kirpa Ram's shop, a really fascinating material which the proprietor said was French (half the cloth shops of Asia used to buy the offcuts and remnants of material made in Europe). It was black, printed with sprays of flowers, and I yearned to buy a dress length of it and would certainly have done so except that (a) I couldn't afford it, and (b) I knew only too well that I hadn't the figure for it. However, it was just as well that I didn't buy it because next week I attended a cocktail party at which no fewer than *five* women turned up wearing dresses made from the same material. The first two had glared at each other like a pair of angry cats when number two entered, and a deathly and embarrassed silence fell when number three made her appearance; but when number four arrived there was a moment or two of stunned silence, and then the guests collapsed into shrieks of mirth. Then number five walked in, whereupon the shrieks redoubled; the unfortunate five laughing with the rest of us. In fact it made the whole party into a howling success — literally.

Returning from Kohat, Mother got her usual rapturous welcome from Angie, who had been left behind in the charge of Kadera, and later that year, when the snows melted and the almond trees made a pink froth in the valley, we moved back into a houseboat which we moored once again at the Moons' *ghat* at the end of their garden. The only drawback to a riverside mooring was the risk of floods; and once again, as a result of an exceptionally heavy monsoon at the beginning of June, the Jhelum river rose until, with appalling rapidity, we found ourselves dangerously near the top of the bund and looking down into what had once been the Moons' garden but was now an unkempt wilderness, because at some time during the winter their house had been destroyed by a fire that had left only the outer walls standing. Everything else had gone, and the ruined garden was now a shallow lake.

The Jhelum, according to the few newspapers that managed to get through, had risen over sixteen feet above its normal level, and seventy-five feet in the gorges, where it had ripped away a span of the Kohala Bridge. Both the Banihal and the Rawalpindi roads were flooded for several miles, and the papers reported that 'rocks and rafters are blocking the road at several places' — *Rafters*? What on earth do you suppose they meant by rafters? Logs? Roofs of houses? — No, I am not quoting from memory (I have a very good one, thank heaven, but it's not as good as all that!). I am quoting here from a couple of newspaper cuttings that Mother pasted alongside snapshots in her 1931 album. A later one says that 'a large number of motor vehicles, with stores and hundreds of passengers, are held up on the roads. So far no loss of life has been reported though much damage has been caused to property.'

They don't report that among the 'motor vehicles' held up in the valley (in the Moons' garden, actually, where they had been given asylum) were half the vehicles and members of a French expedition, sponsored and launched by Monsieur Citroën of Citroën cars, who had already pulled off a Trans-African crossing in a fleet of specially designed trucks, fore-runners of the Jeep and the Land Rover. That African crossing had been a wild success, and with a book and film about it, *The Black Journey*, already on sale, the enterprising French had decided to attempt an even more hazardous feat, this time by two expeditions: one would start from Syria and drive overland by the way of Kashmir and Gilgit to Kashgar, where they would meet up with the other lot, who were to set off from Peking. Both expeditions were filming as they went, and someone or other would be writing it all up, this time under the title of *La Croisière Jaune*, the 'Yellow Crossing' (China, Mongolia and the Gobi Desert), as a follow-up to the original 'Black Journey'.

The leader of the first Citroën expedition, and most of its top brass, including the official artist, were to do the toughest stretch, Syria to Kashgar, and it was they who were stranded in the Moons' garden on the other side of the bund from where we were moored. Never have I been angrier with myself for not learning to speak French when I was at school. It had never occurred to me that I should need to. It wasn't France I intended to make for when school was over, but India. Oh dear, how silly can one be? However, having instantly made friends with the stranded Citroën on the other side of our bund, I managed somehow, though only because their leader, Georges-Marie Haardt, his number two, Louis Audouin-Dubreuil, better known as 'Little Louie', the expedition's artist, Alexandre Yacovleff, a young Russian, and 'Waddy', Colonel Waddington (who was up in Srinagar again that season) all spoke enough English to cope with uneducated little twerps like me.

I don't remember if I have mentioned 'Waddy' before. He was a friend of the Moons and we had seen a lot of him when he had been visiting them in a previous summer. He was a Frenchman who spoke English like an Englishman, which was only natural, because his family had originally been English, and had emigrated to France in the seventeenth century. One of his forefathers had helped to hide Charles II — then only Prince Charles — in an oak tree on the family farm, after the Royalists were defeated at the Battle of Worcester.

It must have been after that that Waddy's ancestor fled to France, and when Charles came back to England as King, the ancestor was given a pension amounting to five pounds a year, 'in perpetuity', by the Government — in those days, quite a tidy sum, I gather! This 'pension' had been solemnly paid ever since, right up to the time of Waddy's father, though by then they had been French for generations. But Waddy's father, an unromantic type and obviously no historian, accepted an offer of a lump sum in lieu.

Anyway, Waddy was up that year, and naturally spending a lot of time with his compatriots. In fact, for as long as the French expedition was there he used our boat as a home from home, and there were always some of them parked on it, drinking and chatting. I was charmed when Tacklow told me that Little Louie had said my French was '*ver*' *ver*' bad!' but this didn't matter, because 'When she talk, she talk like a Frenchwoman — with her hands and her face; she make them speak for her.'

The young Russian, Alexandre, had a stack of paintings with him and we persuaded him to let us see some of them. He brought a huge portfolio to our boat one morning and gave us a private exhibition. It was wonderful. He had used tempera mostly, using white-of-egg as a medium because, he said, even in the wildest and remotest parts of the world, one could always get chickens. I have never seen anything quite like some of those pictures. They seemed to jump off the canvas at you; portraits of light-haired men and women who claimed descent from the Greek and

Macedonian captains and governors that Sikandar Dulkhan — Alexander the Great — had left behind him to hold the vast Empire he had conquered. Wrinkled faces of old, old men and smooth-cheeked young ones; pretty girls and grey-haired grandmothers; mountain people who had been born and lived all their lives in little, lost valleys that no westerner had ever heard of before.

Their faces looked back at one as though they were alive. And the larger canvases showed the country through which the expedition had come so brilliantly that afterwards you could almost swear that you had actually been there yourself and seen it with your own eyes. There were magical paintings of the smoky interiors of Mongolian *yurts*, crammed with duffel-clad figures huddled around a small cooking-fire; and others of men on small shaggy ponies, riding herd on a string of yaks and dwarfed to pygmies by the enormous size of the land they rode across — a vast plain streaked with patches of snow and rimmed along the far horizon by low barren hills, snow-topped and very far away.

The only sad thing about those pictures was that they very nearly drove me into throwing all my painting gear, pencils, paintboxes and blocks, into the Jhelum, and stopped me from painting for months afterwards. What on earth was the use of my messing about with producing my half-baked little pictures when there were artists like that around? Not in a hundred years could I *begin* to approach that standard. To this day, when I am writing a novel — even if it is only a whodunit — I never read anything by an author I really admire, or am afraid I may admire, because it puts me off my own.

Mike turned up again somewhat unexpectedly. He walked on to the boat one morning, looking a bit apprehensive and as if he wasn't sure of his reception. It was good to see him again, and more than good to find that I was still fond of him but not in the least bit in love with him any more. All that was over and done with, and we laughed ourselves into hysterics over that row and its results and ended up the best of friends. I introduced him to the members of the expedition, with whom he got on like a house on fire since, unlike me, his French was good enough to stand the strain. And the rest of the summer was a repeat of the picnics and bathing-parties and amateur theatricals of a typical Srinagar season.

A magnificent party was given at the City Palace for the Citroën Expedition, where *The Black Journey*, the film they had taken of their Trans-African crossing, was premièred. And later on in the year, all

Srinagar — or as many of its inhabitants and holiday-making visitors as could fight their way through the cheering crowds that lined the river-bank from His Highness the Maharajah's *ghat* at the turn of the river above the Club, down to the City — were given a magnificent spectacle as His Highness showed off his baby son and heir, who earlier that summer had been born in the South of France and was now being brought back by his parents to be shown to his people.

They came down the river in the glittering royal barge, escorted by a fleet of flower-decorated boats rowed by men in gold-trimmed uniforms, and accompanied by an armada of coloured *shikarras*. Her Highness the Maharani shimmered with gold brocade and tissue and sparkled with diamonds, while her tiny son, the centre of all this splendour, slept placidly on his mother's knee. We had a splendid view, having arrived early enough to stand against the wooden railing that surrounded the Club's pier, which was crowded by members, many standing on chairs and the ones at the back on tables. Bill was up on short leave at the time, and he and a friend of his, one Jeff Dimsey, were standing with Bets and myself, squashed up against the rail and leaning far out to watch the approaching boats, when a girl some way further up, and also leaning out as far as she could, turned her head and looked back at us. '*Wow!*' breathed Bill.

I did not know then that she would become one of the best of my friends; and although more than sixty years have passed since that sunny morning on the pier of the Srinagar Club, she still is. Bill, riveted, clutched my arm and said, 'Gosh, what a girl! Did you see her? I must find out who she is, Jeff. — did you see that smashing girl? I *must* find out who she is!'

'Yes,' agreed Jeff, apparently answering both questions, and equally smitten. Being a man of action, he turned and vanished into the packed masses of the crowd behind and around us. Which is why Bill never even got to first base with young Yda Reynolds — who, as it happened, had been totally unaware of my susceptible brother's admiring gaze, her own having been caught by Jeff Dimsey's equally smitten one — and by the fact that Jeff had burrowed through the crowd like a purposeful mole until he managed to end up just behind her, after which the rest was comparatively easy. To make this a better story, he should, of course, have married her and lived happily ever afterwards. But then Yda always had a whole set of suitors, and though she may have shown a momentary preference for Jeff, that was all it was — he ended up as just one of her many admirers. Bill for his part continued to adore, but by the time Jeff had been crossed off the list, he was back with his battery and that was that.

Odd, this attraction that she had, because she wasn't especially pretty: a little damsel, with dark curly hair and a figure not much better than my own, whom men fell for like ninepins and of whom women used to say, 'I can't think *what* they see in her!' Which was silly, because there was plenty to see. She played an excellent game of tennis and an equally good game of golf, and at the age of fifteen had been selected to represent Australia (the country in which she had been brought up by her grand-parents and gone to school) at the Olympic Games in both the junior tennis and the swimming and diving, and would have done so if her father had not refused to allow her to do any such thing, on the grounds that 'well-bred young ladies did not make public exhibitions of themselves'.

I have just been talking to her on the telephone, and getting the latest news of the progress of one of her granddaughters who is playing in the Junior Tennis Championships. Yda still resents the fact that she was done out of playing for Australia at the Olympics, and, when reminded of that day on the pier of the Srinagar Club, said that if she *had* a preference, she thinks it was for Bill rather than Jeff, but that she didn't take either of them seriously. Poor deluded young chumps.

Later that month there was another glittering ball in the Old Palace; this time in honour of His Highness's birthday. Having heard that a fabulous price had been paid in order to persuade the most famous *nautch*-girl in all India to travel to Kashmir and entertain the guests for the occasion, I had been looking forward to seeing this famous lady. But as the evening wore on, I could see no sign of anyone who looked spectacular enough to fill the bill, so I latched on to one of His Highness's ADCs and demanded to be told what had happened to the celebrity. Had she missed the train or the plane or been held up by a landslide? No, no. Nothing like that, my handsome young friend assured me. She was here all right, but her performance was strictly for men only.

It needed a lot of coaxing, but in the end I managed to inveigle the poor man into letting me have just a peep. And that was all it was. He hurried me down a series of red-carpeted corridors and stopped by a door from behind which came the sounds of sitar and tabla accompanying a shrill Indian soprano, punctuated by and almost lost in roars of male laughter. The door-keeper, looking startled and disapproving, began to protest in a hushed whisper, and after a brief colloquy, and the passing of something that I took to be a five-rupee note, he opened the door just wide enough for me to stick my head inside . . .

So *this* was why there was such a shortage of Englishmen on the ballroom floor and in the rooms immediately surrounding it! I had thought they must have become bored or drunk too much champagne, and left early. But here they all were — or far too many of them, anyway — laughing their heads off at the most famous *nautch*-girl in India, and clapping almost every word she said. As for the 'dancing-girl' herself, she may have been pretty once, but now, to my young eyes, she was just a fat old woman bundled up in a glittery sari over a Rajputana-style skirt, lavishly embroidered with gold thread and spangles, that stopped just above her ankles; her feet were bare below jingling anklets, and like the lady who rode a white horse to Banbury Cross, she had 'rings on her fingers and bells on her toes' — and more in her ears and her nose as well. As for her dancing, it was restricted by the fact that she had a brought a small carpet with her, one that couldn't have been larger than the average bathmat, and she never moved off it. Standing on it, she stamped and shimmied and swung her massive hips so that her skirts whirled and undulated to the twanging of the sitar and the thumping of the tabla. Her arms and her bejewelled neck did more dancing than her stamping feet, and the movements of her eyes and chin and those supple, elegant hands were a marvel to behold.

I haven't got a good enough ear to appreciate Indian music, and, perhaps fortunately, my Hindustani was no longer good enough to take in more than a fraction of the words she was singing, for they were undoubtedly not of the kind that Mother would have approved. But her strictly male audience, which included His Highness and every man, Indian or British, who could manage to sneak off while his womenfolk were not looking, were literally mopping their eyes and rocking in their seats with laughter. And from that brief look at her I realized that however much she had been paid for her performance she was worth every anna of it. I wish I could have seen more of it, but my agitated young friend tugged at my arm and pulled me back after a mere minute or two, and hurried me back along the corridors to the ballroom.

I was aware that a lot of correspondence was going on between Tacklow and Mother's friends and relations in China about our move there, and was relieved to learn that there was no chance of our booking one of the

Brysons' bungalows at Pei-tai-ho that summer, or of getting a passage to Shanghai and Tientsin that would land us up there at the right time of year — Mother did not fancy getting involved with the typhoon season, and I don't blame her. And though Tacklow, if he had had the choice, would have left at once, our departure for China was eventually arranged for the spring of the following year, when a bungalow at Pei-tai-ho would be at our disposal for the summer — and for as many of the following summers as we chose — and a passage booked on a China-going ship at a time that would miss the freezing North China winters, and land us in Shanghai at the best time of year to fit in with visits to those of Mother's relations whom she particularly wanted to see.

I still had a whole year stretching out before me — more than a full year. A whole summer and part of autumn in Kashmir, and after that a cold weather season in Delhi. Why worry about anything after that? I had a wonderful summer.

ꗂ That party, plus a final cabaret show and dinner-dance at Nedou's, and Bets's birthday on 13 October, for which Ken Hadow again laid on a party at the Hadows' hut in Gulmarg, brought the Kashmir season to a close for us.

The summer visitors had already begun to leave in droves as the nights became colder and the snow-line crept downward across Apharwat. And now the long avenue of Lombardy poplars leading from Srinagar to Barramulla turned from green to gold, and Mother, Bets and I, who with Tacklow and Angie would be among the last to leave, were out with our paintboxes nearly every day. I have never been able to decide whether the valley was more beautiful in autumn than in spring. Spring in the valley was Paradise regained. But then autumn can be spectacular, for the grass and the poplars turn gold and the willows bright yellow, and with the first touch of frost the leaves on the chenars turn every shade of red from scarlet to magenta, and all this gorgeous bonfire of colour blazes up against a background of chalk-white snow-peaks and a deep blue sky.

ꗂ We left Kashmir in early November, without knowing when, if ever, we should see it again. And this was one time when I would have welcomed sullen skies, a whingeing wind and spitting rain, not only because it suited my mood, but because it would have made saying goodbye to the valley easier. Instead, Kashmir chose to give us a royal send-off with one of its most brilliant days. The kind of day that stays fresh in your mind for ever.

The snow-peaks glittered against a cloudless sky, and there was just enough breeze to make the last of the poplar leaves flutter down and carpet our road with gold coins. The whole valley sang with colour and the red and orange and gold of the leaves that flickered and floated down in the brilliant air in a ballet of colour seemed to dance to the strings of an unseen orchestra. Every yard of the road was beautiful that morning. I could not help wondering if anything in China could possibly compare with this.

Chapter 33

~❧❧❦~

We left Kashmir by the Banihal route because the Baramulla one was blocked, and we stopped at the last turn on that long zig-zag road that leads to the tunnel near the crest of the pass, through which one leaves the valley. We climbed out and walked back to stand by the low stone wall that edged the road, to look down at the red and gold valley that now lay so far below us. Bets and I were probably sharing the same thought: would we ever come back? And Tacklow and Mother, at a guess, were thinking of a future in the country where their married life had begun, Tacklow thankful to be leaving a country in which he felt he had been publicly disgraced for one in which he had been so blissfully happy.

I don't remember that any of us said anything. We just looked for about five minutes, then got into the cars again and drove through the tunnel and down another twisting, winding, zig-zagging road on the other side of the mountain and away to the plains, where after a night or two on the way we reached the same flat-roofed bungalow, 80/1 The Mall, which Tacklow had once again rented for us for the Delhi season.

Burma Shell happened to have set up a chummery in Old Delhi that year, and since one of the members, Oliver de St Croix (known to one and all as 'Crux'), was a particular friend of ours, almost as soon as we arrived we found ourselves involved in a round of parties. That was the gayest of seasons, a last merry-go-round of fun and party-going.

It began with a staid dinner party, hosted by Crux, which proved to be a launching-pad from which other parties proliferated. At one of the earliest of these, given by the members of the Burma Shell Chummery in Underhill Lane, Old Delhi, Bets met, and fell instantly in love with, one of its members, W. H. Pardey, a tall rugger-playing type with a Bulldog Drummond moustache, known to his friends as 'Cecil', though that was not his name. It was, however, Tacklow's name. As far as Mother was concerned there was only one Cecil, so she jibbed at having another one as a constant caller at 80/1 and demanded to know why he was always called 'Cecil' when his initials were W. H.? The explanation, blithely given by a member of his chummery, was that the young Pardey had acquired the nickname of 'Cess' because he was credited by his little schoolmates with having 'a mind like a cesspool'. This was not, as you may have imagined, well received.

This unfortunate nickname had followed him out to India, where someone, hearing him hailed as 'Cess' by a chum, leapt to the conclusion that his Christian name must be Cecil. And since no one had bothered to correct it, 'Cecil' he became. And would have remained, if Mother had not flatly refused to use it. Tacklow thought it was all rather funny, and pointed out to her that a cavalry general of their acquaintance had originally been introduced to him, many years earlier when Tacklow was doing an attachment to his regiment, with the unforgettable words, 'And this chap, if you can believe it, rejoices in the name of Offley Bohun Stovin Fairless Shaw. But you don't have to let that worry you, because we always call him "Stinker".'*

Mother refused to be amused, and told Bets that if she was going to spend most of her time dancing and picnicking and playing tennis in this young man's company, she had better decide on what she wanted us to call him, because 'Cecil' was *out*. And if Bets thought that it was time her parents stopped calling him 'Mr Pardey', when all the other young men she knew were addressed, or referred to, by their Christian names, then what did his *family* call him? 'Bill,' said Bets — in a '*so there!*' tone of voice. Those initials stood for 'William Henry', and Mother objected to using Bill — or William either — on the grounds that she would never be sure which Bill (or William) was being referred to. It would have to be Henry. She had a shot at it the next time he was around (which was practically every minute of his out-of-office hours) and encountered an obstinacy equal to her own.

Our Mr Pardey — or rather *Bets's* Mr Pardey — had no intention of answering to the name of Henry. It seems he had an uncle or a cousin or someone named Henry with whom he was not on speaking terms and disliked intensely: something to that effect. I forget the details, but 'Henry'

* Offley, more often called 'Offley Boffley', married an enchanting little American, whose letters to him over a period of many years soldiering in the Empire have recently been published under the title *An Enchanted Journey*.

was a non-starter, and that was that. Mother compromised by deciding to call him by his initials, and he became 'W. H. P.' from then on. I suspect he resented this, though he never said so: at least it put him apart from the Toms, Kens, Sammys, Johns, Jimmys et al. with whom Bets went out dancing and picnicking every night of that light-hearted season.

There had always been as many, if not more, young men than girls around during those summer seasons in Kashmir, most of them footloose and fancy-free, and on leave. So all one had to do was to pair up with a temporary 'summertime soul-mate', collect a gang of like-minded friends, and in their company enjoy oneself in one of the loveliest and most romantic settings that anyone could dream of. Never mind that there were wars and rumours of wars in far-away Europe, and that people were beginning to talk about a man called Hitler and laugh at another called Mussolini. We were young and in love with love; and Noël Coward wrote a song that said it all for all of us, about not regretting past happiness or fun that didn't last. Anyway, some of the fun did last and ended in a haze of orange-blossom and wedding bells and (we hoped) 'happy-ever-after'. Some led to broken hearts and high words, but the majority were remembered with deep affection and no regrets. So I didn't realize until very late in the day that Bets was seriously taken with W. H. P. And also of course, because he wasn't my type at all, I didn't really see him, except superficially and in passing, and thought that Bets was still playing the field and that W. H. P. would just be a pleasant memory to take with her when we sailed for China in the spring.

Bets, however, had fallen in head-first at the deep end. And I suppose she had some excuse, for she had always had a weakness for men with moustaches (I preferred them clean-shaven myself) and when she met him he was convalescing from some operation or other — kidney, she thinks — which had led him to losing a lot of weight. He was a big man who needed to watch his weight and did not always do so. But he was looking his very best when Bets first saw him, and she says that the minute she laid eyes on him she thought, '*Oh*, what a *gorgeous* man!' And was lost. I don't think I can have been paying much attention, because it was at that same party that I was introduced to a charming, high-spirited young *box-wallah* by the name of Neil Pierce, who turned out to be a friend of W. H. P.'s — they had often played against each other in Madras, where both had been members of their respective firms' rugger teams.

Neil was the greatest fun, and would, we thought, have made excellent

Nageem Bagh Navy material. We collected a 'gang' in time-honoured fashion, and manoeuvred in company, as the NBN had done two years earlier, attending the various seasonal gaieties *en masse* — the Christmas party at the Club, the Horse Show and the Horse Show Ball, the fancy-dress ball and the Bachelors' Ball, and the Saturday night dances. And every Sunday, after morning service at 'Sikandar-Sahib's' Church, St James's by the Kashmir Gate, Neil, W. H. P., Bets and I would make for whatever spot had been arranged to picnic, where we would meet the others and spend the rest of the day. Sunday was always picnic day. But whenever the moon was full we arranged a moonlight picnic, or, if that was not possible, then the night before or just after it was full, either at Tuglukabad or, preferably, Haus Khas, the ruined remains of a tank and a college built in the reign of the Emperor Feroz Shah.

Those moonlight picnics, like the ones at Chasma Shai in Kashmir, were pure magic, accompanied by the sugar-sweet melodies of a wind-up gramophone in the enormous night silence of a moonlit world that had not yet become too besotted by petrol-driven engines, aeroplanes and transistor radios blaring out rock-'n'-roll. And where, when no gramophone was playing and no one happened to be talking, you could hear the breeze whispering through the broken sandstone and marble tracery of buildings that had in their day been part of great cities and centres of learning. Better still, when the moon was low, one could see the stars as our children and grandchildren will never see them: clear and sharp and sparkling in a sky that even in dusty India was, compared to today's, still almost free from pollution.

Our numbers at these parties were seldom more than fourteen, at most, and six at the least, though now and again someone would dream up a 'treasure-hunt' party, which involved anything up to and even over twenty-four. And on one occasion — the fancy-dress ball during Horse Show Week — at least eight or nine men got together and hired the Lodi Golf Club's sitting-room and dining-room for a dinner party before the ball, and decreed that everyone should go as a cowboy or a cowgirl. In those days the Club House was one of the least ruined of the ruins that were scattered all over the plains around Delhi and could have been part of a king's palace, or a pavilion for his *zenana*. It was an unlikely setting for eighteen to twenty palefaces dolled up as cowboys and their girls.

It was a hilarious party, and the hosts had hired *tongas* to take the party out to the dance. Paper cowboy hats and sheriffs' stars (both easily obtainable from shops in the bazaar that sold carnival junk), were provided for the *tonga* drivers, who entered with enthusiasm into the spirit of the thing, and the entire party arrived at the IDG, whirling ropes or banging toy guns and whooping at the top of their voices, with the *tonga-wallahs* racing each other to arrive first.

I'd had a lot of fun concocting a very fetching cowgirl outfit from white American cloth (boots, belt, cuffs and hat) with a white flannel skirt cut to look like fringed leather, and about a million little silver metal stationery studs which I used for the nail-head decoration on the belt and its holsters, and on the cuffs and the band round the hat. Very taking it was, too. Neil concocted a white outfit for himself, complete with toy revolvers, and we made a nice pair.

Another of our fancy-dress parties was far less successful. Bill had managed to wangle himself some leave and, having joined us at 80/1, collected himself a girl in record time — Pam Cosgrave, the eldest daughter of great friends of my parents who were temporarily stationed in Delhi. The six of us, chaperoned by Mother, had spent a weekend in Agra, from where we arrived back in the late evening just in time to bathe, change and eat a hasty dinner, before leaving for the Old Delhi Club. But we had failed to read the small print on the leaflet that advertised the ball, in particular a brief announcement towards the end of the leaflet that said, 'Fancy dress optional'.

Well, most women enjoy dressing up in exotic costumes, but the average man shrinks into his shell like a startled hermit-crab at the very idea of 'making a fool of himself parading about in spangles and a ruff, or whatever' — much as they enjoy themselves once they have been bullied into it! So one and all, they had grabbed the lifeline offered by that one word, and chickened out. And minus their loved ones' support, the women had decided, 'I can't go all togged up as Mary Queen of Scots when George insists on wearing a dinner-jacket and a black tie!' and they too had tamely followed suit and worn the old blue taffeta again. Our party, arriving late at the Club just as the second or third item on the dance-programmes was finishing, walked out in all our glory on to the raised platform at the entrance to the ballroom. To be faced by a crowd of around 200 soberly clad dancers and received by a roar of laughter and a storm of cheers and hand-clapping. We were the only people in fancy dress!

Poor Pam was the one who suffered most. She was new to Delhi, and since she hadn't got a fancy dress and could not spare the time to have one made for her, Mother had lent her one that she had worn early on in the days of the First World War. She had gone as Autumn, wearing her opals, complete with tiara, and a dress made of leaves cut from cotton cloth, and shading from green through orange to yellow to varying shades of red. Mother had painted each leaf herself, and it had fitted her then fashionable hourglass figure like a glove, as far as the hip, below which there had been a full skirt of tulle, spangled with tiny beads and ending just above the ankle — very saucy, for Edwardian days. The tulle had perished years ago, but we had kept the exquisite bodice for our dressing-up box, and now produced it for Pam, on whom it reached just above the knee. The whole effect was charming, but exceedingly skimpy, though it showed off Pam's long and lovely legs a treat. But she was a shy child, only just out of school, and finding herself standing there, 'half-naked' as she protested on the verge of tears, being uproariously applauded by a ballroom full of women in floor-length dresses and openly appreciative men in dinner-jackets, all yelling with laughter, she turned, scarlet-faced, and bolted like a rabbit for the Ladies' room, followed, to the Gents', by a red-faced Neil, disguised as the Knave of Hearts in an equally scanty costume that we had made for Sandy Napier and which he had sub-sequently donated to the Kaye dressing-up box. Grabbing his overcoat, our cowardly knave (normally a terrific extrovert) took refuge in our parked car where the rest of us hastily joined him.

You would have thought after all that that we would have given up and gone to bed. Not at all. The young us are appallingly resilient, and all that happened was that W. H. P. drove us back to 80/1, where he dropped three Kayes and a Cosgrave before streaking back to the chummery, where he and Neil swapped their motley for dinner-jackets before returning to pick us up, now more conventionally clad (Pam borrowed an evening dress off one of us), and take us back to the Club. Here we rejoined our friends and danced until the band packed up sometime in the small hours, when the sky began to turn grey and snuff out the stars, and the yawning *khitmatgars* served a lavish British breakfast of ham and eggs, imported sausages, toast and marmalade and cups and cups of tea or coffee. Then the tougher half of the revellers made for their homes or the Club dressing-rooms to change into riding clothes and drive off, as the sky turned primrose yellow, to join a meet of the Delhi Hunt at some previously designated spot in the empty, ruin-strewn lands that stretched away from left to right of the Mall, where their horses and their *syces* would be waiting for them. You can see that the Raj took its amusements, and the more energetic of its exercises, seriously. Thank goodness I have no use for horses.

Tacklow laughed his head off at our account of sweeping into the Old Delhi Club to find ourselves faced by a sea of the correctly clad members of the Establishment, and he told me a fascinating story of his early years in Simla and a fancy-dress ball at Viceregal House.

Cards of invitation to any Viceregal function were valued above rubies among certain members of the social-climbing set, some of whom went to extraordinary lengths to wangle one of the coveted invitations, while others were quite capable of leaving Simla, ostensibly on holiday or to visit friends, rather than let it be seen that they had not been invited. It was impossible to gatecrash the average Viceregal bash, since a printed table plan was issued to each guest. Only at the annual fancy-dress ball, which was a buffet-supper affair for which private dinner parties would be held all over Simla, was it possible for the uninvited to gatecrash, and one year, said Tacklow, after all the invitations were out and every *darzi* in Simla had worked like mad, when the great day came round, news was received that some truly royal Royal had died and all festivities must be cancelled. There were only hours to go before the guests were due to arrive, but by around tea-time every guest had been warned, and the exhausted staff were congratulating themselves on a job well done.

Aware that they had missed no one, they were therefore unprepared for the arrival of several rickshaws pulling up before Viceregal Lodge and decanting passengers in fancy dress at about the time when, but for that eleventh-hour cancellation, the main flood of guests would have been arriving. What *do* you say, when you arrive at a party to which you were not invited, all dressed up as Mephistopheles, complete with scarlet tights and cloak and a crêpe-hair beard, or Madame de Pompadour in a white wig and twenty yards of petunia satin and spangles?

✶ The Delhi season ended for us with another ball at Viceroy's House, after which Mother and I got mentioned in the social column of the newspaper write-up next morning, as 'looking charming (me) in a delightful ball-gown of green satin' (actually, last year's model, courtesy of our verandah *darzi*, who had lengthened it by tacking on a wide hem of mosquito netting dyed to match) and Mother 'looking as young and as pretty as ever in black chiffon-velvet'. Mother was very chuffed! So was I, because it was the first time I had ever been mentioned in the society column. And the last, as far as I remember. Bets's dress didn't rate a mention, so posterity will have to get along without knowing if it was her old pink or the one with spots on. But she danced every dance, mostly with W. H. P., and announced the next day at breakfast that she was engaged to him.

Well, it wasn't exactly a surprise, considering that she had spent almost every available moment in his company during the past two or three months, but Tacklow, who had only seen us *en masse*, so to speak, and hadn't really noticed which young man out of the half-dozen or so in our particular set was attached to whom, was distinctly taken aback. Not that he had anything against W. H. P., or had ever considered him as a possible husband for his younger daughter. For me, perhaps: but not for Bets. I think he must have tried to discuss her choice of chap with Bets. But she was so tremendously happy that it wouldn't have been the least use trying to get her feet back on to solid ground. So he discussed it with me instead, because he presumed that I must have seen almost as much of W. H. P. recently as Bets had.

Well, I had, of course — though only superficially. So I assured my anxious parent that W. H. P. would make an excellent husband for Bets, for they had so many things in common. Bets liked parties and ballroom dancing. So did W. H. P. She liked playing tennis and golf, and going to the cinema; she liked to paint pictures and do pastel portraits, and she liked to play the piano and accompany W. H. P., who had rather a good voice. He admired her artistic talent, her skill on the piano and the tennis court; and as for Bets, she not only thought him fantastically good-looking, but on top of having all their tastes in common, she was wildly in love with him. What more could an anxious father want in a prospective son-in-law?

Tacklow said that he was glad to hear all that, and if I had been W. H. P.'s choice it wouldn't have worried him so much. When I wanted to know why, he said that I was a lot tougher than Bets, that Bets was too gentle, and that he suspected that young Pardey was a bully. I remember laughing at that and explaining that he had been taken in by W. H. P.'s expression, which was inclined to be slightly sneering and superior, as though he were permanently looking down his nose at people. It had put me off him too when I first met him, but he had always been nice to me — and so obviously devoted to Bets — that I came to the conclusion (which I still think is true) that he suffered from an inferiority complex, probably acquired from discovering, on his arrival in India, that he was a *box-wallah*, and that except in such centres of trade as Calcutta and Madras, where the *box-wallah* is king, occupied one of the lowest rungs of the social ladder. That superior sneer was, I thought, a reaction to this discovery that had become a form of nervous tic.

I did my best to reassure Tacklow and, I have to admit it, myself. Because that sneer had worried me too. Somehow it didn't fit in with all the rest. But when you have partied and danced and picnicked, laughed and had fun, discussed politics, life, art and theology, books and all the 'isms' of the age, day after day for weeks on end with the same group of people, you accept them all as 'us' — friends, in fact. Even when they don't agree with you. And anyway, I was half-way in love with Neil Pierce, and wondering what I was going to do about it.

The day didn't end so well, for as soon as his office closed that evening W. H. P. arrived to break the news that Bets had already given us at breakfast, and to ask Tacklow for permission to marry his younger daughter. The two of them, father and suitor, disappeared into Tacklow's study to discuss the position, and emerged after a shortish interval with Tacklow looking rather taken aback, to tell us what had been decided. To begin with, there was no question of a wedding taking place for at least another two years, by which time W. H. P.'s salary would be enough to support a wife, and his seniority enable him to qualify for a married quarter. This meant, since we would be sailing for China in the spring, that he and Bets would not be able to see each other for a considerable time. But at the end of it, he would come to China for the wedding, and they could return to India together on honeymoon. In the meantime, they would like the announcement of their engagement to be sent to the *Civil and Military Gazette* and the *Statesman*, to make it official. There was the usual party on that evening — I rather think it was a supper party at the Underhill Lane Chummery, followed by a visit to the Kashmir Gate Cinema (known to all as the Flea Pit). All I can be sure of is that on arrival at the chummery, Bets and W. H. P., full of the joys of spring, announced their engagement to the assembled company, and that at some time that evening, Neil, caught up in the general euphoria of the occasion, proposed that he and I should follow their example and announce ours.

Had he put the idea to me a few days earlier — or even a few days later — I might have agreed. But as it was, I felt sure that marriage hadn't even crossed Neil's mind until that evening, and that he was, in effect, only copy-catting his friend Cecil's behaviour, the 'if Cecil can do this, cheered on by one and all, then why not me?' reaction. I may be maligning him, but I still don't think so. Anyway, the thought made me step back from the brink, and demand more time to think it over.

I was not given it, for the very next day Neil rang me up from his office to give me the dire news that Head Office was transferring him to Rawalpindi, to take the place of one of their men who had to be sent away on sick-leave. He had been given only two days in which to pack and make arrangements to leave Delhi and that was that. I have forgotten who laid on the party we attended that night, but I do remember that it was another moonlight picnic, this time at Humayun's tomb. Also that our numbers had already begun to shrink drastically with the coming of the hot weather. Pairs were being split up. Bill, for instance, had returned to his battery on the Frontier and Pam had left with her parents for, I think, Assam; and now Neil too would be leaving us. The boys and girls who had joined forces to 'come out to play' at the beginning of the Delhi season would soon be scattered. But tonight 'the moon was shining bright as day' for them, and Humayun's tomb had never looked more entrancing.

It is strange to think that of all the boys and girls in our party who came out to play on that moonlight night, only Bets and myself still survive. And also that no one will ever again see the tomb and its gardens as we saw it then, and as it was to remain for the best part of another three decades. The plain beyond its guardian wall was empty space, dotted with kikar-trees and camel thorn and the romantic traces of other cities of the plain — the 'Seven Cities of Delhi' that had been built long centuries ago, and had each in turn crumbled into ruins and been forgotten. That was half the charm of Humayun's tomb. Its loneliness. But it is lonely no longer. The last time I saw it it stood against a background of tall modern buildings, the beginnings of factories, a railway station — that, admittedly *had* been there in the old days, but only the lines and a signal box and a small, unobtrusive platform at which the mail trains did not stop. Now another suburb of Delhi has grown up about it, and there was telegraph and telephone wires with the usual untidy tangle of electric-light wires, illegally looped from the mains and fed into numerous jerry-built sheds, shops and *bustees* (slums).

But on that last moonlight picnic of the dying season the plain seemed to stretch away emptily to the horizon, and at intervals, from somewhere far out on that moonlit waste, the inevitable jackal-pack would wail in the silence. I still have a clear mental picture of the tomb, and of Neil and myself strolling arm-in-arm around the wide, white marble platform, on which the central building and the dome stand, while he tried to persuade me to become engaged to him. He admitted that he hadn't thought of proposing to me until W. H. P. and Bets announced their engagement, because he knew that he couldn't afford to marry me for several years, and I was about to leave for China — possibly indefinitely. But W. H. P.'s argument had been that he had more chance of marrying Bets if she was known to be engaged to him, and their engagement had been announced in two newspapers in India and another two in England, than if they merely 'had an understanding'. Bets was bound to meet a lot of other men in China, and before she left he wanted to stick a label on her announcing that she was already spoken for — so hands off!

Well, he was to be proved right there. But I was not persuaded. My argument was that since we would have to wait a minimum of two years — possibly more — it was much better to leave the question open. If we were still in love in two years' time, well, obviously we were *really* in love, not merely in love with love. So in the end we left it like that. For which I have always been grateful, though Bets couldn't understand it. She had seen what she wanted, and she wanted to make sure of it. How *could* I take such chances? Neil was so good-looking, and such fun, and even if, as Tacklow insisted, India was *bound* to become independent in the foreseeable future, if we were both married to *box-wallahs* — whose pay and prospects were, incidentally, a good deal better than those of the armed forces! — we should still be able to stay in India; for although the British would have to leave, lock, stock and barrel, including the 'Heaven-born', men 'in trade' would still be expected to stay and represent their firms, and compete with other countries to sell their products.

I admit I hadn't thought of that, and it was a powerful argument in Neil's favour. Especially with China looming up ahead. And I did waver slightly when, on the following night, we all went down to the Old Delhi station to see Neil off to Rawalpindi on the Frontier Mail. I wept a bit after he'd gone, and missed him dreadfully during the week or two that was left before we ourselves took the same train in the opposite direction.

Earlier in the season, Mother had paid a last visit to Tonk, leaving

Tacklow to keep a parental eye on Bets and me. She went to collect all the luggage that had been left there in storage after Tacklow's abrupt departure, and was put up in the State Guest House where it seems they all came to see her, the Begum and several minor begums (all of whom hugged her and wept all over her), poor Nunni-mia, who also would soon lose that title, and a number of state officials and their wives who had been our friends. Even Saadat came, alone except for the driver of his car, and after dark on the night she was leaving; looking incredibly sheepish and mumbling incoherent apologies — it was all a mistake! A terrible mistake — he had never intended, etc., etc. He too had eventually wept genuine tears before hurrying away. Tacklow would probably have melted, but not Mother. She never forgave him.

The notice of Bets's engagement duly appeared in the appropriate columns of the *Civil and Military Gazette* and the *Statesman*, and the days got hotter and dustier and there were no more 'group' parties or picnics. Our few remaining 'pairs', such as W. H. P. and Bets, still patronized the Club dances and the cinema, but nowadays when they went out on the town of an evening, they went strictly *à deux*. And now that Neil had left, I spent most of my time packing up for the approaching move, and wondering if I hadn't made a dire mistake in refusing to commit myself to marrying Neil. I missed him badly. He was a darling, loaded with good temper and charm, and with none of his friend W. H. P.'s complexes and chip-on-shoulder moods. I never saw him in a bad temper, and if he had a fault, it was that he was almost too cheerful and light-hearted. Life was a terrific joke to him, and he could always find something in any situation to laugh at. You could not see him as a successful tycoon in embryo, and I don't imagine that he had much in the way of brain or any ambition to become a captain of industry. His ambition (if any) was to have fun, and his motto was 'Watch and Pray, and it'll come right one day!' A cheerful youth. But not quite what I was looking for. What *was* I looking for? I didn't really know, and all that I was certain of was that I would know when my love came along.

Our packing was finished, the back verandah was piled with trunks, suitcases and assorted boxes, each one sewn tightly into a covering of *tart*, which is India's name for sacking, on which Mother had painted our name and destination in white oil paint. She always insisted on this, on the grounds that she had seen too many pieces of luggage dropped while being unloaded on to stone docks, to explode like a bomb as every lock and hinge broke, scattering the contents among the crowd of dock coolies who considered these bits and pieces as a gift from heaven, and immediately swiped the lot. Mother's boxes might be dropped, but they never exploded, because *tart* is the toughest of tough material; and though the box it was sewn around might be reduced to the consistency of porridge, it was still all there, and practically unlootable.

The packing had been finished just in time, for Delhi put on one of its most tiresome tricks by the way of wishing us farewell — a dust-storm that seemed to lift up every grain of sand in the sandy wilderness in which our little house stood, whirling it away in a howling smother in which one could neither see nor breathe, only to drop it down some ten or twenty miles away, when it grew tired of carrying it. We spent our last morning sitting indoors with every door and window closed — not that this ever kept much of the stuff out, and our last afternoon was spent sweeping as much of the debris as we could out of the empty rooms.

The Bombay Mail left Delhi in the evening, and Kadera and Mahdoo helped load the luggage on to a fleet of *tongas* which they accompanied to the station ahead of us. Mother said a sad goodbye to Angie, whom she was leaving in the care of Kadera — he being the only one of the servants whom she consented to be nice to — and we were off. To be met by a pleasant surprise, for when we reached the station we found various friends of ours had got together and planned a terrific farewell party for us on the departure platform, complete with a bar loaded with glasses and bottles of assorted drinks, soft for the Indians and alcoholic for the British, and attended by several uniformed *khitmatgars*.

All our Indian friends had brought garlands of flowers and tinsel with them which they put round our necks, and the party had obviously started without us, for in spite of the sadness of the occasion, everyone seemed to be in the best of spirits, and the only person missing from the scene was W. H. P. Not to worry, said a member of the chummery bracingly; he'd be along any moment now. He was only meeting a friend on the Frontier Mail which pulled in at another platform on another side of the station just before we arrived. Ah, here he was — ! And with him was a wild-eyed young man who broke into a run at the sight of me, caught me into his arms and kissed me with considerable fervour.

It was Neil of course. And no wonder he looked dishevelled, for he had spent a night and day in an overcrowded carriage on the Frontier Mail. And, what's more, he would have to catch the return Mail train that evening in order to get back to Rawalpindi in time to turn up at his office on the next day but one. I still regard this gesture as the greatest compliment I have ever been paid. For it was not only the discomfort of that long and dusty journey, and the fact that almost as soon as our train left he would have to board one that took him back to 'Pindi, but the fact that he had laid his job on the line by taking two days' leave 'off the record', and, on top of everything else, had kissed a girl in public, before a pop-eyed audience of scores of his friends and acquaintances, and a vast crowd of interested third-class travellers whose code of morals outlawed kissing except in strict privacy.

That gesture of Neil's must have taken considerable courage, for, extrovert as he was, he was also very much a young man of his time and class, and Englishmen did not make an exhibition of themselves in front of all their friends, let alone a shocked crowd of strangers. Embarrassed as I was, I had the sense to realize that I had been paid an enormous compliment.

I don't remember what I or anyone else said or did after that. It was all a confused memory of garlands of flowers and prickly tinsel around my neck, and the ranks closing in, laughing and fooling, turning it all into a joke. I remember saying goodbye to Kadera and Mahdoo and finding that I had tears in my eyes, and Kadera, who missed nothing, telling me not to worry because I would surely be back — 'for if not, why should the Lady-Sahib have left the *chota bandar* (little monkey) with him, instead of letting her loose?' The Burra-Sahib, said Kadera, did not wish to return; and who could blame him? And because he did not, he had made arrangements that each month he and Mahdoo would call at the bank in Srinagar where they would receive pension money from the head sahib there, which would enable them to live comfortably. But he, Kadera, and Mahdoo also, did not believe that they would draw it for very long, because it was said in the bazaar by the *Chinni-wallahs* (the Chinese merchants from beyond the passes who traded between India and China by the old Silk Road that Marco Polo had used) that the Chinni folk, having abolished their King and overthrown their rulers, were now fighting each other as to who should rule. The Burra-Sahib would see for himself when he got there; and since no man with a family to care for would wish to live for long in a country torn by war, he would come back to

Kashmir, where he, Kadera, and Mahdoo and Angi-*bandar*, would be waiting.

I didn't read the newspapers in those days. There were too many other far more pleasant things to do; and anyway headlines were always either alarming or depressing. So Kadera's information about trouble in China was news to me and, far from being daunted by it, I could only hope it was true; provided that it led to our speedy return to Kashmir. Cheered by Kadera's confident predictions, and with my self-esteem considerably boosted by Neil's spectacular 3,000-mile dash from 'Pindi to Delhi and back again, just to say goodbye and 'bon voyage', I boarded the train in far better spirits than I had expected.

Neil, who had stuck as close as he could to me for the short time that remained, jumped up into the carriage and managed to ask me briefly if I had changed my mind. And once again, for about a minute, I admit I wavered, remembering that my parents liked him — he was exactly the type of blond, clean-living, rugger-playing, 'What-ho, chaps!' young Englishman that mothers feel their daughters would be safe with — and I would be able to stay on in India, as Bets, too, would eventually be doing. Better still, with both of us married and settled for life, Tacklow and Mother would be free to retire whenever they liked — in England, China or Kashmir . . . They wouldn't have to worry about us any more.

But it was no good. If marriages were expected to last for only a couple of years (as, worse luck, they seem to now), I wouldn't have hesitated, since a couple of years with Neil would be the greatest fun. But a lifetime of 'What ho, chaps! watch and pray!' until death did us part? No, no and *no*! *Darling* Neil, I was so sorry. So *very* sorry. But the answer had to be 'No'.

'I was afraid of that,' said Neil gloomily. He kissed me again, regardless of the scandalized ethnic majority on the platform, and as the train guard forced his way through the crowd and indicated that he was about to blow his whistle or wave his flag, or both, Bets got an equally fervent farewell embrace from W. H. P. and was pushed up the step into the carriage, followed by Mother and Tacklow. Glasses were raised to us by the revellers on the platform, someone started to sing: 'Should auld acquaintance be forgot' and everyone else took it up. I didn't hear the whistle blown, but I saw the guard waving his flag and as the train began to move Neil ran alongside it and yelled, 'You will write, won't you?' and I yelled back, 'Of course I will!' And then those members of the goodbye party who had started their drinking before we arrived at the station, or perhaps were just naturally high-spirited, started to run with the train too, while Bets and I leant out waving and calling goodbyes, and several members of the party pelted us with the streamers that are thrown around at New Year's parties. It was quite a send-off.

When we could see our well-wishers no more, Bets and I turned our attention to the view outside the windows, and I think both of us sent a silent farewell to places we had known since childhood, and had said goodbye to once before when we were leaving India to go to boarding-school in England, not knowing whether we would ever come back. Well, we had done so. And now we were leaving again for another unknown land. But at least we had both Tacklow and Mother with us this time, and were not going to be abandoned for years on end. But would I come back a second time? That was the question . . . Oh, please God, let me come back!

�֍ When we woke the next morning we were in a different world. The south. The train wound through the long, breathtakingly beautiful canyon that is called the Ghats, and which nowadays few visitors and no tourists ever see, because it is easier and quicker to fly. A few hours later we were being shown to our rooms in the hotel where we would spend the night before boarding the SS *Conte Rosso*, bound for the 'dragon-green, the luminous, the dark, the serpent-haunted sea' to that legendary land of Far Cathay, whose borders had only recently been forcibly broken down by western merchants greedy for trade, and which Tacklow loved as I loved India. Well, it was only fair that he should get the chance to go back there, and I hoped that China would be as kind to her prodigal son as India had been to me, her prodigal daughter. But as I looked out of my bedroom at the twinkling lights of the fishing boats, along the islands and the shoreline of the bay that some Portuguese adventurer, centuries ago, had named '*Bom-baya*' — 'Beautiful Bay' — and that Lockwood Kipling, Rudyard Kipling's father, had described as 'this blazing beauty of a city' — I knew that however enchanting China turned out to be, I would return to India as surely as a homing pigeon, or a pin to a magnet.

Bets, secure in the knowledge that there was no doubt about her return, was already sound asleep, but I stayed by the window, watching the lights and the stars reflected in the water, listening to the crowd around the romanesque gateway to India, and the mixture of Indian and European night-noises — the faint strains of a dance band playing 'The music goes round and around' — tom-toms and tablas, and 'conches in a temple, oil-lamps in a dome/and a low moon out of Africa says "This way home" . . .'

I leant out over the windowsill at a dangerous angle and repeated in an undertone, so as not to wake Bets: 'I'm coming back — *main wapas ana . . . zarur!* We both are. I promise! Tomorrow or tomorrow or tomorrow — Some day, anyway!'

And we did, of course.

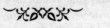

Glossary

abdar	butler
Angrezi	English
Angrezi-log	English folk
barra-durri	open-sided outdoor pavilion
bhat	talk, speech
Bibi-ghur	women's house
bistra	bedding-roll
burra	large, e.g. Burra-Sahib, great man
butti	lamp
charpoy	Indian bedstead
chupprassi	peon
chatti	large earthenware water-jug
chokra	small boy
chota-hazri	small breakfast
chowkidar	watchman, caretaker
dâk-bungalow	resthouse for travellers; originally for postmen (*dâk* means post)
darzi	tailor
dekchi	metal cooking-pot
dhobi	washerman, or woman
Diwan	Prime Minister
ferengi	foreigner
galeri	the little striped Indian tree-squirrel
ghari	vehicle; usually horse-drawn
gudee	throne
gussel	bath (*gussel-khana*: bathroom)
halwa	sweets
Jungi-Lat-Sahib	Commander-in-Chief
kutcha	rough, unfinished
khansama	cook

khitmatgar	waiter
Kaiser-i-Hind	the King (or Queen)
lathi	stout, iron-tipped and bound bamboo staff
Lal Khila	Red Fort
log (pronounced *low'g*)	people, folk
mahout	elephant rider
mali	gardener
manji	boatman
masalchi	washer-up, kitchen boy
maulvi	religious teacher
mufussal	countryside ('the sticks')
murgi	chicken
namaste	the Indian gesture of respect, greeting or farewell: hands pressed palm to palm and lifted to the forehead
noker	servant (*noker-log*: servant folk)
powinders	tribe of gypsies who are always on the move
shikari	hunter
shikarra	canopied punt that is the water-taxi of the Kashmir lakes
tonga	two-wheeled, horse-drawn taxi of the Indian plains
topi	pith hat — almost a uniform in the days of the Raj
vakil	lawyer